GRANDMA KNOWS BEST

GREAT KITCHEN SECRETS

BY
CHEF TONY NOTARO
&
DR. MYLES H. BADER

+ The science behind the secrets
GRANDMA'S KITCHEN & COOKING SECRETS
MORE FOOD SECRETS THAN ANY BOOK EVER PUBLISHED

GRANDMA KNOWS BEST
GREAT KITCHEN SECRETS

BY

CHEF TONY NOTARO

&

DR. MYLES H. BADER

Illustrations: Deborah, Randy & Veronica Peek
Cover design: Al Cavallo & Diana Barbetti

ISBN: 978-0-9882955-6-8
Printed and bound in the United States of America

10 9 8 7 6 5 4 3 2

Telebrands Press
79 Two Bridges Road
Fairfield, NJ 07004
www.telebrands.com

Please note: While this compilation of Kitchen Secrets will solve many problems, total success cannot be guaranteed. Neither the authors, publisher, manufacturer, nor distributor can assume responsibility for the effectiveness of the suggestions.

A WORD ABOUT CHEF TONY

Chef Tony was born into an Italian/Sicilian family in Brooklyn, New York, and from an early age helped in the family fresh produce market stall business which sold fresh vegetables to the neighborhood in Brooklyn. As a young teenager he was taught all the secrets of great Italian/Sicilian cooking by his mother, who provided him with the passion and knowledge which he has taken with him through his professional life.

A natural salesman, Chef Tony researches, tests and uses every product he sells. Kitchen Secrets is his favorite book because in it he shares family secrets that can make your life easier.

A WORD ABOUT DR. BADER

Dr. Myles H. Bader (known as the wizard of food) has been interviewed on over 6,000 radio and television shows in the United States and Canada and is internationally recognized as a leader in Preventive Care and Wellness fields. Appearances on television shows include The Oprah Winfrey Show, The Discovery Channel, Crook and Chase, America's Talking, Trinity Broadcasting, QVC, Smart Solutions; Help at Home, Fox & Friends, HGTV, etc.

Dr. Bader received his Doctoral Degree from Loma Linda University and is board certified in Preventive Care. He has practiced weight control, exercise physiology, stress management, counseled in all areas of nutrition and has lectured extensively on anti-aging for 36 years. During this period he established prevention and executive health programs for numerous safety departments, city governments, and Fortune 500 companies.

Dr. Bader has authored 24 books including Grandmother's Kitchen Wisdom Series, Club the Bugs & Scare the Critters, Cookbook's Companion, 1,001 Secret Money Saving Formulas, Household Hints, 5,001 Mysteries of Liquids & Cooking Secrets, 250 Future Food Facts & Predictions for the Millennium, To Supplement or Not to Supplement, and The Wellness Desk Reference. Dr. Bader's books have been sold through Reader's Digest, Doubleday, Book of the Month Club, QVC, HSN and Barnes & Noble.

INTRODUCTION

There is no doubt over the last 100 years many food secrets have been lost and not passed down from great-grandmother to grandmother to son or daughter. However, after years of research and interviewing many grandmothers' as well as mine I have managed to locate thousands of food secrets and usable facts, most of which will not be found in other food-related books or cookbooks.

The food secrets contained in this book have all been tested for accuracy and have been found to be still very useful in everyone's kitchen. The facts will save you money, provide you with a better understanding of food in general and in many instances help you prepare food the way grandma did.

The book also includes insight into the science of many of the facts providing you with in-depth information that is difficult to obtain from any other source.

The beginning of the book has the most popular and greatest food secrets that grandma could think of and will provide you with an idea of what you will find in the book. The balance of the book is in alphabetical order making it easy to locate anything you wish to look up.

Great Kitchen Secrets will never leave your kitchen and before you prepare any dish you will want to check the book to see if there are any secrets grandma knew to make the dish better.

Dr. Myles H. Bader

SOME OF GRANDMA'S GREATEST SECRETS

BAKING & GRAIN PROBLEMS

PROBLEM: My baked goods keep getting tough and not light and flaky.
SOLUTION: Over-mixing baked goods will cause them to become tough

PROBLEM: My rice burned, can I fix it?
SOLUTION: If you accidentally burn rice, just remove the good rice and place it into a clean pot. Place a fresh piece of white bread or a thin layer of onionskins on top of the rice and continue cooking for about 10-15 minutes before removing the bread or onionskins and discarding them.

PROBLEM: My piecrust will not turn out flaky
SOLUTION: There are a number of ways to make a flakier piecrust. The following are just a few: (1) adding a teaspoon of vinegar to the pie dough; (2) substituting sour cream or whipping cream for any water; (3) replacing the shortening or butter with lard. Lard has larger fat crystals and 3 times the polyunsaturated fat as butter.

PROBLEM: How can I stop the juices from bubbling out of my pies when baking them?
SOLUTION: If you have a problem with juices bubbling out or oozing out when baking a pie, try adding a tablespoon of tapioca to the filling. This will thicken the filling just enough. Another method is to insert a tube wide macaroni in the center of the top allowing air to escape.

PROBLEM: How can I stop the bottoms of my pies from becoming soggy?
SOLUTION: If you have a problem with fruit or fruit juices soaking the bottom of your pie crust and making them soggy, try brushing the bottom with egg whites. This will seal the pie crust and solve the problem.

PROBLEM: How can I stop bread from becoming mushy when I freeze it?
SOLUTION: Add a piece of paper towel to the bread inside the wrapper to absorb the moisture.

PROBLEM: How can I prevent flour from getting bugs in it?
SOLUTION: Place a piece of spearmint gum in the flour.

PROBLEM: My cakes are coming out too heavy.

SOLUTION: Remember, cake flour will make a lighter cake due to its lower gluten content. If you don't have cake flour, try using all-purpose flour, but reduce the amount by 2 tablespoons for each cup of cake flour called for. One of the best recipes for making a light textured cake is to use 50% unbleached cake flour and 50% whole-wheat flour.

PROBLEM: How can I make my pancakes light and fluffy?

SOLUTION: Just replace any water or milk with club soda.

PROBLEM: Every time I make dumplings they get soggy.

SOLUTION: Mix the dough as little as possible, just blending the ingredients. Never drop them into the boiling water, just gently lay them on top of the chicken pieces. Never simmer the dumplings for more than 10 minutes uncovered then cover and cook for another 10 minutes. The other trick is to use a dome lid so that the steam does not make them soggy.

COFFEE & TEA

PROBLEM: How can I stop my coffee from becoming stale?

SOLUTION: Coffee will only stay fresh on a warming unit for 30 minutes. To freshen it up, add a pinch of salt to the cup and then re-heat it.

PROBLEM: My tea is going bad too fast.

SOLUTION: Loose tea should always be stored in a cool, dry location. Humidity and heat will reduce the quality of the tea significantly. A sealed container works well allowing as little oxygen to come into contact with the loose tea. Containers should only be large enough to hold the tea and be opaque since the light can have a negative effect as well. A large container will retain too much oxygen and may cause undue oxidation to take place.

Teabags should be stored in the container they are purchased in and also stored in a cool, dry location.

COOKING PROBLEMS

PROBLEM: How can you tell if water is getting too low in a double boiler?

SOLUTION: When you are using a double boiler, be sure and place a few marbles or a small metal jar top on the bottom of the pot. They will start to rattle when the water gets too low and save you from scorching the pot.

Stop Smoking Oil..201
PROBLEM: How can I stop oil from smoking when frying or sautéing?
SOLUTION: To use butter, margarine or lard for frying or sautéing, add a small amount of canola oil to the oil to raise the smoke point.
This will allow you to cook with them without them breaking down and smoking creating trans-fatty acids.

Fryer Splattering?...216
PROBLEM: How can I stop food from splattering when I place it into the fryer?
SOLUTION: Salt tends to draw moisture from foods. If a food is salted before placing it in the fryer, it will draw moisture to the surface and cause splattering when the food is placed into the heated oil.

Reduce Fat When frying..174
PROBLEM: How can I reduce the amount of fat absorbed into foods when I fry?
SOLUTION: Add a teaspoon of white vinegar to the frying oil before you heat the oil to help seal up the food.

DAIRY PRODUCTS

Extending the Life of Milk..276
PROBLEM: How can I extend the life of milk?
SOLUTION: If you want your milk to have a longer shelf life, just add a pinch of baking soda to the carton. When you place a small amount of baking soda in milk, it will reduce the acidity level, just enough to add a few more days to the expiration date.

However, milk will normally last for a week after the expiration date and still be useable if stored properly and no one drinks out of the carton. Another method is to transfer the milk from a carton to a screw-top glass jar, to reduce the effects of oxidation.

Store Eggs for Long Period..189
PROBLEM: How can I store eggs for a longer period?
SOLUTION: If the eggs are stored with the wide end up they will last longer since it will maximize the distance between the yolk and the air pocket in the egg. The air can harbor bacteria and the yolk is more perishable than the white.

Even though the yolk is attached by two chalazas holding it centered, there is just enough give to allow it to move away from the air pocket.

No More Green Eggs...180
When eggs are overheated or cooked for a prolonged period of time there is a chemical change that will take place. This change tends to combine the sulfur in the egg with the iron in the yolk, which form the harmless chemical ferrous sulfide.

This reaction is more prevalent in older eggs since the elements are more easily released. Eggs should never be cooked for any reason more than 12-15 minutes to avoid this problem.

Stop Boiled Eggs from Cracking
PROBLEM: My eggs keep cracking when I boil them.
SOLUTION: You can prevent boiled eggs from cracking by rubbing a cut lemon on the shell before cooking.

Eggs Sticking to the Pan?
PROBLEM: My eggs keep sticking to the pan when I make an omelet.
SOLUTION: Never fry eggs, scramble eggs or make an omelet in salted butter since it causes the eggs to stick to the pan. It is best to use unsalted butter or vegetable oil.

Cleaning Cheese from Grater
PROBLEM: When I grate cheese it is almost impossible to clean the grater.
SOLUTION: When grating cheese, try spraying a liquid vegetable oil on the grater before grating and cleanup will be easier.

Stop Moldy Cheese
PROBLEM: How can I stop cheese from getting moldy?
SOLUTION: Place the block of cheese in a well-sealed plastic container with a piece of paper towel in the bottom lightly dampened with white vinegar and 3-4 sugar cubes and seal well.

Ice Crystals on Ice Cream
PROBLEM: How can I stop ice crystals from forming on ice cream?
SOLUTION: Place a piece of plastic wrap directly on top of the leftover ice cream.

Cottage Cheese Long Lifespan
PROBLEM: My cottage cheese is getting moldy after a few days.
SOLUTION: Cottage cheese will last 7-10 longer if you store it upside down. When you open cottage cheese spores enter from the air and live on the oxygen layer. When you turn cottage cheese upside down and allow it to fall to the top, you eliminate a percentage of the oxygen layer. Many of the remaining spores then suffocate and ones that remain cannot grow as fast allowing the cottage cheese to last about 7-10 days longer.

FATS & OILS

Food Sticks to Pans
PROBLEM: When I use a greased pan the food sticks to it.
SOLUTION: When the recipe calls for a greased pan, make sure you always use unsalted butter. Salted butter has a tendency to cause food to stick to the pan.

Stopping Fat from Getting Rancid
PROBLEM: Oil is getting rancid too fast.
SOLUTION: Oxygen has been found to be eight times more soluble in fat that in water, which is why fats tend to oxidize so easily and turn rancid.

Every time you open a bottle of oil, more oil leaves and is replaced by oxygen. You can preserve the oil a little longer by refrigerating it.

Oil Getting Cloudy?

Oil Getting Cloudy? 192

PROBLEM: How can I stop my oil from getting cloudy?

SOLUTION: When oils are refrigerated and become cloudy, it is due to the buildup of harmless crystals. Manufacturers will sometimes pre-chill the oils and remove the crystals in a process known as "winterization." These oils will remain clear when refrigerated. Lard has larger fat crystals than butter, which has a lot to do with the texture of these fats and is controlled during processing. The large fat crystals in lard will make it the choice for a number of baked goods where a flakier crust is preferred, especially pies. Moderation in eating these lard products, however, is the key word.

Never Re-Use Oil 219

PROBLEM: What happens to oil when I re-use it?

SOLUTION: When oil is used for frying the temperature is raised to such a high level that a percentage of the oil is broken down (begins smoking) and decomposes into trans-fatty acid oil, as well as turning a percentage of the polyunsaturated oil into saturated oil. Trans-fatty acids even though edible, tends to cause an increase in free radicals (abnormal cells) in the body and may also raise the bad cholesterol levels (LDL) and lower the good cholesterol levels (HDL). Best to use fresh canola oil every time you fry.

FUDGE

Fudge Too Soft 221

PROBLEM: My fudge is not setting up.

SOLUTION: Add 1 teaspoon of cornstarch when you start mixing in the ingredients. Fudge tends to attract moisture and cannot be made on humid days. Too much butter is a common problem. If the water content is too high, it won't set properly. Poor grades of margarine that have been substituted for quality butter will also cause the problem.

HOLIDAY

Get Tender, Moist White Meat 388

PROBLEM: How can I get moist white meat on a turkey?

SOLUTION: If you place your turkey breast-side down on a "V" rack that has been placed in a low-sided cooking pan and allow it to cook for ½ the cooking time, some of the juices will go to the breast and moisten the meat. Purchasing a bird with basting solution injected into the breast, just adds calories and fat to the lean white meat.

Turn the bird right side up after the first hour and continue cooking for the balance of the time. A low-sided pan is now recommended since it was found that a high-sided pan tends to steam the bird too much.

MEAT PROBLEMS

Tough Meat?...270
PROBLEM: What can I do with a tough piece of meat if I don't have meat tenderizer?
SOLUTION: Try rubbing baking soda on the surface of a piece of tough meat and allow it to stand for 2-3 hours in the refrigerator before rinsing it off and cooking it.

Meat Dried Out?..340
PROBLEM: How can I stop meat from drying out when I am cooking it?
SOLUTION: Sealing in the juices by lightly flouring the surface of meats works very well. When storing a roast always place the roast back into its own juices whenever possible. When re-heating meats, try placing the slices in a casserole dish with lettuce leaves between the slices. This will provide just the right amount of moisture to keep the slices from drying out.

Unsafe Nitrites in Meat...35
PROBLEM: How can I neutralize the nitrites in bacon and lunch meats, which I know are bad for me?
SOLUTION: Bacon and lunch meats are highly nitrated, the higher nitrate content is found in the fat, which means that you need to choose the leanest bacon and lunch meat you can find. If you chew up a vitamin C tablet or drink some orange juice it will neutralize the nitrates.

Ham Too Salty?..232
PROBLEM: How can I stop ham slices from being too salty?
SOLUTION: If you soak them in milk before cooking them it will eliminate a large percentage of the salt. If you are cooking a large ham then place the ham in the oven and cook for ½ the time, remove and pour a can of ginger ale over the ham and then rub salt on the outside and finish cooking. The ginger ale and salt will draw salt water out of the ham and should de-salt the ham about 60%.

Fat Getting Into Roast?..340
PROBLEM: How can I stop the fat that is layered on top of my roast from entering the roast?
SOLUTION: Just sprinkle dry mustard on top of the fat and it will not enter the roast.

Meatloaf Cracking?..271
PROBLEM: How can I stop meatloaf from cracking?
SOLUTION: By rubbing water around the meatloaf, it keeps the meatloaf moist and stops it from cracking. Tomato sauce does not have the same effect but can be added about 15 minutes before the end of the cooking time to flavor the meatloaf.

Bacon Shriveling?...34
PROBLEM: How can I stop my bacon from shriveling?

SOLUTION: Bacon will not shrivel if you rinse the bacon under cold water before frying. This reduces the amount the bacon shrinks by almost 50%.

Choosing Tender Steak
PROBLEM: I don't know how to choose a tender steak at the market
SOLUTION: Look at the color of the fat. If it is white the steak will be tender, if it is yellow the steak will be tough.

If the steer was grass-fed, the color of the fat will be yellow and the beef will be somewhat tough. If the color of the fat is white, it means that the steer was corn-fed or grain-fed and will be more tender and cost more.

Tough Beef Stew Meat?
PROBLEM: How can I tenderize the meat in beef stew?
SOLUTION: Wine corks have been used for hundreds of years in France to tenderize beef stew and octopus tentacles. Enzymes in the cork are released when the water reaches a very hot level. Place 2-3 wine corks in the stew when you first start to heat the stew for the best results. The rule of thumb is one wine cork per quart of water.

Meat Sticking to Pan?
PROBLEM: How can I stop meat from sticking to a pan when cooking?
SOLUTION: If you are having a problem with meats sticking to the pan, just allow the meat to stand at room temperature 1 hour before cooking: It will cook more quickly, brown more evenly, and stick less when pan-fried. (Do not do this with highly perishable meats like ground beef and organ meats.)

Roast Too Dry?
PROBLEM: My roast is too dry, what can I do?
SOLUTION: A roast should never be carved until it has had a chance to rest and allow juices to dissipate evenly throughout the roast. When you cook a roast the juices tend to be forced to the center as the juices near the surface evaporate from the heat. A roast should be left to stand for about 15 minutes before carving. This will also allow the meat to firm up a bit making it easier to carve thinner slices.

REFRIGERATOR

Soggy Vegetables?
PROBLEM: How can I stop my vegetables from getting soggy in the crisper drawer?
SOLUTION: Try placing a few sponges in your vegetable drawer to absorb moisture. You can also add a piece of paper towel to the bottom of the drawer.

Avocados in the Refrigerator?
PROBLEM: Avocados will not last long when ripened.
SOLUTION: To ripen an avocado, just place it in a wool sock in the back of a dark closet for 2 days. Avocados should never be stored in the refrigerator if they are not fully ripe.

When they are ripe, they should be stored in the vegetable drawer in the refrigerator and should stay fresh for 10-14 days. Avocados may only be frozen for three to six months if pureed.

SOUPS, STEWS & GRAVY

Fix Burnt Gravy..230
PROBLEM: How can I fix burnt gravy?
SOLUTION: If you really burn the gravy badly, throw it out. If you only burn it a little bit, change the top portion to another pan and add a teaspoon of peanut butter to cover up the burnt flavor without altering the taste.

Remove Fat from Stews, Soups & Gravy................................229
PROBLEM: I can't easily remove the fat from stews, gravies and soups.
SOLUTION: There are two methods; first you can place some ice cubes in a piece of cheesecloth and swirl it around in soup, stew or gravy and fat will be attracted to the ice. Then remove and discard. Second you can use iceberg lettuce leaves in place of the ice.

Lumpy Gravy..229
PROBLEM: My gravy is always lumpy.
SOLUTION: You will never have lumpy gravy if you just add a pinch of salt to the flour and mix it in before adding any liquid.

Help for Too Much Garlic..357
PROBLEM: I have added too much garlic to my dish.
SOLUTION: When you overdo the garlic, just place a few parsley flakes in a tea ball to soak up the excess garlic. Garlic tends to be attracted to parsley.

No Bones in Your Soup..365
PROBLEM: I am having trouble getting all the bones out of my soup.
SOLUTION: Next time you make soup or stew, try using a metal pasta cooker basket. Just place the basket into your pot and cook all your ingredients. When you remove the basket it will contain all the veggies or bones you may not want.

SPICES & CONDIMENTS

Is Baking Soda Fresh?..44
PROBLEM: How can I tell if my baking soda is fresh?
SOLUTION: If you are not sure of the activity level of baking soda, try placing ¼ teaspoon in about 2 teaspoons of white vinegar. If carbon dioxide bubbles appear it still has good activity.

Over-Salted Foods..356
PROBLEM: I over-salted a dish I was cooking.
SOLUTION: Place a piece of raw potato in the soup, stew or soup and swish it around for a few minutes then remove it.

PROBLEM: How can I keep summer herbs all year long?
SOLUTION: If you would like summer herbs all year long and preserve them for winter soups and stews, just make herb cubes in the freezer. Chop up your herbs and place them in ice cube trays, then cover with water and freeze.

VEGETABLE & FRUIT PROBLEMS

PROBLEM: How can I keep beans from becoming mushy?
SOLUTION: If you add molasses to baked beans it will help them retain their shape for a longer period of time. The cell walls in beans prefer the sugar in molasses over other sugars when it comes to keeping their cells walls more stable. Raw beans contain a very small amount of a toxin that is destroyed with cooking.

PROBLEM: Is there a way to use lifeless frozen vegetables?
SOLUTION: These are an important staple; don't be embarrassed to use them. No need to cook before adding to dishes; simply pour boiling water over them in a colander and then add them to your casserole or stove-top dish to finish cooking.

PROBLEM: What is the best way to store ½ onion?
SOLUTION: If you are only going to need half an onion, use the top half since the root half will store longer in the refrigerator.

PROBLEM: How can I reduce the acid in dishes caused by tomato sauce?
SOLUTION: Some people are unable to eat spaghetti sauces and other tomato-based products due to their high acid content. If you add some grated carrots to these dishes it will reduce the acidity without affecting the taste.

PROBLEM: How can I stop asparagus from getting tough when I cook it?
SOLUTION: To tenderize the asparagus stalks, just use your potato peeler and remove the first layer of the stalk. Another method is to break off the top where the woody stem attaches by holding the spear in just the right spot (about halfway down the spear) and with your thumb and index finger of the opposite hand, bend the stalk and it should snap the top away from the bottom.

PROBLEM: My tomatoes have no aroma or flavor.
SOLUTION: Leave the tomatoes at room temperature for 20-30 minutes before serving them to re-activate the aroma & flavor.

PROBLEM: How can I stop potatoes from sprouting?
SOLUTION: If you place ½-apple or a piece of ginger root in a bag of potatoes, they will not sprout.

Perfect Mashed Potatoes
PROBLEM: My mashed potatoes are always heavy and soggy.
SOLUTION: Never pour cold milk into the potatoes. It has a tendency to mix with the starch that has been released through the mashing process and may make the potatoes heavy, soggy, and even create lumps. The milk should be warmed in a pan with a small amount of chives for flavor before being added. Buttermilk will give the potatoes a great flavor. A pinch or two of baking powder will give them extra fluff.

Potato Salad Secret
PROBLEM: How can I stop potatoes from getting soft when making potato salad?
SOLUTION: Always choose new red potatoes and add a small amount of white vinegar to the cooking water to keep them firm.

No Soggy Pickles
PROBLEM: My pickles keep getting soggy.
SOLUTION: Add a piece of horseradish root to the pickle jar to keep the vinegar active and the pickles firm.

Stop Soggy Salad Greens
PROBLEM: How can I keep my salad greens from getting soggy?
SOLUTION: You will never have another soggy salad if you just place an inverted saucer in the bottom of a salad bowl. The excess water left after washing the vegetables and greens will drain off under the saucer and leave the salad greens high and dry.

Stop Premature Lettuce Wilting
PROBLEM: My lettuce in the salad keeps wilting too fast.
SOLUTION: After you tear or chop up your lettuce, place a pinch of salt in the bowl and shake it. This will keep the lettuce crisp and prevent premature wilting.

Keep Celery Fresh Longer
PROBLEM: My celery doesn't last too long.
SOLUTION: One of the best methods of storing celery for a prolonged period of time (2-3 weeks) is to wrap the celery tightly in aluminum foil.

Eliminate Gas from Beans
PROBLEM: How can I eliminate my family getting gas from eating beans?
SOLUTION: When you are soaking the beans at night, just add a teaspoon of fennel seed to the water to neutralize the complex sugar causing the gas or just serve rice with the beans.

Sweeter Corn with Husks On
PROBLEM: Will leaving the husks on corn when cooking make it sweeter?
SOLUTION: Corn on the cob does not have to be shucked when you are going to boil it. If you cook it with the husks on, the corn will be sweeter.
The method is to remove the silk by gently opening up the husk then replace the husk and tie the top with string to keep it shut while it is cooking.

No More Mushy Pumpkins
PROBLEM: My pumpkin gets mushy too fast?

SOLUTION: One of the biggest problems every Halloween is that the pumpkin will get soft and mushy a few hours after it has been carved. The problem is the result of the air coming in contact with inside flesh, thus allowing bacteria to grow at a rapid pace.

Spraying the inside of the pumpkin with an antiseptic spray will retard the bacterial growth and reduce the time of deterioration. Make sure you do not eat the pumpkin or the seeds after it has been sprayed.

Remove Bitterness from Cucumbers

PROBLEM: How can I get rid of the bitterness in cucumbers?

SOLUTION: Next time you purchase a standard cucumber, not the long skinny English variety, cut about one inch off the end and then rub the two exposed areas together in a circular motion while occasionally pulling them apart. This will cause enough suction to release a substance that causes some cucumbers to have a bitter taste. Then discard the small end you used to release the bitterness.

Stop Crying When Slicing Onions

PROBLEM: How can I stop from crying when working with fresh onions?

SOLUTION: When you slice into an onion, a gas is released that affects the lachrymal glands in the eyes and causes a defensive reaction by the body against the chemical "propanethiol S-oxide" which reacts with the fluid in your eyes forming sulfuric acid. The body protects itself from the acid by tearing action, which washes out the eyes ridding itself of the irritant. One of the best methods to avoid tearing is to wear solid plastic goggles.

Other methods if you prefer not to shed tears is to cut the root off last, freeze the onion for 10 minutes, or refrigerate for 1 hour before slicing. Other tricks that have worked are to ball up a piece of white bread and place it on the tip of the knife or hold it between your teeth to absorb the fumes. Chewing gum may also help. Another method that works well is to light a candle to absorb the fumes.

MISCELLANEOUS

Tomato Stains on Plastic

PROBLEM: How can I remove odors and avoid tomato stains from a plastic container?

SOLUTION: To remove onion and garlic odors from plastic containers and to deodorize a plastic storage container in which onions or garlic were stored, wash thoroughly then stuff a crumpled piece of newspaper in the container and snap on the lid. In a few days the smell will disappear. To stop tomato products from staining plastic containers, just spray vegetable oil lightly on the inside before adding the sauce.

Be Careful Storing in Aluminum Foil

PROBLEM: Can you store food in aluminum foil?

SOLUTION: If you plan on storing food for more than 2-3 days in the refrigerator in aluminum foil you should probably wrap the food in plastic wrap first. Aluminum foil will react with foods that are acidic or salty and may impart a strange taste to the food.

Aluminum foil should never be used next to a warm or hot meat product then frozen. It keeps the food warm for too long a period and bacteria may grow and if the food is not re-cooked to a high enough temperature after it is thawed the bacteria may be reactivated.

No More Fishy Smell..203
PROBLEM: How can I avoid a fish smell when working with fish?
SOLUTION: Before handling fish, try washing your hands in plain cold water. Chances are you won't have a fish smell on them afterwards. A small amount of white vinegar placed into the pan you have fried fish in will eliminate the odor.

Lake Fish Lack Flavor..197
PROBLEM: River fish seem to have more flavor than lake fish.
SOLUTION: River fish tend to exercise more than lake fish, which make flesh more flavorful. River fish must swim against the current, while lake fish just lazily move around. This why trout are so flavorful! Cold-water fish will also have more flavor, since they need more of a fat layer, which contributes flavor.

Griddle Temperature for Pancakes..299
PROBLEM: What is the best griddle temperature for pancakes?
SOLUTION: Pancakes should be cooked on a griddle that is approximately 325^0F for the best results. To be sure of having the proper temperature, just dribble a drop or two of cold water on the hot griddle. The water should bounce around on the top of the griddle close to the spot you drop it because of steam being generated and gravity forcing the water back down to the griddle.

Lightest Pancakes Ever..300
PROBLEM: My pancakes are always too heavy.
SOLUTION: When chefs make pancakes, they never use milk or water. They substitute club soda or seltzer to make the pancakes so light they will float around the house and you will have a problem finding them. You can also substitute fruit juice in place of the milk or water.

Eliminate Burnt Food from Pans..334
PROBLEM: I can't get burnt food out of my pan.
SOLUTION: You first need to fill the pot or pan with two inches of water then, add a quarter cup of baking soda and a quarter cup of white vinegar. Bring pot to a boil and allow it to cook for 15 minutes. Turn off the heat and allow the pot to sit until cooled before draining the water and clean the pot as you normally would. If any burnt food residue remains, repeat the process.

You can also substitute dish washing liquid to replace vinegar. Fill the pot with water and add one to two tea spoons of dish washing liquid and the baking soda then bring to a boil and simmer for 10 minutes. Cover the pot, turn off the heat and allow the pot to soak for 30 minutes.
Another method that might work is to fill the pan with water and place a dryer sheet in the water. Allow the pan to soak overnight and the food will wipe right out!

Clams Tough in Chowder?
PROBLEM: Every time I make chowder the clams are like rubber.
SOLUTION: Chefs will always add sliced clams during the last 15-20 minutes of cooking time. When clams are added early in the cooking of chowder they tend to become tough or too soft.

De-Salted Anchovies
PROBLEM: I don't know how to get rid of the salt in anchovies.
SOLUTION: Anchovies can be desalted to some degree by soaking them in ice water for about 15 minutes. They should then be placed into the refrigerator for another 45 minutes before adding them to a recipe.

Garlic Smell on Hands
PROBLEM: How do I get rid of the garlic smell from my hands?
SOLUTION: To remove the garlic odor from your hands, try rubbing your hands with salt on a slice of lemon or rub your hands across the blade of a stainless steel knife.

AAAAA

ABALONE

Abalone is becoming one of the more rare shellfish to be found off the coast of California. The **"foot"** is the tough edible portion, which must be literally pounded into tenderness. The price is high and they must be cooked 12-24 hours after they are captured otherwise they will become bitter.

- The method of tenderizing abalone is to cut the abalone into the thinnest slices possible and then pound those slices even thinner using a special meat-tenderizing hammer. If this is not done properly the abalone will be tough.
- When abalone is cooked it should never be cooked for more than 30 seconds on each side. Overcooking makes it tough. Before cooking place small slashes about an inch apart across the whole piece to avoid curling.
- When purchasing abalone, make sure that the exposed foot muscle moves when you touch it. Never buy shellfish if it is dead!
- Abalone should smell sweet and never fishy, small ones are the best.
- Canned abalone is available in some specialty markets, however, if you open the can, be sure and finish the contents since it will only last for about 4-5 days under refrigeration, if sealed properly.

ACID

A sour tasting substance that is soluble in water. There are a number of acids that are common in foods. The following are a few of the more common ones:

Citric Acid

Citric acid is a weak acid and is present in all citrus fruits such as oranges, grapefruits, lemons and limes. It is also used as an additive for flavoring in a variety of food and soft drinks, to remove color and for flavoring wine and some beer. In human metabolism citric acid plays a role in the conversion of fat, carbohydrates and proteins into energy.

Lactic Acid

Lactic acid is found in common in milk products, such as yogurt, cottage cheese, cheese and even sourdough bread. It can also be a byproduct produced by your body in your muscles when you break down glucose for energy. When you have too much lactic acid in your muscles, your muscles cannot handle contractions and fatigue sets in and you may get painful muscle cramps.

Fatty Acids

Triglycerides, which are fats acids, are made up of glycerol and three fatty-acid chains. These contain excellent levels of energy and are made up of carbon and hydrogen bonds. They are an integral part of many fruits, vegetables and dairy products, in various amounts. Some foods that contain significant amounts of fatty acids are coconuts, avocados, seeds, nuts, milk, cheese, yogurt and whole grains.

ACIDULATED WATER

This is a mixture of water and an acid usually a citrus acid derived from lime, orange or lemon. It is commonly used on fruits or fruit salads to prevent them from browning when their surfaces are exposed to the air. Oxidation takes place very rapidly in many fruits and vegetables. When oxidation takes place the vitamin C is lost in the brown areas.

To prepare acidulated water, add 1½ tablespoons of white vinegar to one quart of water. If you prefer 3 tablespoons of pure lemon juice can be substituted for the vinegar.

ALCOHOL (cooking with)

FREEZING FOODS WITH ALCOHOL

If you are going to try and freeze any dish that has alcohol in it, remember alcohol will not freeze like water and may need to be frozen at a lower temperature.

BRANDY

Brandy is one of the most versatile spirits and can be used in many different dishes. It is especially complimentary to soups, shellfish dishes, beef, lamb, peaches, pears, and a number of puddings.

GIN

May have too much of an overpowering flavor for most dishes. It is best used on game dishes to mask the gamy flavor. An age-old favorite is to use a small amount of gin in tomato soups or a tomato sauce. It will also compliment the flavor of sauerkraut.

LIQUEURS

Since liqueurs are sweet, they tend to go well over desserts and especially fruit salads. Ice creams are excellent with a small amount of a flavored liqueur. Grand Marnier goes well with any dish that has oranges included. Benedictine is an age-old favorite on sponge cake.

RUM

Rum is very effective in flavoring sweet dishes, especially desserts. It is commonly used on rum cakes, fruitcakes, and Bananas Foster.

WHISKEY

Small amounts of quality whiskey will aide in bringing out the flavor in many foods and specialty dishes. It is typically used to replace brandy in many recipes. It is especially good when used in shellfish recipes but will compliment almost any type of meat or poultry dish. Commonly used on chocolate mousse, coffee sorbet, and fruitcakes.

The boiling point of alcohol is 175^0F (79.4^0C), which is lower than the boiling point of water at 212^0F (100^0C). When alcohol is added to a recipe it will lower the boiling point until it evaporates.

For example: if you decide to change your recipe by adding some wine to replace some of the water, you will need to increase your cooking time by about 10 percent.

ALCOHOL (flambé)

If you want to flame a mixed drink safely, try using a teaspoon with a small amount of the preferred liquor and hold a match under the spoon for a few seconds until some of the fumes burn off. Then ignite the liquor in the spoon and pour it over the mixed drink. Never place your face too close to the drink you are flaming, just in case there are more fumes rising. Rum flames up better than most alcoholic beverages.

ALCOHOL, IN RECIPES

The following will provide information regarding cooking with alcohol and how much alcohol is left after a dish is cooked. Some alcohol will dissipate, but not as much as most people may think.

Method of preparation	% Alcohol Remaining
Alcohol not added to boiling food until after food removed from heat	86%
Alcohol added to a flambé and ignited	75%
Alcohol used in a marinade, no heat added	70%
Alcohol stirred into baked dish and simmered 15 Minutes	40%
30 Minutes	35%
60 Minutes	25%
2 Hours	10%
3 Hours	0%

Science of Alcohol in Foods		
Alcohol remaining after preparation	Baked or simmered	
100% Immediate consumption	40%	after 15 minutes
85% Boiling liquid, remove from heat	35%	after 30 minutes
75% Flamed	25%	after 1 hour
70% Overnight storage	20%	after 1½ hours
	10%	after 2 hours
	5%	after 2½ hours

ALLSPICE

The flavor is similar to that of cinnamon, cloves, and nutmeg. The majority is imported from Jamaica, Central America and South America and it is sold in both whole and ground forms. The spice is used in pickling, meats, fish, baked goods, relish, puddings and fruit preserves. Allspice is a common herb and can be found in a number of ready-to-serve foods such as, hot dogs, soups, and baked beans. Allspice is the herb used to prepare Jamaican jerk seasoning used in Jamaican soup, stews and curries.

ALMOND

Almonds can be blanched by covering them with boiling water, removing from the heat and covering them for about 3-4 minutes. After removing them from the water, the skins should easily slip off by squeezing them between your fingers.

Almond with and without its shell

After blanching the almonds, lay them out on a cookie sheet and bake for 10-12 minutes at 325°F.

- If you wish to have a richer almond flavor then just add ¼ teaspoon of pure almond extract to the baked goods.
- Be sure not use the almond skin in dishes or they may impart a bitter taste.

Almonds are an excellent source of calcium. A small handful equals the calcium in 4 ounces of milk. You will still have the fat content of the almonds, which will be higher than non-fat milk. Almonds are actually a member of the peach family.

ALMOND PASTE

Almond paste is prepared from blanched almonds, sugar and glycerin or some other liquid.

- Marzipan, which is a candy contains more sugar and is stiffer and lighter in color and usually sold in small fruit or vegetable shapes.
- Since almond paste, contains more blanched almonds, therefore it costs more.
- In California almond orchards are second only to grapes in orchard space and are California's major food export.
- Almond paste can be purchased in plastic tubes or sometimes found in small cans.
- The paste does not hold up when exposed to the air and needs to be wrapped well and used as soon as possible.
- Marzipan or almond paste can be softened in the microwave for about 3 seconds on high.

ALUMINUM FOIL

Foods wrapped in aluminum foil may be subjected to two problems. The first is that since aluminum foil is such a great insulator it tends to slow down the heat transfer and the food will not freeze as fast as you may want it to. Bacteria may grow and not be killed when the food is re-heated.

Secondly is that when you crinkle the aluminum foil to place it around the food, micro-cracks develop which may allow air and moisture to penetrate the food.
- If you plan on storing food for more than 2-3 days in the refrigerator in aluminum foil you should probably wrap the food in plastic wrap first. Aluminum foil will react with foods that are acidic or salty and may impart a strange taste to the food.

- Aluminum foil should never be used next to a warm or hot meat product then frozen. It keeps the food warm for too long a period and bacteria may grow and if the food is not re-cooked to a high enough temperature after it is thawed the bacteria may be reactivated.

Aluminum foil develops micro cracks and is only good next to a cold food in the refrigerator for no more than 1-2 days. Also, never place aluminum foil on top of a meatloaf with tomato sauce. It will deteriorate from the acid in the tomato sauce. The acid in citrus fruits will also eat away aluminum foil.

If you want to keep food wrapped in aluminum foil from over-browning, keep the shiny side of the foil out.

ANCHOVIES

Anchovies are a popular poultry feed. Most of the over 200 million pounds caught annually are ground up and used for feed. Anchovies used for canning range in size from 3-5 inches, they are also used as a pizza topping and in "real" Caesar salad.

Anchovies can be desalted to some degree by soaking them in ice water for about 15 minutes. They should then be placed into the refrigerator for another 45 minutes before adding them to a recipe.

APPLES

Apples have been enjoyed since 6500 BC. They are native to Europe and Asia; however, the United States produces about 25% of the world's crop. There are over 7,000 varieties grown in the U.S. but only about 50 varieties make it to the market. Apples are grown in 35 states producing 145 million barrels annually. The word apple comes from the old English word *"aeppel."*

The Pilgrims brought the first apple seeds to America in 1620. Apples are a member of the rose family and have similar leaves to rose hips.

Certain varieties of apples may have a different taste depending on the time of year it was purchased. If you buy large quantities, it would be best to purchase a few and taste them. They should be firm, have no holes, should not be bruised, and have a good even color. If the apple is not ripe, leave it at room temperature for a day or two, but not in direct sunlight.

- Before using frozen apples, they should be thawed for at least 1 hour or more. If you added sugar before freezing, be sure to allow for the sugar when using the apples in a recipe.
- The biggest apple on record weighed in at 3 pounds 2 ounces and was picked in Cairo, Michigan.
- Three fruits have been successfully modified to retard softening for longer periods of time. The three fruits are apples, raspberries, and cantaloupe and will be available in supermarkets.
- The popular applesauce apple "granny smith" was named for chef Maria Ann Smith who lived in a suburb of Sidney, Australia.
- Apples will absorb odors of other foods very easily and should be kept away from other foods.

Science of Floating Apples

Apples are about 25% air, which is higher than most fruits. The cells in an apple do not fit very well together and allow for larger air spaces between them. This is also why when you first bite into a freshly picked apple they tend to have a cracking sound, which releases some in the air.

- Apples will ripen very quickly at room temperature. If you are not sure of their level of ripeness, just leave them out for 2-3 days before refrigerating them.
- Apples should be stored in the refrigerator, ideally at 36-38°F to stop the ripening process. They may be washed, dried and placed into a plastic bag.
- When refrigerated, apples will stay fresh for 2-4 weeks.
- Apples may also be stored in a cool, dry location in a barrel that has sawdust in it. The apples should never touch each other and will last 4-6 months.
- To freeze apples they need to be cored, peeled, washed, and sliced. Spray them with a solution of 2 teaspoons of ascorbic acid (vitamin C) in 12 tablespoons of cold water then place them in a container leaving ½ inch at the top.

Unripe apples should be stored at room temperature until they are fully ripe. They should then be placed into the refrigerator to stop the ripening process and help them retain their freshness. Apples will pick up refrigerator odors and should be stored in a drawer.

APPLE FACTS

- Never store an apple near a banana unless you wish to ripen the banana in a very short period of time. Apples tend to give off more ethylene gas than most other fruits (except green tomatoes) and will hasten the ripening of many fruits and vegetables. Ethylene gas is a natural gas that is released by all fruits and vegetables as they ripen. Ethylene has been used for centuries to ripen fruits and vegetables.

- Fruits and vegetables may be gassed to ripen them as they are trucked to market. Ethylene increases the permeability of the cell membrane allowing the cell to respire more and use oxygen to produce carbon dioxide up to five times faster than it ordinarily would. This increased activity of the cell causes the fruit or vegetable to ripen faster.
- If you see a dry, brownish-colored area on an apple, it is called the "scald." It is a slightly tough area, but will not affect the flavor when cooked.
- Apples are capable of floating since 25% of their volume is made up of air pockets between the cells. The soft texture of cooked apples; is caused by the heat collapsing the air pockets between the cells.
- Pare apples by pouring scalding water on them just before peeling them. This will make the skin loosen and they will be easier to peel.

Science of the Apple

Apples will be best if tree-ripened since their starch content is not that great. The vitamin C that is present in an apple is concentrated in the skin, but will only give you about 10% of your daily requirement. Red and yellow delicious apples cannot be used for cooking since they lack sufficient cellulose, have weak cell walls, lose their shape and become mushy. They also do not contain enough acid to balance the sugar content added by the cook.

The wax coating is placed on apples to make them look better and not to help them retain their natural moisture. A bruise on the surface of an apple is no different from the browning that occurs when the flesh is exposed to air. The phenolic compounds and enzymes in the cells react with oxygen and turn the area brown. If the skin is not broken then the air pocket formed from the bruise reacts with the damaged cells and causes a soft area to form. This brown area is still safe to eat.

If you want apples to retain their shape when cooking them, add any sugar the recipe calls for at the beginning of the cooking time. The reason apples stay relatively firm in apple pies and baked apples is that chefs sprinkle powdered calcium on the apples to reinforce the cell walls.

- If the apples are losing their moisture and taste, try slicing them up, placing them in a dish and pouring cold apple juice over them and refrigerating for 30 minutes.
- Frozen apple concentrate will only last for a few weeks after it is thawed.
- The tartness of an apple is derived from the balance of malic acid and the fruit's natural sugars.
- Apples will yield one pound of fresh apples = 2 large, 3 medium or 4 small apples. Also, about 2½ cups if they are chopped or sliced.

APPLES, BAKED

When most chefs prepare baked apples they always add a little cinnamon on top. Chefs will occasionally remove the top of the core with a melon corer and place cinnamon, raisins or nuts in the opening. If you do this be careful not to puncture the blossom end or everything you put in will leak out.

♦ To avoid wrinkled skin on apples when baking them, just cut a few slits in the skin to allow for expansion or remove a ½-inch horizontal strip of peel from an area around the middle.

♦ The best apple for baked apple is the Golden Delicious, Baldwin, Cortland, Ida Red and Northern Spy.

Science of Baked Apples

If you place a whole apple in the oven and bake it, the peel will withstand the heat and manage to retain its shape as long as it can. The peel contains insoluble cellulose and ligan, which reinforce the peel and keep it intact. The flesh of the apple, however, will partially disintegrate as the pectin in its cell walls are dissolved by the water being released from the cells. The cells rupture and the apple turns to applesauce.

APPLES, REPAIRING

Loss of Moisture
When apples lose their moisture, just slice then up and pour apple juice over them and refrigerate for about 30 minutes.
Poor Flavor
Quarter the apples and dip them in powdered anise or sprinkle them with cinnamon.

APPLE COBBLER

Science of Apple Cobbler
If you prefer the cobbler can be topped with graham cracker crumbs and baking until the fruit is tender and the crumbs are golden. If you find that the crumbs are getting too brown before the apples are tender, gently drape the top of the cobbler with a piece of aluminum foil to prevent burning.

APPLESAUCE

Whether your applesauce is smooth or chunky usually depends on when you add the sugar to the recipe.

- If you would prefer chunky applesauce, you should add the sugar before cooking the apples.
- If you prefer a smooth applesauce, then add the sugar after the apples have been cooked and mashed.
- If the applesauce is too sweet, just add a small amount of lemon juice.
- Commercially prepared sweetened applesauce can contain as much as 77% more calories than unsweetened varieties.

Science of Chunky Applesauce
Sugar tends to strengthen the cell walls of the apples allowing them to retain their shape to some degree when being cooked.

- If you use different varieties, you will have a unique flavor.
- Tart, cooking apples are best for applesauce.
- Try using some honey as the sweetener for a great flavor.

ARROWROOT

Arrowroot is derived from the rootstalks of a South American tuber, which is finely powdered and used as a thickener.

- Its thickening power is about 1-2 times that of all-purpose flour and like cornstarch should be mixed with adequate cold water to produce a paste before adding it to a hot mixture.
- One of the best features about arrowroot is that it will not impart a chalky taste if it is overcooked.
- Best not to over-stir a mixture that contains arrowroot or it will revert and become thin again. If your recipe calls for arrowroot and you don't have any just use 2¼ teaspoons of cornstarch.

ARTICHOKES

Artichoke history can be traced back as far as 250 BC. However, the artichoke; was first brought to the United States by a French immigrant in 1806 who settled in the Louisiana Territory. The first commercial crop was grown in Louisiana. In 1922 artichokes were grown in California, which now produce almost 100% of all artichokes grown worldwide. The artichoke is a member of the thistle family, a group of the sunflower family.

Marilyn Monroe was the first artichoke queen in 1949, crowned in Castroville, California, which is the artichoke capital of the world with a festival every year.

Artichokes are all harvested by hand, making it a very labor-intensive crop and costly.

One 12-ounce artichoke is a good source of vitamin C, potassium and folate as well as being low in sodium. It is a fat-free food with only 25 calories.

This large globe-like vegetable tends to scare people away and many people never get to taste one. If you do eat an artichoke remember that the best part to eat is at the base of the leaves, since the rest of the leaf is bitter and tough.

Place the leaf into your mouth and draw the leaf through your teeth removing the tender meat. After eating all meat on the leaves you will be left with the "choke" or the heart of the artichoke, which can be eaten with a fork and is the most succulent portion of the vegetable.

The artichoke is actually an unopened flower bud from a thistle-like plant. They tend to vary in size and produce a sweet aftertaste caused by the chemical "cynarin." When artichokes are sliced and mixed with other vegetables, the "cynarin" will impart the sweet flavor to the other vegetables.

Science of Artichokes

When you eat artichokes a chemical reaction occurs in the mouth that will make other foods and even beverages taste sweeter. This reaction is caused by the compound "cynarine," stimulating the sweetness taste buds on your tongue. This is one reason that it is recommended to serve artichokes by themselves or with a neutral-tasting food such as pasta.

The chemical "cyanarin" stimulates the taste buds that are involved in the sweet taste and keeps them stimulated for 3-4 minutes. After eating artichokes it's best to rinse your mouth with a glass of water. If you are going to make marinated artichoke hearts, be sure that you only use the hearts from the youngest artichokes you can find. To improve the color and to make the artichoke more tender chefs soak them in somewhat acidic water and never cooked them in an iron or aluminum pot.

There are 50 varieties and it is best to purchase them March through May

- Choose from compact, tightly closed heads with green, clean, looking leaves. Their size is not related to quality. Avoid ones that have brown leaves or show signs of mold.
- Artichokes should be soaked in acidulated water for about 1 hour before you prepare them to help them retain their color and tenderness.
- Be sure and wash the artichokes well, since dirt tends to hide between the leaves.
- Leaves that are separated show that it is too old and will be tough and bitter.
- Best to wear rubber gloves when working with artichokes.
- Artichokes should be drained on a rack upside down.
- They are easily burned and should be kept covered by water while they are cooking; however, they are also easy to overcook.

- Stainless steel knives should be used to cut artichokes. Carbon blades tend to react with the chemicals and darken the flesh.

Artichoke bottoms may be used as a container for dip or small vegetables.

- Steaming or boiling is the preferred methods of cooking artichokes.
- A better flavor may be obtained when cooking artichokes if you add a small amount of sugar and salt to the water. They will have a sweeter taste and will retain their color better. If they are still too bland, try adding a small amount of fennel to the cooking water, about ⅓ – ¼ teaspoons.
- Artichokes can be stored in an airtight plastic bag in the refrigerator; however, they should be sprinkled with a small amount of water before placing them in the bag. However, after about 6 days, their flavor starts to deteriorate and they lose their moisture fairly rapidly.
- Baby artichokes can be purchased in most supermarkets, sold either loose or repackaged.
- Older artichokes can be revived when cooking then by adding 1 teaspoon of sugar and 1 teaspoon of salt to the water.
- If you see a slight browning on the leaf edges, it is called "winter's kiss" and is caused by frost damage. This will, however, not affect the quality of the artichoke.
- Do not purchase artichokes that have a large amount of browning. They are old and not good quality.
- Never wash artichokes until they are to be used. Artichokes have a protective coating that can be removed by excessive washing.

Whole, trimmed artichokes need to remain upright if you are going to steam them so that the leaves on one side don't cook faster than the leaves on the other side. You do not want stuffed artichokes to fall over. To accomplish this, try cutting very thick slices (about 1½ inches thick) from medium onions and use your fingers to remove the outer three or four rings from the rest of the slice. Place the onion rings on the bottom of the pan and place one artichoke on top of each ring. The onion rings not only steady the artichoke, but it lifts the stem end off the bottom of the pot, keeping it from overcooking.

Science of Artichoke Color
When an artichoke is cooked, the chlorophyll in the green leaves reacts with the acids in the artichoke or cooking water and forms the compound "pheophytin," which turns the leaves brown. This is why many cooked artichokes have a bronze tint. If the artichoke is cooked fairly rapidly, this reaction will not take place and it will remain green. Also, if you rub lemon on the leaves that have been cut they will not discolor. Another method is to soak the artichoke for 20-30 minutes in a quart of water with 1½-tablespoons of white vinegar. The vinegar will stabilize the chemical that produces the color and the taste is also improved.

Soaking artichokes for 1 hour in acidulated water using 3 tablespoons of lemon juice in 1 quart of cold water improves their color and tenderness. If you cook artichokes in an aluminum or iron pot they will turn a grayish color and not be very attractive. The chemicals in the artichokes tend to react with certain metals.

Serving Artichokes
♦ If artichokes are to be served cold, cool them immediately in cold water; scoop-out the choke and remove the leaves from around the choke.
♦ An artichoke is completely cooked when pierced easily with a fork or skewer.

Basic Boiled Artichokes
Cook the artichokes in a heavy pot with about 2 cups of water and a very small amount of salt. The water should be brought to a boil before adding the artichokes and only place them in a single layer. They only need to be simmered for about 35 minutes. When a leaf comes off easily, they are done.

ASPARAGUS

Asparagus can be traced back to ancient Greece and has been referred to as the "aristocrat of vegetables." Asparagus received the name "Food of Kings" by King Louis XIV of France who had special greenhouses made so that he could have the delicacy year round. The Roman emperors actually kept a fleet of ships to get the asparagus so that they would not run out.

It is a member of the lily family and related to onions and garlic. It is an excellent source of vitamins and minerals. There are two types of asparagus, white and green.

Science of Cooking Asparagus
The major component in the cell wall of fruits and vegetables is a complex carbohydrate called "cellulose." The higher the cellulose content the firmer the fruit or vegetable. To tenderize the cellulose, heat and moisture are used. However, certain vegetables have different levels of cellulose in their various parts. Stems and stalks have more cellulose than tips, which is why it is necessary to remove the outer covering with a vegetable peeler before cooking broccoli or asparagus, otherwise the tips will be mushy and the stalks, tender.

When heat or moisture is applied to the vegetable, it tends to destroy the cell's capability to retain and release moisture, which causes a structural breakdown resulting in tenderness. It also dissolves some of the pectin, which is active in holding the cell walls together.

Asparagus contains a sulfur compound that is converted during the digestive process into a foul smelling chemical. When some people urinate after eating asparagus their urine may have a foul smell. Almost 40% of all people that eat asparagus have this problem caused by a specific gene that causes the harmless reaction. Beets contain a pigment called "betacyanin," which will harmlessly turn the urine and feces red. Only 15% of the population has the problem of not being able to metabolize this substance.

To tenderize the asparagus stalks, just use your potato peeler and remove the first layer of the stalk. Another method is to break off the top where the woody stem attaches by holding the spear in just the right spot (about halfway down the spear) and with your thumb and index finger of the opposite hand, bend the stalk and it should snap the top away from the bottom.

- Canned asparagus contains less vitamin C due to losses by heat and water in the can. It is recommended to use the water in other dishes.
- When choosing asparagus the stalks should be green with compact, closed tips and tender.
- Asparagus loses approximately 50% of its vitamin C content within 2 days after picking as well as some of its sugars. Fresh asparagus should be eaten within a day of purchase.
- Asparagus can be cooked in a microwave for about 8-9 minutes on high.
- The best time of year to purchase asparagus is March through June.
- Refrigeration will help to retain the nutrients providing you cut a small piece off the ends, wrap the ends in a moist paper towel and seal them in a plastic bag.
- Fresh asparagus loses sugar very rapidly and each day it is stored in a plastic bag in the refrigerator it will lose about 10-15% of its natural sugar. As the natural sugars are lost the asparagus will also become tougher.
- The tips should be kept as dry as possible or they will become mushy and fall apart when they are cooked.
- If the asparagus is too thick, you can cut an "X" on the bottom of each one to speed-up the cooking time.

Another method chefs use to tenderize the asparagus stalk is to remove a strip from either side of every stalk allowing the heat to penetrate more efficiently and tenderizing the tough fibers. It depended how old the asparagus is and which method is used.

When choosing asparagus, always choose the asparagus that has the darkest stems, they will be the sweetest. The white-stemmed asparagus is usually bitter and somewhat tough. The greener ones also will have a higher content of vitamin A, C and potassium.

Only male asparagus plants are sturdy enough for genetic engineering. The female plants do not respond well and are being weeded out. The female plants have been found to be tougher and not suitable for eating.

The best asparagus are the thicker, heartier stalks. They contain more nutrients and are almost always more tender. The thin stalks will be phased out and new varieties that are at least $\frac{1}{2}$ inch in width are now available.

The male asparagus flower has a stamen that will produce a spore. The female asparagus flower has a pistil or ovary. The male asparagus stalks are thinner, while the female stalks are fatter. The darker the color of asparagus the more tender and the greener or the more white the better.

Cook asparagus in the center of a Bundt pan for great results.

ASPARAGUS, COOKING OF

Preparing Asparagus

♦ Cook asparagus only until they are barely tender, since they will continue cooking for about 45 seconds after they are removed from the water. Overcooking will ruin asparagus.
♦ Wrap the asparagus stalks in damp paper towel when cooking them and only cook them in about 1-1¼" of water, covered and standing upright.
♦ To freeze, blanch in boiling water after removing 2 inches off the stems for 2-4 minutes. Freeze in a plastic bag.
♦ To stabilize asparagus in a tall pot, place a thick ring of aluminum foil around the tied bundle.
♦ The most common seasonings for asparagus are lemon juice, mustard sauce, parmesan cheese and butter

Cooking Asparagus

♦ Microwave asparagus in 2-3 tablespoons of water for about 6-7 minutes on high.
♦ Microwave cooking can also be done in a 12" round microwave-safe dish with all asparagus spears aimed toward the center with 2-4 tablespoons of water, then cook on high for about 10 minutes.
♦ Asparagus can be steamed in about 10 minutes.
♦ Grill asparagus for 3-5 minutes, precooked and tied in bundles.
♦ Stir-fry asparagus in 1 tablespoon of olive oil or 1-2 tablespoons of unsalted butter for about 1 minute or until tender.
♦ Bundles of asparagus should be cooked in about 1" of water with 1½ teaspoons of salt per quart of water.

AVOCADO

Originally grown in Central America and were first grown in the United States in the 1800's in Florida and California. The name "avocado" is derived from the Spanish word "aguacate," which was derived from the word "ahuacati" meaning testicle. California produces 90% of all avocados sold. The most popular varieties are "**Fuerte**," which is green and thick-skinned, and "**Hass**," which is almost black with a smooth skin.

The Florida avocado has half the fat of the California varieties and only 2/3 of the calories. Approximately 71%-80% of the calories in avocados are derived from fat.

However, most of the fat is the monounsaturated type, the same type found in olive and canola oil. They are available year round and should be fresh in appearance with colors ranging from green to purple-black. They should feel heavy for their size and be slightly firm. Avoid ones with soft spots and discoloration. Refrigerate if ripe, and use within 5 days after purchase.

Avocado is often used as a substitute for butter in some countries, since it has about a 20% fat content.

Avocado Facts

Always choose avocados that are a little soft at the stem end, so that it can be used right away and not left in a dark closet for 2-3 days in a wool sock to ripen. When I make an avocado dip (guacamole) I rarely throw the avocado pits away and grow them all over the house. Just force 3-4 toothpicks into the middle of the avocado and place it narrow end up in a glass of water. Be sure that the water is kept just over the bottom half of the pit, just under the toothpicks.

♦ To ripen an avocado, just place it in a wool sock in the back of a dark closet for 2 days. Avocados should never be stored in the refrigerator if they are not fully ripe. When they are ripe, they should be stored in the vegetable drawer in the refrigerator and should stay fresh for 10-14 days. Avocados may only be frozen for three to six months if pureed.

Neatness Counts

If you would like nice neat slices of avocado to place on a salad, just leave the skin on and make your slices without breaking through the skin. Using a thin rubber spatula, place it between the slices and the skin and move it around to loosen the slices and pop them out.

32

Science of Avocado

Never cook an avocado because a reaction will take place that releases a bitter chemical compound. It would be rare to ever see a recipe that calls for cooked avocado. When restaurants do serve avocado on a hot dish they will always place the avocado on the dish just before serving it. If you just slice an avocado, the enzyme "phenoloxidase" is released from the damaged cells and converts "phenols" into a brownish compound. Ascorbic acid will neutralize this reaction for a period of time, slowing the reaction.

Have you ever heard someone say that if you leave the pit in the guacamole, it will not turn black? I'm sure you have and you have probably tried it to no avail, unless you covered the entire dish tightly with plastic wrap.

The plastic wrap, not the pit, did the trick because it would not allow oxygen to oxidize the guacamole turning it black. Guacamole will oxidize on the surface in about 60-90 minutes if left out uncovered. The area under the pit was not exposed to the air, which is why it never turned black.

Oxygen is not our friend when it comes to exposed-surfaces on food. Another method that works is to spread a thin layer of mayonnaise on the top of the guacamole dip. Spraying the surface with a solution of powdered vitamin C and water also will work as well as actually placing the plastic wrap directly on top of the guacamole.

If you just slice an avocado, the enzyme "phenoloxidase" is released from the damaged cells and converts "phenols" into a brownish compound.

- ♦ Ascorbic acid will neutralize this reaction for a period of time, slowing the reaction.
- ♦ To remove an avocado pit, just thrust the blade of a sharp knife into the pit, twist slightly and the pit comes right out.
- ♦ If an avocado is too hard and needs to be used, try placing it in the microwave using high power for 40-70 seconds. Make sure and rotate it half way through. This procedure won't ripen it but will soften it.

BBBBB

BACON

Bacon is one of the oldest meats in history and dates back to 1500 BC. The earliest reference to bacon was in 1560 by a London Cheesemonger. In the 16th Century, European peasants would actually display the small amount of bacon they could afford.

...e and Tamworth pigs are two of the best, bred specifically for bacon. 70% of all ...e US is consumed at breakfast. There is more than 2 billion pounds of bacon ...d each year in the US.

If bacon was still produced the old fashioned way by curing it slowly and using a dry salt it would not be splattering all over the place. Today's bacon is cured using brine, which speeds up the process. The brine tends to saturate the bacon more causing the grease to be released and splatter more.

♦ To reduce splattering when cooking bacon, use a lower heat setting this will also reduce the number of nitrites you will convert into a carcinogen since the higher heat tends to convert the nitrites faster.

♦ Another method that might work is to soak the bacon in ice cold water for 2-4 minutes, then dry the bacon well with paper towels before frying. Also, try sprinkling the bacon with a small amount of flour, if that doesn't work, as a last resort poke some holes in them with your golf shoes.

♦ If you start the bacon cooking in a cold pan, it will reduce the shrinkage.

♦ Sliced bacon will only stay fresh for 1 week under refrigeration once the package is opened and the bacon is exposed to air.

Never pour bacon grease down the drain, since it solidifies very quickly.

♦ A one-pound package of sliced bacon has about 33 slices.

♦ If you allow bacon to sit at room temperature for 20-30 minutes before cooking it will separate more easily.

♦ Microwave bacon slices for 30 seconds and they will separate more easily.

♦ If you roll the package of bacon into a tube shape and place a rubber band around it, the slices will separate more easily.

♦ Never buy bacon if it looks slimy, chances are that it's not fresh.

♦ Slab bacon costs less than sliced bacon. Remove the rind before slicing it.

♦ Cracklings can be made by chopping up the bacon into small bits and frying it. Be sure that the bacon is partially frozen so that it will be easier to chop up.

♦ Bacon will not shrivel if you rinse the bacon under cold water before frying. This reduces the amount the bacon shrinks by almost 50%.

♦ To quickly and easily make real "bacon bits," hold slices of raw bacon over a frying pan, cut off little pieces into the pan with kitchen shears, then brown, stirring often; drain off grease.

SPEEDY BACON

If you ever wondered how chefs serve bacon fast and have it be crisp and not greasy, here's the secret:

ROLLING-UP THE BACON

Once you open a package of bacon it may become rancid before you have a chance to use it all up. If you freeze it in the original package, the slices will be difficult to separate and allow you to just use a few slices. When chefs can't use all of a bacon package and need to freeze the rest of the package, they just remove 3-4 slices and roll them into a cylinder.

They would do this for the balance of the package then place all the rolled cylinders in a large plastic freezer bag. When they wanted a few slices for a recipe, they would just remove the number of cylinders they needed and leave the rest in the freezer.

Bacon is one-meat that is highly nitrated. The higher nitrite content is found in the fat, which means you need to choose the leanest bacon you can find. Bacon can be prepared in the microwave on a piece of paper towel or under the broiler so that the fat drips down. When shopping for a bacon substitute, remember that almost all of these products still contain nitrites. Check the label and try to find a *"nitrite-free"* product. Chewing up a vitamin C tablet just before eating a nitrated food may neutralize the nitrites converting to a carcinogen.

BAGELS

The name bagel comes from the German word "beugel" meaning "a round loaf of bread." The first mention of the bagel was in 1610 in Kracow, Poland when it was mentioned in a piece of literature that it would be given to women in childbirth. The earliest picture of a bagel was in 1683 in an advertisement by a Jewish baker in Vienna, Austria.

♦ With the increase in bagel shops and delis the sale of bagels has skyrocketed over 175% in the last 12 years. Bagels now rank as one of the most popular breakfast foods in the United States. However, the size is increasing as well, turning a normally low fat, low-calorie food into a high-calorie food.
♦ The largest bagel ever made was on July 23, 1998 in Mattoon, Illinois. It was a blueberry bagel and weighed in at 714 pounds.

BAGEL LANGUAGE

Baglette.................. It is a mini-bagel that weighs around one-ounce.
Bracelets................ It is a bagel with a center hole that is too large.
Bull Bagels.............. It is a big bagel that may weigh over 6 ounces.
Everything Bagel..... It is a bagel that is topped with a little of everything. Usually salt, garlic, poppy seeds, sesame seeds, onion, etc.
Pocketbook Bagel.... It is a bagel that is often round with an off-center hole.
Twisters.................. Bagels made with two coils of twisted dough.
Winkers.................. Bagels that swell too much due to over-boiling and when baked have no hole.

GRANDMA'S OLD FASIONED BAGELS

Ingredients:

1	Package of dry yeast (fresh)	1½	Cups warm water (110^0-115^{0}F)
3	Teaspoons salt	3	Tablespoons sugar
5½	Cups unbleached white flour	1	Gallon of water
1	Tablespoon sugar		
1	Egg yolk beaten with 1 tablespoon of water		
	Poppy seeds, toasted onion flakes, caraway seeds, celery seeds, coarse salt, etc. for toppings.		

Making the dough

- Dissolve the yeast in the 1½-cups of warm water in a large mixing bowl.
- Allow it to stand for 5 minutes or until foamy.
- Stir in the salt and the 3 tablespoons of sugar.
- Start adding the flour one cup at a time, beating well after each addition (use your hands after adding about 3 cups of flour).

- The dough should be stiff, but still workable.
- Turn the dough out on a lightly floured board and knead for 10-15 minutes.
- Place the dough in a greased bowl, turning to coat all sides and cover with plastic wrap.
- Allow it to rise in a warm location for 30 minutes or until it has doubled in size.
- Turn dough out and punch down.
- Divide into 12 equal pieces and shape into rounds.
- Cover with a clean kitchen towel and let rest for 10 minutes.

Shaping the dough

- Work with one dough-round at a time keeping the others covered.
- Holding the dough round in both hands, poke your thumbs through the center.
- With one thumb in the hole, work the dough around, gently stretching, pulling and smoothing until the circle of the dough is about 3-3½ inches in diameter.
- Place on a lightly floured board and cover with a kitchen towel.
- Repeat with the remaining rounds.
- Let bagels rise for about 20 minutes or until puffed.
- Meanwhile bring the quart of water and 1 tablespoon of sugar to a boil in a large stockpot; reduce the heat and simmer until needed.
- When the bagels are puffed, slip 3 or 4 of them at a time into the water.
- They will sink at first then rise to the top.
- Simmer for 5 minutes, turning at least twice.
- Remove the bagels with a slotted spoon and drain briefly on paper towels then transfer them to cornmeal-dusted baking sheets.
- Repeat with remaining bagels.
- When all have been boiled, brush the top of each with the yolk-water glaze and sprinkle on toppings of your choice or just leave them plain.
- Bake in a 400⁰F oven for 35-40 minutes or until golden brown and crusty. Remove to cooking racks.

If you cut bagels in half before freezing, they will defrost very quickly.

Science of Bagels
Most bagels are water-based products that will not do well if placed in a microwave. The microwave will dehydrate the bagel. It is best to use a toaster oven or toaster. Bagels freeze well since they are made without using salt or dairy products. Malt is used to replace sugar and it is cooked in boiling water and then browned in the oven. Some bagels are now made with egg, but most are made with water in the dough.

BAKED GOODS, FAT USED
We need to realize that fat has a number of important purposes in baked goods. They extend shelf life, tenderize the product, add flavor and contribute to the texture.

When fat is replaced, the baked product may be altered to such a degree that the finished product will not be acceptable. Replacements include skim milk, egg whites, and certain starches and gums. These will all lower the fat content and reduce the total calories. The gums and starches cannot replace the fat completely; however, they do help to retain moisture.

BAKED GOODS, FREEZING OF

Certain foods need care when freezing and also special preparation techniques after they have been removed from the freezer. The following foods are some of the more popular that most people freeze:

Biscuits

Prepare as per instructions then freeze in a well-sealed bag. They should be heated unthawed at 350^0F for about 20 minutes.

Bread (homemade)

Prepare as usual and allow the bread to cool before placing in freezer. Thaw at room temperature and if wrapped in aluminum foil, bake at 300^0F for about 10 minutes.

Sandwiches (closed)

If you are going to freeze sandwiches use day old bread and spread butter, margarine or salad dressing to the edge of the bread before adding any filling. Do not use crisp vegetables, cooked egg white, preserves, mayonnaise or tomatoes.

Package sandwiches in aluminum foil and freeze. Thaw at room temperature in original wrapping for about 3-4 hours or in a lunch pail.

BAKING

Fat is used to produce tender baked good products by coating the gluten strands. The more the strands are coated, the more tender the product.

Fat is also needed to add texture to baked goods and other products. Chilled solid fat is recommended when preparing flaky pastry dough since it does not combine with the flour. This creates a flaky texture effect of alternating layers of fat and flour, which is why lard is the preferred fat for piecrusts.

- When greasing a pan with oil or butter, try not to overdo the amount you are using. A common problem of over-browning baked goods and other foods is caused by placing too much of an oil in a pan.
- If you see the slightest sign of mold on baked goods throw the item out. Mold tends to send out feelers that cannot be seen in most instances.
- Baking is a dry-heat method of cooking foods, which surrounds the food with heated air. Baking for the most part dries the food and therefore the need to control the amount of moisture lost is important.
- When mixing batter, spray the beaters with a vegetable oil spray before using them and the batter won't climb up the beaters.

♦ Airspace is important between pans, never place pans next to each other. Hot air needs to circulate and not be blocked.

♦ For the best results when baking always make sure that your oven has been pre-heated for at least 10 minutes before placing the product in. In most instances it is also best to bake on the center shelf so that you will get an even circulation of the heat.

BAKING TIMES

Baked goods should always be baked at high temperatures such as 425^0-450^0F. This will allow the expanding gasses to sufficiently increase the dough volume before the protein has a chance to coagulate, which will set the structure for the food. Small biscuits, because of their size, can easily be baked at the above temperatures without a problem.

However, a lower temperature is preferred for breads of about 400^0F since the higher temperature would probably burn the crust before the insides were baked. If you are baking bread with high sugar content you need a lower temperature of about 325^0-375^0F since sugar will caramelize at a very high temperature and cause the crust to turn black.

GREASE & FLOUR

When baking a variety of foods the recipe may call for you to *"grease and flour"* the pan before adding any ingredients. The standard method is to grease the pan with oil and then sprinkle flour in and tap the pan or move it around to allow the flour to distribute as evenly as possible. However, sticking still may occur unless you place a piece of waxed paper on top of the grease; then grease the waxed paper and then flour.

One of professional chef's secrets is to use what is known as the *"baker's magic"* method, which is to prepare a mixture of ½ cup of room temperature vegetable shortening, ½ cup of vegetable oil, and ½ cup of all-purpose flour. Blend the mixture well and use the mixture to grease the pans. The mixture can be stored in an airtight container for up to 6 months under refrigeration.

OIL CAN'T BE USED FOR BAKING!

Because of its liquid nature, oils tend to collect instead of evenly distributing through the dough. This may cause the baked goods to become grainy. When solid fat is used, baked items tend to be more fluffy and retain their moisture better. Especially bad are the *"all-purpose"* oils, which even though they say that they can be used for baking and frying are not up to the standards that most cooks desire. To produce these oils a number of additives are used which may affect the flavor and taste of the food.

BETTER WEAR DARK SHADES

If you would like the crust on your fresh baked bread to have a great sheen, just brush the top of the bread with vinegar about 5 minutes before the bread has finished baking. Remove the bread before brushing on the vinegar, as the oven can get very cramped.

BAKING, ACIDS IN

NEUTRALIZE ME OR ELSE

Any time a baking powder recipe, especially muffins, cookies and cupcakes by adding an ingredient that had acid in it such as sour cream, yogurt, buttermilk, vinegar, chocolate, any citrus fruit or tart apples; the baked product needed to be neutralized with a base, such as baking soda to produce the best tasting product.

Science of Acids in baking

If you use any of the above mentioned acidic ingredients you will have to decrease the amount of baking powder called for in a recipe. Baking powder also falls into the acid category and for every $\frac{1}{2}$ teaspoon of baking soda used; you will need to reduce the amount of baking powder by 1 teaspoon.

The more difficult acids to work with when baking are lemons, limes, white vinegar, wine vinegar, cider or malt vinegar. Balsamic vinegar is not as difficult to work into a recipe; however, it still has to be neutralized.

BAKING, CHOCOLATE

This is also called bitter or unsweetened chocolate and is pure chocolate liquor that has been extracted from the cocoa bean. Usually has lecithin and vanilla added for flavor and to keep it in a usable suspension.

BAKING, DRY INGREDIENTS

Many recipes call for a variety of dry ingredients to be added all at once (such as baking powder, baking soda, cream of tartar, salt, etc.) If you lose track and are interrupted it can cause a problem. Next time you are working with a recipe that calls for numerous dry ingredients, just place all measured dry ingredients in separated mounds on a sheet of waxed paper.

BAKING, OVEN TEMPERATURES

The temperature of the oven is very important; chefs use a small metal thermometer to make sure that the oven temperature is correct. For regular dough, the oven temperature is normally set at 400^0F to 425^0F and between 350^0F to 375^0F for sweetened dough.

Science of Oven Temperature

When the oven temperature is too low, the dough will expand to its maximum before the gluten and starch have set properly and the loaf will probably collapse. If the oven is too hot, the protein and starch in the outer layers will solidify too fast and form a crust that will prevent the loaf from expanding causing poor texture. When the temperature is correct, the yeast cells will become active for a short period and produce a little more carbon dioxide. This happens when the dough is placed into the hot oven and stops when the yeast cells die as soon as they reach 140^0F.

BAKING, TYPES OF FAT

Low-fat margarine or whipped butter should not be used for baking purposes. They both have too high water and air content and this may cause your cakes or cookies to collapse or flatten out. For the best result, always try and use the type of fat recommended in the recipe.

When the recipe calls for a greased pan, make sure you always use unsalted butter. Salted butter has a tendency to cause food to stick to the pan.

BAKING, USING WATER

GLUB, GLUB

When it came to adding water to baked goods, grandma always added a little extra yeast. At the bottom of one of her bread recipes, she has a note that said:

"If using hard water add a small amount of extra yeast or use a small amount of vinegar."

Science of Water

The hardness or softness of water will make a difference in the final baked product. Water with a high mineral content will affect the rate of fermentation of yeast and the pliability of the dough. You need to reduce the pH of the batter by adding a small amount of vinegar (mild acid) or increasing the yeast.

BAKING, WITH HONEY

The best honey for baking is the mildest-flavored, which is the white or golden honey.

...oney is added to a batter, it should be added in a slow stream with continuous
...g. Remember, if you use honey in baked goods they will brown faster and you
...y want to reduce the oven heat by about 25^0F (-3.9^{0}C). The addition of honey will
...also produce baked goods that will remain moist for a longer period of time.

BAKING POWDER

Baking powder was invented in 1849 and combines sodium bicarbonate and an acid
salt to make the leavening agent. In 1854 self-rising flour was invented, which combined
baking powder with flour.

Baking powder is a mixture of a number of chemicals that will leaven
breads. The main chemicals are calcium acid phosphate, sodium aluminum
sulfate or cream of tartar and sodium bicarbonate. This mixture of acids and
bases and a starch produce a chemical reaction when water is added to it
producing carbon dioxide, a gas. When this occurs, the gas creates minute
air pockets or will enter already existing ones in the dough or batter.

Double-acting baking powder means that the baking soda contains one acid that is
capable of bubbling at room temperature and another acid that will only react at oven
temperatures. All recipes use the double-acting type unless the recipe asks for another
kind. If the recipe calls for single-action, better use single action for a better product, but
be aware that the single-acting baking powder will start to work as soon as it hits the
liquid. On the other hand don't use single acting if the recipe calls for double-acting
baking powder or the baked good will rise too much.

When you place the mixture in a hot oven or hot plate, the dough rises because the
heat causes additional carbon dioxide to be released from the baking powder as well as
expanding the trapped carbon dioxide gas creating steam. This pressure swells the
dough or batter and it expands or rises for the occasion.

- Always combine the wet and dry ingredients separately.
- A wet measuring spoon should never be placed into a baking powder box.
- Use 1 teaspoon of baking powder for each 1 cup of flour. If you're mixing a batter
  for fried foods, reduce to half the amount for each. This will give you a lighter
  coating.

FORMULA

The formula for making one teaspoon of baking powder is to use ½ teaspoon of cream
of tartar and ¼ teaspoon of baking soda.

If you plan on storing a quantity of the powder for a few days, then add ¼ teaspoon of
cornstarch to absorb moisture from the air preventing a chemical reaction to take place
before you are ready to use it. This formula tends to cause the release of carbon dioxide
faster and the mixture should be used as fast as possible when you use it.
Commercially produced powders work at a higher temperature giving them a longer
period of time before they react.

LOSS OF POTENCY

Baking powder does lose potency over time (about 6 months) and if you are unsure of its freshness you should test it before using it. Place ½ teaspoon of baking powder in a small bowl then pour ¼ cup of hot tap water over it.

The more bubbling activity there is, the fresher the baking powder. The activity must be at a good active level or the dough will not rise sufficiently. Try this test on a box of fresh baking powder so that you will be familiar with the activity level of the fresh powder. Be sure to check the date on the box when you first purchase it to be sure it's fresh.

Science of Baking Powder

Baking powder will influence the characteristics of the product, such as the crust, volume, grain and texture as well as the overall quality of the product. It is a leavening agent composed of an acid and an acid-reacting salt or an acid-reacting salt and bicarbonate of soda releasing carbon dioxide gas. The gas causes creaming by entering the air cells in the batter. The recipe proportions must be exact and the baking powder fresh.

Single-acting baking powder will only release the carbon dioxide gas once. Double-acting releases gas twice, once when you mix it into the product and again when it encounters heat.

BAKING SODA

Sodium bicarbonate (baking soda) is an inorganic powder, which simply means that it is not produced from living matter and is sold in very fine particles with a high surface area. House odors are composed of organic oils that become stuck in the powder and neutralized as if taken into a sponge. When the oils remain in the soda they eventually become inactivated permanently.

Baking soda is actually derived from the manufacture of common washing soda, also known as "sal soda." Baking soda is composed of carbon and oxygen molecules, which combine to form carbon dioxide gas. If batter has a sufficient acidic nature then only baking soda is needed to produce carbon dioxide. If the batter does not have sufficient acid then baking powder, which carries both acid and alkali is needed.

All baking soda in North America is mined from the mineral, Trona, which is found in Green River, Wyoming. The large deposit was discovered in the 1930's. Trona is actually composed of sodium bicarbonate and sodium carbonate, a very close relative. The ore is mined from deep mines, crushed, rinsed and heated to produce sodium carbonate. The sodium carbonate is then dissolved in water and carbon dioxide is forced through the solution releasing the sodium bicarbonate crystals, which is washed then dried and packaged as baking soda.

...g soda will not help vegetables to retain their color when added to the cooking ...er. It is best to add a small amount of milk or white vinegar to the cooking water.

♦ When baking soda is added to a recipe, it has an immediate rising action with the release of the gas, which means that your oven must be preheated and your pans greased before you even combine the ingredients.
♦ Baking soda should be added to dry ingredients first and the wet ingredients just before placing the food into the oven.
♦ Baking soda will last for approximately 6 months if stored in an airtight container and in a cool, dry location.

If you are not sure of the activity level of baking soda, try placing $\frac{1}{4}$ teaspoon in about 2 teaspoons of white vinegar, if carbon dioxide bubbles appear it still has good activity.

Sodium bicarbonate is produced in the human body to assist in maintaining the acidity (pH) level of the blood as well as being found in saliva. It will neutralize plaque acids, which might otherwise dissolve our teeth. Another action in the body is to neutralize stomach acid so that we don't get ulcers as well as assisting in the breathing process by transporting carbon dioxide from the tissues to the lungs for disposal.

Avoid using baking soda around fruits and vegetables. Baking soda is a base and many fruits and vegetables are somewhat acidic. When you mix a base and an acid, you may end up with a salt and significant loss of taste.

♦ If baked goods contain molasses (somewhat acidic), they will have better texture if you add ¼ teaspoon of baking soda for every 1/3rd cup of molasses used in the recipe.
♦ If you use a box of baking soda in the refrigerator to get rid of odors, it will only remain active for about 3 months.
♦ Once a month you should pour about ¼ cup of baking soda into the garbage disposal to clean out the odors. Allow it to remain for about 1 hour before washing it down.

BANANA

The banana has been mentioned in history as far back as 327 BC when they were found growing in India by Alexander the Great. They are available all year round since they grow in a climate with no winter. They should be plump and the skin should be free of bruises as well as brown or black spots.

Bananas contain less water content than most other fruits. They are actually a **"berry"** from a plant classified as an herb tree, which is capable of reaching heights of 30 feet. The banana tree is also the largest plant in the world with a woody stem.

♦ Bananas should be purchased green or at least with some green tint and allowed to ripen at home. There are over 500 varieties of bananas.
♦ The banana tree is actually an herb. It is a fruit, herb and a berry all in one.
♦ Bananas are mainly grown in a tropical climate; however, they are also grown in Iceland in soil heated by volcanic steam vents.
♦ If you are not sure if a banana is ripe, just insert a toothpick in the stem end. If it comes out clean and with ease, the banana is ripe.

As soon as a banana ripens at room temperature, they should be stored in the refrigerator to slow down the ripening process. The skin will turn black; however, this does not affect the flesh for a number of days.

♦ Bananas contain less water than most other fruits. They are a type of berry from a tree classified as an herb tree which can grow up to 30 feet high, and are the largest plant in the world with a woody stem. Bananas were one of the first plants ever grown on a farm.
♦ Ripe bananas may be stored in a sealed plastic bag in the refrigerator after they have ripened.
♦ If you are going to cook with bananas, use ones that are just under ripe for the best results. They will retain their shape better!
♦ If bananas become overripe, just place them in the blender and puree them, then freeze them for use at a later date for banana bread.

SUGAR CONTENT

Bananas are always picked when they are green. If they are allowed to ripen on the tree they tend to lose their taste and become mealy. The sugar content increases as soon as the banana is picked and increases from 2% to 20%.

• The more yellow the skin becomes, the sweeter the banana.
• Brown spots are the result of the sugar level increasing over the 25% level.
• The more brown, the higher the sugar content.

FREEZING BANANAS

Bananas will freeze for about 6-7 months if left in their skins. Ripe bananas can be mashed and frozen in one-cup portions and can be used for baking. If you peel the whole ripe banana, place it in a plastic bag and it can be frozen whole.

BANANA BREAD

> ### Science of Banana Bread
> When bananas ripen, the acid level decreases and if you only use baking soda in the recipe, the bread will not come out very good. Chefs always use both baking powder and baking soda when preparing banana bread to assure perfect leavening.

A VERY RIPE FACT

When you use those old bananas that are overripe for banana bread, be sure and add both baking powder and baking soda to the recipe for the best results. To tell if a banana is ripe, just insert a toothpick and pull it out. If it comes out clean, the banana is ripe enough to eat.

BARBECUE SAUCE

Barbecue sauces are prepared to provide a particular flavor to the food and are usually brushed on meat and chicken.

They are not designed to tenderize the food and do not penetrate very deeply into the food. Almost all barbecue sauces contain oil, which keeps the surface of the food moist and helps avoid burning. The sauce is applied a number of times during the cooking process with a natural bristle brush or a special barbecue brush.

- Commercial barbecue sauces that are purchased in the supermarket can be turned into homemade sauces with the addition of finely chopped garlic, diced onions or green pepper.
- If you want to spice up the barbecue sauce, just add some finely chopped fresh chili peppers, Tabasco sauce or some cayenne.
- Fresh herbs can be added as well as sweetening it up with some molasses.
- Keep track of what you are adding so that if the family likes it, you can duplicate the flavor.

BARBECUING

The word "barbecue" originated from the Spanish word *"barbacoa,"* which means *"frame of sticks."* The Spanish used the word to describe the Haitian Indians' method of grilling their meats outdoors.

When you need to barbecue for a large crowd and your grill isn't big enough, you can save time by using a cookie sheet and placing a few layers of hamburger between layers of tin foil and baking the burgers at 350^0F for 25 minutes.

Then complete them on the grill in only 5-10 minutes. Hot dogs may be done the same way but only bake for 10 minutes.

THE BARBECUING CHEF

Grandma had the heaviest round barbecue I ever saw. It's a good thing it had wheels or it would never move anywhere. The top grate was a shiny stainless steel, which made it easier to clean especially since I had the chore.

Science of Barbecuing

When barbecuing beware of flare-ups since they will char the food and place a black soot coating on the food affecting the flavor and texture of the food. Allow 30-45 minutes for the coals to heat up and develop a light gray coating. All visible fat needs to be trimmed off any meat to avoid flare-ups. The heat can be increased by adding more coals or placing the food closer to the heat source. If you have air vents under the bottom close them and it will increase the heat. The thicker the metal the more heat will be retained.

- ♦ A number of different herbs can be placed on the coals to flavor the food. The best are savory rosemary, or dried basil seedpods. Lettuce leaves can be placed on the coals if they become too hot or flare up.
- ♦ Charcoal briquettes should always be stored in airtight plastic bags since they will absorb moisture very easily.
- ♦ Coat your grill with a spray vegetable oil before starting the fire then clean it shortly after you are through. Never spray the oil on the grill after the fire has started, as it may cause a flare-up.
- ♦ Window cleaner sprayed on a warm grill (not a very hot grill) will make it easier to clean. This should be done shortly after removing the food.

BARBECUING, CHICKEN

If you are going to use a barbecue sauce on chicken you need to know when to apply it otherwise the chicken will have an acid taste.

- Barbecue sauces contain sugar and high heat tends to burn sugar very easily as well as some of the spices.
- The barbecue sauce should never be placed on the bird until about 15 minutes before the bird is fully cooked.
- Another secret to the perfect barbecued bird is to use lower heat and leave the bird on for a longer period of time.
- Never place the bird too close to the coals or the fat in the skin may cause a flare-up.

BARBECUING, CORN

When wrapping corn in tin foil for barbecuing, try placing a sprig of marjoram next to each ear of corn.

BARBECUING, STEAK

When you eat a 16-ounce steak prepared on a charcoal barbecue, remember that you may be ingesting the equivalent cancer forming agents (carcinogens) that would be found in 15 cigarettes. The problem only exists if there is sufficient fat dripping on the *"real"* charcoal briquettes, which causes a chemical reaction to take place coating the meat with *"pyrobenzines."*

- Wrapping the meat in foil or scrapping the black material off will help to reduce the risk.
- There is no risk if you use artificial charcoal or a gas grill.
- Americans spend over $400 million dollars each year on charcoal briquettes.
- Always turn steaks with tongs to avoid puncturing the steak and allowing the juices to run out. This is one of the more common mistakes backyard chefs make and will dry out the meat.

BARDING

This is the process of covering meats or fowl with added fat to keep the flesh moist. It is usually done to meats that only have a small fat covering and is accomplished by basting the meat with any fat source.

- ◆ If you want to use bacon, be sure to boil the bacon strips for 4-5 minutes to reduce the salt content.
- ◆ The barding fat needs to be removed about 15 minutes before the meat is fully cooked to allow the meat to brown.

BASIL

There are more than 60 varieties of basil found worldwide. It is a common seasoning for fish, meat, tomato dishes, soups, stews, pizza sauce, dressings, and used on salads. Basil is a relative of the mint family and is usually imported from India. Basil is also grown in the United States and known as "sweet basil." It is best to store fresh basil in the refrigerator in a slightly moistened plastic bag. It should retain its flavor and aroma for about 4 days.

- ◆ Basil tends to lose much of its flavor after about 15 minutes of cooking and should be added about 10 minutes before the food is done for the best results.
- ◆ There are a number of varieties of basil, which include lemon and cinnamon basil, which have green leaves and opal basil, which has purple leaves.
- ◆ When preserving fresh basil in oil only fresh leaves should be used and removed carefully from the stems. Place the leaves into a jar and cover them with extra virgin olive oil. Seal the jar well and refrigerate until ready to use.
- ◆ Fresh basil is excellent in salads and used in pesto, which is a puree of basil, pine nuts, olive oil and Parmesan cheese.
- ◆ Basil will freeze well and can be used year round.

- ➤ **Scrambled Eggs**

  Add 1 teaspoon of fresh leaves with the eggs before you cook them.
- ➤ **Roasts**

  Sprinkle the roast lightly with crushed dried basil before roasting.
- ➤ **Tomatoes**

  Mix basil with extra virgin olive oil.
- ➤ **Shrimp**

  When boiling, add ¼ teaspoon of the dried herb to the water before boiling.
- ➤ **Stew**

  Place 1 whole sprig in stew the same time meat is added and before it starts to boil.
- ➤ **Vegetables**

  If baking vegetables, sprinkle dried herbs lightly before placing in the oven.

BAY LEAF

 It is usually sold as whole leaves and commonly used in vegetables, stews, sauces, soups, French dressing, dill pickles, meat dishes, veal, and poultry. Also, used in numerous ready-to-serve foods. Remember to remove bay leaves from foods before you serve them. If someone eats a piece it will be like eating a mouthful of straw. Never crumble up a bay leaf when using it in a recipe and stir gently so as not to break the bay leaf up. The Turkish variety of bay leaf has a milder flavor than the California variety and is wider and shorter.

Bay Leaf

Bay leaf was used for a number of dishes, the most common of which was tomato soup. Only one bay leaf was added to 2 cups of soup to flavor it while the soup was cooking. Grandmother used bay leaf in pickling and especially when cooking carrots.

Rule of Thumb

For every 4 servings use approximately ¼ teaspoon dried leaves and tips or 3 teaspoons chopped fresh leaves or 1 small sprig of fresh leaves.

BEANS, BAKED

Canned baked beans will no longer cause flatulence since they are treated with an enzyme called "b-oligosaccharidase." This enzyme neutralizes the complex sugar in the beans.

Science of Baked Beans

If you add molasses to baked beans it will help them retain their shape for a longer period of time. The cell walls in beans prefer the sugar in molasses over other sugars when it comes to keeping their cells walls more stable. Raw beans contain a very small amount of a toxin that is destroyed with cooking.

BEANS, CANNED

 Canned beans should be rinsed before using them to remove any excess salt and discard the liquid. They are excellent pureed and used in soups.

BEANS, LEGUMES

Almost all legumes, including beans, peas, and lentils (fresh or dried) contain a toxin called a "lectin," which is capable of causing abdominal pain, nausea, diarrhea, and severe indigestion. To destroy this toxin, legumes must be cooked at a rolling boil for 10 minutes before lowering the heat to a simmer. Peas and lentils only need to boil for 2-3 minutes to kill the toxin.

STORING

If legumes are kept in a dry, cool location below 70^0F they will last for up to 1 year and retain most of their nutrient content. They may be stored in their original bag or container or transferred to a sealed glass jar.

- Never mix old beans with new beans, as they will not cook evenly. It is not necessary to freeze dried beans since it will not help to retain their nutrient content any longer.
- Beans in cooked dishes may be frozen, however, they may be somewhat mushy when thawed but can last for up to 6 months.
- Pinto beans contain about 22% protein while beef has only 18%, and eggs 13%.

Science of Beans, Peas & Lentils

To remove the gas problem from dried beans, add 1 teaspoon of fennel seed to the water that the beans are soaking in. The fennel will neutralize the complex carbohydrate called oilgosaccharides causing the gas. These sugars cannot be digested by normal stomach acids and end up in the lower intestinal tract and fermented by friendly bacteria causing gas. If the water is changed that the beans are soaking in 2-3 times overnight it will also reduce the chances of intestinal gas forming.

Beans, peas and lentils all contain the chemical group called lectins. This is a toxin that can cause abdominal pain, nausea and diarrhea. They cannot be consumed raw and should to be cooked for a minimum of 10 minutes at a full boil then reduced to a simmer. The toxins are destroyed after about 3 minutes of boiling. This is not the source of the flatulence problem, which is caused by a complex carbohydrate.

When you cook dried beans, try adding 2 tablespoons of white vinegar to the pot. This will tenderize the beans and will reduce the gas problem in susceptible individuals.

BEANS, LIMA

Gas-free lima beans are now being grown. They will contain less of the hard-to-digest complex sugar that causes the problem.

Poisonous Lima Beans

Lima beans tend to produce an enzyme called "cyanogen" which is a form of cyanide. Some countries have laws that restrict certain varieties of Lima beans from being grown. European and American farmers have developed new breeds of Lima beans that do not produce as much of the toxin and are safer to eat. These potentially harmful toxins may be removed by boiling the beans in a pot without a lid allowing the hydrogen cyanide gas to escape with the steam. Neither raw lima beans nor their sprouts should be eaten raw.

BEANS, PINTO

Pinto beans are a dried bean that is an excellent source of protein. They should have a bright uniform color. Fading is a sign of aging or long storage periods.

- ♦ When preparing pinto beans, try and purchase ones of uniform size, the smaller ones may become mushy before the larger ones are cooked. If you feel that this may be a problem, try adding a small amount of baking soda to the water while they are cooking.
- ♦ When you are cooking dried beans, make sure you add 3 teaspoons of a pure vegetable boil to the water, this will help prevent boil over.
- ♦ To tell whether a bean is fully cooked squeeze the bean, you should never feel a hard core.
- ♦ Be sure and check dried beans for any extraneous material that may be in with the beans. Even small stones have been found in bean packages.
- ♦ If you are cooking the beans in an acid medium, such as with tomatoes, this will slow down the cooking time and testing the tenderness of the beans is a must.

A chef's trick to soften beans in a short period of time is to cover the beans with cold water about 2-3 inches over the top of the beans then bring the pot to a quick boil and allow it to simmer over low heat for 2 minutes. Remove the beans from the heat and allow them to stand for about 1 hour. Do not use the water.

If you over soak them bubbles will start rising to the surface and they will look shriveled. If this does occur, just remove the beans from the pot and allow them to remain in a colander for one-half hour before using them.

To reduce the gassiness, chefs may change the water 2-3 times then cook them in fresh cold water.

Remember, salt and any acid like the type found in tomatoes will make beans tough. Never add beans to a tomato sauce until they are fully cooked.

- The taste of beans can be improved by adding a small amount of brown sugar or molasses.
- Dried beans can be stored for up to 12 months if placed in a cool, dry location and in a well-sealed container.
- Dried beans can be frozen and will last for many years, almost indefinitely.
- One pound of dried beans will equal about 2½ cups uncooked and 5-6 cups cooked.
- Be sure and re-hydrate all dried beans before using them in cooking.

The fast method of re-hydrating dried beans is to place them into a large pot and cover them with water then bring them to a boil. Remove them from the heat and allow them to stand for 1-2 hours before using in a recipe.

Many people worry about the loss of nutrients due to the long cooking and soaking times for beans and other legumes. Studies performed by the USDA, however, have proved that legumes even if they require 1-1½ hours of cooking time will still retain from 70-90 percent of their vitamin content and almost 95 percent of their mineral content. The most affected were the B vitamins of which about 45-50 percent is lost.

Instead of soaking beans in water overnight, try soaking them in cider, then use applesauce to thicken the syrup.

BEANS, SHELL

These are actually mature fresh seeds that are between the fresh seeds and dried seeds. Shell beans have a higher level of vitamins and dried beans are higher in protein, potassium and iron.

- Shell beans should have a bulge and a tightly closed pod.
- If the pods are sealed, they should last for 2-3 days.
- When they are cooked, add a small amount of baking soda to the cooking water to help stabilize their color.
- Cooked beans have a refrigerator life of approximately 5 days.
- If you boil the beans whole without even removing the ends you will retain 50% more of the nutrients.
- If you place a very small amount of sugar in the cooking water of beans it will bring out the flavor.
- Baking soda should never be added to green beans while they are being cooked, as it will reduce the nutrient content of the beans.
- Acid foods such as tomatoes will cause the color of green beans to be lighter.
- You can store unwashed beans in a well-sealed plastic bag in the refrigerator for up to 4 days.
- One pound of fresh beans will yield about 3½ cups whole and almost 3 cups trimmed and cut up with the stem and string removed.

- Excellent used raw in salads when blanched for about 10 seconds and the placed immediately into ice cold water to help retain their color.
- Frozen beans can be thawed in cold water for about 8 minutes.

If you want your snap beans to produce over a longer period of time, just pick them when the beans are about pencil width. Make sure that the seeds are just visible. If you wait too long the plant will make the seeds larger instead of the meat of the bean and use up all its energy.

BEEF

In many instances when we purchase meats the outside is a nice red color and the insides are darker almost with a brownish tint.

Butchers have been accused of dying or spraying the meats; however, it is really not their fault. Actually, when the animal is slaughtered and the oxygen-rich blood is not pumped to the muscles, the myoglobin tends to lose some of its reddish color and may turn a brownish color. Then when the meat is further exposed to the air through the plastic wrap, oxidation tends to turn the myoglobin a red color.

Butchers call this process the *"bloom"* of the meat. If you would like to see the insides a bright red color, just slice the insides open and leave the meat in the refrigerator for a short period of time. The air will turn the meat a reddish color. Remember, however, that if the meat is exposed for too long a period the oxygen will eventually turn the meat brown.

Science of Fat Color

If the steer was grass-fed, the color of the fat will be yellow and the beef will be somewhat tough. If the color of the fat is white, it means that the steer was corn-fed or grain-fed and will be more tender and cost more.

A well-marbled piece of meat will always be more tender that a lean cut of meat with little fat showing.

- Any meat that has been ground up has had a large percentage of its surface exposed to the air and light. Oxygen and light cause a breakdown in the meat and tend to change the color as well as making the meat go bad in a very short period of time. Exposure to oxygen, especially, leads to deterioration known as "self-oxidation." Grinding meats also speeds up the loss of vital nutrients.
- If you would like nice brown meat, be sure and blot the excess moisture from the surface, of the meat before cooking it. A light dusting with flour also works well after blotting.
- The beef chop is really a T-bone steak, which is much larger than a pork chop or a lamb chop.

- Dark-colored beef is only 1-2% of all beef. The fresh beef tends to turn a dark color very quickly making it unsuitable for sale at the supermarket, since we like to see our beef red instead of brown. Simply: it is caused by the cow being under too much stress before being slaughtered and drawing on glycogen stores to covert the glycogen to lactic acid. Normal lactic acid levels in beef will cause the meat to become red.

> Chefs never look for beef that has fresh bright red color, which is very appealing. They always look for meat that is more reddish brown, which means that the beef had been exposed to oxygen and will have a better flavor.

- There is a healthy movement going on to educate the public in the benefits of grass-fed cattle, bison and chickens. This is definitely the healthier way to go if there will be enough to go around and the products are easy to obtain.
- The animals that are grass-fed are higher in a number of antioxidant nutrients as well as omega-3 fatty acids. There are no hormone residues to be concerned about and no feed antibiotics to stimulate their growth. These animals live a normal life and provide us with the best quality meats.
- Fresh beef can be left in its original wrapper if cooked within 6-8 hours of purchase. If you plan on keeping it without freezing, it is best to re-wrap it.
- Ground beef can be left in its shrink-wrapped package for up to 2 days in the refrigerator.

When beef is cooked it becomes more easily digested and utilized by the body. Cooking beef to medium-well (170^0F) will increase the availability of vitamin B_1 by 15% over well-done beef (185^0F). Amino acids, the building blocks of protein will be absorbed more efficiently and more fully utilized when they come from beef. The absorption-rate of beef is about 90%; grains are 80% and legumes (beans) at 60-75%.

> As we cook beef we can see that the color of the meat changes depending on how long we cook it. The red pigment of the myoglobin changes from a bright red in a rare steak to brown in a well done one. The internal temperature in a rare steak is 135^0F, medium-rare is 145^0F, medium is 155^0F, and well done is 160^0F.

HOW MUCH BEEF TO BUY FOR EACH PERSON?

BEEF ONLY:

Type of Beef Per Serving

Chuck Roast/Rib Roast.........½ lb.
Filet Mignon ....5 oz.
Hamburger.........................¼ lb.
Pot Roast with bone.............¼ lb.
Ribs..................................1 lb.

Round Beef Roast with bone.. ¼ lb.
Round Steak........................ ½ lb.
Sliced Lunch Meats.............. ¼ lb.
Steaks with bones................ 12 oz.
Steaks without bones............7 oz.
Stew Meat......................... ¼ lb.
Tenderloin of Beef................½ lb.

THE INSIDE STORY OF A COW

There are eight major cuts of beef butchered in the United States, they are called shank, flank, brisket, chuck, round, rib, plate and loin. The eight cuts are given a number of additional names, which will be more recognizable to the consumer. These include names such as: sirloin, porterhouse, top round, eye of the round, New York, T-bone, etc. These explain the way the eight major cuts are actually cut up. The tenderness of beef will depend on the location of the cut and the

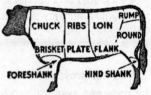

Beef showing various cuts

method of cutting. Some cuts are tougher than other cuts. These include pot roasts (chuck roasts), which are cut from the neck area of the cow and will be the least expensive.

CHUCK CUTS (ROASTS)

These are the toughest cuts and should be cooked in a small amount of liquid and they may need to be tenderized.

RIB CUTS (RIBS)

Markets may label these as baby back ribs, rib steaks, rib roasts, or just back ribs. For the best results they should be prepared by grilling or placed in the oven and cooked slowly. The taste can be improved by adding a sauce or using a marinade.

LOIN CUTS (TENDERLOIN)

Cut from behind the ribs they are the most tender. They include filet, Spencer, porterhouse, and New York steaks. A New York steak is a sirloin steak that has been cut about 1" thick and was popularized in New York City.

ROUND CUTS (ROASTS)

Most of these will be tender and can be cooked a number of different ways. They include top round, eye of the round, and bottom round. They can be pot roasted or spit barbecued.

FLANK AND PLATE CUTS

Most of the time if USDA Good grade is purchased they will need tenderizing. Prime and Choice are much better choices for these cuts. They are usually cut in strips and used for stir-frying. London broil is made from flank steak, best if marinated.

BRISKET CUTS

The brisket is cut from behind a cow's front leg or may be cut from the leg itself. Normally a tough cut of beef it needs to be cooked in liquid for about 2-3 hours.

If you wish to get the best results when preparing a brisket, rotate the roast ¼ turn every 25 minutes. The brisket is fully cooked when you see the fat just starting to roll off. However, if the fat can easily be removed with your fingers the brisket is overdone.

THE BODY PREFERS WELL DONE BEEF

When it came to cooking roasts, grandma would usually cook the meat close to well-done most of the time. She said that she could more easily digest it and it caused her fewer digestive problems. However, the meat seemed to be somewhat dry and gravy was usually needed when she made it this way.

♦ It would be best not to salt any meat that is going to be broiled, grilled or sautéed until after they have browned.

Science of Well Done Beef

Science has proven that when meat is cooked well done it is more easily digested by the body and even utilized better. Cooking meat to medium-well at an internal temperature of 160°F (60°C), however, should suffice and will actually increase the availability of vitamin B_1 by 15 over well done beef at 185°F (82°C). Amino acids (protein) are better absorbed from beef than from any other source. The absorption rate from beef is 90% and from beans only 60-70%.

Science of Beef

Beef is mainly composed of protein (in the form of muscle tissue), fat and water. If you remove the fat, beef is actually about 60% water. Beef muscle fibers are supported by small bands of connective tissue: either collagen or elastin. The cut of meat from a muscle that gets a lot of exercise has more connective tissue, resulting in a tougher cut of meat.

Since the connective tissue in these areas usually have a fat layer surrounding the connective tissue, melting it away with heat and liquid (such as stew) allows the meat to become tender. This tenderizing process actually turns the collagen into gelatin.

The other type of connective tissue, elastin can only be broken down by slicing the meat into small strips or pounding the beef with a tenderizing hammer. Another method of tenderizing beef is to marinate the beef in an acidic solution, which softens the collagen.

Marinating for too long a period may, however, cause the meat to lose moisture when it is cooked and lose juices. When any cut of cooked beef cools, the meat may become tough since the collagen, which has turned to liquid, turns back into a solid.

In the last few years the bacteria E. coli has been associated with the risks of eating beef. However, more of an explanation is needed regarding the actual risk and how it can be eliminated if it is present at all. The bacteria E. coli is an intestinal bacteria; that is usually not be washed off the beef after processing. It is capable of causing severe illness or even death. The bacteria, if present, would normally be found on the surface of the meat and searing or cooking a piece of meat on both sides would easily kill the bacteria.

When you cook a steak or roast all sides are normally cooked and the risk is eliminated. This means that if you wish to eat a medium or medium-rare steak there is no risk if the meat is properly cooked.

The problem is more significant in regard to hamburger or raw meat dishes, such as steak tartar. Since hamburgers are ground beef: if the bacteria is present on the surface it will move to the inside during grinding, then if the hamburger is not cooked thoroughly, the bacteria may still be lurking inside. The following facts are meant to be usable in the choosing and preparation of meat and poultry as well as providing some general information that might be of interest.

BEEF, REFRIGERATION OF

When cooked beef is refrigerated the flavor changes noticeably. After only a few hours, fat, which is the main source of the flavor, tends to produce an *"off-flavor"* within the meat. This off-flavor is caused by the heating process, which tends to release reactive substances from the muscle tissue and produces oxidation of the fats, especially the phospholipids and the polyunsaturated fats in the muscle itself. One of the reasons this occurs is that the iron in the muscles is broken down and released from the hemoglobin and myoglobin and encourages the oxidation reaction.

BEEF BRISKET

Science of Cooking Brisket

+ You can use any combination of vegetable you wish, such as celery, leeks, carrots, potatoes, mushrooms or bell peppers. Preheat oven to 325°F. In a large casserole or Dutch oven, heat oil over medium heat.
+ Sauté onions, garlic and celery lightly, remove from heat and set aside. Season brisket with salt and pepper, and in the casserole, brown all sides of the meat. Return onion mixture to pan. Add enough broth or water to cover the meat. Bring to a boil and skim off any froth.
+ Cover the casserole and transfer to the oven. Braise for 3 hours, checking periodically to make sure the liquid still covers the meat.

- Add more liquid if necessary. Add desired vegetables and cook for 1 hour more. If you put tomatoes in only cook them for about 30 minutes.
- To brown the vegetables, allow the liquid to cook down to a depth of about 1 inch in a partially covered casserole. The brisket should be allowed to cool to room temperature before refrigerating.
- After the brisket cooks wrap it in plastic wrap and chill overnight.
- In the morning remove the brisket from the pan and scrape the vegetables back into the pan. Brisket should only be sliced across the grain.
- If the meat shreds when you cut it you are not cutting across the grain.
- After you slice the whole brisket, place the slices back into the pan.
- Distribute the vegetables and sauce both below and above the meat, cover with foil and continue to chill until 30 minutes before time to begin cooking. Allow the meat to come to room temperature before placing in a 350°F oven to warm before serving. Takes about 30-40 minutes.

- To slow the process down and fight the off-flavor problem, try to avoid using iron or aluminum pots and pans, and try not to salt meats until you are ready to eat them.
- Pepper and onions may also slow the process down and even inhibit the off-flavor problem.

BEEF JERKY

Preserving and drying meats have been done for thousands of years using salting, smoking and drying methods.

Making jerky from beef was the only way that the early settlers had to incorporate meat into their diet safely. Jerky was sun-dried back then, however, it is now made in the oven with controlled temperatures. Making your own jerky is still somewhat popular these days, however, it is easier to just buy it at your local supermarket.

BEEF KABOBS

Only the Best

The two top cuts that are best for kebobs are top sirloin and top blade.
Butterfly the cubes before marinating and more of the surface will be exposed to the marinade. The marinade will work faster and the beef will be more flavorful and more tender.

BEEF STEW

If you add 3-5 wine corks to your beef stew it will tenderize the meat very quickly. The cork is a fiber material from a tree and contains enzymes that have the ability to tenderize meats. Best to remove the corks before serving the stew, they are not very appetizing.

◆ Never add hot water to beef stew when adding water or it will make the meat tough. Only add cold water for the best results.

BEEF TENDERLOIN

Beef tenderloin tends to narrow on one end, which is called the "tip." If you roast or grill the roast as is, the narrow tip will be overcooked before the thicker end is done.

Don't Make a Bow

Chefs always fold the thinner tip (about 6-inches) under the roast to cook the roast more evenly. They then tie 12-inch lengths of cooking twine crosswise along the length of the roast about 1-2 inches apart.

A Flick of the Wrist

Tenderloin roasts also have the tendency to bow when they are cooked due to a shiny silver membrane. The membrane tends to contract during cooking. The problem can be solved by sliding a knife under the silver skin and just flicking the blade upward to cut through the membrane. If you do this in 5-6 locations along the length of the roast it will eliminate the bowing problem.

BEER, COOKING WITH

When you cook with beer, the heat will cause the alcohol content to evaporate allowing the flavoring agents to remain intact. The acid, however, will react with certain metals and it is recommended that you do not use aluminum or iron pots to prepare dishes that contain beer. The best cookware to use is glass or an enameled pot. If your pot does get discolored, just boil a small amount of rhubarb juice in the pot to remove the stain.

When cooking with beer: pale lager can be used for thinning a batter; lighter ales or lagers and some water can be used for steaming mussels.

Scottish ales can be used for a substitute for chicken or beef stock; light or medium bodied lager beer can be used for marinades. Beer can be mixed with soy sauce and full-bodied lagers or ales can be used for strong flavored marinades.

◆ The best beer that recommended by sushi chefs is Kirin Ichiban lager. It has a mild, sweet taste that compliments the sushi without detracting from the sushi flavors.
◆ Honey ale goes with lamb, India pale ale goes with soups (especially if they contain cheeses), brown ale pairs up nicely with chicken dishes, and a smoked beer with appetizers.
◆ When preparing any recipe with beer, chefs will always use a light beer and allow it to remain open at room temperature for 15 minutes. When using beer in a recipe you do not want to add the carbonation when it is too active.
◆ Beer can be substituted on a one to one for any liquid in a recipe.

BEER, STORING

Beer should always be stored in an upright position whether it is a can or a bottle.

When beer is allowed to rest on its side for any length of time a larger percentage of the beer is exposed to the oxygen in the container. The more oxygen it is exposed to and the longer the duration the less flavor the beer will have.

BEETS

Beets have the highest sugar content of any vegetable; however, they are low in calories and are an excellent source of vitamins and minerals. Both the roots and the leaves are edible. Beets; are a relative of spinach. It is best to buy only small or medium-sized beets the larger beets are not very tender and may have a stronger flavor. Never purchase beets if they look shriveled or flabby, they should be firm.

Salt to the Rescue
Beet juice will stain your hands and is hard to clean off. To remove the stain on your hands, just sprinkle salt on the stained area and allow it to remain for a few seconds before washing the area with soapy water.

- Beets have the highest sugar content of any vegetable, are low in calories and are an excellent source of vitamins and minerals.
- Both the roots and the leaves are edible. Beets are close relatives of spinach.
- It is best to buy only small or medium-sized beets since the larger beets are not very tender and may have a stronger flavor.
- Never purchase beets if they look shriveled or flabby, they should be firm.
- Beet greens should be used as soon as purchased and roots within 5-7 days.
- When preparing any dish that contains beets, be sure and add the beets last.
- Beets should not be blemished when purchased.
- Never allow more than 1"-2" of the greens to remain after you get the beets home since they will leach liquid from the bulb.
- Beet greens are very high in nutrition and should be prepared similar to spinach.
- Beet greens should be used as soon as purchased and the roots within 5-7 days.
- Beets should be cooked whole and not peeled to retain their nutrients.
- When preparing any dish that contains beets, be sure and add the beets last.
- Beets will lose some of their color and color the other foods red. If you add 2 tablespoons of lemon juice or vinegar to the water you are cooking beets in, it will stabilize the red color and it won't fade.

Science of Buying Beets
The beet top greens are an indication of freshness and if they show signs of wilting, the beets are not fresh and have been stored too long. The tops should still have about ½ inch of the stem left on or the beets will leak their juices. Try and purchase the smaller beets since they will not have large unusable woody cores. Be sure the root tip is about two inches long.

Beets will discolor other vegetables and should only be added to them just before serving.

OFF WITH THEIR TOPS

As with any vegetable with a leaf top, the leaf top should be removed when they are purchased and stored. The leaf top will leach moisture from the root or bulb and shorten their shelf life.

Science of Beets

Beets contain the chemical pigment "betacyanin" which gives the beets their red color. Some people cannot metabolize this pigment and it turns their feces and urine red for a few days, however, it is harmless. If you use beet, greens in salads, just use the leaves and be sure and remove the stems and discard them, since they may be bitter.

BERRIES (General Information)

In cultures that have to survive by adding a significant amount of berries and nuts to their diet, there is little if any incidence of cancer. Most berries and a number of nuts contain ellagic acid, which researchers are investigating to find out if the acid has an effect on cancer cells. In tests on mice, the mice that were fed ellagic acid had 45% fewer tumors. Berry juice is also an important source of iron.

- ♦ All berries should be firm and their color bright.
- ♦ Berries should be refrigerated and never allowed to dry-out.
- ♦ They should be used within 2-3 days after they are purchased for the best flavor and nutritional value.
- ♦ Berries do not ripen after being picked.
- ♦ Choose only bright red strawberries and plump firm blueberries that are light to dark blue.

Checking the bottom of berry containers is a must to be sure they are not stained from rotting or moldy berries.

- ♦ Mold on berries tends to spread quickly and you never want to leave a moldy one next to a good one. This actually goes for all fruits.
- ♦ Berries; can be defrosted by placing them in a plastic bag and immersing them in cold water for about 10-12 minutes.
- ♦ If you're making a dish with berries, make sure the batter or consistency is thick enough to hold the berries in suspension. Berries placed into thin batters just go to the bottom.

61

- Acid rain has stimulated the growth of many natural stands of "low bush" blueberries in many inland areas by reducing the pH level and increasing the acidity level of the soil.

- The largest producer of blueberries in the United States is New Jersey followed by Michigan. Blueberries are second only to strawberries in berry consumption.

If you need to store berries for a short period of time (one day or less), place a piece of paper towel on a cookie sheet and place the berries out in a single layer then cover them with a paper towel and refrigerate. Berries will not last more than a week in their original container without starting to deteriorate or get moldy.

Berry, Berry Interesting
Every raspberry or blackberry, contain a 75-125 druplet cluster and each druplet contains a seed. Blueberries are the top source of antioxidants in the produce department.

- Blackberries can grow either upward like a bush or trailing on the ground. When they are grown trailing they are called a "dewberry."

Gently Now
If you are going to prepare a fresh fruit salad or a tart, it is very difficult not to crush the berries in a mixing bowl or keeping them intact when you are trying to sugar them. Try chef's method of placing the berries in a large plastic bag and adding the sugar. Hold the bag closed with one hand and gently move the berries about with the other hand. If you are going to use the berries in a tart, just empty the berries directly into the pastry shell.

BISCUITS
When making biscuits, never overwork the dough be gentle if you want to have light biscuits. Overworking the dough makes them tough and continually re-rolling may cause the biscuits to become tough.

- An inverted water glass can be used to cut biscuit dough. Cookie cutters make wild looking biscuits.
- If you want your biscuits to be soft, try brushing them with milk or melted unsalted butter then place them in the pan so that they touch each other.
- Whatever recipe you are using, it probably calls for you to use yeast. Instead of the yeast, substitute 1 teaspoon of baking soda and 1 teaspoon of powdered ascorbic acid (vitamin C) for the yeast.

By doing this, you will not have to wait for the dough to rise. The addition of these products will react with the other ingredients and the dough will rise naturally during the baking process.

Before baking rolls, try glazing the tops. Just beat one egg white lightly with one tablespoon of milk and brush on. When glazing a cake, try using 1 tablespoon of milk with a small amount of brown sugar dissolved in it.

♦ Check your baking powder for freshness and make sure that you sift all the dry ingredients together. This will provide you with the texture you desire. If you don't have a sifter, then just place all the ingredients into a large sieve and shake them all out, it's the even blending of the ingredients that is the key. Shortening is also the preferred fat over butter since shortening is a more refined product and is capable of adding lightness. Butter tends to make biscuits more solid.

TEENEY WEENEY BUTTER

If you leave the butter in very small pieces and don't melt it into the dough, the biscuits will be flaky. Only knead a few strokes, never more than 6-8 for the best results and only use soft wheat flour. Use a high heat setting of 425°F, any lower and the biscuits will dry out.

♦ Use the best quality, unbleached all-purpose flour, unless the recipe says otherwise.
♦ Be sure that the shortening is cut into very small bits in the flour. The mixture should resemble coarse meal (about ¼ inch crumbs).
♦ If biscuits cool off too much, be sure and brush the tops with melted butter before reheating, loosely wrapped in aluminum foil at 350°F for only 30 seconds.

It is important to cut out as many biscuits as possible from the first rolling of the dough. The more you roll out the dough, the tougher the biscuit will be.

♦ If you like your biscuits and rolls to be a rich golden color, just add one teaspoon of sugar to the dry ingredients. It only adds 16 calories to the whole batch.
♦ The best method of re-heating biscuits or rolls is to put them into a slightly dampened paper bag sealed with a tie. Place the bag into the oven at a very low temperature. It should only take about 5 minutes and it is best if you keep your eye on the bag just to be safe.
♦ If you dip a biscuit cutter in flour, it will keep the dough from sticking to it.
♦ Biscuits should always be baked in a very hot oven of 400-425°F.
♦ Always use cold shortening and cold liquids for the best results.

Patty Cake, Patty Cake

Chefs never have to re-pat biscuits. They use a biscuit cutter or use a **"wedge-method"** and press the dough into a round cake pan that is large enough to hold dough that is ¾-inches thick. They turn the dough out on a lightly floured surface and with a large knife, cut the dough into equal-sized triangular wedges.

Science of Mixing Biscuits

When kneading flour by hand or in a mixing machine, the dough gets very elastic. The amount you knead will determine how much gluten is developed. If you are making bread, you want maximum gluten developed. However, when it comes to making biscuits, the more gluten you develop, the less tender the biscuits will be.

To prevent brown spots and a bitter taste, be sure and mix the dry ingredients with a whisk to be sure they are well blended.

BLANCHING FOODS

There are different methods of blanching or parboiling foods. The following are two of the more popular methods:

- Place the food in a bowl, then pour boiling water over the food and allow it to stand for 30-60 seconds.
- Drain off the water and immediately place the food into ice-cold water to stop the cooking action.
- Place the food in a large pot of boiling water, add ¼ teaspoon of salt to the water and boil rapidly for 1 minute. Immediately drain and plunge the food into ice water.
- Soft vegetables, such as tomatoes do not need to be boiled for one minute to be blanched. Tomatoes only require 15 seconds in the boiling water. Cabbage and spinach only requires 30 seconds. Use your judgment depending on the hardness of the food when blanching or parboiling.
- Vegetables that are frozen and not blanched are still good to eat, however, the quality, color, texture and flavor will be considerably lower than those that have been blanched before freezing.
- Corn must be handled just right or it will not be very edible. Corn should be blanched according to directions and chilled immediately in a bowl of ice water until the cobs are completely cooled down. Before you cook the ears, allow them to partially thaw at room temperature and place a small amount of sugar in the water.

Most microorganisms are not destroyed by freezing and may even be present on fruits and vegetables. Blanching does help lower the microorganism count significantly but enough of them do survive and are ready and waiting to destroy the food as soon as it thaws. Inspect all frozen foods, which may have accidentally thawed by leaving the freezer door open or from an electrical failure. The botulism microorganism does not reproduce at 0^0F.

MICROWAVE BLANCHING

If you choose to blanch in a microwave, I suggest you read up on the procedure in your manual. It is not as efficient as boiling water blanching and cold spots are possible, which will not kill the enzymes that must be destroyed.

♦ When vegetables are frozen, enzymes may still remain active and cause changes in the color, texture, and taste in the vegetable even if they have been previously stored under refrigeration. Freezing will slow down the changes; however, it will not totally inactivate the enzymes.

♦ If vegetables are blanched by either boiling them in water that has boiled for 2 minutes first (to release oxygen) or steaming them for 3-4 minutes it will not cook them but will inactivate the enzymes and the vegetables will retain their color, texture, and taste.

♦ The enzymes are important to good nutrition and it would be more desirable to only purchase enough for a few days at a time.

Science of Blanching Before Freezing

When vegetables are frozen, enzymes may still remain active and cause changes in the color, texture, and taste in the vegetable even if they have been previously stored under refrigeration. Freezing will slow the changes down; however, it will not totally inactivate the enzymes. If vegetables are blanched by either boiling them in water that has boiled for 2 minutes first (to release oxygen) or steaming them for 3-4 minutes it will not cook them but will inactivate the enzymes and the vegetables will retain their color, texture, and taste. Of course, the enzymes are important to good nutrition and it would be more desirable to only purchase enough for a few days at a time.

BLEU CHEESE DRESSING

Fresh bleu cheese will provide a stronger flavor with a great aroma. Bleu cheese was created in 1854 in France and originally called "bleu d'Auvergne." After milking, the milk that will be used to produce "bleu cheese" is allowed to stand for about 8 hours before it can be processed. A mold, similar to penicillin mold derived from wheat bread is introduced into the cheese as it is being processed.

Science of Bleu Cheese

To produce the blue streaks throughout the cheese requires a process that would puncture the cheese, allowing oxygen to assist in the growth of the bacteria. Automatic machines actually prick the cheese, as it is developing to allow the oxygen to enter. As the bacteria, grows the oxygen provides the nourishment to allow the bacteria to send out the blue feelers throughout the cheese.

BLINTZES

Blintzes originated with the Jews of Russia and were first mentioned in an English cookbook in the late 1800's. Blintzes are a very thin pancake that is stuffed with a variety of ingredients depending on the occasion or holiday and no one made them better than grandma.

GRANDMA'S BLINTZES RECIPE

Ingredients:

Blintzes:

2	Large eggs
½	Teaspoon of salt
1	Cup water
1	Teaspoon of salt

Filling:

1	Pound of cottage cheese (put in ricer)
1	Large egg
4	Teaspoons of sugar
1	Cup all-purpose flour (sifted)

- Beat eggs enough to blend yolks and whites thoroughly.
- Add salt and water then stir into batter and mix until smooth.
- Lightly grease a small frying pan (about 6 inches in diameter) and pour in 2 tablespoons of batter.
- Cook over low heat on one side, just until it holds its shape.
- Turn out onto a clean cloth and repeat until all batter has been used.
- Mix all ingredients of filling together and put heaping tablespoons of cheese mixture on each blintz, fold sides in, roll up and fry in butter until golden brown.
- Serve with sour cream or applesauce.

Science of Blintzes

The normal blintz batter is made from 3 beaten large eggs, ¾ cup of matzo meal (flour may be substituted), ½ teaspoon table salt and 1½ cups of tap water. Frying pans used for blitzes should be heavy and in the size of the blintz. The pans should only be used for blintzes and kept seasoned and never washed. Blintzes are only browned on one side in a very slight layer of oil. Most chefs use a brush to just brush oil on the pan before adding the batter. The blintzes are folded over three sides then rolled into shape. The most common filling is a mixture of cottage cheese, sugar and sour cream. After the blintz has been filled they are placed back into the pan and lightly browned so that the filling is warmed before serving.

BOILING

When we see water bubbling; either lightly or more rapidly the temperature will always be the same 212^0F (100^0C). There is, however, the possibility of 1^0F difference at times but for the most part it remains constant.

The only difference in the rapidly boiling water is that the food may cook somewhat faster due to the increased activity of the heat-carrying molecules.

The food will cook more evenly and the food will retain more nutrients if the water is not rapidly boiling. Hard water, due to its high mineral content will boil 1-2^0F above soft water.

When sugar, salt, or almost any other solid are added to water, the boiling point is raised and the freezing point lowered. If you add one ounce of salt to a quart of water it will raise the boiling point 1^0F-2^0F (17.2^0C-6.7^0C). An example of this; If you lived at an elevation of 1 mile you would have to add 8 ounces of salt to water to reach 212^0F (100^0C). The molecules of either salt or sugar interfere with the natural breakdown of the water molecule.

- Adding salt to water to cook pasta faster is a waste of time, since the amount needed would be too much to fit into the pot. If you added 1 tablespoon of salt to 5 quarts of boiling water to cook 1 pound of pasta, it would only raise the boiling point by 7/100th of one degree Fahrenheit.
- Cookbooks that advise you to add salt to the cooking water of pasta should advise you that it is only done for flavoring. However, other studies tell us that adding salt sometimes makes certain pasta get tough.
- It is OK to salt the water for foods that have a short boiling time such as vegetables. Never salt the water when cooking corn or it will toughen the corn, instead add 1 teaspoon of sugar to the water to sweeten it. When cooking foods for a prolonged period of time, never salt the water, especially for stews, stocks and beans. Beans especially tend to get tough. The safest way to use salt on many dishes and foods is to salt the foods just before they are finished cooking.
- When the weather is bad and stormy, the atmospheric pressure goes down. The lower the pressure, the lower the boiling temperature of water becomes.
- The decreased temperature is usually about 1-2 degrees and it will take a little longer to cook boiled foods.

If you are having problems keeping a pot from boiling over, try placing a toothpick between the lid and the pot. Other tricks include placing a wooden spoon across the top or rubbing butter around the inside lip of the pot. Also, if you add $1\frac{1}{2}$ teaspoons of butter to a cooking pasta or soup, it will not boil over. This doesn't work with vegetable oil and of course, adds calories and cholesterol.

PUT A LID ON IT?

When a chef needs to boil water he never bothers to place a lid on the pot of water until it starts steaming. He knows that it doesn't really matter if the pot had a lid on or not until the water gets very hot.

BRAISING

This method of cooking is usually used for cuts of meat that are not very tender. The food is browned and then covered as airtight as possible and cooked in a small amount of liquid at a low temperature for a long period of time.

- If you are going to braise a piece of meat, be sure that you pat it as dry as you can and then lightly dust the meat with flour before braising.
- Use a large, heavy pot and as close to the size of the food you are going to braise.
- The pot should be hot before adding the meat to be browned.
- Only use a small amount of liquid when braising, you do not want to poach the food.
- If any other liquid is called for in the recipe only add it after the meat has browned.
- Be sure that liquid only simmers and is not boiling away.
- If you are going to braise in the oven, the temperature should be around 325°F. This is an ideal way to braise since the heat surrounds the pot and the food cooks more evenly.

OVEN BRAISING

When a tough piece of meat needs some tenderizing, braising is usually one common method. However, chefs don't use the top of the stove method that most people use.

They use the oven instead, since using the stovetop tends to cause the liquid to boil too easily and the texture and flavor of the meat will suffer.

BREAD (general)

When making bread and the recipe calls for water, you can substitute milk and it will make the texture softer and the crust darker. The milk should be scalded first to improve the volume.

♦ Sweeteners such as honey, molasses, and cane sugar are really not required in bread making; however, they tend to slow down the coagulation of the protein allowing the dough to increase in volume making a fluffier loaf. They do add a few more calories to the bread, but they also extend the shelf life.
♦ If you do plan on using honey or molasses, always add a small amount of extra flour to offset the liquid sweetener.
♦ If you are in a hurry for whole wheat bread to rise, try adding one tablespoon of lemon juice to the dough as you are mixing it.

THE BREAD SLASHER

A proofed loaf of bread needs to be slashed across the top, which allows trapped air to escape. Be sure you do not use a knife that will snag and tear the bread. If you want a clean slash, just spray the knife blade lightly with vegetable oil before slashing the loaf.

♦ The structure of the bread is supported by the coagulation of the proteins and the gelatinization of the complex carbohydrates. If this did not occur, all baked goods would collapse once they started to cool and the steam and carbon dioxide would dissipate.
♦ The water from boiled potatoes contains just the right amount of starch to substitute for the water you might use in a bread recipe. It will also help keep the bread fresher for a longer period of time. If you are using raw milk that is not pasteurized in your recipe, make sure you scald the milk before using it. Raw milk contains an organism that tends to break down the protein structure of the gluten.
♦ To replace lost moisture in a loaf of bread that has hardened, try wrapping it tightly in a damp towel for about 2-3 minutes then place the bread in the oven at 350^0F for 15-20 minutes. Moisture can easily be replaced in French or Italian bread by just sprinkling the crust with cold water and placing them in a 350^0F oven for 8-10 minutes.
♦ Always check baking bread at least 10-15 minutes before the baking time is completed to be sure your oven temperature is accurate.
♦ If you are having a problem with bread browning too fast, try placing a dish of water on the shelf just above the bread. The added humidity in the oven will slow down the browning. This will work with cakes as well.

THE LOAF OF PERFECTION

To bake the perfect light loaf of bread, chefs use a 14 X 16 inch, thin piece of stone and place it on the lowest position shelf in the gas oven.

They also place a small pan with about $\frac{1}{2}$ inch of boiling water in it to produce steam. This method produces the greatest tasting bread ever.

- To help your bread rise and provide a great texture, just add 1 tablespoon of cider vinegar for every 2½ cups of flour you use. Remember to reduce the liquids you normally use by the amount of vinegar that you add.
- If your bread is a "low-riser" it may mean that you used old yeast, too little water, or water that was too cold or hot. Remember too high a heat kills yeast activity. Try again with fresh yeast and warm water.
- For the best results, never use a shiny bread pan. It is best to use a dull finish aluminum pan to bake your bread in. A dark pan may cool too quickly and a shiny pan reflects heat to such a degree that you may not get even cooking.

Hard to Slice Bread

Some bread has thick and heavy crusts that make the bread difficult to slice. The knife may not cut through the bottom crust and you end up tearing the slice to remove it. To slice a loaf neatly, just turn the loaf over on its side and slice through the top and bottom crust at the same time.

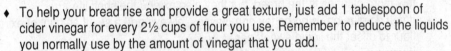

- Occasionally, dough rises too much before the bread starts to bake, thus causing the gluten strands to become weak and too thin, leading to the escape of carbon dioxide gas. When this occurs, the bread may rise then collapse and have a sunken top.
- For thick dough that is difficult to knead, just place a small amount of vegetable oil on your hands. Placing the dough in a plastic bag also may help.
- If your bread is a "high-riser" or has collapsed you may have added too much yeast or water. Use less next time. Remember a small amount of sugar is **"yeastie food"** and will feed the yeast and make the dough rise faster. If too much sugar is used then it will actually act to inhibit the rising.
- If your bread has a crumbly texture you might try adding a small amount of salt, which will give the bread a more even texture.
- Salt is really not needed when making bread. It does, however, make the crust a little crispier as well as slowing down the growth of the yeast, which will prevent the dough from increasing its volume too fast.

Science of Bread

Baking on tiles or "pizza stones" is an excellent method of making bread. It produces a light loaf of bread with a crust that is not too dark. Pizza stones are easily available at a kitchen shop and sell for about $25-35. The stone is placed on the  bottom shelf and should be preheated to 450°F for about 20-30 minutes before reducing the temperature to your normal baking temperature. Keeping the bread away from the top of the oven also slows crusting.

- If you ever wondered how pumpernickel bread gets its dark color, it comes from adding a dark caramel to the white or rye flour. The better pumpernickel breads are made from rye flour only.
- If you burn bread, try removing the burned area with a grater.
- If white bread is your bread of choice, only purchase the bread if it clearly says: "enriched," on the label, many do not.

If you are going to freeze a loaf of bread, make sure you include a piece of paper towel in the package to absorb moisture. This will keep the bread from becoming mushy when it is thawed out.

- Fresh bread will not get moldy as fast if you wrap it in waxed paper and place it in the refrigerator.
- When kneading dough, always knead on a wooden board. Plastic boards do not have the tacky surface needed to knead the bread or the grabbing quality.

BREAD BOX

The dry air in the refrigerator actually draws moisture from the bread. Bread develops mold faster at room temperature, however the freshness of the bread is lost in half the time. Freezing maintains the freshness, however, liquid is released as cells burst from the freezing and the texture of the bread is never the same. Storing bread will depend on the length of time it will take for you to use the bread. For short periods of up to 5-6 days, the breadbox works great. It provides a closed compartment and will keep the bread fresh, otherwise it has to go into the refrigerator or freezer to avoid mold forming.

- The best method of cooling hot bread after it has been removed from the oven is to place the bread on an open wire rack. This will allow air to circulate around the bread and should eliminate any soggy areas.
- Save the bread bags from store bought bread for use when you bake bread.
- Remember, when you are making 100% whole wheat bread, it will come out more moist if you slowly add the flour to the water and mix gently.

It is the nature of whole wheat to absorb water slower than other types of flour.
- Don't be fooled by bread labeling. If the package reads whole-wheat flour, cracked wheat, or wheat bread it is probably made from white flour.
- Whole wheat bread cannot be expected to rise as high as white breads since it has more volume due to lack of refining.
- When purchasing rye bread, it would be best to read the label. Most rye bread contains white flour and very little rye flour. For the best quality, the label should read "whole rye flour."
- To purchase the highest quality white bread, make sure the list of ingredients reads "unbleached flour" instead of "white flour" or just "flour."
- Non-dairy creamer can be used to replace dry milk in your bread recipe.
- An old trick is to put a small piece of aluminum foil under the cloth in your breadbasket before placing the bread or rolls in. This will help the food retain its heat for a longer period of time.

TO CRUST OR NOT TO CRUST

If you're worried about your bread crusts becoming too hard, just place a small container of water in the oven while the bread is baking. This will provide just enough moisture and steam to keep the bread soft.
- Do you ever wish that you could bake a loaf of bread without the crust becoming too crispy? Well the secret to a softer crust is to open the oven door and throw in a few ice cubes about midway through the baking time. This will produce a dense steam and provide just enough extra moisture to keep the crust from becoming too hard and too crispy. It also will allow the bread to rise more easily giving you a nice firm, chewy inside.
- A baker's secret to the greatest-looking crust on top of homemade bread is to brush the top of the bread with cider vinegar 10 minutes before the bread is done. Remove the bread, brush on the vinegar and return the bread to the oven for that last 10 minutes.

Re-sealing a Loaf

When you need to seal up a loaf of bread and you have lost the metal tie, just twist the bag shut and fold the excess back over itself and over the remaining bread. This will only work after some of the slices have been removed and you have enough of the bag to fold over.

HARD WATER

The high mineral content of hard water may retard fermentation by causing the gluten to become tough. The minerals will prevent the protein from absorbing water the way it normally would. To counteract this problem there are a number of methods you may wish to try, such as using bottled water, adding a small amount of vinegar to reduce the pH, or adding more yeast. Water that is too soft can cause the dough to be sticky. If you are having a problem you may want to consider using a dough improver.

LIQUIDS CREATE DIFFERENT TEXTURED BREADS

Liquids tend to impart their own significant characteristics to bread. Water, for instance, will cause the top of the bread to be crisper and significantly intensifies the flavor of the wheat. Water that remains after potatoes are boiled (potato water) will add a unique flavor and make the crust smooth as well as causing the bread to rise faster due to the higher starch content.

- Any liquid dairy product will change the color of the bread to a richer creamy color and leave the bread with a finer texture and a soft, brown crust.
- Eggs are capable of changing the crust so that it will be more moist. If any liquid sweetener such as molasses, maple syrup, or honey is used it will cause the crust to be dark brown and will keep the crust moist.
- A vegetable or meat broth will give the bread a special flavor and provide you with a lighter, crisper crust.
- Alcohol of any type will give the bread a smooth crust with a flavor that may be similar to the alcohol used, especially beer.
- Coffee and tea are commonly used to provide a darker, richer color and a crispier crust.

MICROWAVE BAKING

It is possible for bread to rise in a microwave oven in approximately 1/3rd of the time it would take through normal methods.

The only problem is that it may affect the flavor somewhat because the slower it rises the more time there is to develop the flavor, and have it permeate throughout the dough. If you do decide to use this method, your microwave needs to have a 10% power setting. If you try to use any higher temperature the dough will turn into a half-baked glob.

To make dough rise for one standard loaf, place ½ cup of hot water in the back corner of the oven. Place the dough in a microwave bowl that is well greased and cover it with plastic wrap, then cover the plastic wrap with a damp towel. With the power level set at 10% cook the dough for 6 minutes; then allow it to rest for 4-5 minutes. Repeat the procedure if the dough has not doubled its size.

TOASTING

A French chemist first discovered the browning reaction of toast. He discovered that when bread is heated a chemical process takes place that caramelizes, the surface sugars and proteins turning the surface brown. The sugar then becomes an indigestible fiber and a percentage of the protein (amino acids) loses their nutritional value. The toast then has more fiber and less protein than a piece of bread that is not toasted. The protein is actually reduced by about 35%. If you're making your own bread, you can increase the amount of protein by just reducing the amount of regular flour by 2 tablespoons and replacing it with an equal amount of quality soy flour.

THE FOUR MOST POPULAR TYPES OF BREAD

Batter Breads

These are yeast-leavened breads that are always beaten instead of kneaded.

Quick Breads

If you ever wondered what quick bread is, it is bread that is leavened with baking powder or baking soda instead of the standard yeast.

- Quick bread does not require any rising time since there is an instant reaction to the water between the oven temperature and the acidic nature of the dough allowing carbon dioxide to form and expedite the rising process.
- To salvage overcooked quick breads, try poking deep holes through the top with a skewer and slowly drizzle fruit juice or honey over the holes, allowing the liquid to penetrate the bread.

When making quick bread you would normally spray the inside of the loaf pan, however, this sometimes may not work too well. To be sure that the loaf can be easily removed, try placing a strip of parchment paper the length and width of the pan. Be sure that the edges overlap the pan and it will be easy to lift the loaf out.

Flat Breads

This would include matzo, which is flat due to the lack of a leavening agent.

Yeast Breads

These are leavened with yeast and are always kneaded to stretch the gluten in the flour. If you use room-temperature ingredients in the yeast and quick-bread types, it will accelerate the rising and baking times.

FRENCH BREAD GETS STALE FAST

French bread is made without fat. The fat content in bread tends to slow down the loss of moisture in bread and keep it softer by reducing the percentage of gluten from forming too strong of a structure. French bread may get stale after only 5-7 hours, which is why the French purchase their bread supplies at least twice a day. To revive French bread that has dried out, just sprinkling the crust with cold water and place the bread in a 350^{0}F (176.7^{0}F) oven for 8-10 minutes.

BREAD, QUICK

This is bread that is leavened by baking soda, baking powder or eggs. The most popular quick breads are biscuits, cornbread, muffins and cranberry or banana bread.

- If you use too much baking powder or baking soda, the bread will have too dry a texture and may have a somewhat bitter taste. The batter may also rise too much and then fall.

- Too little baking powder or baking soda will produce bread with a heavy, gummy texture.
- Both baking powder and baking soda will release gas as soon as they are moistened, always mix them with the other dry ingredients before adding the liquid.
- Since the powder and soda start working so fast, be sure and have the oven preheated and ready as well as the pans greased.
- Don't over mix the ingredients; small lumps will disappear while the product is baking.
- You can check the doneness of quick bread by placing a toothpick near the center of the loaf. If it comes out clean the product is done.

BREAD, SOURDOUGH

Sourdough starter is really *"wild yeast"* that lives in a batter of flour and water. Starters were as valuable as gold in the early days, guarded and treasured. Prospectors actually slept with the starter on cold nights so it would not die from freezing. A 240-year old sourdough starter can be obtained by calling 1 (800) 827-6836.

MAKING SOURDOUGH BREAD

Make sure that no metal comes into contact with the sourdough starter. This can cause a chemical reaction that will kill the starter. If this happens, a black, blue or pink liquid will come to the surface.

- Always use the least-processed flour. King Arthur or quality organic, unbleached flour is best.
- Clay or crock containers may also have metal in them and should not be used.
- Pressure in starters may build up and they need to be covered with loose-fitting lids.
- Starters should always be separated into two batches: one to use now and the other to store as a "back-up."
- If you use a sourdough starter instead of a mix the bread will have a more open texture.
- Starter that are being used should be refrigerated overnight.
- The **"back-up"** starter should be fed about every 2 months.
- Your main starter should be stored in a 3-4 quart container allowing you to build up enough "starter" to use for baking.
- Never use chlorinated water when making sourdough bread. The chlorine can injure the starter.
- Always use a clear container for starter (not glass) so that you can easily see the bubbles when the starter needs to be fed.
- Transfer the starter to a clean container every 2 months.

♦ If you would like to prepare bread with a sourdough flavor, just replace the milk or water with yogurt.

Science of Sourdough Bread

To make your own starter, it would be best to acquire the directions from a baker's cookbook or the Internet. It is a must if you are to make sourdough bread. You must have yeast that will work in an acidic environment. Standard baker's yeast works by breaking down the sugar maltose, which the acids in sourdough bread will not work. The acids in sourdough bread are 75% lactic acid and 25% acetic acid. While the bacteria in sourdough bread, requires maltose, it cannot break it down. The bacteria, prefers a temperature of 86°F (30°C) and a pH of (acid/base level) of 3.8 to 4.5 ideally. Standard bread prefers a pH of 5.5. Starters for sour dough bread survived for hundreds of years and thought to be protected by bacteria; that is related to the penicillin mold in cheese.

BREAD, YEAST

There are two types of yeast breads, those where the dough is kneaded and those that are beaten, called *"batter breads."* The batter breads use extra yeast and need more beating, however, they do not need to be kneaded. Since the gluten is not completely developed through the long kneading process, the texture of the bread becomes more coarse and the flavor more yeasty.

♦ If the dough is slightly tacky when touched, it will make a lighter loaf of bread. If too much flour is used, the bread will be dry and somewhat dense.

♦ If you are going to work with sticky dough made with rye flour, be sure and oil your hands so that the dough won't cling to them.

♦ Thin plastic gloves work very well and you won't have to get your hands sticky.

♦ If you're going to use an electric mixer when preparing these breads, it would be best to spray the blades with vegetable oil to stop the dough from climbing up the blades.

♦ When the dough is rising, make sure that there is no draft to cool it off in spots and make the dough rise unevenly.

♦ Yeast dough needs to rise to double its original size.

♦ When baking, be sure that bread pans are at least 4 inches apart.

♦ You can freeze yeast dough before you bake it if you let it rise once then punch it into a loaf. Lightly oil some plastic wrap, place the wrap oil side up into a loaf pan, add the dough then seal it as best you can with the wrap.

♦ If you want the crust to be crisp, just place a shallow pan filled halfway with hot, water on the bottom shelf of the oven. The water will create steam and help to make the crust crispier.

BREAD MACHINE

These machines are now operated by a computer chip and are capable of mixing bread, kneading dough, doing punch down, bake and even cool the bread. Measure the ingredients, tell the machine what cycle to use and push a button.

SECRETS OF THE BREAD MACHINE

- Do not use rapid-rising yeast, only instant active yeast.
- The flour used should contain at least 12 grams of protein per cup.
- Use only flour that has not been treated chemically from only hard wheat.
- If you use a delayed cycle, never use fresh eggs and fresh milk. Use powdered eggs and milk.

Never add any ingredients including hot butter unless it cools or you may kill some or all of the yeast.

- Always check the dough after 5-10 minutes in the first kneading cycle. You may need to add more liquid depending on the weather. Dry weather may require additional moister.
- If you are using sweet dough, place the dough in a plastic closed bag in the refrigerator for about 12 hours to allow extra rising time.
- For all heavy flour, such as whole wheat, buckwheat, rye, etc. Use the whole-wheat cycle.
- Any bread that is low in sugar or fat should use a shorter knead time cycle, such as the French bread cycle.
- If the breads are high in fat and sugar or you are using ingredients that burn easily, use the sweet bread cycle.
- To prevent soggy crusts, remove the pan and the bread before the cool down cycle starts and allow the bread to cool for 15-20 minutes.
- Most bread machines are timed for the use of dry yeast. Compressed fresh yeast should never be used in bread-baking machines.
- Remember that adding extra salt, fresh garlic, cinnamon or sugar to the dough may slow down or even stop yeast action.
- If you have a problem with the paddles sticking to the shaft, apply a small amount of vegetable oil before you add any ingredients to eliminate the problem.

If you substitute honey, molasses or other liquid sweetener for the sugar called for in the recipe, it may cause over-browning.

- If the top of your bread is raw, it means that the bread has risen too much and hit the top of the bread machine.

♦ Machines that produce 1 pound loaves of bread use about 2 cups of dry ingredients and ½ cup of liquid. The larger units can produce 1½ pound loaves and use 3½ cups of dry ingredients and1½ cups of liquid.

BREAD PANS

Science of Bread & Cake Pans

When you remove a loaf of bread or a cake from the oven, it is full of trapped steam. As it cools, the steam will go into the air or convert to water and be absorbed into the product. If you allow too little steam to dissipate into the air, the product will become soggy. Allow the baked product rest for about 5-7 minutes until it has settled then remove it and place it on a cooling rack. You then maximize the surface area and allow more steam to escape.

NEED AN EXTRA BREAD LOAF PAN?

If you need to make two or three loaves of bread and only have one loaf pan, you can make additional loafs by using a 9"X13" baking dish. Just place the one loaf pan you have in the center of the baking dish and place the dough on either side. If you need to make three loaves, just use all three areas.

BREAD PUDDING

Science of Bread Pudding

If you can find a good quality Vienna bread you can leave the crusts on since the special baking process used when making the bread will give you a better product. The bread you are going to use should be a few days old. If it is fresh then toast it lightly before buttering it. The 30-minute wait at room temperature will allow the liquid to soak in.. If this is not done the butter will come up to the top and the bread will remain dry and chewy.

BREAD STICKS

Best to read the list of ingredients and check the fat content before you purchase bread sticks. They may contain up to 40% fat.

BREADCRUMBS

Breadcrumbs are getting more and more expensive! You will never have to buy them again if you have a special jar set aside and place the crumbs from the bottom of cracker boxes or low-sugar cereal boxes in the jar.

♦ Break up a loaf of bread into small pieces and place them on a cookie sheet in the oven overnight to dry out. If you have a pilot light that will work fine.

If not heat the oven to 225^{0}F, then turn it off and leave the bread in overnight.

♦ Packaged bread used for stuffing mix can be placed in a food processor and made into breadcrumbs. These are usually seasoned and make a tasty breadcrumb.
♦ Can be used to thicken soup with.
♦ Breadcrumbs can be frozen for about 6 months in a well-sealed container.
♦ If you butter breadcrumbs and then sauté them, it is great on salads. Use 1 tablespoon of butter for every 1½ cups of breadcrumbs.
♦ Certain cereals can be crushed and used for breadcrumbs, especially corn or wheat ones.

SAVE THE HEELS FOR THE CHEF

A chef always makes his own breadcrumbs and always saves the leftover bread heels and cubed them before placing them into the oven on a cookie sheet and baking them for 15 minutes at 250^{0}F or until they just start to brown.

Chefs will crush them wrapped in a towel using a rolling pin; however, they normally use a blender or food processor to make quick work of the job. If the bottom crust of the bread you are going to use is too hard, discard it or it may jam up the blender.

BREADING

Chefs never have a problem making breading stay on a food. There are a few secrets that will really make the difference:

♦ When using eggs, make sure they are at room temperature.
♦ Always place the breaded food in the refrigerator for 45 minutes then allow it to return to room temperature before placing the food in the fryer.
♦ Never over beat the eggs, the more air you put in, the lower the binding ability of the egg.
♦ Milk can be used in place of the egg but won't give you the sticking power.

Toss foods in a well-sealed plastic bag to reduce cleanup and more evenly have the breading placed on the food. Keep shaking until all the food is well coated.

♦ Always use the smallest breadcrumbs you can purchase, large breadcrumbs do not adhere well.
♦ Homemade breadcrumbs are coarser and always adhere better.
♦ Make sure that the food that is to be breaded is very dry.
♦ Homemade breadcrumbs are the best because of their uneven texture they tend to hold better.

FORMULA FOR AN ALL-AROUND BREADING
The following blend should make any food taste better and enhance the flavor.

Mix all ingredients together well and store in the refrigerator until needed. Allow the blend to stand at room temperature for 20 minutes before using.

2	Cups of whole-wheat pastry flour
½	Tablespoon paprika
1	Tablespoon of dry mustard
¾	Teaspoon of finely ground celery seed
1	Teaspoon ground black pepper
1	Teaspoon dried basil
1	Teaspoon dried marjoram
¾	Teaspoon dried thyme

BROCCOLI

There are over 50 varieties of broccoli with only a few varieties containing enough cancer-fighting phytonutrients to be effective. Some varieties have as much as 30 times the phytonutrients than others. The University of Illinois is working on research that will produce a new breed of broccoli that will contain the most effective phytonutrients and the highest levels.

- ♦ Broccoli has a higher nutrient content if eaten fresh.
- ♦ The stem should not be too thick and the leaves should not be wilted.
- ♦ If the buds are open or yellow, the broccoli is old and will have a significant loss of nutrients.

Science of Broccoli

High temperatures will cause broccoli to discolor. It will also cause the broccoli to flower if the temperature goes above 80°F. Cooked broccoli still contains 15% more vitamin C than an orange. They contain 8 times the beta-carotene as the stalks. One cup of broccoli contains 90% of the USRDA of vitamin A, 200% of vitamin C, 6% of niacin, 10% of calcium, 10% of thiamin, 10% of phosphorus, and 8% of iron. Broccoli's color is very sensitive to acidic foods, such as tomatoes. It also provides 25% of your daily fiber needs and even has 5 grams of protein.

Broccoli should be washed in a good organic cleaner since the EPA has registered more than 50 pesticides that can be used on broccoli. Seventy percent of these pesticides; cannot be detected by the FDA after harvesting. In a recent study it was reported that 13% of broccoli still retained pesticide residues even after initial processing.

- ♦ The florets should be closed and should be a good solid green color.
- ♦ Store in a well-sealed plastic bag, unwashed and refrigerated for the best results.
- ♦ Broccoli should always be blanched before freezing.
- ♦ Broccoli leaves are good to eat only if they are young. Older leaves get very bitter.

STORING BROCCOLI

Broccoli should be stored in a plastic bag in the refrigerator. It will keep for only 3-5 days before the florets start opening and a loss of nutrients occur.

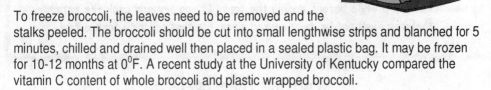

To freeze broccoli, the leaves need to be removed and the stalks peeled. The broccoli should be cut into small lengthwise strips and blanched for 5 minutes, chilled and drained well then placed in a sealed plastic bag. It may be frozen for 10-12 months at 0^0F. A recent study at the University of Kentucky compared the vitamin C content of whole broccoli and plastic wrapped broccoli.

Broccoli that was left out in the air lost 30% of its vitamin C content in four days while the broccoli that was wrapped in plastic only lost 17% and retained its color better. The respiration rate of the broccoli was slowed down conserving the nutrients.

KEEPING BROCCOLI GREEN

Broccoli should only be boiled for 30 seconds if you wish to retain its green color at the highest intensity. This short duration cooking causes the gases that are trapped in the spaces between the cells to expand and escape and the color can be seen more vividly.

However, when broccoli is cooked for more than 30 seconds in boiling water the chlorophyll reacts with acids in the broccoli and the color is lost. The color may now appear to be more olive green, which is caused by a brown substance called "pheophytin." Remember to always add vegetables to the boiling water, never start them in cold water or you will lose nutrients and color. Baking soda may be added to the cooking water to turn broccoli green, but this only works for a short period of time before the broccoli turns mushy. Baking soda will also destroy some of the nutrients.

Science of Broccoli Odor

Broccoli as well as Brussels sprouts contains the natural chemical called mustard oil "isocyanides." Isocyanides when heated breaks down into foul smelling sulfur compound called hydrogen sulfide and ammonia. In fact, you should never cook these vegetables in an aluminum pot or the reaction will cause an even more intense smell. The longer you cook the vegetables, the more chemicals are released and the smellier the kitchen. Cook them for as short a time as possible. If you keep a lid on the pot and place a piece of fresh bread on the top of the broccoli or Brussels sprouts while they are cooking, the bread will absorb some of the odor. Then discard the bread.

Broccoli poses a real problem when trying to cook it. Grandma never placed the whole broccoli in the water but chopped the stems off and cooked them either separately or placed them into the water and allowed them to cook for a while before adding the florets.

If she did cook the stems, she always used a vegetable peeler to remove the first layer so that they would be more tender.

Science of Cooking Broccoli

Broccoli stems have a higher concentration of cellulose (complex carbohydrate) than do the florets. Because of this fact the stems will take much longer to cook and need to be cooked for a while before adding the tops. If you try and cook the entire broccoli, the stems will not be fully cooked since the tops will only take a few minutes.

REMOVING THE FLORETS

Florets should be removed about ½-inch below the head. You can also remove the florets by snapping them off where the individual clusters meet.

BROILING

A few pieces of dried bread placed in the bottom of the broiler pan should absorb fat drippings. This will eliminate smoking fat and should reduce any fire hazard.

When the door is left ajar, it will actually improve the broiling aspects and reduce the roasting aspects.

When the door is left ajar the pan and the air inside the broiler doesn't become as hot as it normally would and reduces the effects of conduction heat cooking. It still allows the same heat intensity to occur and improves the flavor and imparts a more crusty texture to meats.

PEEK-A-BOO

One of the strangest things I remember grandma doing was to leave the broiler door ajar when she was broiling. It didn't seem right to be losing all that heat and taking longer to broil the food.

- ♦ Before starting to broil, be sure and line the broiler pan with aluminum foil or spray it with vegetable oil.
- ♦ If you trim any excess fat off meats it will reduce the risk of a fire.
- ♦ Make sure that any meat you cook is at room temperature before placing it on the broiler pan.

Science of Broiling

When you leave the broiler door ajar, you will improve the flavor and produce a crusty texture to the meat. You are actually increasing the broiler aspect of the cooking process and minimizing the roasting aspect. Also when the air inside the broiler isn't as hot as it would normally get, the cooler temperature reduces the effects of conduction and convection cooking. However, it doesn't affect the radiant heat from the heating element in the broiler.

- Be sure to always pre-heat the broiler and the pan before placing food on it.
- If you place a little water on the bottom of the broiler pan, it will reduce the chance of a fire.

If you baste the meat, be sure that the basting liquid has been warmed.

- Make sure that any food you are going to place on the broiler pan is dried off first with paper towel.
- Thin meats should be closer to the heat source and cooked for a short period of time.
- If possible try and drain off excess fat that has dripped into the bottom pan.

BROWN SAUCE

It is gravy that is prepared using onions, beef broth, butter, flour, vegetables and seasonings.

BROWNIES

YOU DON'T USE A HAMMER & CHISEL

Fudge brownies are very difficult to remove from baking pans unless or use a chef's trick: Just place two pieces of parchment paper perpendicular to each other in the pan before placing the batter in. When they are finished cooking, just remove the batter with the parchment paper and place it on a cutting board ready to be sliced into squares.

BRUSSELS SPROUTS

This vegetable was named after the capital of Belgium, where it originated. A relative of the cabbage family, it even resembles small heads of cabbage. They were brought America in the 1800's from England and were first grown in Louisiana.

They are an excellent source of protein, but not a complete protein unless you eat them with a grain.

- They are easily overcooked and will become mushy.
- Best to store them in the refrigerator to keep the leaves a green color instead of yellow.
- If you cut an *"X"* on the stalk end of each Brussels sprout with a sharp knife before cooking them, the sprout will retain its shape and not fall apart.
- The small opening will allow the steam to be released through the bottom instead of being forced through the leaves.
- If you purchase Brussels sprouts of the same size, they will cook up and be done at the same time.
- Never add an acid like lemon juice to the cooking water or the sprouts will end up a gray-green color.

BUFFALO MEAT

When cooking a beef roast, which has a high fat level, you would normally cook the roast at 325°F; however, due to the lower fat content of a buffalo roast, you only need to cook the roast at 275°F for the same period of time. The roast will also be naturally more tender. In fact, once you taste a buffalo steak, you will never go back to beef, steak.

Beefalo is a cross between a cow and a buffalo and is excellent meat; however, pure buffalo meat is even better. Game meats of all types are lower in fat than most of the beef we normally purchase; however, it is more difficult to find in the stores. Many game meats also contain appreciable amounts of omega-3 fatty acid.

Beware of the wording on meat packages. If the steak packaging reads "lean" the steak cannot have more than 10% fat, "extra lean" cannot have more than 5% fat. The only time I have seen this low a fat content in a steak was a Buffalo steak. Ground beef when labeled "lean" is allowed to have as much as 22% fat.

Buffalo (bison) meat is gaining in popularity throughout the United States. The meat is low in fat, cholesterol, and even calories compared to beef. Today's herds total about 190,000 head and growing steadily. The National Bison Association has 2,300 members.

NUTRITIONAL FACTS ABOUT BUFFALO

3oz SERVING	CALORIES	FAT g.	CHOLESTEROL mg.
Buffalo (bison)	93	1.8	43
Turkey	125	3.0	59
Chicken	140	3.0	57
Beef	183	8.7	75

BUTTER

Butter is made up of 59% water, 40% fat (mostly saturated), and only 1% protein. To be called butter, butter must have a butterfat percentage of 80%. A natural coloring agent called annatto is added to some butter to give it a deeper yellow color.

The USFDA grades butter by taste, color, aroma, texture and body. Grading is done on a point system with 100 being the best. Grade AA must have at least a 93 points, Grade A at least 92, and Grade B a minimum of 90 points. Salt is added to butter to increase its shelf life.

Oxidation will take its toll on butter just like any other fat. It tends to react with the unsaturated fats and causes rancidity. This reaction can be slowed down to a crawl if the butter is either under refrigeration or placed into the freezer. Butter should always be kept tightly wrapped.

♦ There are basically three types of butter used daily: whipped, regular (salted) and unsalted.

- Whipped butter is regular butter with air beaten into it, which creates a more spreadable product. Whipped butter contains 30-45% air.
- Never use whipped butter in baked goods.
- In most recipes salted and unsalted butter can be used interchangeably. However if the recipe calls for unsalted, be sure and use unsalted.
- If you need to grease a pan with butter, always use unsalted since salted may cause the baked goods to stick to the pan.

Butter at the Ready

Chefs always have tablespoons of butter ready when they need them and never have to stop and measure all the time. Next time you unwrap a quarter pound of butter, cut it into tablespoons using the markings on the side of the butter wrapper as a guide. Saves time instead of measuring every time.

Cutting in Butter

While many bakers use their fingertips to cut butter into flour, the problem may arise from the heat of their hands partially melting the butter. A food processor works great but you can also use a food grater. Just rub a frozen stick of butter against the large holes of a standard box grater over the bowl of flour then use a pastry blender or two table knives and work the butter into the flour. Keep cutting only until you have pea-sized pieces.

Temperature of Creaming Butter

When you cream butter for cakes and cookies, the butter needs to be close to room temperature, which is about 67^0F so that it can be worked but not be too soft. Cold butter cannot hold much air as softened butter and the baked product may turn out too dense. When you remove the wrapper from butter, the wrapping should have a creamy residue on the inside. If there is no residue, the butter was too cold. The butter also needs to bend with a little resistance without cracking. The butter should also have a small amount of give when slightly pressed with your finger.

A Real Cut-Up

I always wondered why chefs meticulously cut a quarter pound of butter into almost perfect-sized little cubes when they are going to melt butter. By slicing butter into small pieces it will melt at room temperature in about 15 minutes.

When melting in the microwave from the refrigerator causes a flavor and aroma loss of about 80%.

Science of Melting Butter

It turns out that if you just place pieces of butter or a full quarter pound in a pan to soften, some of the first butter melted will start to burn before the balance of the butter melts. Chefs always add a small amount of oil to the butter allowing them to cook with butter without the butter smoking.

- When butter is heated the protein goes through as change and causes the butter to burn and scorch easily.

85

- A small amount of canola oil added to the butter will slow this process down, however, if you use clarified butter, butter in which the protein has been removed you can fry with it for a longer period and it will also store longer than standard butter.
- Clarified butter, however, will not give your foods the rich real butter flavor you may desire.

A REAL NO, NO

Chefs never cook with salted butter and make sure that they can easily tell the difference by wrapping up leftover butter in waxed paper and labeling it. Chefs never use whipped butter either!

- If you would like to have your butter ready and easy to spread at all times, go to a kitchen store and purchase a "British" butter dish. It is a butter dish made from terra cotta, the top of which needs to be soaked in cold water every day.

Science of Salted Butter

It seems that the salt content of salted butter can vary from brand to brand making it difficult to calculate the added salt need for a recipe. When you use salted butter you do have to calculate the salt that may be added by the butter. When a cookbook calls for butter to be added to a recipe, it means unsalted butter in all instances.

Butter is sold in three grades depending on the flavor rating and milk-fat content. The best grade is U.S. Grade AA, next is U.S. Grade A, which has a lower flavor rating and U.S. Grade B, which is made from sour cream. The milk-fat rating of butter must be at least 80%.

- Butter will go farther and have fewer calories per serving if you beat it well, increasing the volume with air.
- Butter is frequently called for in recipes. Be aware that when it is, make sure that you do not liquefy the butter. Most recipes, especially cake recipes, will have a better texture if the butter is just softened.
- Soften butter and then mix your favorite herbs in it or you can add Parmesan cheese, sesame seeds, mustard, orange juice, etc. If you do add a liquid like honey or any other liquid, be sure and add it slowly for the best results.

BUTTER, CLARIFIED

The whole family loved the flavor of butter and grandma loved cooking with it. However, she knew just how to prepare butter so that it could be cooked with easily and still retain its flavor. Butter breaks down too easily and cannot be used for very many dishes unless it is in a somewhat different form. Grandma always used either clarified butter or ghee.

Science of Clarified Butter

Clarified butter is far superior to regular butter because you are able to fry with it at higher temperatures and it will store longer, even at room temperature. One of the drawbacks, however, is that you do have to give up some of the butter flavor, which comes from the protein (casein) in the part of the butter that is lost during the clarification process. The smoke point of butter will be raised from 250^0 to 350^0F (121.1^0 to 176.7^0C) since it is the protein that tends to cause the butter to scorch and smoke. The protein also reduces the storage time of butter.

When you clarify butter you separate the fat from the non-fat ingredients. When butter is heated it tends to breakdown into three different ingredients: A layer of foam, the thick middle layer of fat (the clarified butter) and a light-colored bottom layer of water, carbohydrates and protein (casein). The bottom layer contains no fat at all. The top layer contains similar ingredients as the bottom layer and trapped air keeps it from falling to the bottom.

HOW TO MAKE CLARIFIED BUTTER:

- Cut up ¼ pound of unsalted butter into very small chunks.
- Place the butter into a clear ovenproof bowl.
- Cover the bowl and place it in the oven on the lowest temperature setting possible.
- After the butter has completely melted, place the bowl in the refrigerator for one hour and do not disturb.
- The middle fat layer (clarified fat) should be solidified.
- Remove the middle fat layer, remove the top foam and the bottom slimy layer, and then rinse the middle fat layer under cold water.
- Dry the fat layer gently with paper towel and will store in the refrigerator for up to 3-4 weeks.

BUTTER, COMPOUND

A compound butter is just a butter that has added ingredients and flavorings. It is usually prepared from unsalted butter; however, unless you prefer a sweet slightly sour taste, you might prefer using salted butter for most recipe variations.

Basically, the butter is softened and beaten and beaten to add air and create a degree of fluffiness before adding any ingredients. When preparing a compound butter, it would be best to start with the highest quality butter available. Many pasta dishes are served using a flavored compound butter instead of a sauce.

BUTTER, CREAMING

If your recipe requires that you cream shortening with a sugary substance, try adding a few drops of water to the mixture. This will make it easier to stir. When you are creaming butter in the blender, cut the butter in small pieces.

BUTTER, DRAWN

When you see drawn butter used on a menu it means that it is clarified butter with the sediment drawn off. It is a very clear butter that has a refrigerator life of about 2 weeks.

BUTTER, GHEE

Ghee is similar to clarified butter and is made using real butter. Ghee has a big advantage over butter in that you can cook and especially sauté with it without it breaking down and burning too easily. Therefore you are able to treat ghee similar to oil. The smoke point of ghee is around 375^0F (190.6^0C), which is still lower than most oils but it is still much better than plain butter. Ghee tends to impart a great flavor to many sautéed foods, which is not possible with standard butter. To prepare ghee, just place some butter in a saucepan on high heat and heat until all the water evaporates.

Butter is approximately 19% water. Continue cooking at the lowest heat point until the milk solids start to coagulate and caramelize (turn a light brown). The excellent flavor is released into the ghee when the milk solids turn brown. The milk solids are easily skimmed off and removed and you are left with the ghee.

Strain the final mixture through a few pieces of cheesecloth to remove any remaining milk solids.

To Prepare Ghee
Just place some butter in a saucepan on high heat and heat until all the water evaporates. Butter is approximately 19% water. Continue cooking at the lowest heat point until the milk solids start to coagulate and caramelize (turn a light brown). The excellent flavor is released into the ghee when the milk solids turn brown. The milk solids are easily skimmed off and removed and you are left with the ghee. Strain the final mixture through a few pieces of cheesecloth to remove any remaining milk solids.

BUTTER, IMITATION

The product "I Can't Believe It's Not Butter" is a spray is made from water, a small amount of soybean oil, salt, sweet cream buttermilk, gums, and flavorings. The average 4-spray serving only contains 15 mg. of salt. If you spray your popcorn it will not make it soggy and 20 squirts will only give you just over 2 grams of polyunsaturated fat.

BUTTER, MAKING IT

Science of Making Butter
You need to start with fresh cream and whip it either in a food processor or an electric hand mixer. If you use the food processor it must have steel blades and you will have to mix the cream for 4-5 minutes.

If you use a hand mixer it will take about 5-7 minutes. If you are really ambitious and want to do it the old-fashioned way then you will have to mix it by hand vigorously for about 45 minutes. The particles in the cream will eventually separate from the liquid. The liquid that remains is the "real" buttermilk not the stuff you buy in the market made with a skim milk culture. The solids that remain are pure unsalted butter. Wash the butter in cold water and then knead it into the form you would like. It will take 2 cups of cream to produce about $\frac{3}{4}$ quarter cup of butter.

BUTTER, MICROWAVE SOFTENING

We all have the experience of softening butter too long in the microwave and ending up with a runny mess or the butter will be somewhat softer on the inside than the outside. When butter is placed into a microwave the inside melts first and causes a rupture in the outer surface and leaks out. Best to microwave for a few seconds then allow the butter to stand for 2-3 minutes before using it allowing the inner heat to warm and soften the outside. However, when you place cold butter in the microwave expect to lose about 80% of the flavor and aroma.

CHEF'S SECRETS

When softening the butter, always allow the butter to soften at room temperature. The butter should be soft enough to be stirred with a wooden spoon. Never soften butter in a microwave or in a pan on top of the stove (unless it is at room temperature), since these methods will affect the flavor of the butter unless it is soft. When adding the other ingredients, never use a blender, mixers or food processor. This will affect the overall texture of the final product.

BUTTER, STORAGE

When storing butter it will be more important where you store it than how long it will last. Butter tends to absorb odors more efficiently than any other food. If you store it near onions it will have an onion smell. If it's around fish, it will smell fishy, etc. If butter is refrigerated it will retain its flavor for about 3 weeks, then it starts losing it rather fast.

If you desire a rich butter flavor it would be wise to date your butter package. Butter will freeze if you double-wrap it in plastic then foil to keep it from absorbing freezer odors. It will last for 9 months if fresh when frozen and must be kept at 0^0F.

BUTTER, UNSALTED

Depending on the area you live in and the particular supermarkets butter product, the salt content of salted butter will vary from 1.5% to 3%. This can play havoc with certain recipes unless you are aware of the actual salt content of a particular butter and how the level of salt in that butter will react with your recipe. It is best in almost all instances to use unsalted butter and just add the salt.

BUTTER, WHIPPED

All recipes that call for butter always calculate the measurements for standard butter. Whipped butter has higher air content due to the whipping. If you do wish to use it, you need to increase the volume of butter used by about 33%.

Make your own whipped butter and just whip up softened butter with electric mixers until fluffy. It will have less cholesterol and fat calories as long as you use less.

Science of Whipped Butter

All recipes are based on the use of stick butter. Whipped butter is about 25% air and is also very difficult to calculate. Whipped butter works great on pancakes or toast since it melts easier than stick butter.

BUTTERMILK

While it is still possible to find the "old fashioned" buttermilk that was drawn off butter, the majority of buttermilk is produced from skim milk cultures. The milk is incubated for 12 to14 hours, which is longer than yogurt and kept at least 400 cooler, while it is fermenting. The buttery flavor is the result of a by-product of the fermentation process and is derived from the bacterium "diacetyl."

Buttermilk can be substituted for 2% or whole milk in most recipes. Buttermilk is less than 1% fat, almost equal to skim milk, however, it has a thicker consistency. When you substitute buttermilk in place of milk, you are adding additional acid to the dough and upsetting the ratio of acid to base needed for the leavening agent to release the maximum amount of carbon dioxide. This will reduce the amount of carbon dioxide that is generated.

To offset the additional acid, you need to add a small amount of baking soda in place of an equal amount of baking powder. The basic rule of thumb is to reduce the amount of baking powder by 2 teaspoons and replace it with ½ teaspoon of baking soda for every cup of buttermilk you use in place of the milk.

- Buttermilk sold today is not the same as your grandmother used to make. It is prepared from a culture of skim milk. However, if a recipe calls for buttermilk, it would be best if you tried to find a dairy and purchase the "real" thing. Real buttermilk has a fuller body, contains butter, and has a much richer flavor, which is what the recipe calls for.
- If a recipe calls for buttermilk and you don't have any, try using slightly soured milk. Soured milk may be used in many baking recipes.
- To make soured milk, just place 1 tablespoon of white vinegar into one cup of milk and allow it to stand for 10-15 minutes. If you are in a hurry, just place the cup in a microwave for about 30 seconds.
- Buttermilk powder, if unopened will last for up to 3 years if stored in a cool, dry location. After it is opened it must be refrigerated and will last for 1 year.

- If you place a piece of aluminum foil on top before placing the lid on, the powder will last longer and remain fresher.

BUTTERMILK, DRY

This milk can be used in a recipe that calls for buttermilk and has a slightly higher fat content than non-fat milk. The shelf life is shorter than non-fat milk.

CCCCC

CABBAGE

Originated in the eastern Mediterranean region and was popular among the ancient Greeks. It is available year round in three main varieties; red, green, and savory, which has crinkly leaves.

- Avoid cabbage with wormholes and be sure to smell the core for sweetness.
- If you are preparing a recipe that calls for cabbage wedges, try steaming them instead of boiling them and they will retain their shape better.
- Use young cabbage, the older cabbage gets, the tougher the leaves and the more bitter it becomes.
- Cabbage needs to be boiled until it is tender, which should take about 5 minutes for shredded and a little longer for wedges.
- Cabbage can be cooked ahead of time, plunged into a bowl of ice water and stored in a plastic bag in the refrigerator. Be sure and use it by the next day.
- Green and red cabbage should have firm tight leaves with good color.
- Cabbage should be refrigerated in plastic bags and used within 7-14 days.
- Cabbage; along with its other cruciferous family members are being studied in cancer prevention, due to its "indole" content. Initial studies indicate that if you consume ½ of a standard cabbage daily you may prevent some cancers.
- An easy method of removing leaves to prepare stuffed cabbage is to cut around the core at the base, remove the core and remove the leaves from the base. Remove one leaf at a time very gently.
- Cabbage will last longer if stored in the refrigerator sealed tightly in a plastic bag. It should stay for about 2 weeks. Cabbage is 91% water.

Science of Cooking Cabbage

Cabbage contains a sulfur compound, which is released when the skin is cut. One of the compounds is called "sinigrin" and with help of an enzyme can change to mustard oil, which causes the raw cabbage to have a biting flavor. When cabbage is cooked a number of the sulfur compounds and other chemicals are released and cause an unpleasant odor and off flavor.

NO GAS PROBLEM

Flatulence problems from cabbage can be eliminated by boiling the cabbage for about 5-6 minutes then draining the water and continuing to boil it in fresh water. The chemical that causes the problem is released during the first few minutes of cooking.

> If you serve pineapple with cabbage or beans it will prevent bloating and gas.

STAYING IN SHAPE

If you are preparing a recipe that calls for cabbage wedges, try steaming them instead of boiling them and they will retain their shape better.

CABBAGE, STUFFED

When you need cabbage leaves for stuffed cabbage try freezing the whole cabbage first, then let it thaw and the leaves will come apart without tearing.

CAJUN STYLE

The definition of "Cajun Style" cooking refers to cooking a dish that contains onion powder/dehydrated onion, garlic powder/dehydrated garlic, white pepper, red pepper, and freshly ground black pepper.

CAKE MIXES, COMMERCIAL

Science of Commercial Mixes

Commercial mixes use special chlorinated flours and fat emulsifiers. These help to make the cakes from mixes to come out light and tender. The chlorinated flours change the surface properties of starch and flour fats and stop the gluten proteins from binding. The flour can also withstand more of the structure damaging ingredients such as sugar and shortening thus producing a sweeter more tender cake. Special emulsifiers are used in the shortening to prevent shortening from reducing the volume of air foam.

CAKES

Many people do not read all the instructions carefully in a recipe. If a recipe states for a pan to be greased, it may not mean to grease the entire pan including the sides. A number of cakes need to go up the sides and only the bottom of the pan should be greased. Always prepare your pans and preheat the oven before mixing the batter.

THE TALKING CAKE

When it comes to baking cakes, chefs have some very strange methods of checking when a cake is done and if the batter is just right. They actually listen to the cake while it is baking and if they hear a bubbling sound, the cake is done.

- Room-temperature fat, when creamed with sugar has the capability of trapping air in a cake batter, creating very light-textured cakes.
- Make sure eggs are all at room temperature when making cakes for the best results.
- If you are going to cut an unfrosted cake and make decorative designs, try freezing the cake first. This will make it much easier to slice and make the designs. Fresh cakes are hard to work with without making a big mess.

If you want a lighter cake, separate the eggs then add the yolks to the butter mixture then beat the whites and fold them into the final batter.

- If you would like an old-fashioned look on top of a cake, just place a paper lace doily on top and sprinkle powdered sugar over it, then remove it. Colored powdered sugar works great too.
- When a cake has finished cooking, the sides will shrink slightly from the pan. The exception to this is chiffon and sponge cakes.

Always check your oven temperature for accuracy at least every few months. Ovens can be off as much as 60^0-70^0 and may need to be adjusted. If the temperature is off by more than 15^0 if could affect your baked goods.

- If you need to store a cake more than 1-2 days you should add ½ an apple to the cake saver. This will provide just enough moisture to stop the cake from drying out too soon.
- Warped pans should be discarded. They will spoil the quality of the product especially if you place batter directly in the pan.
- A baker's trick when placing a design on top of a cake is to take a toothpick and trace the design before sprinkling on the topping.

One of the best methods of keeping the insides of a cake from drying out is to place a piece of fresh white bread next to the exposed surface. The bread can be affixed with a short piece of spaghetti.

- Single layer cakes should always be baked on a center shelf for adequate heat circulation.

- If a cake gets hard and stale, throw it out, don't try and repair it.
- A richer cake can be produced by substituting 2 egg yolks for 1 whole egg as long as you don't have to worry about your cholesterol.
- During the first 15-20 minutes of baking, never open the oven or the cake may fall from the sudden change in temperature.
- When your baked foods get stuck to the bottom of the pan, try wrapping the cake pan in a towel when it is still hot or place the pan on a cold, wet towel for a few minutes.
- If you're having problems with bubbles in the batter, try holding the pan about 5 inches off the floor and drop it. It may take 2-3 times but the bubbles will be all gone, the cake might be too if you're not careful.
- If you have problems keeping a cake together when you are icing it, try holding it together with a few pieces of thick spaghetti.

Remember, never grease tube pans used for sponge, angel food or chiffon cakes. You want there to be some traction for the batter to climb up the sides easily.

- Never place a freshly baked cake on a plate without shaking a thin layer of sugar on the plate first. This will prevent the cake from sticking.
- It really isn't worth the trouble but if you want to revive a cake that has gone stale; just very quickly dip it in low-fat milk and place it in a 350^0F oven for 10-15 minutes.
- When you are going to cream butter and sugar together, be sure and add the spices and any salt included in the recipe.
- If the mixture of the whipped butter and sugar looks like it is curdled, don't be concerned since it will change when the flour is added.
- Chocolate chips, chopped dates, nuts and raisins have a tendency to settle to the bottom unless the batter is thick and will suspend them.
- To get rid of unwanted air from angel food or sponge cakes, just run a knife in a zigzag pattern through the batter.

Altitude Baking

When baking at an altitude of over 3,500 feet, it is necessary to increase the temperature 25 degrees and add 1 tablespoon of flour to the recipe. Then continue adding 1 tablespoon of flour for every 1,500 feet increase in elevation. If you are using leavening and 1 teaspoon is needed at sea level then use $2/3^{rd}$ teaspoon at 3,500 feet, ½ teaspoon at 5,000 feet, and ¼ teaspoon at 6,500 or above.

CAKES, BUTTER TYPE

If you have ever baked a butter cake and it was too heavy, chefs have a trick that works great by incorporating air into the batter making the butter cake light and airy. All you have to do is to cream the sugar with the fat at room temperature. Shortening of any type does not blend well when it is too cold.

94

CAKES, CHOCOLATE

Chocolate has a high acid level, so high that it would upset the balance between the acid (cream of tartar) and the base of baking powder. When baking soda (sodium bicarbonate) is used, it may make the chocolate cake too basic and most recipes also call for the addition of a sour-milk product such as yogurt or sour cream to assure that the batter will not be too alkali (basic).

If the batter did become too alkali, the color of the cake would turn red instead of brown and taste bitter.

CHOCOLATE HEAVEN

When it came to choosing which cake was the most popular, chocolate cake was the winner and grandma's chocolate cake was to die for. She knew all the secrets to making it perfect, such as using baking soda instead of baking powder as the leavening agent.

CAKES, CUTTING

Next time you cut a cake, try cutting it from the center so that you can move the pieces together keeping the edges moist. If you will be cutting cakes regularly, it would be best to purchase a cake cutter. This is long and thin with metal tines and has a handle.

CAKES, FLOURING

Try using dry cake mix instead of white flour, works great and no mess on the outside of the cake.

CAKES, HEART-SHAPED

 A heart-shaped cake is easier to make than you might think. All you have to do is to bake a normal round cake and a square cake. Then cut the round cake in half, then place the square cake so the one of the corners face you and add the halves of the round cake on either side.

CAKES, MIXING

When the batter is beaten too long, excessive gluten is formed and a poor texture is the result. This is true with most baked products. Mixing and beating batter is more important than most people realize and must be done just right for the perfect product.

CAKES, ONE-BOWL

It is a layer cake, which is made by mixing the batter in one-bowl. When this is done you omit the step of creaming the shortening or butter and the sugar. Using the one-bowl method you add the shortening, liquid, and the flavorings to the dry ingredients and beat. The eggs are then added and the batter beaten again.

CAKES, PANS

Cake pans are a very important part of making a cake. Some factors will influence the outcome more than others, such as the thickness of the pan, which is not very important. However, the finish of the pan and its relative volume to the size of the cake is very important. If a cake is heated faster, the gas cells will expand faster and the better the batter will set.

- ♦ Remember never to fill the baking pan more than ¾ full. The cake needs room to expand.
- ♦ To avoid this problem, remove the pan from the oven and allow the product to remain in the pan and to just rest for a few minutes.
- ♦ The product should then be removed and placed on a cooling rack which will allow more of the area to release additional steam and stop any moisture from going to the bottom of the product, causing the bottom to become soggy.

JOLLY GOOD IDEA

If you are short one cooling rack, just use 4-5 dinner knives in a row to keep the baked goods off the counter. Place them in opposite directions for a fairly flat surface.

- ♦ The perfect pan for the job should be the actual size of the finished product. If the side of the pan is too high the unused area can shield the batter from needed radiant energy and slow the rate at which the batter is heated making the cake drier. This is also the cause of humps in the cake.
- ♦ Never use a baking pan with a bright surface since they will reflect radiant heat and transmit the heat too slowly and thereby slowing the baking process.
- ♦ When breads and cakes are baked, they build up steam inside, which needs to be released after they are removed from the oven.
- ♦ If the steam is not allowed to escape, it will convert to water as it comes in contact with the cooler air and be absorbed back into the product, thus making the product soggy.

Science of Removing a Cake – CHEF STYLE

When a cake sticks to the pan and is difficult to remove, just place the cake pan on a wet kitchen towel and let the cake steam away from the sides and bottom of the pan.

CAKES, POUND

Pound cakes occasionally come out underdone; which, was probably due to using two different sugars. If you run out of one sugar and use another brand that you had never used before, it may cause a problem. It turns out that the shape of sugar crystals can make a difference. A cake must rise and uses a leavening agent to make it happen.

Most cakes use carbon dioxide (CO_2), which is released from the baking soda or baking powder. The initial step in making a pound cake is to start with the fat, which can be butter or shortening or both. The fat is beaten with a mixer, which incorporates the CO_2 bubbles in it. The next step involves sprinkling the sugar slowly into the fat.

When the sharp sugar crystals cut into the butter they form tiny pockets, which fill with air as the mixer keeps pulling more fat over the pockets and closes it. This step makes the fat double in volume and produces the creamy texture.

If the sugar crystals in one of the brands of sugar are smaller or it contains edges that are not as sharp it won't cut into the fat as deeply. This results in a smaller pocket and less air is pulled in. Eventually steam fills the air pockets as the cake bakes and the uneven distribution of air causes the insides of the cake to be poorly cooked. Be sure and use the same sugar you are used to using for the same results.

CAKES, SOLVING PROBLEMS

- Cakes will fall if too little flour is used.
- Cakes will rise too high in center and crack if too much flour is used.
- Cakes will brown on top before they rise, enough if oven heat is too high.
- Cakes will be soggy if too much shortening is used.
- Cakes will be too heavy if too much sugar is used.
- Cakes will have large holes and tunnels if you beat too much after flour is added.

ANGEL FOOD, CHIFFON, AND SPONGE CAKES

If your cake has poor volume you may not have beaten the egg whites long enough. Only beat them until they stand in straight peaks. They should look moist and glossy when the beaters are removed. Another problem occurs if you over-mix the batter when you add the flour. The ingredients should be gently folded in and combined until the batter is just smooth.

DON'T MAKE ME DIZZY

Chef's secret to light, perfect angel food and sponge cake is in the mixing of the ingredients. When the foam and other ingredients have been mixed together and stirred, they should always be stirred using a spatula and never in a circular motion. The spatula is moved up and down a few times in the center; moving the batter and bringing it up then occasionally they fold some of the lower layers over each other from the bottom.

- The angel food pan should be inverted after baking. This can be done, by placing the pan tube over the neck of a tall sturdy bottle. If you prefer you can also prop the edges of the inverted pan on 4 cans of equal height.
- An angel food cake may be left in the pan and covered tightly with tin foil for a maximum of 24 hours, or until you are ready to frost it.
- The best way to cool an angel food cake is to turn it upside down on an ice cube tray or place it upside down in the freezer for just a few minutes.

- If your cake shrinks or falls, the egg whites have probably been beaten too long. Another problem may be that you forgot to cool the cake upside down allowing the steam to dissipate throughout the cake, thus creating a lighter, more fluffy cake.
- If your cake is tough you probably over-mixed the batter at the time when the dry ingredients were added. Ingredients should be blended only until they are mixed.
- If your sponge cake has layers, you didn't beat the egg yolks long enough. They should be beaten until they are thick and lemon-colored.
- If your chiffon cake has yellow streaks you have added the yolks directly into the dry ingredients instead of making a "well" in the center of the dry ingredients then adding the oil and then the egg yolks.
- If your chiffon cake has a layer, you probably have either over-beaten or under-beaten the egg whites. Only beat the egg whites until they are stiff and look moist and glossy.

Science of Angel and Sponge Cakes
Ordinary stirring breaks up too many of the fragile air pockets. The cake needs
these kept intact and as the cake bakes, these air cells expand and raise the batter
while the flour starch gelatinizes assisting the heat-coagulated proteins to reinforce
the cell wall.

Safety Measure for Tube Pans
Spilling batter down the center of the tube is very common even among bakers unless
they know the secret to avoiding the problem. Once the pan has been properly
prepared; by greasing or lining with parchment paper, place a small paper cup over
the top of the tube. Gradually scrape the batter into the pan with a rubber spatula.

LAYER CAKES
- If your cake has a coarse texture or is heavy and solid you probably didn't beat the sugar and Crisco™, margarine, or butter long enough. These ingredients need to be mixed together very thoroughly for the best results.
- If your cake is dry, this may indicate overcooking and failure to check the doneness after the minimum cooking time. Another reason this occurs is that you may have over-beaten the egg whites.

- If your cake has elongated holes this is a sign of over-mixing the batter when the flour was added. Ingredients should be mixed only enough to combine them totally.

DIVIDE PROPERLY OR FAIL

When making a layer cake it is important to divide the batter evenly between pans so that the layers will be the same height. It is best to use a kitchen scale to measure the weight of the batter for each layer.

Cakes need to be rotated during baking to assure that they will brown evenly. Using a glove does not work very well and it would be best to use a long-handled pair of tongs.

Spaghetti Tester

If you need to test a deep cake, try using a long piece of spaghetti. If the spaghetti comes out with moist batter on it, the cake needs more time in the oven.

CAKES, SPLITTING LAYERS

If you want to split cake layers, just loop a piece of unflavored dental floss tightly around the center of the cake horizontally then cross the ends and slowly pull on each end. Do it firmly, but slowly so as not to damage the layer.

CAKES, SWEETENERS USED

The texture of a cake will change depending on the type of sweetener used. Sweeteners may determine how tender the cake will be so make sure you use the right one. Never substitute a standard granulated sugar for a powdered sugar. Powdered should only be used for icings and glazes. Granulated is recommended for baking. If you're baking any cake that has a crumb texture, make sure that you use oil in place of solid fat.

CAKES, TRANSPORTING OF

THE GRANDMA-MOBILE

When transporting cakes it is almost impossible to keep the plastic wrap from touching the frosting and making a mess. Next time try placing toothpicks around the top of the cake and attaching mini marshmallows to the tips of each toothpick, leaving a small end of a number of the toothpicks so that you can push the plastic wrap on to the tip above the marshmallow.

CAKES, UPSIDE DOWN

Any single layer cake can be made into an upside down cake.
Grease a pan then place about 1/3rd cup of melted butter on the bottom then sprinkle ½ cup of brown sugar over the butter then sprinkle some ground cinnamon and nutmeg over it.

99

Top this with chopped nuts and canned pineapple or other fruit then pour the batter over the fruit and bake. After the cake is done baking, place it on a serving plate upside down and allow it to remain for about 5 minutes before removing it.

CANDY

When you're making candy, be sure and follow directions to the letter. Candy recipes are very exacting and variances can cause a poor quality product.

Candy must be cooked at the temperature that is recommended, never try and speed up the process by increasing the heat.

The lower the final temperature of the candy after it is cooked will determine the softness of the final product. In fact, if the humidity in the kitchen is over 60% it will adversely affect the final product.

- ♦ If you have a problem with candy boiling over, try placing a wooden spoon across the top of the pot to break the bubbles.
- ♦ When adding water to a candy recipe, always add very hot water for a crystal clear candy. Cold water may contain contaminants that cause cloudiness. Freshly prepared candy will keep for about 2-3 weeks.
- ♦ If you have a problem with candy boil over, just place a wooden spoon over the pan to break the bubbles.
- ♦ Candies stored in the refrigerator can pick up foreign odors and should be stored properly in a closed container. Also, be sure and place a piece of waxed paper between the layers when storing candy.

Cane sugar should always be used for candies, beet sugar tends to cause more foam.

- ♦ To successfully defrost candy, the temperature should be raised gradually. Place the candy to be thawed, still in the original wrapper, in a brown paper bag lined with a paper towel. This will absorb any moisture that may collect during defrosting.
- ♦ If you are making candy and the weather is hot and humid, don't try and make chocolates unless the room is well air-conditioned. The best temperature to make chocolates, divinity, hard candy, and fudge is between 62^0F and 68^0F with low humidity. These candies absorb moisture from the air very easily.
- ♦ When adding water to a candy recipe, always add very hot water for the best results and a clearer candy. Most freshly made candy will remain fresh for 2-3 weeks.
- ♦ Be sure and have a candy thermometer handy when preparing candy recipes.

The microwave can be very handy since it is a source of direct heat. This means that scorching and overcooking can be held to a minimum. Best to avoid boiling over when preparing candy in the microwave: by using a bowl that holds about twice as much volume as you are preparing.

CANDY, CRYSTALLIZATION OF

Sugar crystallization is one of the more frequent problems when making candy. This usually occurs when the slightest grain of sugar that may be trapped on the side of the pan falls down into the syrup mixture. This can easily be prevented by heating the sugar over low heat and do not stir, until the sugar is completely dissolved.

If any sugar crystals are still clinging to the sides of the pan, tightly place the lid on the pan and continue cooking the syrup for 3-4 minutes. The steam that is generated will melt the clinging sugar grains.

TRAPPED SUGAR PROBLEM

When making candy, a frequent problem is that of sugar crystallization. This may occur when the slightest grain of sugar gets trapped on the side of the pot and falls down into the syrup. Chefs prevent this by heating the sugar over low heat and never stirring until all the sugar is dissolved.

Another method is to tightly place a lid on the syrup and continue cooking it for 3-4 minutes. This will produce steam and will melt the sugar crystals that are clinging to the sides of the pot.

Science of Sugar Crystals

Placing sugar crystals (sucrose) into water causes them to dissolve. However, the hotter the water, the more sugar you can add to the water and eventually the water will become saturated. By boiling the water it can even become more saturated then adding an acid such as lemon juice or cream of tartar it will cause a chemical reaction that tears the sugar molecule apart. The result is two simple sugars: fructose and glucose and since neither will form crystals when the water eventually evaporates it make a non-crystalline candy. Another method of stopping sucrose from re-forming as the water evaporates is to add corn syrup or butter to the water, which is a non-crystalline sugar.

CANDY, FREEZING

Freezing has a negative effect on a number of candies and never tastes the same and may lose their consistency. Hard candies may crumble, jellies become granular, cereal products and popcorn candy become mushy, and the rest lose their original consistencies due to the expansion of the liquid in their cells.

CANDY SYRUPS, PREPARATION OF

When using sugar to prepare syrups, remember that sugar has the tendency to attract moisture from the air and thus keeps foods moist. Cakes are lighter because the sugar slows the gluten from becoming stiff. It has the tendency to lower the freezing point of most liquids, which keeps ice cream in a state of a semi-solid.

When used on meats it will help retain the natural moisture. Sugar syrups are easy to prepare and very popular.

Thin sugar syrup
One cup of granulated sugar added to two cups of water.

Medium sugar syrup
One cup of granulated sugar added to one cup of water.

Heavy sugar syrup
One cup of granulated sugar added to ¾ cup of water.

Thick sugar syrup
One cup of granulated sugar added to ½ cup of water.

- In a small saucepan, add the sugar to the water and stir gently over low heat. Do not allow the mixture to boil until the sugar is completely dissolved. When boiling begins, stop stirring and continue to boil (uncovered) for about 1 minute. Flavorings can be added either before or after cooking. If you overcook the syrup, just add ¼ cup of boiling water and cook again.

Stages of sugar syrup

- The thread stage is used to determine the actual temperature of the sugary syrup. In order for the candy to set up it must crystallize into sugary syrup. Cook the syrup in a small saucepan over medium heat until it reaches the desired temperature. If you do not have a thermometer, the following will be useful:

Thread Stage 230^0F to 234^0F (110^0C to 112.2^0C):
Syrup will form a soft light thread.

Soft Ball 234^0F to 240^0F (112.2^0C to 115.6^0C):
Syrup will form a small ball that will flatten out when removed.

Firm Ball 244^0F to 248^0F (117.8^0C to 120^0C):
Syrup will form a firm ball that tends to flatten out when pressed between your fingers.

Hard Ball 250^0F to 265^0F (121.1^0C to 129.4^0C):
Syrup will form a hard ball that has just a little give to it when squeezed.

Soft Crack 270^0F to 290^0F (132.2^0C to 143.3^0C):
Syrup tends to separate into hard threads that are bendable.

Hard Crack 300^0F to 310^0F (148.9^0C to 154.4^0C):
Syrup will separate into threads, which are hard and very brittle.

Caramelized Sugar 310^0F to 338^0F (154.4^0C to 170^0C):
Syrup will become a golden color.

NOTE: When sugar is cooked above 350^0F (176.7^0C) it will turn black and burn.

- When preparing sugar syrup, always watch the bubbles. Bubbles tend to get smaller as the sugar syrup thickens. If the syrup bubbles get too small it's time to start over.

CANNING

When canning anything the jars should always be sterilized regardless of the method used.

The only exception is when you cook the foods in the jars, and then the jars do not need sterilization but should be thoroughly washed. No preservatives, additives, or artificial colorings should ever be added to a home canned product. Always wipe the outside of all jars with white vinegar before storing to reduce the risk of mold forming on any food that wasn't cleaned off well.

- As long as the seal is intact frozen home-canned goods are still safe to eat providing the seal is intact. However, as with all fresh frozen foods the taste and texture may change.
- If you see a black deposit on the lid after you open a canned food it is usually nothing to worry about (as long as the jar seal is intact). The mold-looking deposits are actually caused by tannins in the food or by hydrogen sulfide released by the foods when processed.
- Foods high in starch such as corn, Lima beans, and peas need to be packed loosely since they tend to expand after being processed. Fruits and berries should be packed solidly due to shrinkage and the fact that their texture does not stop the heat penetration.

Science of Canning

Canning was invented in 1810 by Peter Durand; an Englishman, who called it a "tin canister." This would be an improvement over the glass jar, especially for transportation to outlying areas without breakage. The first "tin cans" had to be made by hand with workers cutting the can from sheets of tin-plate then soldering them together leaving a small hole in the top to place the food in. The hole was then covered with a small tin disc and soldered closed. A tin worker was able to produce about 60-cans a day.

The United States started a canning operation in the 1820's and within 20 years the canning of foods was being done all over the country. In 1860 Isaac Solomon in Baltimore found that if he added calcium chloride to the water when it was boiling he could raise the temperature from 212°F to 240°F and thus reduce the processing time from about 6 hours to 45 minutes. A processing plant could now produce 20,000 cans a day instead of 2,500. The longest food to date that has been eaten safely was canned meat that was 114 years old.

- If you see a jar that has a cloudy liquid the food is probably spoiled. Be very cautious, these jars should be disposed of without being opened. Spores can be released that may be harmful.

- When you open any canned food check the liquid and make sure that it is not cloudy. Cloudiness in many liquids indicates spoilage. If you have any doubts about foods, it is best to throw them out without tasting them.
- There are, however, a number of reasons foods may become cloudy and still be good such as different sizes of foods causing the breakdown of the smaller pieces, hard water, salt containing impurities and additives.
- Pickles may frequently become cloudy due to the fermentation process and this is not harmful.
- Pure apple cider vinegar is the best to use when pickling. It has a 4-5% acidity level.
- If you don't want your pickles to become soft, make sure that the vinegar has adequate acidity and that enough is used. Also, keeping the pickles in the refrigerator will help them remain hard.
- As long as the seal is intact, canned foods can last for many years. Nutrient content will be diminished, however, to a great degree.
- After canning the food, tap the top, you should hear a clear "ringing note." If the food is touching the top, this may not occur, but as long as the top does not move up and down, the food does not have to be reprocessed.
- Canned foods need to be stored in a cool, dark location. Summer heat may cause a location to develop enough heat to damage the canned foods. Heat causes dormant bacteria to become active and multiply.

CANNING SALT

Grandma did a lot of canning and used a special salt that she made herself. She called it "canning salt" and is really pure salt and only salt without the iodine added. It can be found in canning sections of the supermarket or you can make your own.

GRANDMA'S CANNING SALT

Ingredients:

1	Cup of **non-iodized** salt	1	Tablespoon Spanish paprika
¼	Teaspoon celery salt	1	Teaspoon ground black pepper
¼	Teaspoon ground white pepper	¼	Teaspoon garlic salt

If you use garlic powder, just a pinch will do.

Science of Canning Salt

The iodine in salt can affect the flavor of some foods by reacting with certain chemicals in the food to produce an off-flavor. While you probably would not notice the flavor difference a trained chef or grandmother could tell the difference.

CANOLA OIL

Produced from the rapeseed plant, which is a relative of the mustard family. It is normally found in the refined state, has a very high smoke point making it one of the best all-around oils.

This is the best oil for frying since it does not breakdown as easily as most other oils. The oil is high in monounsaturated fat and low in saturated fat.

It is also one of the lowest priced oils. Canola oil is one of the few oils that contain omega-3 fatty acids. The name canola was derived from the word Canada and oil.

CAPERS

These are an unopened green flower bud of a wild cultivated bush grown in Italy, France and Algeria. It takes a large amount of manual labor to pick the buds since they must be picked each morning, just as they reach the proper size. Recently, capers are also being grown in California. After they are harvested, they are dried and pickled in special vinegar brine.

- Capers are normally sold either whole or pickled in brine.
- Commonly used on smoked fish, chicken dishes, eggs, or veal.
- Capers provide piquancy, which is why they are used in special sauces and as a condiment.
- Capers are very high in sodium.
- They will store for about 9 months under refrigeration providing the buds are covered with brine.
- Wash then well under cold water before serving.
- They can be served with almost any food and are excellent in salads providing a degree of piquancy.

They are normally sold either whole or pickled in brine. Commonly used on smoked fish, chicken dishes, eggs, or veal. Capers provide piquancy, which is why they are used in special sauces and as a condiment.

CARAMEL

Caramel sauce is prepared from sugar and water. The mixture is cooked until it is a dark brown color. Caramel candy is prepared from sugar, milk or cream, honey or corn syrup and butter. Additional ingredients can also be added such as nuts and chocolate bits.

CARAWAY SEEDS

Science of Caraway Seeds
Somewhat similar flavor to licorice (anise) and are harvested at night before the dew evaporates. The majority sold in the United States is imported from the Netherlands and commonly used in rye bread, cookies, organ meats, dips, cabbage, sauerkraut, soft cheese spreads, sweet pickles, Sauerbraten, and French dressing.

CARROT

Carrots are the best source of beta-carotene of any vegetable. Studies show that carrots may lower blood cholesterol levels; however, drinking an excessive amount of carrot juice may turn your skin orange due to high level of carotenoid pigment. Reducing the intake will alleviate this color problem. They are available year round and should have smooth skin, solid orange color and are well formed. Should be stored in the refrigerator and never placed in water for any period of time, especially if peeled.

♦ If carrots are to be used in a stir-fry, try boiling them first, then place them in cold water until needed. It takes longer to cook the carrots since they are so solid. To slip the skin off carrots, drop them in boiling water, let stand for 5 minutes then place them into cold water for a few seconds.

♦ To curl carrots, peel slices with a potato peeler and drop them into a bowl of ice water. When grating carrots, leave a portion of the green top on to use as a handle. This will keep your fingers from becoming shorter.

♦ Best to wash and scrape the carrots and slice them into 1/8th inch slices. Boil water in a large pot and place the carrots in for 5 minutes, remove, dry and place in food dehydrator for 2-4 hours.

♦ A good rule to remember when purchasing vegetables for freezing is to purchase "young ones." The nutrient content will be higher and they will contain less starch. Freeze as soon as purchased. Remember, fresh produce has stronger cell walls and will handle freezing better.

Reviving

A number of vegetables tend to lose their moisture before you are able to use them up and become limp. There is no need to discard them when all you have to do is immerse them in a bowl of ice cubes and water for 1 hour in the refrigerator. The cells will absorb the water, return to their normal size, thus making the vegetable hard and crisp again. Soaking fresh vegetables for long periods of time, however, may have the opposite effect because of excess water buildup in the spaces between the cells.

Science of Buying   Carrots
If you see a shriveled carrot, they have been improperly stored and any mushy or soft spots indicate decay. The thin hairy rootlets coming out of the skin tell you that the carrot is old and if there is any green tinge around the stem it means that the carrot was allowed to remain in the sun too long. The green areas on carrots will be bitter and should be discarded. The color should be a vivid orange and not a pale orange. Watch out for carrots being sold in orange bags so that you can't tell the real color of a fresh carrot.

Tops

Carrots and beets need to have their tops removed before they are stored. The tops will draw moisture from the vegetable, leach nutrients from the carrot and cause them to become bitter, as well as reducing their storage life. However, leave about two inches of the root if it is still there to keep the bottom sealed. Carrots and beets need to be stored in a plastic bag with holes in the refrigerator. Both are very susceptible to a number of microbes that will cause them to decay. Carrots will freeze well with only minimal blanching. Beets should be boiled until they are fork tender before freezing.

CURLING A CARROT

Use a vegetable peeler to peel long, thin strips from top to bottom of a carrot after it has been peeled and washed. Roll the strips one at a time around your finger and fasten the curled carrot with a toothpick to hold it together. Place the curls in a large bowl of ice cubes and water (the colder, the better) and place them into the refrigerator for about 30-45 minutes. Remove the curled carrot strips, take out the toothpick and keep them cold until used to garnish a salad.

HOW SWEET I AM

If you want the sweetest carrots ever, try adding a teaspoon of sugar to the water and just cook them until they are barely tender. Raw carrots need to be slightly cooked so that the nutrients will be better absorbed.

Science of Carrots

The cell wall of carrots is difficult for the body to breakdown, thus making it more difficult to utilize the nutrient. Therefore the body does not get to utilize 100% of the nutrients unless the carrot is at least partially cooked. This softens the cell walls and makes it easier for the body to utilize more of the nutrients. The carrot is actually the taproot of the plant. The small eyes you see when looking at a carrot is actually small secondary roots that feeds water and nutrients to the center cylinder to feed the plant and leaves.

When carrots are stored in a sealed plastic bag a chemical is released called "terpenoid," which will reduce the sweetness and make the carrot somewhat bitter. Also, if carrots are stored with apples, melons, avocados, peaches, pears or green tomatoes they will develop terpenoids faster. Those fruits and vegetables tend to give off more ethylene gas as they ripen.

The area just under the skin contains a large majority of the nutrients in the carrot. It is best to leave the skin on if possible. A slight scrapping can be done if you don't go to deep.

CASSEROLES

Some casserole recipes call for dishes of certain sizes and volume. To determine the size of your casserole dish, just fill it with water and measure the water.

Dishes are sold in 1, 1½, 2 and 3 quart sizes. If you are going to prepare a casserole ahead of time, be sure and line the dish with aluminum foil before adding the food then seal it with the lid.

Making a casserole can be very difficult if you do not have the right casserole dish to prepare it in. Always use one of two different dishes, either a cast iron casserole dish (preferred) or a ceramic one. Both are very heavy and have heavy lids.

CHEF'S HINTS & TIPS FOR CASSEROLES

- Keep pre-cut and peeled veggies in the freezer.
- Use dried herb instead of fresh herbs because of cooking times.
- Keep the casserole lid off if you want a browned topping.
- If you re-heat a casserole, defrost it in the refrigerator, cover and bake at 350°F.
- Make casseroles in advance allowing enough time for flavors to release and mingle.
- If you would like a crisp topping on your casserole, try leaving the lid off while it is cooking for the last 10 minutes.
- Try sprinkling the top with breadcrumbs for a great looking dish.

Science of Casserole Dishes

The outside of a casserole dish must be kept at the oven temperature while the inside food remains at about 212°F (100°C) allowing the liquid inside to gently boil. The casserole dish should have a thick wall allowing thermal conductivity to withstand the temperature differences to avoid rapid boiling and evaporating of the liquid in the food. The liquid that does escape is in the form of steam from around the lid. The lid must be heavy and fit solidly or thermal expansion will loosen the lid. Be sure that the lid is flat and heavy and the lip of the dish is flat as well maintaining a good seal.

CAULIFLOWER

- Do not purchase if the clusters are open or if there is a speckled surface, this is a sign of insect injury, mold, or rot.
- Should be stored in the refrigerator, unwrapped.
- Cauliflower can be kept white during cooking by just adding a small amount of lemon or lemon peel to the water.
- Overcooking tends to darken cauliflower and make it tough.
- To reduce the odor when cooking cauliflower, replace the water after it has cooked for 5-7 minutes.
- Due to certain minerals that are found in cauliflower, it is best not to cook it in aluminum or iron pot. Contact with these metals will turn cauliflower yellow, brown or blue-green.

THERE GOES MY INSIDES

To cut up the florets properly, first remove and discard all outer leaves then turn the cauliflower on its side and cut off the stem close to the base of the head.

Turn the cauliflower so that the stem end is up and using a small knife, remove the core then remove the individual florets and cut into desired sizes.

♦ It is a common practice to tie the leaves up around a cauliflower plant as it grows to bleach the heads. Instead of the old method, try gathering up the leaves and then place a brown bag over the head. The air will still be able to circulate and will prevent rotting that is common when the leaves are tied.

Science of Cauliflower

Cauliflower is surrounded by green leaves, which protect it from the sun and cause the cauliflower to remain white instead of producing chlorophyll and turning green. When you cook a cruciferous vegetable such as cauliflower, never use an aluminum or iron pot. The sulfur compounds will react with the aluminum turning the cauliflower yellow. If cooked in an iron pot, it will turn the cauliflower brown or a bluish-green. Place a pinch of cream of tartar in the cooking water and the cauliflower will not discolor.

Odor

If you break up a few pieces of fresh white bread and add them to the pot when you are cooking cauliflower it will reduce the smell. Placing a piece of fresh white bread on top of the cooking cauliflower will also work.

Storing

One of the most important things to remember is never bump or injure the florets.
This will cause the head to loosen and spread too fast and cause discoloration. Store the head in a plastic bag that is not wrapped too tight around the head and store it in the vegetable crisper. Never wash the cauliflower before it is stored and it should keep for 4-6 days.
Wash the head thoroughly before eating since a number of chemicals are often used to preserve their freshness. To freeze, just cut the cauliflower into small pieces, wash in lightly cold salted water; then blanch in salt water for 5 minutes. Drain and chill them before placing in a plastic bag.

CELERY

Celery arrived in United States from Europe in the 1800's. Celery has very high water content and is low in calories. It is available year round. Stalks should be solid, with no hint of softness along any of the stalks, which will denote pithiness. If even one stalk is wilted, do not purchase.

♦ Celery will only store in the refrigerator for 7-10 days and should not be placed in water.

◆ Don't discard the celery leaves. Dry them, then rub the leaves through a sieve turning them into a powder that can be used to flavor soups, stews, and salad dressings. This can also be made into celery salt.

Chop, Chop

Chopping celery can be a pain unless you know the easy way to do it. Just leave the celery bunch whole and wash it then just chop away. It is easy to hold on to when it is intact.

Science of Celery

Celery is easy to cook. The pectin in the cells will easily break down in water. However, the "strings," which are made of cellulose and lignin are virtually indestructible and will not break down under normal cooking conditions. The body even has a difficult time breaking them down and many people cannot digest them at all. It is best to use a potato peeler and remove the strings before using the celery. When preparing stuffed celery stalks for a party, always be sure and remove the strings.

Celery contains the chemical "limonene" which is an essential oil and known to cause contact dermatitis in susceptible individuals. This chemical is also found in other foods such as dill, caraway seeds, and the peelings of lemons and limes. Photosensitivity has also been a problem with workers who handle celery on a daily basis unless they wear gloves. The chemical that is responsible for this problem is "furocoumarin psoralens" and increase contact may make your skin sensitive to light.

◆ Celery, carrots and lettuce will crisp up quickly if placed into a pan of cold water with a few slices of raw potato.
◆ To prevent celery from turning brown, soak in lemon juice and cold water before refrigerating for only a few minutes.
◆ When you purchase celery, purchase the greenest you can find, it will be the healthiest and have the most flavor.
◆ One of the best methods of storing celery for a prolonged period of time (2-3 weeks) is to wrap the celery tightly in aluminum foil.

COLORED CELERY

If you place celery sticks into a glass of water with food coloring, the celery will absorb the coloring and change into that color.

CELERY SEED

It is usually added to macaroni salad and scrambled eggs and sold in the seed form and as celery salt and used in soups, stews, salad dressings, fish dishes, salads, pickling, and many vegetable dishes. Celery flakes are made from dehydrated leaves and the stalks are used in the same dishes.

CHEESE

Cheese was first produced in the Middle East when it was found that domesticated animals could be milked. An Arab nomad filled one of his saddlebags with milk to have a source of nutrition while crossing the desert. When he rested and wanted a drink, he found that the milk had partially turned into curds and whey, since the saddlebag was made from the stomach of an animal and contained the enzyme renin. The ancient Sumerians also knew cheese making 4,000 years before the birth of Christ. Cheese was first produced commercially by the Romans. Cheese comes in a wide variety of colors and flavors, few of which are natural. Most cheese is naturally white, not yellow, pink, green or burgundy. The cheese industry has perfected methods of changing a good quality nutritious product into a chemical smorgasbord.

The following is just a partial list of chemicals used by the cheese industry: Malic acid, tartaric acid, phosphoric acid, alginic acid, aluminum potassium phosphate, diacetyl sodium, carboxymethyl cellulose, benzyl peroxide and an unbelievable number of dyes and coloring agents. These chemicals are used to give cheeses their sharp taste, color them and make them smell more appealing or just to change their texture. All of the chemicals have been approved by the FDA and are supposed to be harmless; however, a number of the dyes and coloring agents are being studied and are related to cancer in laboratory animals.

Many of these same chemicals are also being used in other industries for making cement, bleaching clothes, producing cosmetics, printing, and even rust proofing metals.

Be more aware of the type of cheese you buy and try to buy cheeses without the added chemicals, especially cheeses that are low fat or even non-fat.
If the label says "all-natural" you still need to see the wording "no preservatives or coloring agents." Consumers need to read the labels more than ever these days.

- ♦ An ounce of cream cheese may contain as much as 110 calories. As advertised, it does have fewer calories than butter for a comparable weight, but we tend to use more and also use it more frequently.
- ♦ It would be best if you choose cheeses that are low-sodium, low fat, or reduced-fat. There are new varieties appearing almost weekly in supermarkets and health food stores.

- Be sure and read the label. If a cheese is labeled "natural" the name of the cheese must be preceded by the word "natural" if not it is a chemical concoction. **Save Your Hands.**
- When you want to slice up a hard cheese, play it safe and place a kitchen towel folded in half between the top of the blade and the cheese.

This will protect your hand if the knife slips and also make it easier to put pressure on when cutting.

Shaving Cheese
When you have to produce paper-thin slices for a dish, try using a vegetable peeler on a solid block of Parmesan cheese.

- Most cheese substitutes are produced from soybean vegetable fats. Many low-fat cheeses substitute water for the fat reducing their shelf life.
- The wax coating on cheeses will protect it. If there is an exposed edge try covering it with butter to keep the area moist and fresh.

Science of Cooking with Cheese

When cooking with cheese never used cheese directly from the refrigerator. When chefs cook with cheese, they always allow the cheese to come to room temperature first. When this is done the cheese will melt more evenly and as with butter, cut the cheese into small cubes before melting.

When this occurs, the protein separates from the fat and the cheese gets tough and rubbery. Once a cheese hardens, especially in a sauce, it would be wise to discard the sauce and start over. When you melt cheese, it would be wise to grate the cheese first. The cheese will then melt in a shorter period of cooking time. The reason cheese tends to form lumps or strings is that the calcium phosphate present in the cheese binds with the protein.

This can be avoided if a small amount of wine, which contains tartaric acid, is added to the melting cheese. The tartaric acid prevents the calcium phosphate from linking the cheese proteins. If you prefer not to use wine, just use a small amount of lemon juice and the citric acid will accomplish the same thing.

- It requires 8 pounds of milk to produce 1 pound of cheese. One average slice of standard American cheese = 8oz of milk. Best to at least purchase the 2% cheeses or the non-fat varieties.

When chefs melt cheese, they never cook it for too long a period or at too high a temperature.

- To keep cheese longer without mold forming, place a piece of paper towel that has been dampened with white vinegar in the bottom of a plastic container that has a good seal before adding the cheese.

- Also, add 5-6 small sugar cubes in case any mold that does get in will go for the sugar cubes instead of the food.
- Soft cheeses can be grated using a metal colander and a potato masher. A hand grater with large holes will also work.
- Cheeses that have dried out may still be used for dishes that require grated cheese.
- White or yellow cheddar cheeses contain about 70% fat, of which 40% is saturated. When grating cheese, try spraying a liquid vegetable oil on the grater before grating and cleanup will be much easier.
- Many low-fat cheeses substitute water for the fat, thus reducing their shelf life.
- The term that is used to clarify the actual age of a cheese in "affinage." Brie cheese must have an "affinage" of 8 weeks before it can be sold.
- If you use a food processor, be sure and spray the blades with vegetable oil before starting to make cleanup easier.

CHEESE, CHEDDAR

It is one of the first things to look for when purchasing cheddar cheese is uniform color. If the cheese has white spots or streaks it has not ripened evenly or is starting to develop mold. The texture should always be relatively smooth; however, it is not uncommon to purchase cheddar that is grainy and crumbly.

If the cheddar has a rind, be sure that the rind is not cracked or bulging, which may mean that the cheese will be bitter due to poor manufacturing practices. Cheddar will continue to age in the refrigerator for months and should be stored in a container with vinegar dampened paper towel underneath.

CHEESE, MELTING

One of the more frequent problems with melting cheeses is that the cheese is heated at too high a temperature for too long a period of time. When this occurs the protein is separated from the fat and the cheese becomes tough and rubbery. Once this occurs it cannot be reversed and the cheese is ruined.
- Remember to keep the heat on low and best to use a double boiler. If you are going to melt cheese don't try and melt large pieces.
- Cut the large piece into a number of small chunks before you attempt to melt it.
- Cheese should be added last to most recipes.
- Grating the cheese will also make it easier to melt and this method is best for sauces. Certain exceptions are ricotta, Camembert and Brie, which have higher water content and lower fat content. These are not as good for certain dishes.
- Low calorie cheeses that are lower in fat content do not melt as well as regular cheeses.

The reason cheese tends to form lumps or strings, is that the calcium phosphate present in the cheese binds with the protein. This can be avoided if a small amount of wine, which contains tartaric acid, is added to the melting cheese. The tartaric acid prevents the calcium phosphate from linking the cheese proteins. If you prefer not to use wine, just use a small amount of lemon juice and the citric acid will accomplish the same thing.

CHEESE, MOZZARELLA

Slipping and Sliding

If you want to shred semi-soft cheese like mozzarella in the food processor, best to spray the feeder tube, disk and work bowl with a light coating of vegetable spray first. If you prefer to use a box grater be sure and spray it with vegetable spray first. Placing the soft cheese in the freezer also works.

New Use for Egg Slicer

Mozzarella cheese is very hard to slice unless you use an egg slicer. Just place the cheese in and slice away then remove and separate the slices.

CHEESE, REPAIRING

Dried Out/Hard

Grate it and use it for a topping.

Moldy

Remove at least ½ inch or more from the mold area before using.

Rubbery

Place the cheese into a food processor and chop into small bits, then place it in the top of a double boiler and cook slowly. This usually occurs when too high a heat is used or cheese is cooked too fast.

CHEESE, STORING OF

Science of Storing Cheese

Since there are mold spores in the air that can come into contact with a block of cheese every time you expose the cheese to air, you need to protect the cheese by storing it properly.

Using a well-sealed plastic container, place a piece of paper towel in the bottom of the container that has been lightly dampened with white vinegar. Place the block of cheese on top of the paper towel then add 3-4 mini-sugar cubes to the container and seal it as tight as you can removing as much air as possible. If there are any mold spores in the container, they will be killed by the white vinegar or will eat the sugar cubes instead of the cheese.

CHEESECAKE

When preparing a cheesecake, never make any substitutions. Go exactly by the recipe. Cheesecakes will come out excellent if the recipe is followed to the letter. When it comes to making cheesecake chefs follow their recipe to the letter. They make sure the cheese is at room temperature and never bake too fast, chefs know that the slower you bake a cheesecake, the less it will shrink. Also always use one pan that is the perfect size and never use it for any other baked product.

Science of Baking Cheesecake

- Never substitute a different size pan for the exact size recommended.
- Make sure that you blend the ingredients in the order given in the recipe for the best results. Never place fruit inside of a cheesecake. Fruit topping should be added, if desired no more than 1-2 hours before you serve it.
- If you are preparing an unbaked cheesecake, be sure and mix all the ingredients until they are very smooth before gently folding in whipped cream.
- When you are mixing the ingredients, beat at medium speed only and just until the batter is smooth.
- When cream cheese is used in any recipe, make sure you blend it well so that it's light and fluffy before adding any other ingredients to it, especially eggs. Eggs should always be very fresh Grade "AA" large eggs
- Over-mixing at high speeds can cause cracks to form as the cheesecake bakes. The cheese must be at room temperature when starting. Sour cream must be fresh if used.
- Best to use a 9-inch spring-form pan and butter the sides.
- The oven should never be opened for the first 25-30 minutes or it may develop cracks or partially collapse. Bake for 10 minutes at 550^0F then reduce the heat to 200^0F and bake for about 1 hour.
- When the edges are light brown and the center is almost completely set, turn off the oven, open the door ajar and allow the center to set for about 20-30 minutes. This is another method of reducing the incidence of cracks.
- Always bake cheesecake on the center rack in the oven.
- Slowly baking cheesecake will not shrink as much when cooled.
- Egg based cheesecakes should always be baked on low heat for the best results. If you get too much shrinkage, then the cheesecake was baked on too high a heat setting. Cheesecake usually takes $1\frac{1}{4}$-hours to bake. Cracks can be repaired with softened cream cheese or sour cream.
- The center of a cheesecake will firm up as it is cooling. Cheesecake should be served cool. Refrigerate overnight for the best flavor and texture.
- Cheesecake should be allowed to remain in the pan and cool overnight before removing it from the pan.

To avoid your cheesecake cracking from the evaporation of moisture, it will be necessary to increase the humidity in the oven by placing a pan of hot water on the lower shelf before you preheat the oven.

Cheesecake cracks can be repaired with creamed cream cheese or sweetened sour cream.

♦ Sour cream must be fresh if used.
♦ All ingredients must be at room temperature.
♦ Preheat the oven for about 15 minutes.
♦ Always cut cheesecake with dental floss that is not waxed.
♦ To remove cheesecake from the pan, first make sure that it is cool, then invert it on a lightly sugared plate, then transfer them to your serving plate.

Pre-baking a crumb crust for about 10 minutes at 350^{0}F should keep it crisp. Make sure that you cool the pre-baked crust before adding the filling.

♦ Remember never to jar a cheesecake when it is baking or cooling.
♦ Cheesecake should be left out of the refrigerator for about 30 minutes then served at room temperature for the best flavor. You can store it in the refrigerator for about 3-4 days. Plain cheesecake can be frozen for up to 2 months.

CHEESECLOTH

Natural white cotton cloth, which is available in either fine or coarse, weaves. It is lint-free and maintains its shape when wet. Primarily used for straining jellies or encompassing stuffing in turkeys.

♦ Can be used for poaching whole fish.
♦ Bundling herbs and used in soups and stews.
♦ Wrapping fruitcakes and soaking in alcohol.
♦ Lining molds.
♦ Straining soups and stews.
♦ Wrapping around citrus fruits and squeezing the juice from them.

CHICKEN

Commercial chickens; must be cooked to an internal temperature of 185^{0}F to kill any bacteria that may be present. If the chicken is fully cooked and you see traces of pink near the bone, it is not a sign of undercooking. It is probably only the bone pigment that has leached out during the cooking process. This is more common in smaller birds or ones that have frozen and defrosted. The meat is perfectly safe to eat and can be avoided by purchasing older birds.

Any kitchen item, whether it is a washcloth, sponge or the counter must be thoroughly cleaned after working with chicken to eliminate the possibility of contamination of other foods and utensils if any harmful bacteria is present. Recent television shows have uncovered the fact that there is a potential health risk with chicken due to present processing techniques. Most of the pathogens related to poultry are rarely detected using the present poultry inspection procedures. Studies conducted by the National Academy of Science reported that 48% of food poisonings in the United States are caused by contaminated poultry.

EASE THE TRAUMA

When chefs bring a whole chicken to the table for serving, they always make sure that it had sat for 10-15 minutes before serving it. If you cut open a chicken that has just come out of the oven you will lose most of the juices.

GET A GRIP

Trying to cut a raw piece of chicken can be dangerous since it is very slippery. Next time you need to slice the chicken, just wad up 2-3 pieces of paper towels and use that to hang on to the chicken.

♦ When you cook white and dark meat chicken parts together, remember that the white meat cooks faster than the dark, so start the dark meat a little sooner. The higher fat content in the dark meat is why this occurs. The white meat may be too dry if you cook them together.

♦ When you cook giblets, make sure that you place the liver in during the last 20 minutes. The liver tends to flavor all the giblets when cooked with them from the beginning.

♦ The easiest way to skin a chicken is to slightly freeze it first, then grip the skin with a piece of paper towel. The skin will come right off with hardly any effort.

♦ When choosing meat or poultry in the supermarket, make sure that there is no liquid residue either wet or frozen on the bottom of the package. If there is, it means that the food has been frozen and the cells have released a percentage of their fluids. When cooked the bones will be noticeably darker than a fresher product.

Science of Chicken Picking

Free-range chickens will always be more flavorful than one that lives in a closed coop with little if any sunlight and under stress. Coop chickens are also more disease prone. Free-range chickens are able to move around the yard and live normally. They are more flavorful since the exercise develops flavor. Best, however, to purchase a young free-range chicken if you want it to be tender since the exercise also may make them tougher as they age.

Re-Freezing Chicken

Yes! Providing the chicken has been defrosted in the refrigerator and has not remained in the refrigerator for more than 2 days.

Cleaning a Chicken

Chickens need to be cleaned thoroughly inside and out before cooking them to remove any residues that are left from the slaughtering process. While it is impossible to completely clean the bird you should at least do the best you can.

The preferred method is to place 1 tablespoon of baking soda in the water that you will use to clean the chicken and rinse the bird several times with the water then clean water several times. The mild acidic action and abrasives of the baking soda will do the job.

5 pounds of chicken will provide about 3 cups of meat

Which Came First - The Chicken or the Egg?

This is a relatively easy question to answer. The egg came first through a series of DNA changes in the relatives of the present day chicken. Thousands of years ago there were no chickens, just fowl that resembled the bird.

As time passed and evolution took place two non-chickens produced DNA that was different and when two non-chickens produced similar DNA and there evolved a male and female of the new species they found each other and mated, they became the present day chicken.

♦ This is not chicken blood, but is mostly water that was absorbed by the chicken during the chilling process. All blood is drained from the chicken and if there were blood left it would denote a poorly processed bird and the skin would also be a bright red.

Bacteria on Chicken

If a piece of chicken has 10,000 bacteria on a 1 square centimeter area when it is processed and reaches the supermarket it will increase 10,000 times that figure if left in the refrigerator at about 40^0F for 6 days. The Center for Disease Control in Atlanta estimates that 9,000 people die each year from food-borne illness with thousands of others becoming ill from bacterial, chemical, fertilizer, and pesticide residues left on foods and poultry. According to the USDA 40% of all chickens are contaminated with salmonella and even if contaminated they can still pass the USDA inspection. Almost 50% of all animal feed may contain salmonella.

♦ When you make chicken or turkey salad, make sure that the meat has been cooked to 180^0F then allow the meat to cool in the refrigerator before adding the salad dressing or mayonnaise.

Tenderizer

Lemon is a natural tenderizer for chicken and gives it a unique flavor also you might try basting it with a small amount of Zinfandel. Remember; a low to moderate cooking temperature will produce a juicier chicken, since more fat and moisture are retained.

♦ Do-it-yourself bouillon cubes can be made by, freezing leftover chicken broth in ice cube trays. They can be stored in baggies and kept frozen until needed for a recipe or soup. They are easily thawed in the microwave.
♦ Raw poultry and hamburger meat should not be kept in the refrigerator for more than 2 days without being frozen.
♦ If you want to save money when buying chicken, buy whole chickens then cut them with poultry scissors and freeze the sections you want together. When you purchase whole birds, try not to buy the larger ones, they are older birds and not as tender. Young chickens and turkeys also have less fat.
♦ Chickens are Grade A, Grade B, or Grade C. Grades B and C are usually blemished and only used in canning, frozen foods, and TV dinners. Grade A, chickens are sold in supermarket meat departments.

When you broil chicken breast; be sure and place them far away from the heat source or the tops will burn before they get completely cooked.

♦ Poultry in foreign countries are never subjected to the conditions we allow in the United States. You will also notice a difference in taste. If you do notice an odor from the market production chickens, try rubbing a small amount of lemon juice into the skin. The bird will enjoy this and it will totally remove the odor.
♦ If you want to store chicken for 3-4 days in the refrigerator, change the wrapping to plastic wrap or waxed paper.
♦ The supermarket wrapping often contains blood residue.

- A free-range chicken has an average of 14% fat compared to a standard cooped-up production chicken at 18-20% fat.
- If you wish your chicken or its parts to be browned, try brushing them with a low-salt soy sauce.

CHICKEN, BARBECUING

 When cooking chicken on a barbecue rack, always grease the rack well first. The collagen in the skin will turn into a sticky gelatin, which causes it to stick to the rack. To really solve the problem, try baking the chicken for 15-20 minutes in a preheated oven, breast side up, allowing the gelatin time to infuse into the fat and meat or to be released into the pan.

EASY ON THE SAUCE

When chefs barbecue chicken they never use barbecue sauce until the last 10-15 minutes of cooking time. When I barbecue I would start slopping it on when I first started cooking and kept slopping it on throughout the cooking process. Chefs are aware that the sauce will burn before the chicken is done.

Science of Barbecuing Chicken

If your chicken is coming out blackened, charred and sour tasting it is because you insist on placing barbecue sauce on the bird at the beginning of the cooking time. While barbecue sauce will flavor the chicken, the high heat scorches and burns the sugars, which are a major component of barbecue sauce and makes them bitter. Certain spices in the barbecue sauce also react with high heat for a prolonged period and turn bitter instead of adding a nice flavor. NEVER PUT BARBECUE SAUCE ON CHICKEN UNTIL THE LAST 10-15 MINUTES.

CHICKEN, FRIED

Most chefs agree to the following method as being the best. Place the chicken pieces in buttermilk in the refrigerator for 45 minutes, drain and dry well before breading.
Combine all-purpose flour, pepper, salt and any other seasoning you prefer in a brown paper bag and place the chicken pieces in the bag and shake.
The bag will absorb any excess moisture and coat the chicken in the process. Frying oil should be exactly 375^{0}F and be sure not to crowd the chicken pieces.

- If you want "real" crispy fried chicken then use half cornstarch instead of flour. Use your regular seasonings and add ½ teaspoon of baking powder to it.
- If you want the chicken to dry and crispy then only fry the pieces until they are browned then place them into a 350^{0}F oven to complete the cooking process.
- If you would like some extra fiber, just add oat bran to the seasoning.

Science of Chicken Skin

Chicken skin contains collagen (connective tissue). When collagen is subjected to high heat it undergoes a chemical change and turns into a gluey gelatin. This causes the skin to stick to the rack when you remove the bird leaving you with a bird that does not have table appeal. The rack needs to be greased and you need to start the roasting process in a preheated oven with the chicken breast up for the first 20 minutes. This will allow the gelatin that is produced to be absorbed into the fat just under the skin.

THE STUCK CHICKEN

A common problem many cooks have when roasting a chicken is that some or all of the skin tends to stick to the roasting rack. The solution is to grease the rack, since placing aluminum foil over the roasting rack doesn't work either; it just sticks to the aluminum foil.

Science of Breading

> Most breading recipes for chicken call for an egg-milk-water mixture (egg wash).
> Be sure to strain the mixture before using it to avoid large parts of the egg white in the wash.
> Straining the egg wash will also make the coating even.
> To avoid having lumps of flour and bread crumbs on your fingers, which make breading more difficult, just designate one hand as "wet" and the other hand as "dry."
> The "wet" hand will handle the chicken pieces that are not coated and dip the pieces in the milk and then place the pieces in the flour.
> The "dry" hand will then sprinkle flour over the top of the piece coating it and removes it from the flour and places it in the egg wash and remove it with the "wet" hand.
> The above method is how chefs prepared large quantities of chicken pieces without getting lumps on their fingers or leaving clumps on the chicken pieces.

CHICKEN, FROZEN

Science of Buying Frozen Chicken

Next time you are in the supermarket and buying chicken chances are the chicken is fully thawed. If the chicken has been frozen or near frozen it will not be as flavorful as one that was processed properly.

Chickens that are sold thawed are "deep thawed" and not normally frozen. The difference is that the processing plant lowers the temperature of a freshly dressed chicken to 28^0F to reduce the deterioration process and keep the meat fresher.

The bird will not freeze at 28^0F but will retain its freshness longer. Even though the freezing point of water is 32^0F, the liquid inside a chicken contains natural proteins and other solids that lower the freezing point. However, once the chicken leaves the processing plant some shippers and supermarkets store the chickens at temperature below 28^0F and end up freezing the chicken, thus lowering the quality of its flavor and texture.

To protect the shipment shippers may also extend the life of chickens by packaging the chickens in plastic wrap and using nitrogen gas to replace the oxygen in the package. Pathogens cannot survive in nitrogen gas; however, shippers and markets can still freeze the chickens and thaw them when they need them.

CHICKEN, ROASTED

SAVING TIME

To save time when roasting a small chicken, just butterfly the chicken by slicing it in half opening up the bird to form a single flat piece of chicken. Just cut through the bird on either side of the backbone and remove the backbone then turn the chicken over and flatten the bird with the heel of your hand. You will reduce the roasting time about 20 minutes by doing this.

CHICKENS, TYPE SOLD

Organic Chickens

May only be raised on land that has never had any chemical fertilizer or pesticide used on it for at least 3 years. They must also be fed chemical-free grains and are for the most part free-range chickens.

Mass-Produced Chickens

Commercially raised in crowded coops and never allowed to run free. They are marketed in exact sizes in the same number of months.

Kosher Chickens

Chickens: that have been slaughtered and cleaned in compliance with Jewish dietary laws.

Broilers/Fryers

These are 7-week old birds that weigh from 3-4 pounds.

Roasting Chickens

These are usually hens that weigh in at 5-8 pounds with more fat than broilers.

Stewing hens

Usually weigh 4-8 pounds and are one year old. Basically, these are retired laying hens. They are tough old birds and need to be slow-cooked but are flavorful.

Capons

These are castrated roosters, which average 10 weeks old and weigh 8-10 pounds. They usually have large white meat breasts from making a lot of noise.

Poussins

These are baby chicks only 1 month old and weighing about one pound. They lack flavor and are only used for grilling.

Rock Cornish Game Hen

These are small broilers or fryers and weigh about 1-2 pounds. They are best grilled or roasted. They are actually chickens that are only 4-6 weeks old and are a hybrid of Cornish and Rock chickens.

- One hen is only enough for one serving.
- They will take less time to cook than a whole chicken.
- They are normally stuffed and to prepare them for stuffing, just use a sharp knife to cut it down the backbone then use the palm of your hand to put pressure and press down until the bird is flattened out.
- It takes about 1 cup of stuffing per bird.

CHICKEN-FRIED STEAK

Not too many people can agree as to just how this dish got its name. The closest we can come to an answer is that the dish came from the southern United States, probably Mississippi, when someone breaded a small cube steak with a breading similar to fried chicken and fried the steak. The meat used was a tough cut of beef and needs to be pounded into submission with a hammer.

CHICKEN SALAD

Science of Chicken Salad

When preparing either chicken or turkey salad, be sure and place the cooked chicken into the refrigerator to cool before adding any salad dressing or mayonnaise to it. The chicken should also be cooked to 180°F (82.2°C) at the thickest part to be sure that it has cooked through.

CHILI, PREPARATION OF

Chili did not originate in Mexico and can rarely be found in a restaurant there unless it is a popular tourist spot. The first records of chili mix, dates back to 1850 when Texas cowboys needed a hot stew when they were traveling to the California gold fields. They prepared a "brick" that could be stored made from dried beef, salt, pepper, chili peppers, fat and other seasonings. They boiled the bricks in pots along the trail.

The original chili peppers were from wild chilipiquin bushes that grew in Texas and other areas of the southwest. Chili was made the "state food of Texas" in 1977 and stated that the only "real" bowl of chili is made in Texas.

The first aim is to soften the bean and turn it into mush, without it falling apart. The cell wall needs to be weakened and the starch granules need to be gelatinized.

> Occasionally, cooks will try to save time by relying on the acid nature of chili sauce to complete the cooking of the bean and end up with hard beans.

CHILI PEPPERS

When you purchase chili peppers be sure they are firm, not shriveled, have no soft spots and pick those with deep, vivid colors. You can store them in a plastic bag in the refrigerator for up to 2 weeks.

♦ The majority of the capsaicin (80%) is found in the seeds and membrane.
♦ If you remove the seeds and the membrane, the chili will lose a lot of its hotness.

> To neutralize the hotness, try drinking milk, ice cream or any high starch food. Alcohol tends to increase the effects of capsaicin; however, some Mexican beers seem to neutralize it.

♦ Neither, cooking or freezing will inactivate the capsaicin intensity.
♦ The bigger the chili pepper, the milder it usually is. The smaller chili peppers usually have more seeds and veins.
♦ Use rubber gloves when working with chili peppers.
♦ When cooking or roasting the peppers, try not to breathe in the fumes.

The best method of preparing chili peppers for use in recipes is to first roast them. Just use a long handled fork on top of the stove and singe them until the skin blisters. Place the hot peppers on a cloth and cover them allowing them to steam making the skin relax and easily pull away allowing the seeds and veins to be removed. Try not to use too many of the seeds unless you desire a hot fiery dish.

CHIVES

Chives have a light onion flavor and are commonly used in to flavor dips, sauces, soups, baked potatoes, or to replace onion flavor in a recipe. Chives are a good source of potassium, iron and calcium.

- Chives should be cut up only just before you are ready to use them to preserve their vitamins and minerals.
- Heating chives will also cause a big loss of nutrients.
- Frozen chives retain a larger percentage of their flavor than dried chives.
- Diced scallions are a good substitute for dried chives.

- Chives will lose almost all their flavor when dried.
- Frozen chives will not have as much flavor as fresh chives.
- Should be added to dishes just before you finish cooking to preserve their flavor.
- Chives can be frozen up to 6 months. Keep them frozen and just remove what you need. Re-freezing will kill a lot of the flavor.

CHOCOLATE

Forrest E. Mars, founder of Mars, Inc. on a trip to Spain saw some soldiers eating candy that did not melt in their hands and only in their mouth.

The chocolate pellets were covered with a hard sugary coating and even stood up to the heat of the hot climate in southern Spain. Mars got together with Hershey's chocolate and started the M&M Company.

- When you are melting chocolate, water droplets, excess condensation, and high temperatures may cause the chocolate to stiffen prematurely (seize up). To alleviate this problem, add a teaspoon of corn oil to the pan and stir. More oil can be added if needed to assure the proper consistency.
- The chemical theobromine found in chocolate may reduce the amount of available protein that is absorbed through the intestinal wall. Sugar also reduces the body's ability to destroy bacteria. Oxalates, another chemical found in chocolate may unite with available calcium carrying it through the intestine as an insoluble compound, rendering it unusable.
- Never store chocolate in the refrigerator or the freezer or when you thaw it out condensation will form and affect its ability to melt smoothly.

HOW SWEET IT IS

In a study by Dr. Andrew Waterhouse at the University of California at Davis, chocolate was found to contain an antioxidant called *"phenols."*

This is the same compound found in red wine that was thought to lower the risk of heart disease in France. The study found that cocoa powder prevented the oxidation or breakdown of LDLs (bad cholesterol).

When LDLs are broken down they tend to convert into fatty plaque forming particles that may contribute to the clogging of healthy arteries, thus becoming a risk factor for heart disease. A 12-ounce chocolate bar has the same amount of "phenols" as a 5-ounce glass of red wine. Additional studies are also showing that chocolate contains flavonoids, which act as an antioxidant that may have the ability to slow down the deposition of plaque on the walls of the arteries.

- The higher quality chocolate the better.
- You can also melt chocolate in the microwave by placing the chocolate in a microwave-safe bowl and heat on medium (50% power).
- Four ounces of chocolate will take about 3-4 minutes in a 700-watt microwave.
- When you melt chocolate make sure that not even a drop of water gets into the pot or the chocolate may seize up. If this happens, add a small amount of vegetable oil and mix it in well.
- To melt chocolate, just place chopped chocolate pieces into the top of a double boiler over simmering water. Remove the top pot with the chocolate from the heat when the chocolate is just a little more than half melted and stir until it is smooth.

Be aware that semi-sweet chocolate chips and chocolate squares may retain their shape when melted and if you wait for them to look melted you may ruin the chocolate.

- Be sure that the chocolate snaps when broken.
- Why purchase chocolate slivers, when all you have to do is use your potato peeler on a Hershey bar?
- If chocolate is stored in a damp, cool area it may develop white crystallized areas. This chocolate can still be used and the flavor will only be slightly affected.
- If the labeling on a chocolate product states "artificial chocolate" or chocolate-flavored" it is not "real" chocolate and should not be used in a recipe.
- Chocolate needs to be cooled to room temperature before adding it to cookie dough or cake batter.
- To substitute for 1 ounce of unsweetened chocolate use 3 tablespoons unsweetened cocoa plus 1 tablespoon butter. For 1 ounce of semi-sweet chocolate use ½-ounce of unsweetened chocolate plus 1 tablespoon granulated sugar.

Science of Making Chocolate
Real chocolate is made from chocolate liqueur, which is produced from cocoa pods. It is not really liquor in the sense most of us think of liquor, but the name given to the processed product obtained from the fruit of the cocoa tree. The cocoa tree is a member of the evergreen family and can only be found in equatorial climates. The tree grows to about 20 feet and the pods that contain the cocoa bean are about 8-10 inches long with each pod averaging 30 beans each.

In 2012 the cocoa bean crop was about 2.5 million tons most of which came from West Africa. The first step in the processing is actually in the field with the pods being opened then allowing the beans to sit in the sun.

This exposure causes a number of microbes to multiply killing the seeds' embryo as well as producing changes in the structure of the cells. The cell walls deteriorate releasing substances that mix together resulting in the bitter "phenolic" compounds binding to each other and reducing the degree of bitter taste. The beans are then cleaned and dried and shipped to other countries.

The bean now must be processed into the chocolate liqueur. They are roasted for about 1 hour at 250°F, which finally gives them the chocolate flavor. This involves approximately 300 different chemicals and results in the "browning reaction" and the

color of chocolate. After they are browned, they are cracked open and the "nibs" (kernels) separated from the shells. The nibs are then ground up to release the cocoa butter, carbohydrates and proteins, which are all in the thick liquid oil called "chocolate liqueur." The refining process continues until the mixture ends up as a coarse chocolate or a powder.

CHOCOLATE SAUCE/SYRUP

When preparing chocolate sauces, there are a number of tips that you should be aware of. The following will help you obtain the perfect sauce:

CHEF'S SECRETS

If a liquid is used in the recipe, always melt the chocolate in the liquid, not separate for the best results. Use low heat and stir continuously. The microwave is excellent for melting chocolate. Just place the chocolate in a large measuring glass and cook until melted while keeping an eye on it to be sure it doesn't overcook.

Most chefs melt chocolate in a double boiler over simmering (not boiling) water. Always use the type of chocolate called for in a particular recipe and always use the highest quality chocolate you can find.

Science of Chocolate Syrup

If you use low-fat or non-fat milk, the recipe will not turn out good. You need the texture of the fat to give the chocolate syrup a creamy texture. If the syrup is allowed to heat too long, you will end up with a great fudge recipe.

CHOCOLATE, TEMPERING

Tempering chocolate is the process of melting it, cooling it, and then melting it again. This process produces a more lustrous, glossy and stable mixture and is called for in many chocolate recipes. This is an exact science to obtain the right consistency and takes some practice. However, there is a "quick-tempering" method that utilizes a small amount of oil that will speed the process up considerably. The end product will be a little thinner, but will not make a difference in most recipes and decorative uses.

QUICK-TEMPERING METHOD

Use 1 tablespoon of vegetable oil (preferable a neutral oil such as canola or safflower) also clarified butter, is often used by some candy chefs, even a solid shortening. Stir 1 tablespoon of the oil into every 3 ounces of melted chocolate you use over low heat. Quick-tempered chocolate will only hold up for 2-3 days, but the candy is usually long gone before that.

HELP! MY CHOCOLATE HAD A SEIZURE

If your chocolate turns from a shiny, smooth liquid to a dull, very thick paste it has what is called a *"chocolate seizure."* Seizing happens when you do not follow instructions to the letter. The following are the most common problems that cause seizure:

❖ The temperature got too hot and it was not stirred continually.
❖ Milk and white chocolate are more susceptible to seizing.

Even a small amount of moisture from a metal spoon can cause a seizure. Use a wooden spoon.

❖ Fondue chocolate can change if too much moisture gets into the fondue pot from the fruit that is being dipped in.
❖ Never add cold cream or milk; be sure it is the same temperature as the chocolate.
❖ Even large amounts of liquid can be added to chocolate as long as the liquid is the same temperature or has at least been warmed.

CHOWCHOW

Chowchow is a relish made from chopped vegetables, usually cabbage, peppers, cucumbers, and onions. It is packed in a sugar-vinegar solution and seasoned with special mustard and pickling spices and usually served with meats and sausages.

CHOWDER

It is a relatively thick soup that is made with a fish or clam base with vegetables, especially potatoes. Cream is usually used in the base and all the contents stewed.

New England clam chowder was first prepared in the United States by early colonists who were watching wild pigs dig up clams for food. They realized that these were a good food source and started making soup from them.

Different groups made the "chowder" with milk and some with tomatoes and neither agreed on which recipe was the best. The one thing that they agreed on was that the chowder had to have a very strong clam flavor with lots of clams and most was made with potatoes. Quahogs (named after the wild pigs) are hard-shelled clams and are preferred.

Chefs will always add sliced clams during the last 15-20 minutes of cooking time. When clams are added early in the cooking of chowder they tend to become tough or too soft.

Basically, chowders are very thick, chunky and hearty soups. Many times they tend to resemble stews more than soups. The majority of chowders are prepared with shellfish, fish or vegetables or a combination of all three. Most chowder recipes call for the addition of potatoes and milk or cream. The vegetables most commonly used in chowders are corn, celery and onions.

CHUTNEY
Chutney is a combination of different fruits and spices mixed together to make a great tasting relish.
- Can be used as an instant glaze on broiled meats and fish.
- Can be used to enhance the flavor of many casseroles.
- To prepare salad dressing using chutney, just combine 2 tablespoons of chutney with olive oil or mayonnaise.
- If you whip chutney with some cream cheese it will make a great spread for bread.

CILANTRO
Sold as fresh coriander, as a fresh herb and looks a lot like parsley. Commonly used in Mexican dishes and in salad dressings and salsa.

To keep cilantro fresh, just remove the fresh leaves from the stem and place then on a piece of barely moist paper towel in a single layer. Roll the paper towel up and wrap it in plastic wrap or a bag, making sure as much air as possible is removed. Store in the refrigerator and the cilantro should stay fresh for at least 3-5 days.

CINNAMON
Cinnamon is from the inner bark of a tropical Laurel tree. It is imported from China and Indonesia. However, the variety commonly sold in the United States is usually imported from Vietnam and called the "cassia" variety and is used in its whole form for preserving, spiced beverages, chicken, meat, flavoring puddings, pickling, cider, and hot wine drinks.

The ground form is used for baked goods, ketchup, vegetables, apple butter, mustards and spice peaches. However, the "real" cinnamon is from the Laurel tree in China. The color is the giveaway; true cinnamon is actually a light tan color, while "cassia" is a dark reddish-brown.

♦ The stick cinnamon will have a more intense flavor and aroma than the ground cinnamon.

♦ Cinnamon sugar is somewhat expensive in the supermarket, but you can easily make your own for a fraction of the cost. Just combine ½ cup granulated sugar with 1½ tablespoons of ground cinnamon and be sure and store it in a well-sealed container.

♦ Cinnamon sugar is excellent in coffee in place of granulated sugar.

♦ Try cinnamon toast buttered with a small amount of cinnamon sugar sprinkled on top.

CITRUS FRUITS (General Information)

Chefs are very fussy about choosing citrus fruit in the market. They need to be sure that it was ripe and sweet and if they weren't sure, they only buy a few and check them for sweetness before going back and buying more. This seems like a real hassle, but some chefs are very fussy. They also use the white area just under the skin in many citrus dishes.

Science of Citrus Fruit

Chefs know that the vitamin C in an orange is very high, especially in the white area, which is called the albedo. The peel is also high in vitamin C and in fact 75% of the vitamin C concentration is in the peel and white; only about 25% is in the segments and pulp. Also, citrus fruit will not ripen much after it is picked and needs to be picked when it is ripe since there is little starch in citrus to help it ripen after it is picked.

The main source of energy for a fruit is its sugar content, which is also utilized for the manufacture of the fruits' organic materials. The sugar content weight of most fruit averages about 10-15%. The lime, however, has only 1% compared to the date, which is over 60% sugar. The sugar is produced by starch, which is stored in the plants leaves, and as the fruit ripens, the starch is converted into sugar. Also, as the fruit ripens, the acid content of the fruit declines and the sourness is reduced. Most fruit is sour before it ripens. A number of organic acids are responsible for the plants' acidic nature. These include citric, malic, tartaric, and oxalic acids. Almost all fruits and vegetables are slightly acidic.

Chefs use acidulated water to reduce the browning of citrus fruits and vegetables that darken rapidly. To make the water, use 4 cups of cold water and add 4 tablespoons of lemon juice. If lemon juice is not available, you can substitute 2 teaspoons of white vinegar. Just toss the food with the solution or place the food in the water for a short period of time.

CITRUS JUICE

All citrus fruit must ripen on the tree, since they will not continue to ripen once picked. Before the fruit is picked representative samples are taken and evaluated as to their sugar (brix) and acid content. As soon as the percentages are correct the fruit will be harvested. Almost 98% of all citrus fruit is still harvested by hand using wooden ladders and sacks.

CITRUS PEELS, HARMFUL EFFECTS

Unless the citrus is organically grown, it would be wise not to eat any product that uses citrus peels including orange and lime zest, which is often grated into desserts. Citrus crops in the United States are routinely sprayed with a number of carcinogenic pesticides according to the EPA. These pesticides tend to remain in the skin. They include acephate, benomyl, dicofol, methomyl, 0-phenylphenol, chlorobenzilate, and even parathion. A thorough cleaning and scrubbing will not remove most of these chemicals.

CLAMS

The most popular clam is the hard-shell clam (littleneck, cherrystone, Pismo, chowder or butter).

The geoduck clam, a soft-shell clam is unable to close its shell because its neck sticks out too far and is too big. It can weigh up to 3 pounds and is not as tasty as the hard-shell clams. Packaged soups and canned clam products are produced from large sea clams.

All shellfish are called "filter feeders." They rely on food entering their systems in the water that goes by them which may contain almost any type of toxic material and even sewage. Over time any toxic material that is ingested may increase to a harmful level to humans if adequate amounts of toxic shellfish are consumed.

♦ Diseases such as hepatitis can be transmitted if the shellfish were feeding in areas that were contaminated with sewage.
♦ Shellfish are capable of filtering up to 20 gallons of water a day looking for food.
♦ Shellfish are rarely, if ever, inspected. Some of the contaminants are rendered harmless if the shellfish is cooked.

If a clam is found floating, it must be discarded.

♦ Raw shellfish should only be eaten in moderation unless they are aqua cultured.
♦ To open shellfish, rinse them in cold tap water for 5 minutes then place them into a baggie and place it into the freezer for about 30 minutes.

♦ They should be cooked in heavily salted water to draw out the sea salt. Remember, shellfish are naturally high in sodium and not recommended for a low-sodium diet.

♦ Another method of opening clams is to place the clams in a single layer on a cookie sheet and place them into the freezer for 15 minutes. The clams' muscle will relax making them easier to open.

Once saltwater clams are dug up they must be cleansed of sand and debris or they will not be eatable. To accomplish this, the clams should be allowed to soak in clean seawater (never fresh water) for about 20 minutes. Change the water every 4-5 minutes to clear the debris from the water.

♦ A healthy clam should have its shells closed when being cooked; however, they should relax and open after they are boiled.

♦ If you keep the clams on ice they will probably relax and open their shell, to test their condition just tap their shell and they should close. If they don't close then they are sick or dying and should not be used.

♦ After they are cooked if the shells do not open they should be discarded and the shell never forced open.

♦ Live clams can be stored in an open container, covered with a moist cloth for 1-2 days under refrigeration of at least 40°F.

♦ Shucked clams can be stored in their own liquor, under refrigeration at 40°F for 2-3 days or frozen at 0°F for 3 months.

♦ If you are short of liquor to cover the clams, you can make your own by mixing ½ teaspoon of salt in 1 cup of water.

Clams should always be cooked on low heat so that they will not be too tough.

♦ A clam knife is normally used to open clams, however, if you don't have one, just use a beer-can opener.

♦ When cooking clams, they are fully cooked as soon as the shell opens.

♦ Only fresh or frozen clams are recommended for soups and stews. Do not use canned clams since the texture is too soft for dishes that have to cook for a long period of time.

♦ Minced clams should only be added to soups or stews during the last 5 minutes of cooking time for the best results.

CLARIFICATION

It is the process of removing small particles of suspended material from a liquid. Butyl alcohol is used to remove particles from shampoos. Traces of copper and iron are removed from certain beverages and vinegar.

CLOTTED CREAM

If you are ever working from a British recipe and it calls for Devonshire or clotted cream, the following will tell you how to make it:

- Allow non-pasteurized cream to stand in a saucepan for 12 hours in winter, or 6 hours in summer at room temperature then place the pan on very low heat and heat (without boiling) until the cream shows small rings of foam coming to the surface, which will show that the cream is scalded. Remove immediately from the heat and place into the refrigerator for 10-12 hours. Skim off the thick, clotted cream and serve as a garnish for berries or do as the English do and spread it on scones with a dollop of jam or preserves.

CLOVES

Imported from Indonesia and usually sold as whole cloves. A strong spice used in moderation in baked beans, pickling, ham roasts, sweet potatoes, baked goods, puddings, mustards, soups, hot dogs, sausages, and barbecue sauces.

In the year 300 BC the Chinese Emperor had a breath problem and was given cloves to sweeten his breath. Cloves contain the chemical "eugenol," which is the same chemical that is used in a number of mouthwashes. Eugenol (oil of cloves) is also used to stop the pain of a toothache.

- They are very pungent and used in moderation.
- Commonly used to make pomander balls by inserting whole cloves into apples, oranges or lemons. Just pierce a hole in the fruit and insert the whole clove without snapping off the end.

COBBLER

GRANDMA'S COBBLER

This is a relatively easy fruit dessert to make and grandma had the method down perfectly.

Ingredients:

2	Cups all-purpose flour	7	Tablespoon unsalted butter (cut up)
½	Cup granulated sugar	¾	Cup heavy cream
½	Teaspoon salt	5	Cups fruit (sliced)
½	Cup unsalted butter	1	Tablespoon baking powder
2	Tablespoons honey	¼	Cup brown sugar

- Preheat the oven to 350⁰F. Butter the bottom of a 9 X 13-inch baking dish and fill it with fruit then set it aside.

- Mix together the flour, sugar, salt and baking powder then combine the 7 tablespoons of cut-up butter and flour in the bowl and mix with your hands until the mixture resembles coarse meal.
- Add the cream at once then stir with a wooden spoon and form your dough then knead for about 20 seconds.
- Pick up small pieces of the dough and drop then on top of the fruit until the top is covered.
- Bake for 30 minutes.
- Prepare the butter mixture for the top by combining ½ cup of butter with the honey and brown sugar then place on low heat in a pan to melt.
- After the cobbler has baked for 30 minutes, pour the mixture on top then increase the heat to 375^0F and cook for an additional 15 minutes or until a crust is formed.

Science of Cobbler

You can use any fruit you wish; however, my grandmother's favorites were peaches from her tree in the backyard. The "freestone" peaches were as big as grapefruits and the sweetest I have ever tasted. If you use a low sugar fruit such as apples, you will need to toss the pieces with sugar before placing them into the pan. She sometimes combined different fruits, but mostly berries. Raisins were regularly added in all grandmas' cobblers. Ready-made piecrust works well and saves time.

COCKTAIL SAUCE

CHEF'S SHRIMP COCKTAIL SAUCE

Ingredients:

1	Pint of quality ketchup	1¼	Cups of chili sauce (not too hot)
½	Cup prepared horseradish (drained)	2	Ounces of fresh lemon juice
1	Tablespoon of Worcestershire sauce		

COCONUT

Coconuts are always available. When choosing one, be sure that its heavy for its size and you can hear the sound of liquid when you shake it. If the eyes are damp, don't buy the coconut.

- Coconuts can be stored at room temperature for 6-8 months depending on how fresh it was when it was purchased. If you are going to grate coconut for a recipe, make sure that you place the meat in the freezer for at least 30 minutes. This will harden the meat and make it easier to grate.
- Packaged coconut is available in cans and plastic bags and can be purchased sweetened or unsweetened, shredded or flaked.
- If shredded coconut gets too dry just soak it in whole milk for about 30 minutes.

- To make colored coconut, just add 3-4 drops of food coloring to every cup of shredded coconut. Be sure and toss until all the coconut is evenly colored.
- To prepare unsweetened toasted coconut to be used as a garnish, just spread coconut on a cookie sheet that has shallow sides and bake at 325°F for about 10-12 minutes. Be sure and toss the coconut occasionally until a golden brown.

Separating

To easily separate the outer shell of a coconut from the inner meat, just bake the coconut for 20-25 minutes at 325°F then tap the shell lightly with a hammer. The moisture from the meat will try and escape in the form of steam and establish a thin space between the meat and the shell separating the two. The coconut milk (which unlike the coconut and the meat is low in saturated fat) should be removed first by piercing 2 of the 3 eyes with an ice pick. One hole will allow the air to enter as the milk comes out the other one.

COCOA POWDER

If you purchase one of the better brands of cocoa powder, such as Mont Blanc, it should last for at least 1-2 years and be fresh.

- If standard supermarket unsweetened cocoa is stored in a well-sealed container, it will store for about 2 years.
- If you want a richer flavor in stews or chili, just add 1-2 tablespoons of unsweetened cocoa powder.
- When you add unsweetened cocoa powder to brownies or cakes, you will need to decrease the flour by 1 tablespoon for every 2 tablespoons of cocoa you use. You will also need to compensate for the bitterness by adding 2 teaspoons of sugar for every 1 tablespoon of cocoa.

COFFEE

THE STORY OF COFFEE

The coffee tree is believed to have originated in Central Africa where the natives would grind the coffee cherries into a powder and mix it with animal fat, then roll it into small balls, which they would take with them on long journeys or hunting trips. Raw coffee is high in protein (until it is diluted with water) and when combined with the fat provided adequate calories and a stimulant.

The first factual information relating to the actual drinking of the beverage is by the Arabs in the Middle East. The Arabs protected the coffee bean seed to such a degree that they would not allow it to be exported under the threat of death.

However, in 1660 some of the coffee seedlings were smuggled into Holland and then transported to Brazil in 1727 where the climate was more favorable. The climate and soil conditions were ideal and the coffee trees thrived.

Coffee trees need an annual rainfall of over 70 inches of rain with every tree only producing about 2,000 "coffee cherries" to make one pound of coffee. The United States consumes 50% of the world's coffee, which amounts to 400 million cups every day. The average coffee drinker drinks 3 cups per day. Eight out of 10 adults drink at least one cup of coffee daily.

Coffee prices have risen dramatically since 1994 due to major frosts in Brazil, which destroyed 1 billion pounds of coffee, about 10% of the world's coffee supply.

When you keep coffee warm in a coffee pot on a warming unit, it will only stay fresh for about 30 minutes after it is brewed. If your coffee needs to be freshened up, try adding a dash of salt to your cup then reheat it.

THE PERFECT CUP

There are a few factors that you need to be aware of in order to prepare the perfect cup of coffee. They are:

♦ The freshness of the ground beans, always grind the beans just before you are ready to use it.
♦ How long ago the bean was roasted. Is the coffee bean fresh?
♦ Cleanliness of the brewing equipment.
♦ The quality of the bean.
♦ The quality of the water.

The most critical of these factors is the freshness of the ground, cleanliness of equipment and the water quality.

Metal coffee pots, may impart a bitter or metallic taste in your coffee. A glass or porcelain pot is recommended. If you are going to use a metal pot, the only one that is acceptable is a stainless steel one. Copper and aluminum are not recommended at all. If you are using a percolator the brewing time should be no more than 6-8 minutes, while a drip pot should take about 6 minutes and vacuum pots about 1-4 minutes.

When chefs are caught short and don't make enough coffee, I have seen them take instant coffee and boil it for about 30 seconds then reduce the heat and allow it to steep for about 3 minutes before serving it. When you use this method, the coffee tastes just like freshly brewed coffee and not instant.

Science of Ground Coffee

Ground coffee goes stale within one week after you open the can or jar at room temperature. It will last a little longer if you store it in the refrigerator but every time you open the can and remove some coffee you allow more oxygen to get into the can.

Ground coffee exposes so much of the surface of the bean that it allows the oxygen to really do damage easily. The more you open the can and dip out a spoonful the faster the coffee will lose its flavor.

If you grind fresh beans they will only last one week at room temperature or two weeks in the refrigerator.

When you brew coffee, it is necessary to have the proper temperature, which will allow the maximum extraction of the caffeol compounds, which are the taste and aroma enhancers.

The proper temperature also protects the coffee from producing an overabundance of polyphenols (tannins), which will give the coffee a somewhat bitter taste.

Professional coffee brewers will keep the brewing temperature between 185^0F-205^0F (85^0F-96.1^0C). If the temperature is too low, the coffee grounds will not release sufficient caffeols and if too high the tannins take over.

Studies have proven that the ideal temperature for drip coffee making is 95^0 to 98^0F (35^0C to 36.7^0C). If the water is any cooler it will not extract enough caffeine and essential oils from the coffee bean. Coffee that is brewed above the ideal temperature range will contain too high a level of acidity.

- If you blend two or more types of coffee beans it will make a richer, tastier coffee.
- If you want to reduce the amount of caffeine intake, just blend caffeine with a dark-roast decaffeinated coffee.
- Ground coffee can be stored in the freezer and will retain its flavor if wrapped in an airtight container.
- Every time you open a package of coffee and allow air to get in, it will reduce the aroma and flavor. Air is not a friend to coffee!
- To prepare your own instant coffee, just place 2 tablespoons of ground coffee in a strainer or tea infuser that has been lined with paper towel. Place the strainer or tea infuser in a coffee cup and add 6 ounces of boiling water then cover and allow it to, steep for about 3 minutes or until it is at the strength you desire.
- Try using a stick of cinnamon as a coffee stirrer.
- If you need to remove coffee or tea stains from a China cup, try using a paste prepared from salt and white vinegar.

Saving Big Bucks

If you want to make cappuccino without the expensive machine, just place a pan filled with heated milk on a large potholder and beat the milk with a hand-held electric mixer until it the consistency is foamy and velvety. When milk is foamed in this manner, it will hold soft peaks even when you spoon it onto a coffee mug.

Helping the Grinder

If you have ever tried grinding coffee beans in an inexpensive grinder and ended up with powder and bean parts that were not ground try this trick next time. Shake the grinder while you hold the lid tightly and it will do a more even job.

Stabilization

If you have ever used a manual drip coffee maker, you know that occasionally the grounds have spilled down into the pot by bypassing the filter. The filter will fold over itself in one spot allowing the leakage. To avoid the problem, just dampen the filter with water and press it against the sides of the plastic or metal cone. As soon as you start to pour coffee and water, the filter will adhere to the sides.

COFFEE CAKE

Science of Icing a Coffee Cake

The icing for coffee cake is just sifted confectioner's sugar thinned with a little milk and flavored with a small amount of vanilla. It is easily drizzled on top using chef's method by just dipping a large dinner spoon into the bowl of icing then quickly moving the spoon back and forth over the coffee cake allowing the icing to fall in thin ribbons from the end of the spoon. Keep going until it has the desired effect.

COLE SLAW

Chefs like cabbage to be very crisp so they place shredded cabbage in a bowl of ice water in the refrigerator for 1 hour. They would then blot it dry and store it in a plastic bag until they were ready to use it.

Science of Crisp Slaw

Ice, cold water has the ability (unlike warm or hot water) to enter the cells of the vegetable and firm up the cell walls. As long as the vegetable is kept at least well cooled, the cell walls will retain the structure.

By 2013 potato salad and coleslaw will be high-pressure treated with 80,000 psi for 2 minutes, which should inactivate any pathogens and bacteria and increase their shelf life.

CONVECTION OVEN

The standard oven and the convection oven work very similar to each other. The notable difference in the convection oven is that it has a fan that increases the distribution of the heat molecules providing heat to all areas more evenly and faster. Because of the fan and the efficiency of the heat circulation, a lower temperature is usually required, thereby conserving energy. Roasts, especially do well in a convection oven because of the lower heat, the meat tends to be juicier.

Make sure you follow the manufacturer's recommendations as to temperature since you will be cooking at 20^0 to 75^0 less than you would normally.

♦ Since convection ovens heat up so fast, they rarely require pre-heating.
♦ No special cookware is needed.
♦ If you are cooking meats or fish, you can lower the temperature by 25^0.
♦ When using the convection oven for roasting, you can lower the temperature from 20-30%.
♦ Baked goods, however, are easily over-browned and need to be watched closely.

COOKIE PANS

If you don't have a thick cookie pan, try baking the cookies on two pans, one on top of the other. It will eliminate burned bottoms.

Light-colored, shiny cookie pans work best and will brown the cookies more evenly than dark-colored ones. If you are concerned about sticking, just place a piece of parchment baking paper under the cookies.

COOKIES

Cookies are made from dough that are high in sugar and fats and lower in water content than other types of dough. Because of this there is a shortage of available water to starch granules and gluten protein.

The sugar will draw moisture from the mixture, more than other ingredients and between this and the fact that cookie dough mixture is not mixed the same as other dough; the gluten development is minimized.

• If you desire a cookie with a cake-texture this can be achieved by mixing the shortening, eggs, sugar, and liquid together, then gently folding in the flour and leavening agent.
• To prepare a more dense cookie, just mix all the ingredients together very slowly. Because of the way cookies are mixed and the limited use of liquid, the starch is only able to gelatinize slightly.
• Save your used coffee cans, they make excellent containers to store cookies in. Use the original plastic lid or a piece of plastic wrap sealed with a rubber band.
• When making oatmeal cookies, try lightly toasting the oatmeal on a cookie sheet before adding it to the batter. The best way to do this is to heat the oatmeal at 185^0F for about 10 minutes. The flakes should turn a golden brown.

The Disappearing Chip

When making a batch of cookies, the last few cookies always seem to be short some of the goodies such as raisins, nuts or chocolate chips.

To solve this problem chefs only place half of the goodies in half the dough saving the balance of the dough and goodies to be added after they use up the first half.

It's the Rule

If you want the best looking cookies, they should all be the same size. The best way of doing this is to use a 12" ruler and place it on top of your bowl of dough. When you are making the cookie balls of dough, you can eyeball the measurement with the ruler and make all the cookies come out uniform.

The other method is to use an ice cream scoop dipped in cold water after every few cookies.

Help! I'm Cooking Too Fast

Never use a dark-colored pan since they absorb heat and may cook the cookies too fast. Dark pans will cook the outside of the cookie before the inside is done. Grandmother always used a bright, shiny baking pan, which also cooled faster between batches and baked more evenly.

How Dry I Am

Drying frosted cookies can be a real pain, unless you know the chef's trick. Just place the cookies on a sturdy paper plate and separate the layers with small sturdy paper cups. You can usually go up to 4-5 plates without a problem.

Saving Burned Bottoms

Use parchment paper to bake the cookies on since it will withstand high temperatures, is non-stick and strong enough so that it won't easily tear apart. Also try cooling the bottom of the pans between batches on a damp kitchen towel.

Never bake with two baking sheets touching each other on the same rack since it creates hot spots and your product will bake unevenly.

I Need My Space

Some cookies have the tendency to spread and may end up touching each other. To eliminate this problem, do not place the dough in even rows lining up the cookies.

It is best to alternate the rows of three cookies in the first row, two in the second and three in the third and on and on.

The Jelly Holder

If you're making cookies that require an indentation in the center to hold jelly or other goodie, you would normally just make the indentation with your thumb. However, the indentation is never rounded, but can be repaired by using the back of a metal melon ball scoop to round it out perfectly.

You Need to Circulate More

One of the more important lessons about baking and ovens is that you never crowd foods you are baking. The heat has to be able to circulate evenly around the baked goods. The more you place in the oven, the slower it will all cook. If you must put a number of dishes in the oven, allow additional cooking time.

- ♦ If you have a problem with burning the bottoms of cookies when making a number of batches, all you have to do is to run the bottom of the pan only under cool water before placing the next batch on the pan.

- When you start with too hot a surface the cookies may burn their bottoms. The desired shape of the cookies may also change if placed on the hot pan.

MARGARINE IN COOKIES

When margarine is used to make cookies, the firmness of the dough will depend on the type of margarine you use.

One of the most important things to remember when choosing margarine for cookies is that the package says *"margarine"* not *"spread."* If the margarine is made from 100% corn oil, it will make the dough softer. When using margarine you will need to adjust the *"chilling time"* and may have to place the dough in the freezer instead of the refrigerator. If you're making *"cutout"* cookies the chilling time should be at least 5 hours in the refrigerator. Bar and drop cookie dough does not have to be chilled.

MOISTURE

If you are having difficulty keeping your soft cookies moist and keeping the moisture in cakes and pancakes, just add a teaspoon of jelly or sour cream to the batter.

- Cookies tend to burn easily. One method of eliminating this problem is to remove them from the oven before they are completely done and allow the hot pan to finish the job.
- Whipped butter, margarine, or any other soft spread that is high in air and water content should never be used in a cookie recipe.
- When making cookies, sifting the flour is usually unnecessary.
- Cookies should be cooled on an open rack not left in the pan. They should be fully cooled before you store them or they may become soggy.

When cookies are placed on a rack to cool, they must be at least 6-inches off the counter or steaming will occur. Try placing the rack on a tall bowl.

- Never use imitation vanilla when baking cookies, always use the real stuff. Also, never use chocolate-flavored morsels, only 100% "real" chocolate.
- Use a saltshaker filled with powdered or colored sugar for sprinkling candy or cookies. Make the holes larger if needed.
- When mixing the cookie dough, remember that if you over stir, the cookies may be tough.
- If your cookie dough is cold, it will not stick to the rolling pin. Chill the dough for no more than 20 minutes in the refrigerator for the best results.
- If you would like a sharp edge on your cookies when using a cutter, try dipping the cutter in warm oil occasionally during the cutting.
- When cookies do not brown properly, try placing them on a higher shelf in the oven.

COOKIE SECRETS

❖ Place all the ingredients into a mixing bowl and blend them until they were smooth.

❖ Allow 2-3 minutes at low speed for mixing.

❖ Add the sugar, butter or shortening, salt, and any spices to the mixing bowl and cream them all together.

❖ Add the eggs and any liquid.

❖ Add the flour and leavening agent last.

◆ Unbaked cookie dough may be frozen for 10-12 months. Wrap as airtight as you can in freezer bags.

◆ Cookies should be turned half way through the cooking time.

◆ Soft cookies will always stay soft if you add a half an apple or a slice of fresh white bread to the jar. This will provide just enough moisture to keep the cookies from becoming hard.

◆ If you are using 100% whole-wheat flour and want the crunchiest cookies ever, try using butter instead of any other shortening. Never use oil or it will make the cookies soft.

Science of Soft Cookies

Bakers make soft cookies with honey since honey has a high affinity for moisture. They always use margarine or shortening and maintain an oven temperature of 375°F (190°C). They also remove the cookies from the oven just before they were finished cooking then allowed them to cool. The cookie sheet was always greased, which reduced the chance of spreading.

Science of Crisp Cookies

One of the ways bakers make cookies crisp is to make sure that the cookie has high sugar content. Sugar will delay setting giving cookies more time to spread. The sugar also ties up moisture so that less is available to steam and make the cookie soft. Oven temperature is also very important and should be at 350°F (180°C) to slow browning allowing cookies to dry as they bake.

COOKIES, REPAIRING

Burned

Stop using brown cookie sheets; use shiny ones. Make sure that the cookie sheet is full and does not have just a few cookies on it.

Dough Crumbly

Allow the dough to remain at room temperature for 30 minutes and cover the dough with a lightly dampened kitchen towel.

Dough Sticks to Hands
Place your hands in a bowl of ice water (with ice cubes) for 20 seconds.
Dough Sticks to Rolling Pin
Store the rolling pin in the freezer.

COOKIES, TYPES
Bar Cookies
Soft dough is used and the batter is then placed into a shallow pan and cut into small bars after baking. Always trim off the hard outer crust before serving. Never use diet or whipped margarine or any fat that is labeled "spread" and never use salted butter. Bar cookies should be cooled and stored in their baking pan and cut after they are cooled unless they are crisp-style, which need to be cut while they are still warm.

If you would like an instant glaze, try placing chocolate chips on the surface of the bar as soon as they are removed from the oven. It should take about 5 minutes for the chocolate to fully melt.

Drop Cookies
They are made by dropping small amounts of dough onto a cookie sheet. To make uniform drops, best to use a measuring teaspoon. If you want to freeze drop cookie dough, just drop it on a cookie sheet and freeze until it becomes solid. After it freezes solid transfer the cookie dough to freezer bags. Allow the dough to thaw on a cookie sheet, covered with waxed paper for about 35 minutes before you bake them.

Hand-Formed Cookies
They are made by shaping cookie dough into balls or other shapes by hand.

Pressed Cookies
They are made by pressing the cookie dough through a cookie press or bag with a decorative top to make fancy designs or shapes.

Refrigerator Cookies
Made by shaping cookie dough into logs, then refrigerated until firm. They are then sliced and baked.

Make a mold from a paper towel core, cut lengthwise and line with wax paper. Wrap a thick rubber band around it to keep it in shape until it hardens.

If you are cutting a log of refrigerator cookies, be sure and turn the log a quarter turn, every 5 slices to keep it round.

Rolled Cookies
The cookie dough is rolled out and made into thin layers. Cookie cutters are then used to make different shapes.
Dip plastic cookie cutters in warm vegetable oil or spray them lightly. Use as little flour as possible when rolling out the dough. Try using a pizza cutter for cutting rolled-out dough.

CINNIMON'S SUGAR COOKIES

Ingredients:

2	Cups bread or high-protein flour	2	Teaspoons baking powder
½	Teaspoons salt	2	Large eggs
¾	Cup granulated sugar	2/3	Cup corn oil
2	Teaspoons "real" vanilla extract	1	Teaspoon grated lemon zest

Sift together, flour, baking powder and salt. Whisk the eggs until well blended then add sugar, corn oil, lemon zest and vanilla extract and mix well. Place in refrigerator and chill for 30 minutes. Place rounded teaspoons of the cookie dough on an un-greased cookie sheet (about 2-inches apart).

Bake the cookies in a preheated 400°F oven for about 7-9 minutes. Remove from oven and allow them to cool on wire rack.

You should never use all-purpose flour when making sugar cookies, since the all-purpose flour may cause the cookies to spread too much. Freezing the dough before baking also helps as well as not greasing the baking sheet.

The Perfect Sugar Cookie

These cookies should have an even thickness and lightly coated with granulated sugar. You can do both in one motion after rolling the dough ball in sugar and placing it on the cookie sheet. Using a glass with a 2" rounded bottom, butter the bottom of the glass and dip the bottom in granulated sugar, then flatten the dough. Shape and dip after every cookie.

♦ If you want your sugar cookies to remain a little soft, try rolling the dough out in granulated sugar instead of flour.

COOKING

There are three main methods of transferring heat to food, radiation, convection, and conduction. Basically, you are transferring heat from a hot object to a cold one. Radiant heat is in the form of electromagnetic waves, such as those from a toaster to the toast. It does not require any assistance from air and water. The energy travels at 186,000 miles per second, the speed of light.

♦ Convection cooking employs circulating molecules, which are propelled by either gas or liquid. The heat is placed at the bottom of the food or liquid and as the heat rises, it allows the colder food or liquid to fall toward the heat.

- The air or water currents provide the convection cooking as a vehicle for the heat.
- Conduction cooking utilizes an oven where the hotter molecules pass along the heat from the surface to the interior of the food.

Gas vs. Electric

There is no contest here, it is definitely gas that wins on the range top, since you are able to change the temperature quickly, as well as have instant heat control, which is preferred by all chefs.

Boiling over is more easily controlled with gas than electric in all instances. The oven, however, is a different story. Electric ovens will reach the desired temperature more rapidly and hold it more evenly with excellent accuracy.

COOKING, BAD WEATHER

OH, THE WEATHER OUTSIDE IS GLOOMY.........

> **Science of Cooking in Bad Weather**
> When the weather is stormy and the atmospheric pressure decreases, it lowers the boiling point of water a little. The decrease only amounts to 1-2 degrees and it only takes a little longer to cook foods that need to be boiled.

COOKING, GENERAL

When you use heat to cook food, basically you are increasing the speed of the molecules of that food. The faster they move, the more they collide, the more heat is generated, and the hotter the food gets. This changes the texture, flavor, and even the color of the food. For every 20^0F you raise the temperature over the normal cooking temperature you will actually increase the molecular activity by 100 percent, not 20 percent.

Foods that contain a large percentage of connective tissue, such as meat, or have a tough fibrous structure, such as those found in certain vegetables, should be cooked using moist heat. These foods are not naturally tender; therefore must be tenderized by the moist heat. There are, of course, exceptions to the rule, one of which is if the meat is heavily marbled or frequently basted.

- Always slice, chop and prepare all ingredients for a recipe before starting to prepare it.
- Have more than one kitchen timer available.
- When foods are at room temperature they will cook faster than cold foods.
- When using a mixing bowl on the counter, be sure and place a damp towel under the bowl so that it won't move.

- ♦ If you are going to use a spoon, spatula or other utensil for a sticky food, be sure and spray the item with vegetable oil before adding the sticky substance.
- ♦ Be sure and turn off the burner before removing a pot from the range top.

> **Oven mitts and pads need to be dry when you are going to use them. If they are wet or even damp, they will transfer heat to your hands.**

COOKING, ODORS

Unless you really like the smell, try placing a few unshelled pecans in your saucepan when cooking kale, cabbage, or collard greens to reduce the odor. When cooking onions or cabbage, boil a small amount of vinegar in a pan to remove the odor.

> **Make a paste of baking soda and lemon juice to get rid of the odors from your hands.**

COOKING OILS

The following are some of the more common oils that are used for cooking and baking. Oils will vary as to the type of fats they are composed of, color, aroma, nutrients, and smoke points. Oils may be categorized in many different ways, such as how refined the oil is, the plant or animal it was extracted from, the method of extraction (cold or hot), smoke point, consistency and color. All fat content figures are for one tablespoon of fat or oil that includes saturated fatty acids (SFA), polyunsaturated fatty acids (PUFA), monounsaturated and fatty acids (MUFA).

COOKING PROBLEMS (weather related)

The weather can adversely affect certain foods and it would be wise to take a chef's advice regarding the following before attempting to cook them, especially since anything made with sugar absorbs additional moisture from the air, especially after it has cooled. Before it cools evaporation takes place, after it cools the problem occurs from high humidity.

Candy-Making

If you make candy on a hot or humid day, the candy will not set up properly. Candy should be made in a room that is ideally 60^0-68^0F with low humidity outside. This affects chocolate, divinity, fondant, hard candy and fudge.

Jams & Jellies

On rainy or humid days, jams and jellies will not gel.

Mayonnaise

Never prepare it during a thunderstorm since the static electricity will stop it from thickening. The heat and humidity will also cause it to become heavy and somewhat greasy.

Meringue

The peaks will flop over if you attempt to prepare meringue in damp weather. Egg white tends to absorb just enough moisture from the air to cause it to become limp.

Pastry Dough

It is best to make it on a cold, dry day for the best results. When the weather is hot and humid the butter will absorb moisture and become greasy making the finished product somewhat greasy as well.

Yeast Dough

If the day is humid or very hot yeast dough will be hard to knead and may rise too fast and even lose elasticity. The added moisture causes the yeast to absorb additional moisture.

Yeast actually feeds on the sugars in flour and produces carbon dioxide causing leavening. The carbon dioxide makes thousands of mini-balloons in the dough filled with the gas and provides bread an airy texture.

COOKING TEMPERATURES

SPEEDY MOLECULES

Cooking any food increases the speed of the molecules inside the food. The faster they move, the more they collide and the more heat that is generated, the hotter the food becomes. Heat changes the texture, flavor and color of food. Some cooks want to speed up the cooking process by increasing the temperature; this can be a real problem and one that chefs will never do.

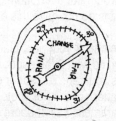

Science of Increasing Cooking Temperature

For every 20°F (6.7°C) you raise the cooking temperature over what the food should be cooked at, you will actually increase the molecular activity by 100%, NOT 20%. The quality of the food being cooked usually suffers from the higher cooking temperature. Chefs prefer to partially cook certain foods that will take too long to cook at normal temperatures and complete the cooking when they need the food. They will only do this with foods that will not be affected by a change in the flavor, color or texture they desire.

SOLVING THE DISBURSEMENT PROBLEM

Grandpa made a wooden handled tool with a large round head with holes in it, which grandma placed under a number of pots and pans while they were being used to disburse the heat evenly.

Science of Heat Disbursement

Unfortunately even today many range tops whether gas or electric do not disburse the heat evenly. The more professional range tops do a much better job than most units produced for the home. Heat diffusers are commonly used by many cooks to provide an even heating surface. Diffusers are available in all kitchen supply stores.

COOKWARE

There are a number of materials that are used to manufacture pots and pans, many of which do not really do the job adequately. Remember, the thicker the gauge of the metal, the more uniformly it tends to distribute the heat. The finish on the metal will also affect the efficiency of the cookware. The names of product lines of a number of cookware companies for 2013 have changed, but the materials have, for the most part, remained the same.

Stop Finger Burning

Save your wine corks and place a wine cork under the handle of pot tops. Just wedge it in and if you don't have a potholder handy you can just use the cork to remove the lid.

Your cooking pans should be made of a material that will dissipate the heat evenly throughout the bottom of the pan so that the food will cook evenly. Unfortunately, many pans do not have this ability and develop cold spots.

To check your pan, place a thin layer of about 4-5 tablespoons of sugar that has been mixed with 2 tablespoons of water on the bottom of your pan and spread it out as evenly as you can. The sugar over the hot spots will caramelize and turn brown forming a pattern of the hot spots. Hopefully, you will not have a pattern and the sugar will caramelize all at about the same time. If you do have a problem, use a heat diffuser under the pan or try the same test using a lower heat setting.

HOW TO CLEAN OUT BURNT FOOD

You first need to fill the pot or pan with two inches of water then, add a quarter cup of baking soda and a quarter cup of white vinegar. Bring pot to a boil and allow it to cook for 15 minutes. Turn off the heat and allow the pot to sit until cooled before draining the water and clean the pot as you normally would. If any burnt food residue remains, repeat the process.

You can also substitute dish washing liquid to replace vinegar. Fill the pot with water and add one to two tea spoons of dish washing liquid and the baking soda then bring to a boil and simmer for 10 minutes. Cover the pot, turn off the heat and allow the pot to soak for 30 minutes. Another method that might work is to fill the pan with water and place a fabric softener sheet in the water. Allow the pan to soak overnight and the food will wipe right out!

ALUMINUM

The majority of cookware sold in the United States in 2013 was still aluminum, which is an excellent heat conductor. Current studies report that there is no risk from using this type of cookware unless you are deep scraping the sides and bottoms of the pots continually, allowing aluminum to be released into the food. Rarely does anyone do this. Excessive intake of aluminum may lead to Alzheimer's disease.

Aluminum cookware stains very easily, especially if you are using hard water to cook with.

Certain foods, such as potatoes, will also cause the pans to stain easily. If you cook a high-acid content food such as tomatoes, onions, wine or if lemon juice is used in aluminum, it will probably remove some of the stain. If a pan is already stained when the acidic foods are cooked, it may transfer the stain to the food possibly turning your foods a brownish color.

Aluminum pans also tend to warp if they are subjected to rapid temperature changes, especially if they are made of thin gauge aluminum. If they are made of a thick gauge, they will have excellent heat-flow efficiency and will not rust, thus making the thick pan, the best pan for use as cookware. Water and cream of tartar will clean aluminum. Just fill the pan with water and add 1 tablespoon of cream of tartar then boil for 15 minutes before washing.

Lime-soaked pickles should never be made in an aluminum pot even though the instructions state that aluminum is recommended. A chemical reaction takes place, which is not healthy.

CAST IRON/CARBON STEEL

A cast Iron/carbon steel pot may only supply a small amount of iron in elemental form to your diet, but not enough to be much use nutritionally.

Certain acidic foods such as tomato sauce or citrus fruit may absorb some iron but not enough to supply you with adequate daily supplemental levels. Iron does, however, conduct heat fairly well. These are both non-stainless steel, iron-based metals that have a somewhat porous, jagged surface.

These pots need to be "seasoned." To accomplish this, you need to rub the cooking surfaces with canola oil and heat it at 300^0F for about 40-50 minutes in the oven, then allow it to cool to room temperature before using. The oil has the ability to cool and seal the pores and even provide a somewhat nonstick surface. Another factor is that when the oil is in the pores, water cannot enter and possibly cause the formation of rust.

These pots should be washed daily using a mild soap and dried immediately. Never use salt to clean the pot, since this may cause rusting. If a cleaner is needed, be sure it is a mild one. Iron pots tend to release metal ions that react with vitamin C and reduce its potency. Cast iron pots can be cleaned, by just filling the pot with warm water and dropping in 3 denture-cleaning tablets, then allow the pot to sit for 1 hour. This method will not affect the seasoning. To remove rust, just use sand and vegetable oil and rub lightly.

Seasoning a Cast Iron Pot

- Wash the pot in warm soapy water.
- Use a scouring pad to remove any residues and rough up the surface.
- Fill the bottom of the pot with salt and allow it to remain on a medium gas flame for 1½-hours.
- Remove pot from stove and discard salt in sink. Remove any plastic liners.
- Clean the bottom of the pot with a piece of paper towel to remove any salt residue.
- Place ½ inch of vegetable oil in the pot (prefer canola or soy) and place on low heat for 30 minutes.
- Remove from heat and discard the oil.
- Clean the bottom with paper towel to remove the oil residue.
- Rub the bottom with fresh oil before storing away. This will make the bottom non-stick.

COPPER

These will not react with any food and are safe to cook in. Copper is one of the best heat conductors and is preferred by many chefs. Copper pans, however, should only be purchased if they have a liner of tin or stainless steel to be safe, otherwise they may leach metals into the food. When you cook in glass, remember to reduce the oven temperature by 25^0F. One of the worst types of cookware is the thin stamped stainless steel pots with a thin copper-coated bottom. The copper coating is approximately 1/50th of an inch in thickness and too thin to distribute the heat efficiently and uniformly.

The "real" copper cookware provides excellent heat distribution on the bottom as well as the sides of the pan. The copper, however, needs to be kept clean and if black carbon deposits form to any degree it will affect the heat distribution significantly. These pots are usually lined with tin, which must be replaced if it wears out. Otherwise, excess copper may leach into the food, causing a health risk. Foods that are high in acid will increase the release of copper. The metal ions in copper will also react with vitamin C and reduce the amount available.

ENAMELED COOKWARE

While the enamel does resist corrosion, it is still metal coated with a thin layer of enamel. The coating is produced; by fusing powdered glass into the metal surface, which is in most instances cast iron. The cookware can chip easily if hit against another object and can even shatter if placed from a very hot range into cold water.

GLASS COOKWARE

Rapid temperature changes may cause the glass to crack or break in many brands. Glass has a very low "heat-flow" efficiency rating and when boiling water is poured into the glass cookware, the actual heat that is transferred from the boiling water to the bottom of the cookware will travel slowly back to the top of the pot. Because of this, the bottom of the pot will swell and the top of the pot does not expand creating a structural type of stress and a crack is very possible. Corningware® and Pyrex™ in that order would be the only choices for glass cookware, since both will resist most stresses.

NON-STICK

These are made of a type of fluorocarbon resin that may be capable of reacting with acidic foods. For 2013 there were a few minor coating improvements but basically stay with the top brands.

If you do chip off a small piece and it gets into the food, don't be concerned it will just pass harmlessly through the body. Never allow any brand of "non-stick" surface pan to heat to a high temperature dry.

The pan may release toxic fumes if heated above 400^0F for more than 20 minutes. This could be a serious problem for small pets and birds. Proper vegetable oil seasoning of most pots will produce a non-stick surface without risk and last for months. These non-stick surfaces are the result of a chemically inert fluorocarbon plastic material being baked on the surface of the cookware or other type of cooking utensil.

Science of Non-Stick Cookware

Food sticking to the pan is a result of the protein in the food reacting with the surface of the pan. Protein is very reactive above 175^0F (80^0C) with the metal ions in the surface. If the protein adheres to the surface, the temperature of the protein can rise over 212^0F (100^0C) and burn. To prevent burning the proteins you can either use non-stick cookware since it does not contain metal ions in the pan surface or stir the food, keeping it moving around, until the outside of the protein substance gets browned.

Safe Stacking

When you store non-stick cookware and need to stack them, try placing the pans into a large plastic bag so that they won't scratch or chip each other. You could also just place a couple of sheets of paper towels between them.

The food is actually cooked on jagged peaks that protrude from the bottom, which will not allow food a chance to stick to a smooth surface. The surface is commercially "seasoned" producing the final slick surface. The major contribution of a non-stick surface is that of allowing you to cook without the use of fats, thus reducing the calories of foods that would ordinarily be cooked with fats. The less expensive non-stick cookware usually has a very thin coating and will not last very long with everyday use. With heavy usage and continual cleaning, the coating will eventually wear thin.

STAINLESS STEEL

The best is All-Clad Stainless, which has a heavy aluminum core. The aluminum core extends up the sides of the pan and is sandwiched between a stainless steel cooking surface and an exterior layer of magnetic stainless steel. Excellent choice for gas ranges where flames can reach around the sides of the pans. Experts consider this to be the best cookware choice.

It is heavier than cheaper pots and pans and is oven-safe up to 500^{0}F. The non-stick versions are also great. To be a good heat conductor, pans need to have a copper or aluminum bottom. High acid foods cooked in stainless steel may leach out a number of metals into the food, which may include chlorine, iron, and nickel.

CORIANDER SEED
Relative of the carrot family, it has a sweet musk flavor. The seed or ground form is used in gingerbread, cookies, cakes, biscuits, poultry stuffing, pork, spiced dishes, pea soup, and cheese dishes.

CORN
Corn was first grown in Mexico or Central America and was an early staple of the American Indian.

Corn is a good source of protein and can be part of a complete protein by serving it with rice. When corn is ground for tortillas, an excellent amount of niacin is released. Corn contains 5-6% sugar making it a taste favorite. Americans consume about 25 pounds of corn per person annually. It is available May through September and the kernels should be a good yellow color. Do not purchase if the husks are a straw color, they should be green. The straw color indicates decay or worm infestation. Yellow corn usually has a more appealing flavor than white and is higher in vitamin A content.

The easiest method of removing kernels from an ear of corn is to slide a shoehorn or spoon down the ear. The best tasting corn is grown in Florida and is known as "Florida Sweet."

Choosing
Choosing fresh corn can be a difficult task unless you have some "corn knowledge." If the corn still has its husk, it will be necessary to peel back a small area and examine the kernels. The kernels should be packed tightly together with no gaps between the rows. Gaps between rows mean that the ear is over mature. If the tip has no kernels the corn was picked too soon and not allowed to mature. The kernels should always be plump and juicy and should spurt a milky, starchy, liquid. If the center of the kernel is sinking inward it is drying out and will not be as sweet. Always purchase corn with the smaller kernels at the tip of the ear since larger kernels, are a sign of over maturity.

Cooking
When corn is cooked, the protein goes through a chemical change called "denaturization" which simply means that the chains of amino acids (proteins) are broken apart and reformed into a network of protein molecules that squeeze the moisture out of the kernel turning the corn rubbery.
The heat also causes the starch granules to absorb water and swell up and rupture the kernel, thereby releasing the nutrients.

- Corn should be cooked just long enough to cause the kernels to barely rupture, which allows the protein to remain tender and not tough.
- When corn is boiled in water, 50% of the vitamin C is destroyed, however, if you cook it in a microwave without water almost all of the vitamin C is retained.
- Worldwide, there are 200 varieties of corn; however, corn ranks as a vegetable low on the overall nutritional scale.

- Steaming corn for 6-10 minutes is one of the preferred cooking methods. To store corn longer, cut a small piece off the stalk end, leave the leaves on, and then store the ears in a pot with about an inch of water, stems down.
- The more you cook corn, the tougher it will get.
- Try cooking corn in an equal amount of milk and water for a very sweet corn.
- You can microwave corn by using high power and figuring 3 minutes for each ear.

Removing Kernels

The trick to removing the kernels from an ear of corn is to place the bottom of the ear in the small funnel of an angel food cake pan then hold the point of the ear and shave down with a knife or shoehorn. Remove all kernels from leftover corncobs and use them in salads or soups the next day.

Making Creamed Corn

When you make corn fritters or creamed corn you need the sweet milk from the kernel as well as the ground up kernels. The best method of releasing the milk and preparing the kernels is to remove them with a box grater using the largest holes. Be sure and scrape the balance of the kernels off the cob after you finish grating.

An excellent base for creamed corn is to use leftover corncobs. Just cover them with milk or a mixture of water and milk and bring to a boil then reduce the heat and cook for about 30 minutes. The liquid is excellent as a starter for creamed corn.

Freezing Your Corn

Corn must be handled just right or it will not be very edible. Corn should be blanched according to directions and chilled immediately in a bowl of ice water until the cobs are completely cooled down. Before you cook the ears, allow them to partially thaw at room temperature and place a small amount of sugar in the water.

Draining Corn

Colanders are usually not big enough to drain corn, however, a clean dish rack is. The dish rack can hold all the ears of corn and allow them to drain.

How Sweet I am

Corn on the cob does not have to be shucked when you are going to boil it. If you cook it with the husks on, the corn will be sweeter. The method is to remove the silk by gently opening up the husk then replace the husk and tie the top with string to keep it shut while it is cooking.

Buttering Corn with Bread

Corn is always difficult to butter. Knives don't work well, neither does using the butter dish, turning the corn in a quarter pound of butter. The best way is to butter a piece of bread and just turn the corn in the bread.

Kebabbing Corn

Corn is very difficult to put on a skewer when making kebabs. However, if you cut the cob into chunks and then run a corkscrew threw each piece, the coiled hole will make it easy to kebab the corn.

The milky liquid in the kernel that makes corn sweet will turn pulpy and bland in only 2-3 days. Corn loses 25% or more of its sweetness in less than 25 hours after harvesting.

- Adding sugar to the water when cooking corn guarantees a sweeter taste, which was probably lost after a few days in storage.
- Leftover fresh corn should be cooked for a few minutes just to inactivate the enzymes and store the ears in a sealed plastic bag for 1-2 days before using it.

Science of Cooking Corn on the Cob

The sugar in corn starts to convert to starch as soon as the corn is picked. The longer the corn is off the stalk, the higher the starch concentration becomes. This reduction of sweetness is a telltale sign of old corn. When the corn is boiled, the high temperature will also cause the conversion rate to increase. Refrigeration slows it down somewhat. Also, never salt the water the corn is being cooked in since the minerals in salt will toughen the kernels. Salting after it is cooked does not have a  negative effect. Place the corn in the boiling water, not in cold water to shorten the time in water.

Yellow corn contains more vitamin A than white corn. When you purchase it, be sure that the silk is not brown.

If you want to grill corn on the cob there are a number of things you need to do first. Before grilling, you will need to remove all but the innermost layer of the husk then use scissors to snip off the tassel. Place the ears on the grill and as soon as you can see the outline of the kernels appearing through the layer of husk that was left on, the corn is cooked.

- Frozen corn will freeze for 1 year.
- If you plan on storing corn, always keep it in a cool, dry location and try not to place the ears touching each other to avoid mold.
- Remember as corn warms up, the sugar tends to convert into starch very quickly. In fact, when corn is piled high in bins in the market and is allowed to stand for days, the bottom ones will be less sweet due to the heat generated by the weight of the ones on top.

CORN OIL

Corn oil is one of the most common oils that is manufactured in large quantities and extracted from the corn germ, a by-product that is obtained from cereal and corn syrup producers.

The oil is a light yellow color and has a mild flavor, which does not overpower recipes. This makes corn oil excellent for baking pastries, and most recipes that call for vegetable oil.

A darker corn oil is sold that is extracted from the whole corn kernel and has a stronger aroma, similar to that of popcorn. Other types of corn oil include unrefined, expeller-pressed oil that has a strong aroma and not recommended for delicate dishes since it will overpower the flavors. This type of oil, however, is good for baking, in sauces and dressings.

The oil cannot be used for frying since it tends to foam and boil over easily. Highly refined corn oil can be used for frying and has a relatively high smoke point. Corn oil is about 87% polyunsaturated fat and contains about 60% of the essential fatty acid, linoleic acid.

Corn oil also contains more vitamin E than most other oils after processing, which normally reduces the vitamin E content significantly.

SFA . . . . . 7 g. PUFA . . . . . 7.9 g. MUFA . . . . . . 3 g.

CORN SYRUP

Corn syrup has been produced in the United States since the mid-1800s and is made by extracting starch granules from the kernels. The starch is then treated with an acid, bacterial, or malt enzyme, which turns it into sweet syrup. Corn syrup is important commercially because of its unique sweetness properties. Even though it is sweet, it can be changed into a sweet substance that does not register on our sweet taste buds. When using corn syrup, remember that there are two colors, dark and light that can both be used interchangeably.

The dark, however, will impart a dark color to your food.

The corn syrup is artificially flavored and used for literally thousands of products including pancake syrups, candy making, ice creams, etc. The fact that corn syrup tends to retard crystallization makes it a good choice for candy, preserves, and frostings. Corn syrup does not store well and should be used by the date on the label.

- ♦ When a recipe calls for corn syrup and does not specify whether dark or light, always use light.
- ♦ Dark corn syrup has a stronger flavor and will add color to a dish.
- ♦ Since corn syrup has the ability to retard crystallization, it is excellent for icings, jellies and most candies.
- ♦ Corn syrup will provide a chewy texture, which granulated sugar will not do.
- ♦ Honey is sweeter than corn syrup. If a recipe calls for honey, use honey.
- ♦ If you don't have corn syrup in the house, just use 1¼ cups granulated sugar plus ¼ cup of cool water to equal 1 cup of light corn syrup.

155

The most common liquid sweetener produced from a mixture of starch granules derived from corn, which are then processed with acids or enzymes to convert it into heavy sweet syrup. The corn syrup is then artificially flavored and used for literally thousands of products including; pancake syrups, candy making, ice creams, etc. The fact that corn syrup tends to retard crystallization makes it a good choice for candy, preserves, and frostings. Corn syrup does not store well and should be used by the date on the label.

CORNBREAD

The texture of cornbread; will be determined by the type of cornmeal you use. If you like an uneven texture, use white cornmeal. If you like a smooth texture, use yellow cornmeal. Make sure that when you are preparing it to beat the mixture until it is smooth.

- If you would like a sweetened cornbread, try adding 2 tablespoons of brown sugar plus ¼ teaspoon of ground nutmeg to your dry ingredients.
- You can add a nice flavor to cornbread by adding a mixture of 1 cup of grated mild cheddar cheese or chopped scallion greens into the batter. Some bacon crumbles will also add a unique flavor.

CORNED BEEF AND CABBAGE

CHEF'S CORNED BEEF & CABBAGE

Ingredients:

4	Pounds corned beef	½	Pound salt pork (cut into chunks)
12	Cups water	¼	Cup granulated sugar
2	Bay leaves	3	Garlic cloves
12	Red potatoes	6	Small turnips (peeled)
12	Small white boiling onions (peeled)	1	Head cabbage
6	Medium carrots (peeled, sliced into ½-inch pieces)		
6	Parsnips (peeled, cut into ½-inch pieces)		

- Soak the corned beef in cold water for 30 minutes.
- Cut the head of cabbage into 6 equal-size wedges.
- In a large pot combine the corned beef, salt pork and water.
- Place over medium heat then bring the mixture to a boil.
- Add the sugar, bay leaves and garlic.
- Reduce the heat to low, cover the pot partially with a lid, allowing steam to escape, and allow the mixture to simmer for 3 hours.

- Remove the bay leaves and add the turnips, carrots, onions and parsnips.
- Continue cooking for 20-minutes more or until the vegetables are just tender.
- Place the cabbage wedges on top of the meat in the pot, cover the pot completely, and cook the mixture for 15 minutes more allowing the cabbage to steam and the vegetables to continue cooking.
- Remove the cabbage and vegetables from the pot and set them aside, keeping them warm.
- Remove the corned beef from the pot and slice into long thin slices.
- Serve the corned beef over the cabbage wedge with the vegetables.

CORNMEAL

Cornmeal may be purchased in two varieties; steel-ground which has the husk and germ almost all removed, and stone or water-ground which retains a portion of the hull and germ and is usually only available in health food stores.

- Steel-ground cornmeal can be stored for up to 10 years if you store it in an airtight container and place it in a cool, dark location.
- Stone-ground cornmeal can only be stored in an airtight container in the refrigerator for about 4 months due to its fat content found in the germ.
- Cornmeal can be purchased in three different textures; fine (corn flour), medium (most common texture) and coarse (polenta).
- Masa Harina is a cornflower that is used to prepare corn tortillas and tamales.
- Cornmeal can be sautéed using a small amount of oil and stirring until golden brown. This is used to prepare polenta before adding any liquid.
- You can dry-roast cornmeal by placing a single layer on a cookie sheet and roasting at 300^0F for 8-10 minutes.

CORNSTARCH

Cornstarch is thick, powdery flour that is made from the corn's endosperm. It is an excellent thickener for sauces but tends to form lumps easily unless it is mixed slowly into a cold liquid and then added to a hot liquid.

Stir the cornstarch until it mixes thoroughly then boil it for a few minutes to thicken the sauce or stew.
- When using cornstarch to thicken a mixture, you only need half as much cornstarch as you will flour.
- For every tablespoon of flour called for in a recipe, you can substitute ½ tablespoon of cornstarch.
- Flour will be more stable than cornstarch when used for thickening.
- When you're cooking a mixture that requires high heat, it would be best to use a combination of the two.
- When you are thickening a stew or soup, be sure and remove as much fat as possible before adding the cornstarch.

- When you add cornstarch paste to a hot mixture be sure and bring the mixture to boil. Cook it for about 2 minutes and stir frequently for the mixture to reach its maximum thickness.
- Another trick to help disperse cornstarch in a liquid is to mix it together with some granulated sugar.
- If you thicken a mixture with cornstarch, it will start to thin if cooked too long, if the temperature is too high or if you stir the mixture too vigorously.
- British recipes call cornstarch – corn flour.

COTTAGE CHEESE

Cottage cheese was originally produced in cottages and was made from a by-product of homemade butter and was eventually called a *"cottage industry."* Cottage cheese is produced from skimming the milk obtained when butter is made and allowed to curdle.

The curds would then be strained from the whey through cheesecloth making cottage cheese.

Cottage cheese is a United States original and is made from skimmed milk either plain-cured, or plain-cured with cream. It is always sold in a soft texture with different size curds. If the label says, "curd by acidification" it will be a synthetic product.

Cottage cheese only retains 25-50% of the calcium from the milk it is made from due to the processing. The higher the water content of cheeses, such as cottage cheese, the sooner they will go bad. Cheddar cheese, however, is so low in moisture that it will last for years with the taste becoming stronger with aging.

Cottage cheese will last 7-10 days longer if you store it upside down. When you open cottage cheese spores enter from the air and live on the oxygen layer. When you turn cottage cheese upside down and allow it to fall to the top, you eliminate a percentage of the oxygen layer. Many of the remaining spores then suffocate and ones that remain cannot grow as fast allowing the cottage cheese to last about 7-10 days longer.

If you want to keep cottage cheese fresh, another method is to add 1 teaspoon of vinegar to the carton and stir it in well. This will really keep it fresh for a long period of time.

CRABS

Crabs and lobsters have the capability to regenerate a new claw when one is broken off. The crab industry in many areas now catch crabs and break off one of the claws then release the crab to grow another one. The crab is able to protect itself and forage for food as long as it has one claw.

 Different species of crabs are found in different oceans or seas. Crabs caught in the Gulf of Mexico or Atlantic Ocean are called Blue Crabs. Crabs caught in the Pacific Ocean are known as the Dungeness. The most prized crabs and the largest are the King Crabs; these are caught off the coast of Alaska and Northern Canada. The smaller Stone Crab is found in the waters off the coast of Florida.

- Crabs should only be purchased if they are active and heavy for their size.
- Refrigerate them as soon as possible and cover them with a damp towel.
- Live crabs should be cooked the day they are purchased.
- If canned crabmeat has a metallic taste, soak it in ice water for 5-8 minutes, then drain and blot dry with paper towels.
- Canned crabmeat is available flaked or as lump or claw meat.
- Once a can is opened, it must be refrigerated and used up within 2 days.
- When picking over crabmeat (fresh or canned), be sure and use your fingers so that you can feel if there are any small pieces of shell.
- You can purchase crab legs and claws cooked and frozen.

The soft-shell crab can be found in a variety of sizes. The smallest are called "spiders" which are almost too small to keep. They only measure about 3½ inches across which is the bare legal size.

The "hotel prime" measure in at about 4½ inches across and the "prime" at 5½ inches. The largest are called "jumbo" and measure in at a whopping 6-7 inches across.

MALE vs. FEMALE

Male crabs are known as a "jimmy" (T-shaped apron) and female crabs are known as a "sally" (V-shaped apron). The female crabs may also be called a "sook" and will always have their fingernails (or claw tips) painted a bright red. Males will never have red-tipped claws.

SHELL COLOR

If crab shells are orange after they are cooked, the crabs were old and may not have the best flavor. Their shells should be a bright red after cooking, which means that the chemical in the shell was still very active.

CRANBERRIES

Cranberries seemed to originate in the United States in the New England states around the Cape Cod area and grow well in sandy soil.

The *"cranberry bogs"* of New England have a story attached that says that in the late 1700's Reverend Richard Bourne made an Indian medicine man mad and he placed a spell on him before placing him into quicksand. The Reverend spent 15 days buried in the quicksand and this aggravated the Indian who thought that he would die fairly quickly.

While unable to move: the Reverend lived on berries that were dropped over him by a white dove. The medicine man became frustrated and released him from the spell and the quicksand.

One of the berries is supposed to have fallen into the sand and rooted starting the cranberry bogs of New England.

> If you add $\frac{1}{4}$ teaspoon of baking soda to cranberries while they are cooking, it will neutralize some of the acid and less sugar will be needed.

Buy berries that are hard, bright, light-to-dark, red and sealed in plastic bags. When frozen they will keep for up to one year.

Only cook cranberries until they "pop."
Cranberries will not handle a great amount of heat before the water inside produces enough steam to burst the berry. When a cranberry pops and bursts it is best to stop the cooking process, otherwise the cranberry will become bitter and very tart.

The addition of lemon juice and a small amount of sugar added to the water will help to preserve the color, since the heat will cause the pigment (anthocyanin) to be dissolved and turn the cooking water red.

- If they bounce they are fresh and firm.
- Only wash cranberries just before using.
- They freeze well if wrapped in an airtight bag.
- Use frozen cranberries in recipes for good results.

> ### Science of Cranberries
> Cranberries are usually too tart to eat raw and are therefore made into sauces, relishes, and preserves. Only 10% of the commercial crop in the United States is sold in supermarkets, the balance is made into cranberry sauce or juice. Canned cranberries have only 14% of the vitamin C content than that of fresh and 3 times the calories.

Cranberries contain "ellagic acid," a phytochemical. When choosing a fresh cranberry in the supermarket, make sure it bounces. Another name for cranberries is "bounce berries." Buy berries that are hard, bright, light-to-dark, red and sealed in plastic bags.

Cranberries grow in bogs that are always kept dry while they grow. When harvest time arrives the bogs are flooded and a special machine shakes the vines underwater releasing them so that they can be harvested as they float to the surface. Early American Indians used cranberries in a poultice on wounds to stop the bleeding since it was found to contract tissues.

♦ Add 1 teaspoon of unsalted butter to each pound of cranberries to eliminate foam and over-boiling.
♦ Frozen cranberries can be used in recipes without defrosting them.

Science of Cranberry Bread
Be sure you do not over mix the dough or it will cause the gluten to become tough. When you remove the bread from the oven, allow it to cool in the pan for 10 minutes before placing it on a rack for complete cooling to stabilize the cake. Never serve the bread until it has remained on the counter wrapped in plastic wrap for one day allowing the flavor to meld in.

CRANBERRY SAUCE

If the cranberries are sliced in half they will not burst during the cooking and will be less bitter.

Science of Making Cranberry Sauce
The acid in cranberries has the tendency to turn bitter the more the cranberries are cooked. Using a large saucepan, combine the cranberries, sugar, water and wine and simmer over medium heat. Stop the cooking process as soon as the cranberries pop, which means that they are done. If they are cooked any further, they will be too bitter. Add the rum and room temperature butter and mix well. The heat should melt the butter and create an excellent sauce. The sauce should gel in the refrigerator in about 3 hours and may be served hot or cold.

CRAYFISH/CRAWFISH/CRAWDAD/MUDBUG
These look like miniature shrimp and are a relative. The largest producer in the world is the state of Louisiana. They produce over 22 million pounds of these little "crawdads" a year.

To begin with, crayfish are always cooked live similar to lobsters and crabs. They have a much sweeter flavor and are affectionately known as "crawdads." All the meat is found in the tail of the crayfish.

To easily remove the meat, gently twist the tail away from the body then unwrap the first three sections of the shell to expose the meat. Next you need to pinch the end of the meat while holding the tail in the other hand and pulling the meat out in one piece. If you wish you can also suck out the flavorful juices from the head.

The tails can be eaten as well as the orange fat, pancreas and even the liver. All parts are used in classic Cajun dishes.

CREAM

To cream is to beat foods until they become light and fluffy: commonly sugar, butter and shortening.

Large centrifuges (spinning machines) are now used in dairies to separate the cream from the milk. A percentage of the fat is extracted from the cream, which determines the type of cream and related to the different uses it is sold for. Heavy whipping cream is 36-40% butterfat, light whipping cream is 30-36%, and butterfat and light cream (coffee cream) can be anywhere from 18% to 30% butterfat (best to check the label). Half-and-Half is 11% butterfat and is produced from half cream and half milk.

Cream is no longer made the "old fashioned" way, which was to allow it to separate to the top of the milk and skim it off. Cream is now produced using a centrifuge, which allows the fat globules to be released in a liquid, become concentrated and easily removed. Light cream is 20-30% butterfat, light, whipping cream is 30-36% butterfat, and heavy whipping cream is 36-40% butterfat.

SAVING THE CREAM

If cream can't all be used and will sit in the refrigerator for a period of time, try placing 1/8th teaspoon of baking soda in the cream.

Science of Saving the Cream

The baking soda neutralizes the lactic acid, which builds up as the cream sours. This will add days not weeks to the cream and it should still be usable, however, taste the flavor or smell it before using it to be sure that it has not gone bad.

BEWARE OF LEFTOVERS

When cream has been placed on the table in a container and has reached room temperature, never place the leftover cream back into its original container or it will ruin the rest of the cream. It can be saved by storing it separately and reused if it has not soured.

- Cream should be refrigerated in the coldest part of the refrigerator as soon as possible after you get home from the supermarket.
- Cream can be frozen as long as there is at least ½ inch on top of the container. The container should be wrapped in a freezer-proof plastic bag and will stay for 4-6 months.

CREAM, CURDLING OF

Dairy Products

To avoid curdling when cooking with dairy products, always cook at a lower temperature setting.

In Coffee

If you want to stop cream from curdling up in your coffee, just add a pinch of baking soda to the cream before pouring it in. The baking soda will neutralize the acid in coffee just enough so as not to alter the flavor, but will eliminate the curdling.

Over Fruit

Cream has the tendency to curdle when poured over acidic fruits. To eliminate this problem, try adding a small amount of baking soda to the cream, then mixing it well before pouring it over the fruit. Baking soda is capable of reducing the acidity level in fruits.

CREAM, IN COFFEE

Almost every coffee drinker at one time or another has been irritated by the presence of floating cream. A thorough investigation was conducted and the results are in. The stronger the coffee, the more acid that may be formed and if the cream is not very fresh it will contain just enough lactic acid to cause a reaction with the coffee and rise to the top. However, if the coffee is too acidic it may cause even the freshest cream to go bad almost instantly and thus rise to the top.

CREAM, SOURING

When cream is having a somewhat off-odor and you need to use it, try mixing in 1/3rd teaspoon of baking soda. The baking soda will neutralize the lactic acid in the cream that is causing the souring. Before you use the cream, however, make sure the flavor is within normal boundaries.

CREAM, SPINNING OFF

Cream is produced by spinning milk in a centrifuge, which causes the fat globules (butter) to release from the watery substance and become more concentrated then removed. Supermarkets carry three grades of cream: Light cream which is between 20-30% butterfat, light whipping cream which is between 30-36% butterfat, and heavy whipping cream which is between 36-40% butterfat as compared to whole milk which is only 3.3-4% butterfat.

CREAM OF TARTAR

Tartar is derived from grapes during and after the process of fermentation. Two pinkish crystalline sediments remain in wine casks after the wine has fermented; they are "argol," which collects on the sides of the cask and "lees" which collects on the bottom. These substances are actually crude tartar. The crude tartar is then de-crystallized by cooking in boiling water and then allowing the remains to crystallize again. This substance is then bleached pure white and further crystallized. As this process concludes a thin layer of very thin white crystals are formed on the surface. The name cream of tartar is derived from this thin top layer that looks like cream. It is used to produce baking powder when mixed with baking soda.

CROCK POT (Slow Cooker)

The Crock pot; was invented in 1971 by Rival. Many consumers still question whether the pot is safe or a breeding ground for bacteria since it advocates all day cooking at a low temperature. The fact is that most slow cookers have settings that range from 170^0F to 280^0F. Bacteria die at 140^0F, which is below the lowest possible temperature that can be used.

However, if the lid is left off it may cause a problem with food not being fully cooked and harboring bacteria that is still alive. To minimize the risk of food poisoning, the following should be followed:

- ♦ All foods should be at refrigerator temperature. No frozen or partially thawed foods.
- ♦ Crock-pots will range in size from 1-6 quarts.
- ♦ Only cook cut up pieces of meat, not whole roasts or fowl and allow the heat to penetrate fully.
- ♦ Make sure that the cooker is at least ½ to 2/3 full or the food will not absorb enough heat to kill any bacteria.
- ♦ The food must be covered with liquid to generate sufficient steam.
- ♦ The original lid should always be used and should be tight fitting.
- ♦ When possible, allow the cooker to cook on the high setting for the first hour then it can be reduced.

- Never use the cooker to reheat leftovers. A number of bacteria are usually found on leftovers and it takes a high heat to kill them.
- Always follow the manufacturer's directions for temperature settings.

CROUTONS

Prepare a mixture of your favorite herbs and seasonings with olive oil and brush the flavored oil over slices of bread. Be sure and do both sides of the bread. Stack as many slices as you can slice easily and cut the bread into bite-sized cubes. Spread the cubes in a single layer on a baking sheet and bake at 300^0F until they are dry and crisp. The time it takes to dry them out will depend on the size of the crouton.

CRUCIFEROUS VEGETABLES

We have all smelled broccoli, cabbage, Brussels sprouts, and cauliflower cooking and it is not a pleasant aroma.

When these vegetables are heated it causes a chemical to break down and release a strong-smelling sulfur compound composed of ammonia and hydrogen sulfide (rotten egg smell).

The more you cook them, the more intense the smell, and the more compounds that are released. If you cook broccoli too long the compounds will react with the chlorophyll (the green color) and turn the broccoli brown. If you cook broccoli in a small amount of water, it will slow down the reaction.

CUCUMBERS

Originated in Asia, cucumbers were brought to the Americas by Columbus. They are grown in all sizes from the smallest 1" gherkins to as large as 20" long. They have very high water content and are an excellent source of fiber. The Greenhouse or English cucumber is becoming more and more popular; however, the price of this thin-skinned skinny "cuke" is considerably higher than the standard market cucumber.

- Cucumbers should be firm and a good green color, either dark or light, but not yellow.
- Purchase only firm cucumbers and refrigerate. Large thick ones tend to be pithy and will give when squeezed.
- Cucumbers only have 13 calories per 3½ ounce serving due to their high water content.
- Cucumbers do not contain any starch therefore they are unable to produce sugar to sweeten them. They will, however, get softer as they age and absorb more moisture into the pectin. If the cucumber gets too soft, just soak the slices in lightly salted cold water to crisp up. The reaction that occurs removes the unsalted, lower-density water from the cells and replaces it with the higher-density salted water.

- Cucumbers should be stored unwashed in a plastic bag with holes to allow air to circulate around the cucumber or should be placed in the vegetable drawer if your refrigerator has one.
- Cucumber seeds may be bitter and can be removed by cutting the cucumber lengthwise in half and scooping the seeds out with a teaspoon.
- If you want to remove excess water to make cucumbers crisp for salads, just sprinkle sliced cucumbers with salt then top with ice cubes and refrigerate for 1 hour. Pat them dry and refrigerate until ready to use them.
- Cucumbers will only keep for 3-5 days and do best in the warmest part of the refrigerator around 40^0F.
- Cucumbers do not freeze well because of their high water content; too many cells tend to burst making the cucumber mushy. Pickle juice should be saved and used for making coleslaw, potato salad, etc.

Bitterness Reducer

This fact really surprised me, and I thought it was just another old wives tale again, one that had been passed down through the years and really didn't work. To my surprise it actually worked. Next time you purchase a standard cucumber, not the long skinny English variety, cut about one inch off the end and then rub the two exposed areas together in a circular motion while occasionally pulling them apart. This will cause enough suction to release a substance that causes some cucumbers to have a bitter taste. Then discard the small end you used to release the bitterness.

Waxed

Cucumbers tend to shrink during shipping and storage. The wax coating is to prevent the shrinkage and is edible. The skin should never be removed until you are ready to eat the cucumber or it will lose most of its vitamin C content. The cucumber is capable of holding 30 times its weight in water and is a member of the "gourd family."

If you can remember back to the 1930's, "cucumber" was a slang word for a one-dollar bill.

- Never use a cucumber that has been waxed when preparing pickles. The wax coating will not allow the liquids to be absorbed.
- Once a cucumber is peeled it will lose a high percentage of its vitamin C very quickly.
- To remove the seeds, just slice the whole cucumber lengthwise and use a spoon to remove them.
- A layer of salt can be placed on the top of cucumber slices that have been placed on a dish in the refrigerator for 30 minutes to drain some of the moisture out and crisp them up. The salt can be removed with a piece of paper towel before adding to a salad.
- The most popular seasonings for cucumbers are mint, garlic and dill.

Science of Removing Water from a Cucumber

Chefs will never put cucumbers into a salad before making sure that most of the water is out of the cucumber since cucumbers have such high water content. If you don't remove the seeds and drain them they will make a salad watery. Slice the cucumber lengthwise then remove the seeds with a spoon. Place the flat side on the cutting board and slice the cucumber on a diagonal into $\frac{1}{4}$" pieces. Toss the cucumber pieces with some salt (about 1 teaspoon for every cucumber) in a colander.

After tossing them in the colander you will need to weigh the cucumbers down. Keep the cucumbers in the colander but be sure it is slightly raised off the surface or placed in a pan then place a one-gallon plastic bag filled with water on top of the cucumbers and allow them to drain for 1-3 hours before using them. The salt will help extract water from the cucumbers. Do not add more salt to the salad.

CUPCAKES

If you want to frost cupcakes quickly, just dip them upside down in a bowl of frosting and twirl them a little.

Cupcake and muffin tins need to be filled to preserve their lifetime use. It is best to fill any empties with water.

CURRY POWDER

Curry powder is a blend of at least 20 spices, herbs, and seeds. Ingredients may include chili peppers, cloves, coriander, fennel seed, nutmeg, mace, cayenne, black pepper, sesame seed, saffron, and turmeric. The yellow color comes from the turmeric. It is usually used in Indian cooking, poultry, stews, soups, sauces, and meat dishes.

- ♦ The real Indian curry powder is ground fresh every day and varies in its flavor depending on the region and the cook.
- ♦ The commercial curry powder can be found in two types; standard and Madras. The Madras is the hotter of the two. Different brands will have different flavors and it is necessary to try several brands to find the one you like the best.
- ♦ It only takes a pinch of curry powder to spice up most dishes for the American taste.
- ♦ If you sauté the powder in a small amount of butter for a minute, you can reduce the "raw" taste to some degree.
- ♦ Remember that curry powder gets hotter the longer it remains in the food. Best to consume the food just after adding the spice.

CUSTARD

The recipe for a basic custard formula calls for 1 egg, 1 cup of milk, and 2 tablespoons of granulated sugar.

If you wish to increase the richness you will need to add 2-3 egg yolks, which increases the fat and cholesterol significantly.

To avoid solid custard it will be necessary to continually stir the mixture using a low heat setting to avoid setting the protein too soon. Milk in custard is really not the main protein source but contributes salts to assist in producing a gel. Never try and replace the milk with water. The milk and sugar will thin out the proteins and increase the volume. Abide by the recipe and never try and speed up the cooking process by increasing the heat, it will end up ruining the custard. To make the perfect custard takes time and patience.

When you heat custard containing egg yolks and whites, the protein solidifies causing thickening. The amount of egg to milk ratio, however, is very important if you really want to prepare great custard.

The perfect milk-based custard should use 1 whole egg for every 2/3 cup of whole milk. If sugar is added, add more egg. If you use a starch, such as rice (good thickener); you will need to reduce the amount of egg. After placing the custard in the oven, **NEVER OPEN THE OVEN DOOR** since the retained heat is needed to cook the center of the custard.

DON'T CURDLE ME UP

One of chef's tricks when preparing custard was to never use high heat. Custard will not be creamy if you use high heat. It will thicken nicely when cooked on low heat. If you cook the custard too fast or too long, it will curdle as well.

Science of Custard

The eggs need to be protected from the hot liquid as much as possible. Place the eggs you are going to use in a small bowl and beat in a small amount of the hot liquid. The eggs will now be safely warmed and will do well when added to the complete mixture. Always cook custard on the top of a double boiler or in a water bath. Never allow more than two bubbles to appear before you stop the cooking.

The custard ramekins are hard to remove from a water bath unless you use a pair of tongs with rubber bands on each tong. Just wrap the rubber band several times around each tong and it will make it easy to grab the ramekin.

CHEF'S SECRET

When preparing custard, eggs are sometimes a problem if not handled properly. The eggs should be beat first with sugar and set aside. The milk or cream must then be scalded until small bubbles form around the edges of the pot. Pour a small amount of the hot liquid into the eggs mixing thoroughly, slightly cooking the eggs. Add the egg mixture into the hot milk and heat on low heat until it starts to thicken. The custard should then be strained into a bowl to remove any solidified egg or film that had formed.

- Custard must be stirred continually to prevent the bottom burning.
- Chefs always use a wooden spoon when stirring custard since some of the eggs minerals may react with certain types of metal spoons.
- When stirring always stir in a figure eight pattern to cover the complete bottom.

FILL'ER UP

When making tartlets and you need to fill the individual shells it can be a difficult messy job. To avoid the mess, just use a bulb baster to release just the right amount into each cup.

SKINHEAD

If you want to eliminate the skin forming on your custard, just cover the dish with a piece of waxed paper while it is still very hot.

Mayonnaise and custard do not come out well using frozen eggs; however, all other dishes are not a problem.

DDDDD

DEGLAZE

The process of adding a liquid to remove and dissolve the residues remaining on the bottom of a pan.

DEVILED EGGS

- If you want your deviled eggs to have greater stability, cut a slice off the end and they will stand up for easy filling.
- To keep yolks centered when boiling eggs for deviled eggs, just stir the water while they are cooking.
- When storing deviled eggs, place the halves with the filling together, then wrap tightly with tin foil, twirl the ends and refrigerate.
- Add 1 teaspoon chopped chives to yolks during seasoning.
- An easy way to mix all the ingredients when preparing deviled eggs is to place the ingredients into a plastic bag and squish them all together until they are mixed well. Cut off a small corner of the bag and pipe the mixture into the egg whites.
- If you want to keep the yolk area centered, just stir the eggs while they are cooking.

DILL

It is sold in whole or ground seed form or as a fresh herb. Usually used in cottage cheese, chowders, pickling, soups, sauerkraut, salads, fish, meat sauces, potato salad, green apple pie, and spiced vinegar. Great for livening up egg salad.

If possible only use fresh dill when seasoning a dish. The freshly chopped leaves are the best. Chefs use dill mainly when cooking fish and lamb and of course in pickling. When cooking fish they sprinkle freshly chopped dill on the fish before broiling it. The lamb is sprinkled with dill as it cooks.

DILL PICKLES

CHEF'S DILL PICKLE RECIPE

Ingredients:

50	Small cucumbers	4	Sprigs of fresh dill
2	Ounces whole mixed pickling spices	2	Cups salt
2	Cups apple cider vinegar	2	Quarts water
¼	Pound fresh garlic	5	Gallon crock

It will take about an hour to prepare everything and the fermentation process will take 3 weeks. Make sure that the cucumbers are small and firm (about 4-5 inches long). Wash and drain them well then separate the garlic cloves, peel them and set them aside.

- Place a layer of dill, 2-3 garlic buds and half the pickling spices in the crock then arrange 25 of the cucumbers in the crock.
- Place more dill and garlic buds over the cucumbers then place the balance of the cucumbers in the crock allowing about 6-inches to the top.
- In a medium bowl blend the vinegar, salt and water then pour over the cucumbers.
- Place the balance of the spices, dill and garlic buds on top.
- Cover with a large plate with a weight on top to hold the cucumbers under the brine then place the crock in a cool, dark location. Be sure it is not a cold location.

When the pickles begin to ferment and foam appears, remove the foam (scum) every day. When the pickle solution is clear you can pack them in smaller jars and place in a cold location or in the refrigerator. If you prefer not to store all pickles in the refrigerator, it is best to place them into small jars and sterilize them.

DOUBLE-BOILER

Marbles to the Rescue

When you are using a double boiler, be sure and place a few marbles or a small metal jar top on the bottom of the pot. They will start to rattle when the water gets too low and save you from scorching the pot.

DOUGH, PREPARATION OF

When preparing dough for baked goods, hard water may cause a problem since too high a mineral content may result in the gluten not being able to develop properly. If the gluten does not develop properly, the crust will be tough.

Remember on humid or very hot days, most yeast dough may rise too fast and may be very hard to knead. When this occurs, there is a loss of elasticity.

If you wish to speed up the rising of bread dough, which takes just a small amount of heat, try placing the pan with the dough on top of a heating pad on medium. This will easily do the trick.

When using a dough mixer, try spraying a small amount of vegetable oil on the hook or blade. This will stop the dough from climbing up the hook.

FLOUR TEST - ENOUGH IS ENOUGH

All too often too much flour is placed into a loaf of bread dough causing the bread to be too dry. To check the dough for too much flour, just squeeze the dough gently using your entire hand. If your hand pulls away clean, there is enough flour in the dough. If your hand pulls away with flour on it, there is too much.

Rising Tips

One of the most frequent encountered problems is that yeast dough doesn't rise adequately. There are a number of reasons for this.

- **First**, the dough may be too cool and therefore reduce the level of yeast activity. The temperature needs to be between 80°-90°F for the best results.
- **Second**, the yeast may have been prepared with water that was too hot, which is a frequent problem. The water must be below 140°F for optimum results.
- **Third**, you forgot to test the yeast and to see if it was ready for retirement.

POKING DOUGH FOR THE FUN OF IT

Since dough needs to rise, it is best to set it aside and allow it to rise to about double its original size.

171

However, before starting to work with the dough, poke the dough with your finger to see if it is ready. If the indentation does not spring back, the dough is ready to work.

Science of Rising Dough

While most cookbooks recommend the best temperature for rising dough to be 95°F (35°C) bakers prefer 80°F (27°C) to prevent the yeast from expelling bad smelling byproducts. Also if the dough is too warm it is stickier and harder to work with. When chefs poke the dough and it does not jump back it means that the gluten has been stretched as far as it will go and has reached the limit of its elasticity. The dough is then punched back into shape, which squeezes out the excess carbon dioxide and redistributes the yeast and its food supply. It also evens out the temperature and makes the dough easier to work.

DOUGH-RISING BUCKET

Chefs have a special clear bucket called a dough rising bucket. They use the bucket to keep track of the dough as it rises to be sure the dough rises to double its size. If you can find a clear container, just place the dough in and place a rubber band around the outside at the level of the dough. It will then be easy to see when the dough has risen to double its size.

RISING TO THE OCCASION

As soon as the dough is ready to rise, recipes normally suggest placing the dough into a bowl and covering it with a damp kitchen towel.

However, the towel does not protect the dough from drafts. Best to place a piece of plastic wrap over the top to keep the drafts out.

NEEDING DOUGH?

Kneading dough is really an art and you need to know just when to stop kneading. Chefs will always knead dough just until it has a satiny appearance. They only continue as long as it takes to get the look of the batter just right. However, if we use a machine to help us with this chore, it will only take a short period of time to accomplish the task.

Science of Kneading Dough

Aerating the dough is hard work and machines are actually more efficient. Kneading should be done as long as the dough continues to become stiffer. If you knead too much it will breakdown certain chemical crosslinks and cause the dough to become sticky and inelastic. The satiny appearance that chefs look for was caused by the fat they use to waterproof the gluten and the sugar absorbing water.

MIXING IT UP

When Chefs make dough, they never mix all the flour with the water and yeast. They mix the yeast and water then add half of the flour and allow the mixture to rest for 20-30 minutes before adding the rest of the flour. This makes for a lighter product.

DOUGH, YEAST

The basic formula for "enriched" white bread was invented by Dr. Clive M. McCay at Cornell University in 1934. The formula was one tablespoon of soy flour, one tablespoon of dry whole milk and one teaspoon of wheat germ to one cup of white flour. The formula added additional protein, calcium and B vitamins and did change the taste of the bread. It was called the "Triple-Rich Formula."

WARM THOSE YEASTIES

Yeast rise best at 80^0F so if the kitchen is too cool it will take quite a bit longer. However, my grandmother used to place the dough on top of the TV (if it was on) or use a heating pad and even a warm hot water bottle. Also, she always started with room-temperature ingredients.

Science of Yeast – Rising Times

Warm location (75^0-85^0F)........................... takes 45-60 minutes

Room temperature (65^0-72^0F)................... takes $1\frac{1}{2}$ -2 hours

Refrigerator (40^0F)..................................... takes 12-24 hours

---

A LITTLE DAB WILL DO YA

If the weather is very hot outside and you know that the dough will rise very fast, just add a small amount of extra salt to the dough to slow it down. The speed at which the dough rises will make a difference in the flavor of the bread. The longer the dough takes to ferment, the better the flavor.

Over-mixing baked goods will cause them to become tough

To tell if the dough is ready after it has risen, try poking the dough very gently with two fingers. There should be an indentation left in the dough and it should have doubled in size.

DOUGHNUTS

The Pilgrims made the first doughnuts in the 1600's, which did not have the traditional hole in the middle.

Later in 1809 a mention was made in print in Washington Irving's **Knickerbocker's History of New York.** He described what sounded like a doughnut made from ball of sweetened dough fried in hog's fat. He called them doughnuts or "olykoeks," which is Dutch for "oil cakes."

Doughnut dough should be allowed to rest for about 20 minutes before frying. The air in the dough will have time to escape giving the doughnut a better texture. This will also allow the doughnut to absorb less fat.

Science of Frying Doughnuts

The reason chefs allow dough to rest is to give the dough time for the air to escape giving the doughnut a better texture. It also causes less fat to be absorbed. Placing doughnuts immediately into boiling water for 3-5 seconds causes fat droplets to be released. Drain the doughnuts on a metal rack. Be sure that the frying temperature is exactly 365°F (185°C) and don't fry for more than 50 seconds on each side.

♦ One of the best methods of reducing the total-fat in doughnuts is to place the doughnut in boiling water the second it is removed from the frying vat. Any fat that is clinging to the doughnut drops off in the hot water, then just remove the doughnut after 3-5 seconds and allow the doughnuts to drain on a metal rack for about 10 minutes.

♦ Frying temperature should be 365°F for about 50 seconds on each side. Never turn them more than once and allow room for expansion in the frying vat.

♦ Doughnuts can be made from either yeast (raised doughnuts) or baking powder (cake doughnuts).

♦ If you choose a recipe that has proportionately more egg yolk, the doughnuts won't absorb as much oil.

♦ The softer the doughnut dough, the softer the doughnut.

♦ Placing the doughnut dough in the refrigerator and chilling it before frying will reduce the amount of fat absorbed.

To keep the doughnuts from becoming soggy, add 1 teaspoon of white vinegar to the frying oil **BEFORE YOU START HEATING THE OIL.** This will give the doughnuts added body and reduce fat absorption.

DUMPLINGS

If you want the lightest dumplings every time, just puncture them when they are through cooking with a fork and allow air to circulate within them.

The bottoms of dumplings always seem to get soggy. To avoid this problem all you have to do is wait until the dish is bubbling hot before you place them on top. They will cook faster, be lighter, and absorb less moisture. For a great fruit cobbler place the top on after it starts bubbling.

Science of Chicken Dumplings

Mix the dough as little as possible, just blending the ingredients. Never drop them into the boiling water, just gently lay them on top of the chicken pieces. Never simmer the dumplings for more than 10 minutes uncovered then cover and cook for another 10 minutes. The other trick is to use a dome lid so that the steam does not make them soggy.

EEEEE

EGGPLANT

Eggplant is a member of the "nightshade" family of vegetables, which also include potatoes, tomatoes, and peppers. It is not very high on the nutrient scale and varieties include Chinese purple eggplant, globular eggplant, Japanese eggplant and Italian eggplant.

- ♦ Eggplant contains the chemical "solanine" which is destroyed when it is cooked. Best never to eat raw eggplant.
- ♦ Since eggplants will only last a few days even under refrigeration it is best to use them the same day or no later than the next day after they are purchased.

Science of Eggplant (The fat sponge)

The cells in a fresh eggplant have a very high air content that will escape when the eggplant is heated. When you cook an eggplant in oil, the air escapes and the cells absorb a large quantity of oil. As the cells fill up with oil and as the eggplant is moved about they eventually collapse and release the oil. Eggplants in a recent study absorbed more fat when fried than any other vegetable, 83 grams in 70 seconds four times more than an equal portion of French fries, thus adding 700 calories to the low-calorie eggplant. Eggplant Parmesan is always served in a pool of olive oil for this reason. Eggplant should never be cooked in an aluminum pot; this will cause the eggplant to become discolored.

Smaller eggplants are the best since they are more likely to be sweeter and more tender. If you go to the Near East, every household has a wooden knife or one carved from bone, which is only used to cut eggplant. If a metal knife (except for stainless steel) is used it will turn black as well as turning the eggplant black.

- Eggplants tend to be a bit bitter and the easiest method of eliminating the problem is to slice the eggplant in ½ inch slices, then lightly salt the slices and this will also reduce the amount of oil that is absorbed when frying.
- Eggplant is available year round but is best during August and September. Their outer purple-black skin should be smooth and glossy, free of scars and they should be firm.
- Soft eggplants are usually bitter. Keep them cool after purchase and use in 2-3 days.
- The bigger the eggplant, the longer it was grown and the more time it had to develop a chemical that tends to make the eggplant somewhat bitter.

Males Are Sweeter

Male eggplants contain fewer seeds than female eggplants. The seeds make eggplant bitter, but are difficult to remove effectively. To determine which gender the eggplant is, just look at the bottom where the flower was attached. The male eggplant will have a well-rounded bottom and the stem area will be smooth. The female will have a smaller, narrow bottom and an indented stem area.

Almost 70% of all the eggplants in the world are grown in New Jersey.

EGG SALAD

The Perfect Cube

If you want the perfect cubed eggs for egg salad and not the chunks, slightly mashed pieces or uneven pieces, there is a simple way to solve the problem.

Just place the hard-boiled eggs into an egg slicer and cut the egg lengthwise then turn the egg a quarter turn and slice it crosswise. Then rotate the egg 90^0 so that one end is facing up and slice it from top to bottom. Only takes a few seconds once you do it a time or two.

CHEF'S EGG SALAD

Ingredients:

6	Hard-boiled eggs	4	Tablespoons mayonnaise
1	Teaspoon Dijon mustard		salt & pepper, to taste

- First, carefully separate the hard-boiled eggs by removing the cooked white from the yolks and placing them in separate bowls.
- Using a fork, mash the yolks until they are fluffy and no lumps exist.
- Add the mayonnaise and the mustard to the yolks and blend well.
- Season with salt and pepper and blend well.
- Next place the egg whites on a cutting board or work surface and roughly chop them, leaving ¼- inch-size chunks.

- Do not over chop the whites or they will lose their firm texture.
- Add the chopped whites into the yolk mixture and stir to combine well.
- If possible, refrigerate the egg salad for at least 1 hour before serving, to allow the flavors to meld together.

EGG WASH

Egg wash is a mixture composed of a whole egg or egg white that is combined with milk, cream, or water and beaten well. The "egg wash" is then brushed on the top of baked goods before they are baked to help the tops brown more evenly and give the top a shiny, crisp surface. It also is used to hold poppy seed or similar toppings on rolls as a sort of glue.

EGGS

The egg is still one of the best and most complete sources of protein, regardless of all the negative publicity it has received. Most of this publicity revolves around cholesterol and the high levels found in the egg yolk (approximately 200mg). New major studies have recently shown that consuming egg yolks do not appreciably elevate blood cholesterol levels. One of these studies related the substance lecithin found naturally in eggs as a factor, which may help neutralize some of the egg's cholesterol. Recommendations are still to limit egg consumption to no more than 4-5 eggs per week.

- There are three grades of eggs: U.S. Grade AA, U.S. Grade A, and U.S. Grade B. Grade B eggs are usually used by bakeries and commercial food processors. All egg cartons that are marked "A" or "AA," are not officially graded. Egg cartons must have the USDA shield as well as the letter grade.

Science of the Inner Egg

When eggs are laid they begin to change in a number of ways. The most significant to the cook is that the pH (acid/base balance) of both the yolk and the white changes. Eggs "breathe" and release low levels of carbon dioxide even after they are laid. The carbon dioxide is dissolved in the internal liquids and causes changes in the pH of the egg. The older the egg the more changes that occur. The yolk and the white tend to increase in alkalinity with time, the yolk going from a slightly acidic 6.0 to an almost neutral 6.6, and the white going from 7.7 to about 9.2. Because of the changes in the alkaline nature of the white, the white tends to change from a strong white color to a very weak almost clear color. Coating the shell of a fresh egg with a vegetable oil will slow this process down. The older egg gets, the more liquid it becomes, which may make it more difficult for the chef to work with as well as the yolk being broken more easily.

Laying the Egg

The making of a chicken egg is really a remarkable feat. The trouble a chicken goes through to make sure we have our eggs for breakfast is the result of her daily reproductive efforts.

A chicken is born with thousands of egg cells (ova) and only one ovary. As soon as the hen is old enough to lay eggs, the ova will start to mature usually only one at a time. If more than one matures then the egg will have a double-yolk.

Since chickens will not produce any more ova when their ova supply is depleted: they stop laying eggs and end up in the pot. The liver continually synthesizes fats and proteins to be used in the egg and provides enough nutrients for the embryo to survive the incubation period of 21 days. The eggshell is 4% protein and 95% calcium carbonate. The shell is porous and will allow oxygen in and expels carbon dioxide.

♦ If an egg cracks when being boiled, just remove it from the water and while it is still wet, pour a generous amount of salt over it, let it stand for 20 seconds, wrap it in tin foil, twirl the ends and replace it in the boiling water.

Chefs are very fussy about the eggs they use for baking. They know that eggs, especially the whites are better during certain times of the year. They may even take frozen eggs and use those for baking cakes. The reason is that it makes for a better firmer-bodied cake.

♦ If you have used the egg whites for a recipe and want to save the yolks for a day or two, try storing them in a bowl of water in the refrigerator. When you break open an egg with two yolks it usually is produced from a young hen whose laying cycle has not fully matured.

♦ Egg whites contain more than ½ the protein of the egg and only 25% of the calories.

♦ The one thing the chef never does is to try and separate egg whites from the yolk when the eggs were cold right from the refrigerator.

♦ Eggshells should be dull, not shiny, if the egg is really fresh. In very fresh eggs the yolk will hardly be visible through the white.

♦ White or brown eggs are identical in nutritional quality and taste.

♦ Egg whites become firm at 145^{0}F, yolks at 155^{0}F. Eggs should be cooked at a low temperature to guarantee a tender white and smooth yolk.

♦ Egg-coated dishes should be washed in warm water. If you use hot water it will cook the egg into the dish's surface.

When eggs are cold, the whites and yolk are difficult to separate and more likely a broken yolk will result. The adhesive properties of the white and yolk are fairly solidly connected and the surface tension of the yolk is higher adding another difficult factor. When the egg is at room temperature the white and yolk relax and will easily separate.

SCIENCE OF EGG WHITES

It seems that during the chicken molting season and for a few months afterwards "Spring-laid eggs" whip up better and give better strength to the body of the cake.

Bakers will purchase these Spring-laid eggs frozen all year long for their baking needs. The yolks also have a higher percentage of fat and the egg yolks have a richer color. During the spring, the hens have more opportunity to get fresh green fodder, which makes the difference.

- The quality of eggs can easily be determined by the amount of spread when they are broken. U.S. Grade AA eggs will have the smallest spread, will be somewhat thick, very white and have a firm high yolk. U.S. Grade A, eggs will have more spread and a less thick white. U.S. Grade B eggs will have a wider spread, a small amount of thick white, and probably a flat enlarged yolk.
- When preparing any dish that calls for egg whites only such as a meringue, remove all traces of egg yolk with a Q-tip or edge of a paper towel, before trying to beat. The slightest trace of yolk will affect the final results. Vegetable oil on your beater blades will also affect the results.
- The total digestive time for a whole egg is about four hours due to its high fat content.

GET A GRIP
You will never have an egg slip from your grip if you just dampen your fingers a little. The eggs will adhere to your fingers and won't slip away.

- Egg will clean off utensils easier if you use cold water instead of hot water. Hot water tends to cause the protein to bind up and harden.
- To remove an unbroken egg that has stuck to the carton, just wet the carton. If the egg is broken throw it out.
- Fresh eggshells are rough & chalky. Old eggshells are smooth & shiny.
- If you forget to remove eggs to allow them to warm to room temperature, just place them in slightly warm tap water for 10-12 minutes.
- The twisted strands of egg white are called "chalazae cords." These hold the yolk in place and are more prominent in very fresh eggs.
- The average hen produces about 2,000-4,000 eggs in a lifetime, laying eggs begins 5 months after they are hatched. Most hens tend to average about 225 eggs per year.
- If you want to cool an egg and not have a grayish coating on the yolk, try placing the egg in ice, cold water after cooking.
- Most cookbooks never mention the fact that when eggs are called for in a recipe and the size not mentioned, you should always use large eggs.

- The volume difference in a small egg compared to a large egg may be enough to change the consistency and the quality of the final product.

HOW TO TELL THE AGE OF AN EGG

Science of the Aging Egg

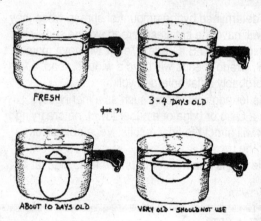

FRESH

dok '91

3 - 4 DAYS OLD

ABOUT 10 DAYS OLD

VERY OLD - SHOULD NOT USE

Using a large bowl, fill the bowl ¾ quarters with cold water. Drop an egg in, not from too high up or it won't matter. If the egg goes to the bottom and lies on its side it's fresh. If it stays on the bottom at a 45-degree angle it is about 3-5 days old. If it stays on the bottom and stands up at a 90-degree angle (straight up) it is about 10-12 days old. If it floats to the top it is bad and should not be opened in the house. Bury it in the backyard and use it for fertilizer and if you are very lucky, you may grow an eggplant (LOL).

When an egg ages it develops a degree of buoyancy as the yolk and the white lose moisture and the air pocket gets larger. Eggshells are porous and moisture will go through the shell.

Black Eggs

Aluminum bowls and cookware tend to darken an egg due to the aluminum reacting with the egg protein.

Green Eggs

Science of Green Eggs

When eggs are overheated or cooked for a prolonged period of time there is a chemical change that will take place. This change tends to combine the sulfur in the egg with the iron in the yolk, which form the harmless chemical ferrous sulfide. This reaction is more prevalent in older eggs since the elements are more easily released. Eggs should never be cooked for any reason more than 12-15 minutes to avoid this problem.

The stamped grade on a carton of eggs is no indication of how fresh an egg is. Eggs can take anywhere from two days to three weeks to get from the hen to the market. The date on the egg carton is based on the day the eggs were packed and not when they were laid.

EGGS, AS BINDER

Many recipes call for eggs to be used as binders to hold everything together; however, egg yolks are high in fat. Egg yolks can be eliminated in almost all recipes and it is not necessary to add additional whites to replace them. If additional whites are used it will make many dishes dry and tough. If the egg yolks are needed for flavor, just eliminate some of them to reduce the fat.

EGGS, BEATEN

If you want to increase the volume of beaten eggs, try using a bowl with a small rounded bottom. This reduces the work area and creates the larger volume.

EGGS, BOILED

HUMPTY DUMPTY PROBLEM

When boiling eggs chefs never let the water go to the boiling point. Almost everyone I have ever seen boiling eggs tends to allow the water to boil and if they are boiling more than one egg at a time, one or more usually end up with a crack and the white coming out.

Need A Lift?

When removing eggs from boiling water; don't bother using a slotted spoon since a small shift in balance could result in losing an egg on the floor. Try using a pasta server spoon that has sides for cradling the egg and providing some security for the egg.

Eggs that are to be used for boiling must always be at room temperature to assure that the cooking timing will be accurate. If you have to use them from the refrigerator, add 2 minutes to the cooking time.

Soft Boiled

Place the eggs in a pan and cover with cold water about 1-inch over the egg and bring it to a boil over high heat. Lower the heat, so that the bubbles just barely break the surface then simmer for 3 minutes.

Medium Boiled

Same as soft boiled but allow 4½ minutes.

Hard Boiled

- Same as soft boiled but allow 10 minutes.
- You can prevent boiled eggs from cracking by rubbing a cut lemon on the shell before cooking.
- Boiled eggs should be cooled at room temperature before refrigerating them in an open bowl.
- To make the eggs easier to peel, just add a small amount of salt to the water to toughen the shell then rinse them immediately in cold water.
- Another trick is to add a teaspoon of white vinegar to the water while the eggs are being boiled this may also help prevent cracking. The vinegar tends to soften the shell allowing more expansion.

- However, they may not be as easy to peel. To remove the shell from a hard-boiled egg, roll it around on the counter with gentle pressure then insert a teaspoon between the shell and the egg white and rotate it.
- Always cool a hard-boiled egg before you try and slice it, it will slice easier and not fall apart.
- Hardboiled eggs will slice easier if you use wax-free dental floss.
- After you make hard-boiled eggs, never place them in cool water once they are peeled.

Hard Boiled or Raw

To tell if an egg is hard-boiled or raw, just spin it, if it wobbles it's raw. If it spins evenly then it's hard-boiled. If you need to store raw eggs with hard-boiled eggs and want an easy way to tell them apart, just add a small amount of balsamic vinegar to the cooking water. The eggshells will come out of the water with a slight brown tint that is easy to distinguish from the raw eggs. You can also just add a few drops of vegetable coloring to the water.

- Hard-boiled eggs will last under refrigeration for 1 week.
- Eggs have a thin protective membrane that if removed or damaged and placed in water or a sealed container, may allow bacteria to grow.
- Hard, boiled eggs should never be frozen since egg white changes texture and becomes tough. When freezing fresh eggs always break the yolk. The whites can be frozen alone and the yolks can be frozen alone unless you plan on using them at the same time.
- If you store your hard-boiled eggs with your fresh eggs, try adding a small amount of vegetable coloring to the boiling water and it will be easier to tell them apart.

Science of Egg Boiling

When an egg is laid it is very warm and tends to cool down, and as it does, the yolk and white cools and shrinks. This cooling and shrinkage result in an air space at the eggs large (non-tapered) end. This air pocket or trapped gas tends to expand as the egg is heated in the boiling water and the gas has no place to go except out of the shell resulting in a crack. When this occurs, the albumen escapes and solidifies in the boiling water almost immediately. To relieve the problem all you have to do is make a small hole in the large end with a pushpin, one with a small plastic end and a small short pinpoint. It is easy to handle and will not damage the egg nor release the white. Also, if you add a small amount of vinegar to the water it will soften the shell and a small amount of salt will harden the shell.

Some eggshells have been found to contain "micro-cracks," which allow harmful bacteria to enter. If you find a cracked egg in the carton when you get home throw it out, it is probably contaminated. Eggshells should be dull and not shiny if the egg is really fresh. In very fresh eggs the yolk will hardly be visible through the white.

ALL CRACKED UP OVER EGGS

To keep the whites where they belong when an egg cracks during boiling, just add some vinegar to the boiling water.

EGGS, FOLDING IN

When you make a cake and you need to fold in the eggs, it can be a difficult process and needs to be done just right. Chefs have a great technique down perfectly and never use a mixer because they don't want to break the air bubbles. The beaten whites will not collapse if you stir using this method.

Science of Folding-In Egg Whites

Use the edge of a large rubber spatula and cut down through the center of the mixture to the bottom of the mixing bowl. Draw the spatula up the side of the bowl then turn it over and cut down through the center of the mixture again. You need to then turn the bowl a quarter turn each time and continue folding and never stirring. This needs to be done until there are no streaks in the mixture. If you have small lumps of egg whites, you have beaten too vigorously. If you over beat the egg whites, just add another egg white and remix.

EGGS, FRIED

Fried eggs should have the white hard and the yolk may be soft. The internal temperature will be approximately 140^{0}F.

To serve the family something different, try cooking fried eggs in cookie cutters in different shapes. Just place them in the pan and break the egg into the cookie cutter. Spray the cutter after it is placed into the pan so that the eggs will be easy to remove.

A No No

Never fry eggs, scramble eggs or make an omelet in salted butter since it causes the eggs to stick to the pan. It is best to use unsalted butter or vegetable oil.

- ♦ To guarantee a white film over the eggs when frying, place a few drops of water in the pan just before the eggs are done and cover the pan.
- ♦ When frying an egg, try adding a small amount of flour to the pan to prevent splattering.

◆ If you have a problem with fried eggs splattering, try adding a small powdering of cornstarch to the pan before adding the eggs. The butter should be very hot before adding the eggs. Reduce the heat once the eggs are in the frying pan.

EASY DOES IT

To prepare old-fashioned fried eggs, chefs will use 1½ tablespoons of unsalted butter per egg. Spoon the hot butter over the eggs as they cook until the yolk has a white film on them. They never cook eggs over high heat.

Science of Frying Eggs

If you cook over high heat too fast, the whites will toughen. Turn the eggs over for about 3-5 seconds and they will be done perfectly. You can also just cover the eggs after you place them in for about 1 minute and they should be done. Melt the unsalted butter over medium heat and as soon as the butter foams and the foam dies down, the butter's moisture has been evaporated. This is when you add the eggs.

Timing Is Everything

Since fried eggs cook very quickly, seconds can make a difference between a runny yolk and one that is set properly. When you place the eggs in the hot pan one at a time, the first egg will probably be done before the last egg. If you add all the eggs at the same time, they will all be done the same.

Use two small bowls that will hold two eggs each (since most of the time you are cooking for two people) then break the eggs into the bowls. Pour the eggs at the same time into the hot pan for perfect results.

This can also work when making poached eggs and all the eggs need to be placed into the water at the same time. Using small cups, place one egg in each cup and hold two cups with each hand. As soon as the water is ready, lower the lips of the cups in the water at the same time and just tip the eggs into the water.

EGGS, MICROWAVE COOKED

When you microwave eggs, remember that the yolk will cook first. Microwaves are attracted to the fat in the yolk.

When cooking eggs in the microwave remember that whole eggs may explode and when cooking an egg with a whole yolk intact, place a small hole in the yolk with a pin to allow for expansion.

EGGS, OMELET

◆ To make the greatest omelet in the world just make sure that the eggs are at room temperature by leaving them out of the refrigerator for 30 minutes before using them.

- Cold eggs are too stiff for an omelet.
- If you always add a little milk to your omelet, try adding a small amount of water instead. The water will increase the volume at least 3 times more than the milk. The water molecules surround the egg's protein forcing you to use more heat to cook the protein and make it coagulate.
- Another great addition is to add ½ teaspoon of baking soda for every 3 eggs. If you try all these tips you will have the greatest looking omelet and your guests will be impressed.
- If you are going to put cheese in your omelet, never add the cheese to the batter always add the cheese to the omelet at the last second before folding to prevent the omelet from sticking to the pan.
- Make sure that the butter is sizzling before adding the eggs.
- Omelets need to be cooked quickly, which is different from other egg dishes.

EGGS, POACHED

If you have problems with poached eggs breaking up, you may have salted the water. Salt tends to cause the protein to break apart. The white will be more firm in a fresh egg and will prevent the yolk from breaking. Make sure you bring the water to a boil and then to a simmer before adding the egg. If you stir the water rapidly before placing an egg in for poaching, the egg won't spread as much and will stay centered.

Vinegar in Poached Eggs

Add vinegar to the water that you are poaching your eggs in and it will create a slightly acidic medium allowing the eggs to set and retain a more desirable shape as well as helping the whites retain their bright white color. The proper amount of vinegar is 1 teaspoon to 1 quart of water. If you prefer lemon juice will also work at ½ teaspoon to 1 quart of water.

- To repair a crack, remove it from the boiling water and pour a generous amount of salt on the crack while it is still wet. Allow it to stand for 20 seconds then wrap it in aluminum foil and continue cooking it.

Science of Poached Eggs

For the best poached eggs, be sure they are fresh. Older eggs with large air pockets do not poach well. Eggs for poaching should be no more than 3-5 days old. Because of its acidity, vinegar lowers the water's pH factor speeding up the setting of the egg whites before they have a chance to spread too far. The vinegar also makes the whites look more shiny. You must use a quality vinegar and never too much. Use only 1 teaspoon of vinegar to 1 quart of water.

To keep the eggs for a few minutes and stop the cooking, just place them into a pan of cold water to stop the cooking and keep them in shape. Just before you serve them, place them into gently simmering water for about 30 seconds to re-heat them.

- When poaching eggs, add a small amount of butter to the tin or plastic cup before placing the eggs in to prevent them from sticking and the yolks from breaking.
- Poached eggs should be placed on a piece of paper towel before serving to drain off all the liquid.
- Hard-cooked poached eggs can be used in egg salad.

EGGS, POWDERED

If you plan on using egg white powder, use 2 level tablespoons of powdered egg white plus 2 tablespoons of warm water to equal 1 egg.

- Powdered egg whites are easy to use and you don't have to separate the yolk.
- Any recipe that calls for just egg whites, just use egg white powder.
- You don't have to wait until the egg whites come to room temperature.
- They are pasteurized and safe.
- Long shelf life.
- Helps reduce fat and cholesterol in dishes.

EGGS, PROTEIN (cooking of)

Science of Cooking Egg Protein

When egg white protein is cooked the bonds that hold the proteins together unravels and creates a new protein network. The molecules of water that are in the egg are trapped in this new network and as the protein continues to cook the network squeezes the water out. The longer and the more heat that is used, the more water is released and the more opaque the white becomes. If you overcook the egg it will release all its moisture and will have a rubbery texture. The nutritional value of dried out eggs is the same as fresh eggs.

EGGS, RAW

You should never pour raw eggs or yolks into any hot mixture. If you need to add them, add them gradually for the best results. Adding the eggs too quickly may cause the dish to curdle.

Never allow anyone in your family to sample batter if it contains raw eggs. Over 392,000 cases were reported in 2012 and 126 people died. Other problem food sources are sauces that contain raw eggs, homemade eggnog and Caesar salad made the old fashioned way.

Chicken ovaries may be contaminated with salmonella and even though eggs look OK and are not cracked they may still be contaminated.

Freeze raw eggs separated. Egg yolks can be frozen by adding 1 teaspoon of granulated sugar for each six, egg yolks or ½ teaspoon of salt. This will keep the yolks from coagulating. Egg whites are easy to freeze by just placing them into a small bowl or ice cube tray. However, foods with cooked egg whites do not freeze well and the consistency changes.

EGGS, REPAIRING
Undercooked
If you crack open an undercooked egg, just place it in aluminum foil and twirl the ends, then place it back in the water to finish cooking.

EGGS, SAFETY
FDA regulations state that eggs should be refrigerated at all times during shipping and in supermarkets, however, in many instances they will be left on pallets in supermarkets without refrigeration. It is best not to purchase eggs left out since the internal temperature of an egg should never fall below 45^0F and no more than 75% humidity.

EGGS, SCRAMBLED
When preparing scrambled eggs, allows allow 3 eggs per person. Most people eat more eggs when they are scrambled. If other ingredients are added, such as cheese or vegetables than 2 eggs per person is sufficient.

When preparing a number of omelets or batches of scrambled eggs, always wipe the pan with a piece of paper towel dipped in table salt after every 2-3 batches. This eliminates the problem of the eggs sticking to the pan.

For the best scrambled eggs, you need to cook them slowly over a medium-low heat starting them in a cool pan.
H_2O TO THE RESCUE
If you want to prepare the fluffiest scrambled eggs you ever served, just add 1-2 teaspoons of water per egg as you are mixing the eggs.

Science of Scrambled Eggs
When you add water to the eggs, the water turns to steam and gives the scrambled eggs a light, fluffy texture. The eggs will also turn out moister since the protein can bind more water molecules as the eggs cook. If you want the ultimate, try using cream instead of water.

EGGS, SEPARATING YOLKS
An easy method of separating egg yolks from the whites is to poke a small hole in the pointed end and drain the white out. If you want the yolk then just break it open.

An even easier method is to use a small funnel placed over a measuring cup. This works very well, just don't break the yolk. Never separate eggs by passing the yolk back and forth from one half of the shell to the other. Bacterial contamination may be present on the shell.

EGGS, SHELF LIFE

The refrigerator shelf life of an egg is approximately 2-4 weeks depending on storage methods. You should always store eggs in a closed container or the original carton for longer life and to avoid the egg absorbing refrigerator odors. If they are stored with the large end up they will last longer and the yolk will stay centered. Also, try rubbing a small amount of vegetable oil on the shell to seal it.

Eggs should be stored with the tapered end down. The larger end should be upright to reduce spoilage since it maximizes the distance between the yolk and the air pocket, which may contain bacteria. The yolk is more perishable than the albumin. Even though the yolk is somewhat centered it does have some movement and will move away from any possible contamination.

EGGS, SIZES

WEIGHT OF ONE DOZEN EGGS
Jumbo.......................30 ounces
Extra Large................27 ounces
Large ....24 ounces
Medium ....21 ounces
Small ....18 ounces
Pee Wee (bakery eggs)15 ounces

CALORIES
1 Large egg = 80 calories
1 Egg white = 20 calories
1 Egg yolk   = 60 calories

MEASURING EGGS
1 Large egg (2oz)   = ¼ cup
1 Med. egg (1¾ oz)= 1/3 cup
1 Small egg (1½oz)= 1/6 cup

EGGS, STORING OF

THE UPSIDE DOWN EGG
When you bring eggs home from the supermarket always open the cartons and make sure that all the eggs are stored with the larger end up and the tapered end down. Also, when I was growing up and looked in the refrigerator, there was always an egg carton in the refrigerator and I always wondered why, since there was an egg holder in the refrigerator door, which made it easier to get at the eggs.

Science of Storing Eggs

If the eggs are stored with the wide end up they will last longer since it will maximize the distance between the yolk and the air pocket in the egg. The air can harbor bacteria and the yolk is more perishable than the white. Even though the yolk is attached by two chalazas holding it centered, there is just enough give to allow it to move away from the air pocket.

Depending on the size of the egg, eggs have between 6,000-16,000 pores and will easily absorb odors from the refrigerator. It is best to store them in their original container or a closed container to keep them fresher. To store and egg for a prolonged period (4-5 weeks) rub vegetable oil on the outside of the shell to seal the pores.

Chefs like to save time and may freeze the egg whites and egg yolks in ice cube trays. The whites and yolks are separated into separate cubicles and then frozen, removed and placed into freezer bags for future use. Remember 1 large yolk = 1 tablespoon and 1 large white = 2 tablespoons.

EGGS, SUBSTITUTIONS

You can substitute 2 egg yolks for 1 whole egg when making custards, cream pie filling, and salad dressings.

You can also substitute 2 egg yolks plus 1 teaspoon of water for 1 whole egg in yeast dough or cookie batter. If you come up one egg short when baking a cake, substitute 2 tablespoons of mayonnaise. This will only work for one egg.

EGG SIZE SUBSTITUTIONS

SUBSTITUTE

Extra	Large	Medium	Small
1 Large	1	1	not recommended
2 Large	2	2	3
3 Large	3	4	4
4 Large	3	5	6
5 Large	4	6	7
6 Large	5	7	8

When preparing any recipe or omelet, try replacing the egg yolks with an equal amount of egg substitute or just reduce the number of yolks.

EGGS, WHIPPED

There are a number of products on the market that sell the egg white only. These are good products and an excellent source of protein. The product should be pasteurized to be safe.

These products can be used for baking and substituted for whole eggs in omelets and other dishes. They can be frozen and are best utilized by the body when cooked instead of consumed raw.

Science of Whipping Egg Whites

Copper bowls should always be used when beating egg whites. Copper tends to absorb the heat friction caused by the beating, which tends to stop the formation of the air pockets needed to form bubbles of air. The copper will also release ions during the beating process that causes the protein in the mixture to become stiffer. If the copper bowl is used, you will not need to use cream of tartar.

Next best is stainless steel; however, a pinch of cream of tartar needs to be added to accomplish the stabilization. Make sure either bowl has a rounded bottom to allow the mixture to fall easily to the bottom and come into equal contact with the mixing blades. Also, be sure that there is not even a trace of egg yolk in your mixture. The slightest hint of fat has a negative effect on the final product. Remove any yolk with a piece of the eggshell.

Never use a plastic bowl for whipping egg whites since plastic has the tendency to hold on to fats. The salt and cream of tartar are added after you beat the eggs and they just barely start to become foamy. The proportion of sugar is important: 2 tablespoons per white for soft meringue and 4 tablespoons per white for hard meringue. Never add the sugar until the foam starts to appear.

When egg white protein is cooked the bonds that hold the proteins together unravels and creates a new protein network. The molecules of water that are in the egg are trapped in this new network and as the protein continues to cook the network squeezes the water out. The longer and the more heat that is used, the more water is released and the more opaque the white becomes. If you overcook the egg it will release all its moisture and will have a rubbery texture. The nutritional value of dried out eggs is the same as fresh eggs.

I could not believe all the trouble some chefs go through to make sure that there was not even the slightest trace of yolk in the vicinity when they are going to whip eggs whites. It seems that even a slight trace of yolk (the fats the problem) will stop egg whites from whipping. They also use a large whisk with many wires to provide as much air as possible to enter the egg whites.

THE FOUR STAGES OF WHIPPED EGG WHITES

It is really important to know when to stop beating egg whites. Recipes usually indicate a stage to which the foam should be beaten.

FOAMY WHITES

The whites should be lightly whipped to just barely frothy and still maintain a fluid consistency. It will consist of large bubbles on the surface that easily pop.

This foam will not hold any peaks as the whisk is lifted from it.

SOFT PEAKS

The foam is moist, shiny and bright white and when the whisk is lifted out, the foam forms a weak peak that will fall over and curl gently. The foam will flow if the bowl is tilted.

STIFF PEAKS

The foam can maintain a glossy sheen and is able to hold an upright peak as the whisk is removed. It will not flow or maybe just barely if the bowl is tilted. When this point is reached, the foam is at its maximum volume.

OVERBEATEN WHITES

It happens more frequently when using an electric mixer. The foam will appear dry and granular. When this occurs you can save it by adding another egg white and beat until you have the desired peaks.

Creating a Foam

Many recipes call for beaten egg whites. They are used to provide rising power, lightness and puffiness to foods. Creating foam is an art and there are many pitfalls that you should be aware of, as well as methods of repairing a foam problem. The following are some of the more common problems and their solutions:

- The slightest bit of fat can affect the foam developing and retaining its shape. This usually is a problem of a small bit of egg yolk being left in with the whites.
- Adding a small amount of an acid, such as lemon juice or cream of tartar will cause the volume to increase.
- Eggs will develop better foam if they are allowed to remain at room temperature for 1 hour before they are used.
- Never over beat, the more you beat, the more the whites will look dry and curdled.
- Add a small amount of sugar and the whites will remain stiffer for a longer period.
- Beating too much will cause the peaks to be too fragile.

Healthy Alternative

A number of companies are selling egg whites. These products can be used the same as you would ordinarily use eggs. However, if your recipe calls for egg yolk, you cannot use only the whites in most instances. If you are making scrambled eggs or any dish that calls for egg whites alone there should be no problem using these products. Be sure the label states that the product is pasteurized and it is salmonella-free. The pasteurization process does utilize high heat so that the products may not respond as well as the fresh egg whites in certain recipes.

EMULSIFICATION

Emulsification is the process of combining two liquids that do not normally wish to come together. A good example of this is oil and water. Oil and vinegar is another example and if they are used to make salad dressing you know that it takes a bit of shaking to bring them together before you can pour the dressing out of the bottle.

When the oil and vinegar solution is shaken the oil is broken into small droplets for a short period of time.

There are a number of emulsifying agents that help keep the liquids in suspension. One of the best emulsifiers for oil and vinegar is lecithin. Lecithin, a natural fat emulsifier, can be obtained at any health food store in ampoules and only one or two of the ampoules emptied into the mixture will place the ingredients into suspension. Lecithin is found naturally in egg whites, which is why egg whites are used in many sauces to keep the ingredients in suspension.

ENTERTAINING

The average-size partygoer at a cocktail party (with no meal included) will gobble-up 10-12 mouthfuls. A large-size partygoer (over 200 pounds) will consume 20-25 mouthfuls. If a meal is included you only have to figure 4-5 mouthfuls. If you are having a wine and cheese gathering, figure 4 ounces of cheese per person. If you're having dip and crackers or chips, you need to figure one cup of dip will serve 8 people, providing you are serving other small goodies.

One quart of dip will provide you with 150-170 cracker-sized servings. If you're having a picnic, figure on 3 beers or soft drinks per person.

FFFFF

FATS, STORAGE OF

STORING FATS IN THE REFRIGERATOR

Fats that chefs have around the kitchen are always stored in the refrigerator since they will last longer and not get rancid.

Science of Refrigerating Fats

When oils are refrigerated and become cloudy, it is due to the buildup of harmless crystals. Manufacturers will sometimes pre-chill the oils and remove the crystals in a process known as "winterization." These oils will remain clear when refrigerated. Lard has larger fat crystals than butter, which has a lot to do with the texture of these fats and is controlled during processing. The large fat crystals in lard will make it the choice for a number of baked goods where a flakier crust is preferred, especially pies. Moderation in eating these lard products, however, is the key word.

FATS VS OILS

The difference between fats and oils is basically that fat is usually solid at room temperature and oil is liquid. If the fat is from an animal source, it is usually solid and from a vegetable source, it is usually liquid. However, all fats are similar in their chemical structure and vary more due to their type of fat saturation. Shortening is solid fat at room temperature and can be either an animal or vegetable fat. The best shortenings will have the word "pure" on the label. If the word pure is not on the label, the product may contain a number of additives that are capable of lowering the smoke point.

Fats and oils should be as pure as possible to obtain the best results when baking or preparing any dish.

FATTY FOOD TEST

THE NAPKIN TEST
There is an easy method of determining whether baked good products have a high fat level, which is simply called the "napkin test." Place the baked goods in question on a paper napkin or a piece of paper towel, if the product leaves a grease stain it contains more than three grams of fat. If you would like to reduce the fat content of pizza, dab a napkin on the surface of the pizza to absorb some of the fat.

FENNEL

Fennel is a member of the parsley family and looks like a very plump bunch of celery. Fennel tastes like "anise" and has a sweet flavor.

It is very low in calories, can easily be substituted for celery, and is high in vitamin A, calcium and potassium. The bulbs should be firm and clean with fresh-looking leaves. If any brown spots are seen, avoid the fennel. It tends to dry out quickly and should be wrapped and used within 3-4 days.

- ◆ Fennel is usually used in pork dishes, squash, Italian sausage, sweet pickles, fish dishes, candies, cabbage, pastries, oxtail soup, and pizza sauce.
- ◆ When you choose fresh fennel, make sure you choose clean, crisp bulbs that are not browning.

- The stalks and greenery should be removed before using.
- Fennel bulbs and the base may be used raw in salads.
- Fennel is commonly used as a garnish.

Chopping Fennel Seeds

The small hard fennel seeds are almost impossible to chop up and tend to fly all over the place. If you need to chop them up, try placing them on a cutting board and pour a small amount of water or oil on them to just barely moisten them before chopping away.

FIGS

Figs can be traced back to ancient Egypt and are one of the oldest known fruits. The majority of the figs grown are sold dried, less than 10% reach markets in their original form. Figs were brought to California by the Spaniards and most are still grown in California. The most common fig found in supermarkets is the Calimyrna. Figs are pollinated by a small fig wasp which if killed off by pesticides ends the crop. Dried figs have 17% more calcium than milk but are very high in calories for their size.

As Tenderizer

It is a fact that figs have the ability to tenderize meats. Fresh figs contain the chemical "ficin" which is called a proteolytic enzyme, one that is capable of breaking down proteins with a similar action to that of "papain" from papayas or "bromelain" from pineapples. Ficin is effective in the heat ranges of 140-160^{0}F, which is the most common temperature to simmer stews.

If fresh figs are added to the stew it will help to tenderize the meat and impart an excellent flavor. However, if the temperature rises above 160^{0}F, "ficin" is inactivated. Canned figs will not work since they have been heated to very high temperatures during their sterilization process. Varieties include Black Mission, Kadota, Calimyrna, Brown Turkey, and Smyrna.

Figs do not like frost and the best method to protect them is to cover the branches that will bear fruit with a plastic bag before a frost appears. If you tie small cans filled with a few stones to each of the bottom of the bags they cannot blow off.

FILE POWDER

A spice used by Cajun chefs is made from ground sassafras leaves to thicken as well as adding a thyme-like flavor to gumbos. The spice tends to become stringy when boiled and needs to be added just before serving.

FISH

The popularity of fish has risen since the 1980's and more varieties of fish have become available. Consumption of fish in 2011 averaged 27.9 pounds per person. More fish than ever are now raised in aquaculture fish farms. The fats in fish are high in polyunsaturated fat and contain the omega-3 fatty acids that may protect us from heart attacks by keeping the blood from coagulating too easily.

Studies show that even canned or frozen fish retain most of their omega-3 fatty acids. However, many fish and shellfish may still harbor certain bacteria and parasites. Cooking is a must for fish and shellfish since they should never be eaten raw. Also, never consume the skin or visible fat on fish as most of the contaminants, if present, will be located there.

NIGHTMARE TIME

The one thing that always bothered me when chefs serve whole fish was staring at the head of the fish. However, they tell me that it was better to serve it that way to make it taste better.

Science of Serving Whole Fish

To serve the tastiest fish ever, you will need to leave the head and the tail intact. This allows the juices to remain in the flesh and they won't leak out very much. If you wish to remove them just before serving that is no problem, but you should cook the fish with the head and tail. The head and tail do contain quite a bit of flavor and are excellent when used in a sauce, fish soup or stock. Also, serving the fish with the head and tail intact will keep the fish warmer when eating it.

SALTY HANDS

When working with fish, chefs usually coat their hands with salt so they can grip the fish more easily.

Science of the Inner Fish

The meat in the center of the fish usually has a higher fat content and will have a better flavor. The tail area will have a more intense flavor and is better used in fish stew or soup. The fish use their tail for propulsion and is somewhat tougher due to the development of the muscle. To tell if you are getting a piece of fish from the center of the fish, just look for the slight horseshoe shape allowing for the stomach cavity.

FILLET SKINNING

To make a difficult job of removing the skin from a fillet easy, just start at the thin end of the fillet and slide a fillet knife between the skin and the flesh until you can grab onto the skin. Use a piece of paper towel to grab onto the skin so that it won't slip out of your hand and use this as a "handle" to steady the skin as you finish cutting the skin away.

SHINY FISH

Sometimes a fish in the market will have a somewhat shiny sheen, which is something chefs tend to shy away from since they don't know whether it was from bacterial decay or chemicals used to preserve the moisture in the fish.

195

Science of Shiny Fish

Sometimes the shiny sheen is caused by bacterial decay, but usually it is the result of the chemical tripolyphosphate ("Tripoli") being used by fishermen and seafood processors to preserve the moisture in the fish. The fish may be soaked for 3-4 hours in the Tripoli solution with the reaction resulting in retarding water loss. Water loss is a result of natural loss of water from the protein when the fish dies.

When the fish dies the protein structure contracts and loses its water-retention ability. Tripoli has the ability to increase the tissue pH resulting in the protein's molecular structure unfolding and increasing its ability to retain water. If the fish can retain water weight, it will weigh more when it hits the market and the fisherman makes more money. Tripoli can provide an increase of 5-10% water weight allowing the fisherman or processor to sell water.

MIDDLE IS BEST

When chefs cut up a fish to serve, I noticed that they only used the center portion of the fish and saved the tails for soup. I didn't notice any difference in the meat, but I'm sure there was a reason for doing this.

Science of Seeing Spots

If a fish was handled roughly when it was caught or after it was processed and the fillet removed, there is a possibility that the damage can be seen as little red spots or bruises. The damage may also be done at the market if the fillet was not handled properly. The bruises ruin the aesthetic appeal of the fish, can cause the deterioration of the surrounding and can even affect the flavor of the fillet.

BIGGER IS BETTER

The one thing I hated when I ate freshwater fish was putting up with the tiny bones and trying to get rid of them as I ate. Since my whole family has this problem they rarely serve fish from freshwater and almost always served ocean fish since they have larger bones, which was easier to remove.

Science of Fish Bones

The ocean water has a high concentration of minerals, especially salt, which fresh water doesn't have. Fish have a better degree of buoyancy in salt water, allowing ocean fish to have a heavier bone structure. Freshwater fish have a more delicate bone structure to compensate for the lack of buoyancy.

LE PEW

Chefs have a secret to getting rid of strong flavor in uncooked fish. Simply, sprinkle a small amount of ginger root juice on the fish, both inside and outside.

LEMON TRICK

When you are grilling fish and are using a lemon sauce to baste the fish, try spearing half a lemon with a long fork and dipping that in the sauce to baste the fish or just to coat the fish with lemon juice.

HERE A BONE, THERE A BONE

Next time you make a salmon fillet, which has small pin bones just place the fillet over the side on an inverted bowl large enough to handle the whole fillet and the pin bones will protrude through the skin. To remove the bones use a pair of pliers or tweezers.

STRONG SWIMMERS

While chefs chose different fish depending on the dish they were preparing, they always try to choose a river fish rather than a lake fish whenever possible.

Science of Where Fish Live

River fish tend to exercise more than lake fish, which make flesh more flavorful. River fish must swim against the current, while lake fish just lazily move around. This is why trout are so flavorful! Cold-water fish will also have more flavor, since they have more of a fat layer, which contributes flavor.

FISH, BAKING

If you are going to bake fish, try wrapping it in aluminum foil with a sprig of dill and a small amount of chopped onion. Another method is to wrap the fish in a piece of well-oiled cheesecloth. This will make it easier to remove the fish from the pan.

LOW FAT, BAKED "FRIED FISH"

It is possible to prepare low fat "fried fish" with using all the fat to fry the fish in. Just dredge them in seasoned flour; dip the fish in egg yolk that has been beaten with a small amount of water and then coat them with breadcrumbs. The fish are then placed in a shallow baking pan that has been lightly greased or sprayed with a vegetable spray. Dot the fish with small dollops of butter or margarine and bake for 6-10 minutes per inch of thickness or until the flesh is opaque.

STAB THAT FISH

Chefs have a sure-fire fast method of telling if the fish was cooked through without using a thermometer.

Science of Cooked Fish

If you are unsure of whether the fish is cooked through or not, chefs have an easy method. Just insert a metal knife into the thickest part of the flesh and wait for 5 seconds before removing the knife. If the knife feels hot, the fish is fully cooked. Be sure that the tip of the knife does not go through and touch the pan.

The flesh of a fish is normally translucent. When it turns opaque and a solid white color it means that the protein has coagulated and the fish is fully cooked. If you wish to be really sure than you will have to cut into the center at the thickest part with a fork and if the flesh flakes, it means that there was sufficient heat to gelatinize the collagen in the myocommata (fish connective tissue). Fish flesh contains very thin, parallel rows of muscle fibers that are held together by the connective tissue. It is these separate sheets of muscle fibers that flake.

FISH, BARBECUING

If you are going to broil, barbecue, or grill fish, be sure and purchase fish steaks that are at least 1 inch thick. Fish will dry out very quickly and the thicker the better, especially for barbecuing. The skin should be left on fillets when grilling, then remove it after cooking. When frying fish, make sure that the surface of the fish is dry.

FISH, BROILING

- ♦ Choose fish that are 1-inch thick to avoid the outer fish cooking before the insides are done.
- ♦ Broiled fish retain their shape better if broiled with their skins on. The skin is easily removed after it has been cooked.
- ♦ The fish should be 4-6 inches from the heat source. The thicker the fish the farther the distance.
- ♦ You do not have to turn the fish when broiling.

FISH, CHOOSING FRESH

Skin

The skin should always have a shiny look to it and when finger pressure is applied it should easily spring back to its original shape. The meat should be firm to the touch with no visible blemishes. Never buy fish if the skin has any dark discoloration.

Eyes

When you look into the fish eyes they should be bulging and not sunken into the head, which is a sign of a dried out fish. The eyes should also be clear and not cloudy.

If the fish winks at you this is a very good sign.

Scales

The scales should not be falling off. If you notice loose scales don't buy the fish. The scales should also have a healthy bright and shiny appearance.

Gills

The gills must look clean with no sign of any slime. Their healthy color is a reddish-pink. Gray gills are a sign of an old fish that has seen better days.

LOOK INTO THEIR EYES

When it comes to choosing a fresh fish, I am surprised that chefs don't use a magnifying glass. They are really picky and want to make sure that the fish is as fresh as possible.

While there are many ways to tell the age of a fish, most chefs prefer to use their gills as the best indicator.

COLD STRORAGE

My grandmother only made fish once a week and always went to the market to purchase the fish a day or two ahead of time. She did not like to freeze fish, unless she knew that the fish were freshly caught and had been gutted immediately after it was caught.

Odor

A fresh fish never smells "fishy." If the fish does have a strong odor about it, it is probably from the flesh decomposing and releasing the chemical compound "trimethylamine." Seafood should be as fresh as possible, usually no more than 2-3 days out of the water.

Science of Fish Gills

The gills are the fish respiratory organs and blood is pumped through the gills, absorbing oxygen from the water. During this process, hemoglobin in the blood undergoes a change, which turns it bright red. If the fish was stored properly on ice, the gills will remain bright red for about 2-3 hours or more.

However, oxidation will start taking place after that and the hemoglobin will change color from the bright red to a brownish red and then turn grayish. When the gills turn gray, the fish may develop an off-odor. Sometimes the gills are removed, making it harder to spot a fresh fish; however, sunken eyes are another sign of an older fish.

Science of Storing Fish

When a fish dies the digestive enzymes erode the alimentary canal walls and get into the flesh. The digestive enzymes in fish are more potent than land animals since they have to break down food supplies, which may be other small fish including their bones. If a freshly caught fish is not gutted soon after it was caught, the digestive enzymes as well as potent bacteria will thrive.

The bacteria are present both inside and on the skin. Freezing a fish may not eliminate the bacteria problem, even at low freezing temperatures. Freezing will also affect the flavor and texture of fish. Fish are also higher in unsaturated fat, which oxidizes faster than saturated fat and will cause rancidity faster than beef.

FISH, CHOOSING FROZEN
Odor
If frozen fish has an odor it has probably thawed and been re-frozen. When it is thawed it should hardly have any odor.

Skin
Be sure that the skin and flesh are frozen solid and that there is no discoloration or soft spots. The skin should be totally intact with no areas missing.

Wrappings
The wrapping should be intact with no tears or ice crystals and be sure that the fish is frozen solid.

FISH, CLEANING
The sooner a fish is gutted the better. The enzymes in a fish's gut tend to breakdown fish very quickly if allowed to remain for too long a period. They are very aggressive and very powerful, which is one reason why fish is easier to digest than any other form of meat. When storing fish you need to remember that the muscle tissue in fish is high in glycogen, which is their energy source. When the fish is killed this carbohydrate is converted into lactic acid, which is usually an excellent preservative; however, the fish tends to use up too much of its energy source thrashing around when it is caught trying to escape.

Another problem with lengthy storage is that certain bacteria tend to be located outside of the digestive tract unlike that of beef and will remain active even below the freezing point.

If you need to scale a fish, try rubbing white vinegar on the scales and then allow it to sit for about 10 minutes.

FISH, COOKING TEMPERATURES
Chefs are very fussy about cooking temperatures when cooking fish. The following are recommendation:

Poaching......................................	180^0-212^0F
Pan Broiling, Pan Frying, Baking....	325^0F
Frying...	360^0F
Broiling...	450^0F

FISH, FILLET
Fillets are so thin, that they cook through in a very short period of time. The meat of the fillet is also so delicate that it has the tendency to flake apart when over cooked or when turned. To avoid the fillet sticking to the pan, just use a liquid oil spray.

A Little Tuck Here, A Little Tuck There

Most fillets taper down to a thin end, which is easily overcooked and too well done to be very appetizing. Chefs, however, have a way of minimizing the overcooking problem by folding the thin tailpiece over so that the fillet is an even thickness.

Be sure and cook it folded side up for the best results.

If you see red spots on fish fillets, it means that the fish has been bruised and has been handled roughly. This may occur from roughly throwing the fish around when it is caught or it has been poorly filleted. Too many bruises may affect the flavor of the fillet by causing deterioration of the surrounding flesh.

If you would like to have a firmer texture to fillets, just soak the fillet in a bowl of 1 quart of water with 2 tablespoons of white vinegar.

FISH, FREEZING

Fish can be frozen in clean milk cartons full of water. When thawing, use the water as a fertilizer for your houseplants.

When fish is frozen it tends to lose some of its flavor. If you place the frozen fish in low-fat milk when it is thawing, some of the original flavor will return. It is recommended by chefs not to completely thaw a frozen fish before cooking since the fish might become mushy. Frozen fish is easier to skin than a fresh one.

FISH, FRYING

Always use the three-container method. The first one should contain regular flour, the second container egg that has been whisked with milk and the third with seasoned flour or cornmeal. The peanut oil should be between 350^0F and 360^0F and no more than 3 inches deep. When the temperature is this high the cold fish will not cause the temperature to drop below 325^0F.

When the oil gets below 325^0F the breading has the tendency to absorb too much oil.

When the fish is golden brown, remove it and place it on a piece of paper towel, patting both sides for a few seconds only then place the fish on a wire rack or serve immediately. If the fish is not eaten or placed on the rack it will begin to steam enough to cause the fish to become soggy.

- ♦ Make sure that the surface of the fish to be fried is very dry.
- ♦ If you use butter or oil with a low smoke point, be sure and add some oil with a high smoke point such as canola oil to the oil to raise the smoke point and avoid an off-taste.
- ♦ Don't bread fish too far in advance or it will end up being soggy!
- ♦ Fried fish can be kept warm in a 275^0F oven on a paper towel lined baking sheet.

FRYING FISH

One of the most important things is the breading for the fish. It has to be just right.

The breading has to be very thick and chefs will use equal amounts of flour and water and also add a few beaten eggs to the batter, which looks a little like cement consistency. Chefs will occasionally add some milk or even beer depending on the flavor they are looking for.

Science of Frying Fish

After you prepare the batter, allow it to remain at room temperature for an hour or more so that the starch in the flour will absorb the liquid. Immerse the fish fillets in the batter then place the fillets on a floured surface for a few minutes, which will allow some of the water to evaporate. Place the fillets in the frying oil heated to 360°F (180°C) and fry. If the batter does not crisp-up, the oil was not hot enough or you placed too many pieces in the fryer. If the batter falls off or the fish falls apart, the batter was not thick enough.

Never reuse oil that has been used for frying fish for any other food, since the oil will pick up a fishy smell and flavor.

CHEF'S SECRETS

- Placing the fillets in the refrigerator helps the breading adhere better.
- Peanut oil tends to bring out the flavor of fish and not overpower it.
- Powdered pepper will not cause the breading to crack.
- Make sure the egg wash coats the fish well or the coating may separate.
- Never crowd the fillets on the cookie sheet for even cooking.
- Use cookie sheet with at least 1-inch sides for even heat reflection.

FISH, GILL REMOVAL

If the fish is caught fresh and prepared shortly afterwards: it not necessary to remove the gills. However, if the fish is not going to be cooked for at least 24 hours after being caught, the gills should be removed. The gills will spoil faster than the rest of the fish and affect the flavor.

FISH, GRILLED

GRILLING WITH A BLOWTORCH

This is by far the easiest and fastest method of cooking fish. It only takes a chef a minute or two to grill each fish. They have a small blowtorch and really like to use it. Unless you have a very powerful grill, grilling fish is not easy.

Science of Grilling Fish

Luckily, chefs have a steady hand when they use the blowtorch and the extreme heat it generates. Just place the fish on a baking sheet, light the torch and slowly bring the flame to the fish. You need to keep the blowtorch moving and never stop on any area. It only takes a minute or so to brown the fish then turn it over and do the other side. The whole procedure for one fish takes 2-3 minutes.

I'm Not Used to Being Dry

Whole grilled fish tend to dry out easily and become overcooked. There is a way to check the flesh without tearing open the skin.

This method will allow you to look into the flesh, as well as producing even-cooking. After the fish has been scaled and gutted, make shallow diagonal cuts about every two inches or so along both sides of the fish from top to bottom starting just behind the dorsal fin

Be Gentle

After the fish has cooked use two metal spatulas and place them under the belly of the fish to easily remove it from the grill and place it on the serving dish or individual plate.

FISH, INSPECTION OF

If you see a seafood product with **"USG INSPECTED"** on the label, report it to authorities, this is not a legal designation. The label should read "Packed under federal Inspection" or (PUFI). This means that it was packed in the presence of or at least inspected by a federal inspector.

FISH, MICROWAVE COOKING

When cooking fish in a microwave, many manufacturers suggest that the fish is cooked at 50% power for more even cooking. Check your instruction manual for your particular microwave oven.

FISH, ODOR

Before handling fish, try washing your hands in plain cold water. Chances are you won't have a fish smell on them afterwards. A small amount of white vinegar placed into the pan you have fried fish in will eliminate the odor.

FISH, POACHED

When poaching fish the contents of the pot are usually somewhat on the alkali side and may react with a pigment in the flesh of the fish known as "flavone." If this is allowed to occur the flesh may become yellow instead of the desired white color. If you add a small amount of wine, lemon juice, or other acid to the pot it will neutralize the alkalinity and render the "flavone" harmless. If the mixture turns slightly acidic it will actually whiten the meat more than it would normally be. Also, when poaching fish keep the fish in single layers and be sure that the poaching liquid reaches the top of the fish.

STEAMING & POACHING

Steaming is done in a steamer, which has a perforated raised platform on which the fish is placed and then water added to the bottom and heated to produce the steam. Poaching has the fish partially in water and utilized steam as well.

Poaching the fish takes place in the oven in a casserole dish with the fish placed on a bed of vegetables and stock added to cover the vegetables.

Science of Steaming & Poaching Fish

Be sure and place the lid on tightly for the best results. The temperature should never rise above 212°F (100°C). Since the temperature is no greater than light boiling, the browning reaction, which is critical in meats for flavor development does not occur and the flavor that results is just that of the fish.

- ♦ Adding a few sprigs of celery leaves to the liquid will reduce the fish odor.
- ♦ If you add 2 teaspoons of lemon juice or white wine to the poaching liquid it will whiten and cause the flesh to be more firm.
- ♦ Poaching liquid can be used in soups and stews.

FISH, PREPARATION OF

Fish and shellfish do not have the extensive connective tissue that is found in land animals. Since the amount is small it doesn't take a lot of cooking to gelatinize the connective tissue with moist heat. If you overcook fish it will toughen the muscle fibers. A fish will be tender when cooked if you leave the head and tail on, this will cause more of the liquid to be retained during the cooking process.

The flesh of a fish is normally translucent. When it turns opaque and a solid white color it means that the protein has coagulated and the fish is fully cooked. If you wish to be really sure than you will have to cut into the center at the thickest part with a fork and if the flesh flakes, it means that there was sufficient heat to gelatinize the collagen in the myocommata (fish connective tissue). Fish flesh contains very thin, parallel rows of muscle fibers that are held together by the connective tissue. It is these separate sheets of muscle fibers that flake.

- ♦ Fish should always be cooked at a relatively low temperature to retain its moisture and provide a more tender product. Fish dries out very quickly and should never be cooked at temperatures exceeding 350°F.
- ♦ To test a cooked fish to see if it is finished cooking, try pressing your finger on the side of the fish. No dent should remain; however, the fish may flake under the pressure.

Science of Turning Shellfish & Fish

Fish and shellfish are difficult for most people to cook since they don't know which to turn and which not to turn when cooking. The meat is more delicate than beef and can be damaged easily or cooked too well done. Turn large or medium shrimp (not small ones), soft-shell crabs, thick fish steaks, large scallops and whole fish. Don't turn lobsters, thin fillets or small fish.

TURNING OVER

One of the more difficult cooking procedures with fish and shellfish is to know when to turn them. Turning makes a difference in the quality of the dish and chefs know just when to turn them.

FISH, REPAIRING

Too Salty

Soak raw fish in cold water for 10-12 minutes, then change the water and store it in water if you are going to cook it soon.

FISH, RIVER

Fish caught in rivers will have more flavor since they must swim against the currents thus exercising more than lake fish. For this reason trout are one of the best eating fishes. Cooler water fishes also have a higher fat content, which tends to make them more flavorful.

FISH, ROASTING

The process of roasting fish is not something everyone should attempt unless your grandmother taught you exactly how to do it. The risk of overcooking and drying the fish out is high. Chefs sometimes roast large pieces of fish on a trivet over a shallow pan and on very high heat. They know by touch when the fish was cooked to perfection.

Science of Roasting Fish

When you roast fish, the oven needs to be at 450°F (230°C). When the fish is done it should have a crisp skin and has not lost its moisture. It takes practice to get the cooking timing just right. You will need to be able to gently press on the fish as soon as you see it becoming dry. If the fish has a burnt taste, it was cooked too long. You may have to protect the fish by placing a piece of aluminum foil on top it.

FISH, SALTWATER

Saltwater fish have thicker more dense bones than freshwater fish, which have thin, minuscule bones. The reason for this is that saltwater has more buoyancy. If you hate fighting the bones, purchase saltwater fish, such as cod and flounder.

FISH, SAUTEING

When sautéing fish it is very easy to burn the fish. Chefs never use butter, instead they use corn oil to sauté and always coat the fish, with either a flour/breadcrumb or ground nut mixture.

FISH, STEAMING (see poaching)

When steaming fish, it should be wrapped in a piece of plain (no design) moistened paper towel. Place the fish in the microwave for 2-3 minutes on each side.

FIVE-SPICE POWDER

Common fragrant spice mixture used in a number of Chinese dishes. It is a combination of cinnamon, aniseed, fennel, black pepper, and cloves.

CHINESE FIVE-SPICE POWDER

3   Tablespoons of ground cinnamon
2   Teaspoons of aniseed
1½ Teaspoon of fennel seed
1½ Teaspoons of black pepper
¾   Teaspoons of ground cloves

Combine all the ingredients in a blender until they are powdered.

FLAMBEING

♦ When you flambé a dish always allow the flame to go out by itself. It is necessary to burn the alcohol for a few seconds to allow any raw alcohol taste to be removed.

♦ Another method of flambéing is to place the alcohol in a metal ladle and either; just warm it before adding it to the dish or actually igniting it and pouring it over the dish.

♦ If you soak sugar cubes in lemon or orange extract they will ignite to provide you with a flaming desert. The alcohol content is just high enough to do the job.

♦ When you flambé be sure and use an alcoholic beverage with high alcohol content so that it will completely burn away and not leave a residue to affect the taste of the dish.

- Choose a beverage that will complement the food.
- Be sure and use a long, handled match to ignite the mixture.
- Ignite the fumes, not the mixture itself.
- Never lean over the dish as you ignite it.
- If it won't ignite, the dish is not hot enough.
- Never blow out the flame or you may end up with the flavor of raw alcohol.
- Once you ignite the food, stir the food to combine the flavors.

FLAVORED OILS

Flavored oils are sold in all food specialty stores and natural food markets; however, it is easy to prepare your own. The best base oils to use are olive, sesame or peanut oil. Any herb or combination of herbs can be added to the oil. All herbs should be thoroughly washed and dried before adding them to the oil since cleanliness is an important factor to reduce the possibility of contaminating the oil. The most common herbs used in flavored oils are garlic, cayenne peppers, fennel, bay leaf, rosemary, oregano, cloves or citrus wedges. The herb needs to remain in the oil until the desired level of flavoring is reached.

When preparing flavored oils, it is necessary to be aware of the potential health problems that are associated with these oils.

The botulism bacteria is commonly found in the soil and brought into the home on vegetables and herbs. Certain precautions need to be taken when preparing flavored oils. Since the botulism bacteria thrives in a low acid, anaerobic atmosphere (low level of oxygen) environment, it is necessary to heat the oil with the herb to 240°F (116°C) to destroy any potential bacteria that may be present. If you are serious about making flavored oils, then you should purchase a book on the subject and adhere to the recipes, preparation and storage methods.

FLOUR

Flour is ground from grains, fruits, vegetables, beans, nuts, herbs, and seeds. Primarily, it is used in muffins, pies, cakes, cookies, and all other types of baked goods.

It is also used as a thickener in soups, gravies, and stews. Many products are "floured" before they are breaded to help the breading adhere better. The production of flour is mainly the "roller process" in which the grain is sent through high-speed rollers and sifters, which crack the grain, separate it from the bran and germ then grind it into the consistency we are used to. Wheat flours are more popular than all other types of flour because of its ability to produce "gluten."
This protein gives wheat its strength and elasticity, which is important in the production of breads.

Place a piece of spearmint gum in the flour to keep the bugs out.

The best flour for all pastries and piecrusts is pasty flour from the South. Unfortunately, this flour is only available in the South and if you can find some it will make the best tasting pastries you ever had. It has just enough tenderness and elasticity to support multiple buttery layers and will not make the dough rubbery. The soil in the South tends to produce this special flour.

ONLY THE BEST FOR THE CHEF

When chefs buy flour, they always buy wheat flour that say **"patent wheat flour"** on the label. This is the best flour you can buy.

- In one pound of flour, there are 3 1/3 cups. In a 5-pound bag, there are 17 cups.
- If you are going to make cookies, biscuits or cakes, be sure and use only cake flour.
- If the dough doesn't need to be stretched too much cake flour is the recommended flour.
- It is almost impossible to purchase flour of any kind without some sort of bug infestation. In fact, the FDA allows an average of 50 insect fragments per 50 grams (about 2 ounces) of grain.
- It is not a danger to your health at this level and is unavoidable. Insects and their eggs may set up residence when the grain is warehoused, during transit, or even in your home.
- To reduce the risk of infestation, just store your grains and flours in the freezer to prevent any eggs from hatching. You can also place a stick of spearmint gum into the container.

Have you ever wondered how to tell the difference in your flours after they have been placed in a flour bin? The plain flour has no taste and the self-rising has a salty taste due to the addition of baking powder.

- Flour can be stored for about 15 months providing you store it in an airtight container and keep it in a cool, dry location. If you want to store it longer, keep it in the freezer but remember to bring the flour to room temperature before you use it.
- When baking, it is important for all the ingredients to be blended well. If the recipe calls for flour to be sifted, try adding other dry ingredients such as the leavening and salt to the flour before you sift.
- Remember, cake flour will make a lighter cake due to its lower gluten content. If you don't have cake flour, try using all-purpose flour, but reduce the amount by 2 tablespoons for each cup of cake flour called for. One of the best recipes for making a light textured cake is to use 50% unbleached cake flour and 50% whole-wheat flour.
- Flour must be at room temperature when you are going to use it. Never use cold flour.

DISSOLVING

Instant flour will always dissolve more readily than regular flour. Regular flour may lump more easily because the exterior of the flour molecule gelatinizes immediately when contact is made with a warm liquid, thus forming a protective shield that blocks the liquid from entering the flour's inner molecules.

This forms lumps with dry insides and wet outsides. Instant flour is produced with irregular shaped molecules with jagged edges so that the liquid can enter. This irregular shape also reduces their ability to clump together to form lumps.

IT'S HOT IN HERE

If you live in a humid climate your flour will absorb moisture easily and adds weight when you try and weigh it out for a recipe. Store your flour in the freezer or in the microwave if you don't have room in the freezer. The microwave is a pain, but removing it when you need the microwave is better than adding moisture to the flour.

SHAK'EM UP FLOUR

When you only need a small amount of flour to dust a cake or small area to work on, this method is great. Just use a funnel to fill a small empty glass saltshaker with flour. Seal the top under the lid with a small piece of cut cardboard and store in the cupboard.

BAG ME SOME FLOUR

If you make cakes very often and do not have a large container to keep your flour in, just place the flour in a large baggie and place the baggie back into the box. When you need flour, it will be much easier to remove flour from a large bag instead of the small opening of the box.

FLOUR, ADDING FAT

Flour will not lump if you add the flour to any fat that is already hot. In fact, you can add flour to any hot liquid without the flour lumping.

FLOUR, ADDING WATER

Regular flour tends to turn into a form of gelatin when it comes into contact with hot water, which tends to block water from entering. Instant flour contains smaller irregular-shaped granules that allow space for the water to enter.

FLOUR, SIFTING OF

- Flour has the tendency to compact during storage and all bakery chefs will sift to achieve a more accurate measurement.
- Occasionally it's somewhat lumpy.
- There may be insects in the flour.
- Some recipes call for other ingredients to be added during sifting to make sure that they are well blended.

FLOUR, TYPES OF

All-Purpose Flour (General-Purpose Flour)

This flour is a blend of hard and soft wheat flour. It has a balanced protein/starch content, which makes it an excellent choice for breads, rolls, and pastries. It may be used for cakes when cake flour is unavailable. Pre-sifted, all-purpose flour has been milled to a fine texture, is aerated, and is best for biscuits, waffles, éclairs, popovers and pancakes.

Bleached Flour

It is white flour with a higher gluten-producing potential than other flours and is used mainly in to make bread.

Bran Flour

It is whole-wheat flour that is mixed with all-purpose white flour and tends to produce a dry effect on baked products.

Bread Flour

Hard-wheat, white flour with high gluten content used to make breads. The flour is unbleached and occasionally conditioned with ascorbic acid. It contains about 14 grams of protein per cup and produces a hearty loaf with a firm crumb.

Bromated Flour

White flour in which bromate is added to the flour to increase the usefulness of the gluten. This will make the dough knead more easily and may be used in commercial bread making plants.

Browned Flour

This is really just heated white flour that turns brown adding color to your recipe.

Brown Rice Flour

Contains rice bran as well as the germ and has a nutty flavor and is commonly substituted for wheat flour.

Cake Flour

Very fine-textured white flour made entirely of soft wheat flour with low protein content, making it best for baking cakes. It tends to produce a soft-textured, delicate moist cake and is highly recommended for sponge and angel food cakes as well as soft cookies.

Corn Flour

Starchy flour; used in sauces as a thickener with a slightly sweet flavor.

Cottonseed Flour

High protein flour; used in baked goods to increase the protein content.

Durham Flour

It is white flour that has the highest protein content of any flour and has the ability to produce the most gluten and usually used in pastas.

Gluten Flour

Very strong white flour: with twice the strength of standard bread flour and used as additive flour with other flours.

Instant Flour

It is white flour that pours and blends easily in cold water and most liquids and is used mainly in sauces, gravies, and stews.

It is rarely used for baking due to its fine, powdery texture.

Science of Instant Flour
The exterior of the regular flour molecule tends to gelatinize immediately when contact is made with a warm liquid and forms a protective shield that blocks liquid from entering the flour's inner molecules, thus forming lumps with dry insides and wet outsides. Instant flour on the other hand is produced with irregular-shaped molecules with jagged edges so that the liquid can easily enter. Also, by having irregular edges it reduces the ability of the flour to clump together forming lumps.

Chefs like instant flour over regular flour. They will tell you that regular flour lumps up too easily.

Pastry Flour
The gluten content is between cake flour and all-purpose white flour and is milled from soft wheat. Pastry flour is best for light pastries and biscuits.

Potato Flour
Provides a thickening texture and used mainly for stews, soups, and sauces.

Rice Flour
Excellent for making delicately textured cakes.

Self-Rising Flour (phosphated flour)
It is soft-wheat, white flour that should not be used in yeast-leavened baked goods. Contains a leavening salt and is low-protein flour. Has the tendency to deteriorate very easily. The flour should be used within 1-2 months of purchase and is recommended for biscuits and quick breads.

Semolina
White flour with a yellow tint made from the endosperm of Durham wheat. It is used mainly in commercial pasta, couscous and some bread and has high protein content.

Soy Flour
It is produced from raw soybeans, which are lightly toasted. It has a somewhat sweet flavor and tend to retain its freshness longer than most baked goods. Soy flour should always be used with, another flour for best results.

White Rice Flour
This type of flour will absorb more liquid and may need additional liquid added as well as increasing the mixing time.

Whole Wheat Flour
Reconstituted flour made from the white flour with the addition of the bran and endosperm. It is sometimes sold as graham flour and has small specks of brown. Whole-wheat flour is more difficult to digest than white flour. It tends to cause flatulence and intestinal upsets in susceptible individuals.

UNBLEACHED VS BLEACHED FLOUR

Unbleached flour would be the best choice for most baking projects that call for one or the other. The unbleached will have a more natural taste since it lacks the chemical additives and bleaching agents used in bleached flour. Bleached flour is also less expensive to produce since it doesn't require aging.

Aging, however, strengthens the gluten content of the unbleached flour. Best not to skimp when buying the unbleached flour as not all companies may allow the flour to age adequately.

YELLOW FLOUR

When flour is processed, it still tends to retain a yellowish tint, which is not very appealing. This yellowish tint is caused by a chemical group called "xanthophylls," which remains in the flour. Bleaching is needed to remove the yellow tint; however, when this is done it destroys the vitamin E in the flour. The yellow color is left in pasta, which is why semolina is never white. The bleaching is done by using chlorine dioxide gas. Higher quality flours are naturally aged thus allowing the air to bleach them.

FOOD, KEEPING HOT

Restaurants use a steam table or heat lamps to keep food hot until it is served. However, at home these methods are not available. My grandmother, however, did have her way of keeping foods hot. To keep most dishes hot, just use a shallow pan and pour boiling water in it then place the pan over one or two burners that are set on their lowest setting. Place the dishes in the water bath.

Fried Foods

Use a cookie sheet or similar sheet with sides; place paper towels on the pan then preheat the oven to 300^0F before turning off the heat and adding the fried foods to the pan.

Hollandaise Sauce

Place the sauce in a wide-mouthed thermos and it will last for 3-4 hours.

Pancakes

Pre-heat the oven to 200^0F and place them on a cookie pan in layers between kitchen towels.

Rice

Place the rice into a double boiler with about 2-inches of gently simmering water in it. Cover the rice with a piece of paper towel and it should last for about 1 hour.

Waffles

Place them on a wire rack in single layers on baking sheets in a 300°F oven. Never stack waffles or they will become soggy. This method will keep them crisp.

Liquid food colorings have a safe shelf life of about 4 years if stored in a cool, dry location.

FOOD PROCESSOR

BUY THE BEST

Best not to buy a budget-priced food processor unless all you use it for is to chop a few vegetables. The lower-priced food processors are all belt driven and do not have the power to do many jobs efficiently, such as chopping meats.

You should purchase a food processor that works with the motor's drive shaft directly rotating the blades.

- ◆ Best to have an extra food processor bowl handy so that you don't have to stop and wash the bowl every time between uses.
- ◆ Be sure and spray the slicing or grating discs with vegetable oil.
- ◆ If you have a problem with the lid going on easily, just spray the inside edges with vegetable oil.
- ◆ If you are working with a metal blade for chopping, try pulsing.
- ◆ When you are pushing foods in, be sure and just use even pressure. Don't force the foods in.
- ◆ If mixing liquids, be careful never to overfill the bowl.
- ◆ Always start with the driest foods.
- ◆ Foods with a similar texture can be chopped or shredded together.
- ◆ The tiny holes in the bottom of the food pusher are for slowly drizzling liquids, such as oil.

FOODS, FLAVOR LOSS

There are a number of foods that should never be refrigerated since the cold causes either loss of flavor, sprouting, or the starch turning to sugar. These include garlic, onions, shallots, potatoes, and tomatoes.

FREEZER BURN

The flavor will be gone from those areas but the product is still safe to eat. Freezer burn makes the surface of the food a lighter color than normal, dries out the food, makes it tough and takes away its flavor. Freezer burn may be caused by a damaged package, food that has been packaged in product that is not moisture or vapor resistant or too much air was allowed into the package.

Before sealing up foods to be frozen, be sure and remove all the air you possibly can.

Poorly wrapped food or slow freezing allows moisture to evaporate and cause freezer burn. This produces a grainy, brown spot on the food that becomes dry and very tough. The area will lose its flavor; however, the food is still safe to eat (if you really want to).

FREEZING SANDWICHES
Frozen sandwiches will thaw by lunchtime. If the bread is buttered prior to freezing, the bread will not become soggy and absorb any filling.

FROZEN JUICE CONCENTRATE
Commercial fruit juice concentrates can be frozen at 0^0F for 1 year and most vegetables for 8 months. Bread can be frozen for 3 months and ground beef for 4 months, roasts and steaks for 1 year. Whole chicken can be frozen for 1 year, while parts are only good for 6 months.

> **If you need to use frozen juice concentrate, just use a potato masher to soften it.**

FRUIT
There are a number of fruits that contain pits, which contain the chemical "amygdalin." If a pit containing this chemical is crushed and heated, it may release the poison cyanide in very small amounts. Fruits such as apricots, apples, pears, cherries, and peaches may contain this chemical.

I WANT MY SWEETS
Fruits can be frozen without sugar. Sugar is only used to maintain the sweet flavor, help retain the texture and stabilize the color and is not needed as a preservative.

- If you want to ripen fruits faster, just place any fruit in a brown paper bag with an apple or a green tomato.
- Both give off harmless ethylene gas, which will speed the ripening of fruits.
- Remember, when you place fruit into the refrigerator it will stop the ripening process. The only exception to the rule is bananas.
- Be sure and wash off waxes that are used to coat fruits and help them retain their moisture. The wax may contain pesticide or fertilizer residues.
- Best to use a vegetable brush on fruits and vegetables before eating the outer skin.
- Try not to soak fruits in water for any length of time or you will wash out any water-soluble vitamins.

FRUIT, BROWNING OF
The best method of reducing or eliminating the browning of fruits can be achieved with the use of ascorbic acid or vitamin C. Pure ascorbic acid is available in most supermarkets or drug stores.

While some people tend to use lemon juice, it is not as effective and may impart more of a lemon flavor, which may not be desirable for many foods.

To stop potatoes, apples and pears from browning when they are cut and exposed to the air, just dip them into a bowl containing water and 2 tablespoons of white vinegar. This also works well with avocados.

FRUIT, CANDIED

Always wash off the sugary candy coating first. Rinsing the fruit in cold water or steam it for 5 minutes in a strainer over boiling water. Be sure that the fruit does not touch the boiling water.

FRUIT, COOKING

The last thing a cook wants is mushy fruit. This frequently encountered problem can be resolved by just adding some sugar to the cooking syrup.

This will strengthen the cell walls with an artificial sugar "cell" wall.

The sugar will also have the effect of drawing some of the fluid back into the cell to slow down the drying out of the fruit and retaining the desired appealing consistency.

FRUIT, DRIED

Vitamin C is lost when fruits are dried or dehydrated. However, most of the other vitamins and minerals are retained. Sulfites are commonly used to preserve dried fruits. This chemical may cause an allergic reaction in susceptible individuals. Best to shy away from any product that contains sulfites. Most fruits and dried fruits are graded extra fancy, fancy, extra choice, with choice and standard being the lowest grade. The grading is based on size, color, condition and water content after being dried.

♦ Dried fruits, if frozen in a liquid, should be thawed in the same liquid to retain its flavor.
♦ If you store dried fruits in airtight containers, they will keep for up to 6 months. If placed in a cool dry location or refrigerated, they will last for about one year.
♦ Refrigeration tends to place the fruit cells in a state of suspended animation and helps retain their flavor. After refrigeration storage, it would be best to allow the fruit to remain at room temperature before eating for about 30 minutes to acquire the best taste.

If you want to revive dried fruit faster, just combine the fruit with ½ cup of water and microwave it on high for 1-2 minutes then let stand for 4-5 minutes before using.

- Dried fruits will be easier to chop if you freeze them first.
- If you have trouble chopping dried fruit in a food processor using the metal blade, just add 1-2 teaspoons of granulated sugar.
- Try using kitchen scissors to cut up dried fruit.
- Spray any utensil you use the cut up dried fruit with vegetable oil to stop the sticking.

ORDER OF THE NUTRITIONAL QUALITY OF FRUITS

1. Fresh, if brought to market in a short period of time.
2. Dehydrated, if Grade A or No. 1.
3. Freeze Dried, if packaged at the site where it is grown.
4. Frozen, if packaged within 12 hours of harvest.
5. Canned.

Using Dried Fruits

If you are going to use dried fruits in a dish it is best to re-hydrate them first by soaking them in cold water for about 2 hours or until they are somewhat plump. Another method is to pour boiling water over the fruit, just enough to cover and simmer for about 15 minutes. However, if you overcook, the fruit will become mushy and not be very good to use.

FRUIT, FREEZING OF

Fruits can be frozen without sugar. Sugar is used to maintain the sweet flavor and help to retain the texture and stabilize the color and is not needed as a preservative.

FRYING

It is never wise to fry at too low a temperature, especially if the food is breaded. The oil will not be hot enough to seal the breading or outer surface of the food and too much of the oil is allowed to enter the food before the sealing takes place.

When the oil is too hot then the food may end up being burned on the outside and not allow the insides to be cooked through. Most breaded foods that are fried are normally fried at 375^0F (190.6^0F).

It is best to check the recipe for the particular food you are frying for the correct frying temperature. Chicken needs to be fried at 365^0F (185^0C) for 10-20 minutes depending on the thickness of the piece. Meats should be fried at 360^0F (182.2^0C).

One of the first rules a chef learns is not to place too much food in a deep-fat fryer. Smaller batches will not cause the frying temperature to drop too low.

When you do fry, remember to always make sure the oil is about 15^0F (-9.4^0C) above the temperature that you want to fry in. Foods that are placed into the fryer at room temperature will cause a drop of about 15^0F (-9.4^0C). Never place food directly from the refrigerator into the fryer since this will cause splattering and may cause a 30^0F (-1.1^0C) drop in temperature

- Fast food restaurants may deep fat or par-fry French fries before they arrive at the restaurant to save time. This may cause a higher level of trans-fatty acids in the fries. As much as 10 grams of fat may come from the par frying.
- When you deep fat fry, try adding ½ teaspoon of baking powder per ½ cup of flour in your batter to produce a lighter coating and fewer calories.

> When chefs fry and don't have a temperature thermometer on their deep-fat fryer to tell if the oil is at the perfect 365°F for frying, they may use a different method. I once saw a chef in China place a wooden chopstick in the hot oil. When the oil started to climb the chopstick, the oil was at the right temperature. Works great!

Fried foods will not pick up and retain as much fat if you add a tablespoon of vinegar to the fryer or skillet before adding the oil. Coat the pan as best you can and leave the balance of the vinegar on the pan.

- Tests have been conducted that prove that the hotter the oil, the less oil will be absorbed by the food. The frying time is also lessened, which also contributes to the fewer fat calories retained.
- When you fry above sea level it is necessary to lower the frying temperature 3°F for every 1,000 feet increase in elevation. If you live in Denver, Colorado, you will need to lower your frying temperature by 15 degrees.

FRYING SECRETS TO REDUCE FAT

When chefs place food in the fryer, the food is always at room temperature so that the food did not reduce the temperature of the oil. Also, food will absorb more fat if the temperature of the oil is too low.

> ### Science of Reducing Absorbed Fat When Frying
> The high fryer temperature will seal the food quickly by instantly cooking the breading giving the food a crisp outer crust allowing the food to cook without the oil hardly penetrating the coating and being absorbed. Also, placing too much food all at once in the fryer has the same negative effect and the food absorbs too much fat. Fry in small batches for the best results then place the fried food in the oven that has been preheated to 300°F then turned off. Place the food on paper towels to keep it crisp and warm and to absorb any fat dripping. The best starting temperature for frying is 365°F, however, if you are at a high altitude remember to reduce the frying temperature by 3°F for every 1,000 feet above sea level.

- If the frying fat is not hot enough, food will absorb more fat. However, if you get it too hot it will smoke, burn, and produce trans-fatty acids. Use a thermometer; the temperature should be 360° to 375°F.

♦ When my grandmother fried foods she always cleaned the oil out with a few slices of raw potato, then threw them away and stored the oil in the icebox to reuse it. When oil is reused the level of trans-fatty acid rises until it is 100%, which doesn't take too long. Oil should never be reused.

Science of Used Frying Oil

When oil is used for frying the temperature is raised to such a high level that a percentage of the oil is broken down (begins smoking) and decomposes into trans-fatty acid oil, as well as turning a percentage of the polyunsaturated oil into saturated oil. Trans-fatty acids, even though edible, tend to cause an increase in free radicals (abnormal cells) in the body and may also raise the bad cholesterol levels (LDL) and lower the good cholesterol levels (HDL). Best to use fresh canola oil every time you fry.

♦ The best oil for deep fat frying is canola. It has the highest smoke point and will not break down easily. Most oils can only be cooked to 400^0F before serious deterioration starts to occur.

CHEF'S FRYING SECRETS

If frying temperatures are not controlled properly, the food will absorb more fat, the batches will not be consistent and the flavor will vary.

The oil will also break down faster. The following are a few facts that should be followed when frying foods:

• A thermometer should be used to check the temperature of the oil and the oil should never exceed 380^0F.
• If the time period elapses between batches, it would be best to reduce the oil temperature to 250^0F slowing down the deterioration of the oil.
• When using shortening to fry with, always heat the shortening slowly. If you heat shortening too quickly, it will scorch. Always start shortening at 225^0F and keep it there until it the shortening has completely melted then you can turn the heat up.
• Too low a temperature will result in poor coloring and usually a greasy product.

To make fried foods less greasy, just add 1 tablespoon of white vinegar to the pan or deep-fat fryer before adding the oil.

• When frying batches, remember to allow the temperature to go back up or return to the normal frying temperature before adding more food to be fried.

WHY FRYING OIL DARKENS PREMATURELY
The following are the more common reasons for frying oil darkening:
- Your frying pan or fryer is not as clean as it should be.
- When you did clean it, you failed to rinse it well and there was some soap film left in the fryer.
- You are overcooking the food.
- The fat has been broken down and is mostly trans-fatty acids.
- The temperature has been consistently too high.

WHY FAT WILL SMOKE
The following are the most common reasons:
- Foreign material has gotten into the fryer and burning while you fry.
- Too much breading has fallen off and is building up.
- The fat has broken down and is no longer good.
- The temperature is too high.

THE CASE OF THE FOAMING FRYER
There are a number of reasons why foam will form on the top of foods being fried. The following are a few of the more common ones:

- The fryer is not as clean as it should be and was not rinsed properly leaving soap scum.
- Too much salt or food particles accumulating in the fryer.
- Using brass or copper utensils in the fryer, which react with the oil creating foam.
- Poor quality fat or old worn out fat.

Up, Up and Away
A frequent problem that occurs when frying is trying to fry too much food at once. The fat may overflow (bubble over) from the temperature difference of the cold food and the hot fat. Also, to avoid food from sticking together, the basket should be lifted out of the fat several times before allowing it to remain in the fat.

To avoid foods splattering when fried, be sure and dry them thoroughly before placing them into the hot oil. Also, place all fried foods on a piece of paper towel for a few minutes before serving to allow the excess oil to drain off.

FUDGE
Fudge should be stirred or beaten with a wooden spoon. Beating the fudge is one of the most important techniques. Beat the fudge from its glossy, thin consistency to a slightly thick consistency. This is when you will need to add raisins or nuts and place into a pan to cool.

Also, next time you prepare fudge, try adding a teaspoon of cornstarch when you first begin mixing the ingredients, this will make the fudge set up better.

A FIX FOR THE SWEET TOOTH

If you are going to prepare fudge, the weather has to be just right. If the weather is too hot and humid, never make anything chocolate. The kitchen should also be cool and sometimes the air conditioner may have to be turned on.

Science of Temperature & Chocolate
The best temperature when preparing chocolate or fudge is between 62° to 68°F (20°C) and the humidity must be low. Chocolate and fudge tend to absorb moisture from the air and it affects the end result.

MELTING CHOCOLATE

Best to melt chocolate at 50% power in a microwave since it is too hot on the stove.

PAULETTE'S FUDGE RECIPE

Ingredients:

5	Ounces of quality unsalted butter (stick)
2¾	Cups of granulated sugar
2/3	Cups of evaporated milk (not condensed milk)
12	Ounces of semi-sweet chocolate chips or bits
7	Ounces of quality marshmallow crème
¾	Cup of fresh walnuts (chopped)
¼ -½	Cup of raisins (good quality)
1	Teaspoon of pure vanilla extract, (best quality)

- Use a 13 X 9-inch pan or equivalent and grease it lightly with the butter wrapper.
- Mix the sugar and milk in a 3-quart saucepan, stir continually and bring to a boil. The butter should be added after you mix the sugar into the milk and after it starts to boil.
- Boil gradually and start with a medium heat and then go to high.
- Do not allow crystallization around the inside top of the pot. Wipe clean.
- Boil for about 7-8 minutes on medium-high heat. Should be a rolling boil.
- Use a candy thermometer and boil until the temperature reaches 238°F (114°C).
- Remove from heat and stir in butter.
- Chocolate chips, marshmallow and vanilla should be in a separate heat-safe bowl.
- Carefully pour the hot butter, sugar and milk mixture over the chocolate chip mixture and stir until combined.
- Add any remaining ingredients or raisins and mix well then pour into pan.
- The fudge should be cooled at room temperature and should set up perfect.
- Slice as soon as it sets up but is not completely solid.

Science of Fudge, Setting Up

If you have a problem with fudge setting up, just add 1 teaspoon of cornstarch when you start mixing in the ingredients. Divinity fudge tends to attract moisture and cannot be made on humid days. Placing the fudge in the refrigerator may harden it temporarily, but when it gets back to room temperature it will start to soften again. Too much butter is a common problem. If the water content is too high, it won't set properly. Poor grades of margarine that have been substituted for quality butter will also cause the problem.

Science of Fudge

Plastic or rubber spatulas may melt if the fudge gets too hot and should not be used. A wooden spoon is recommended. Raw sugar is not the best sugar for fudge. The best chocolate is Hershey's for fudge. Corn syrup and honey do not produce good results. If you use any other nut except walnuts, only use $\frac{3}{4}$ cup instead of 1 cup. It is OK to make fudge when it is snowing since the humidity is usually low. If it is a wet, heavy snow the humidity will be too high. Powdered sugar should not be used in fudge.

Brown sugar can be used to replace white sugar but only up to $\frac{1}{2}$ of the total sugar used in the recipe. If you want to use milk chocolate only use half milk chocolate and half semi-sweet chocolate. Using milk chocolate as your base, the fudge may be too milk chocolate unless it is to your liking. Using milk chocolate will make very sweet fudge, which many people do not like.

When making fudge you need to continue with all procedures until completely done. A variety of extracts can be added to fudge to produce great flavors. Some of the favorites include mint, lemon, vanilla, orange and maple, however, only add $\frac{1}{4}$ teaspoon of an extract to fudge. If you do not add any nuts or raisins a 9 X 9-inch pan will do. Insulated pots may cause the fudge to cool too slowly.

GGGGG

GARLIC

Grown worldwide and sold in fresh clove form or as garlic salt or powder.

It is commonly used in hundreds of dishes especially Italian cooking, sauces, chicken dishes, etc. Garlic has been used as a medication for a number of illnesses throughout history. Americans consume 250 million pounds of garlic annually with a large percentage grown in Gilroy, California. Garlic can be peeled easily by placing it in very hot water for 2-3 minutes.

When actually peeling garlic, try rinsing the garlic under hot water first to loosen the skin. For a special flavor rub a clove of crushed garlic on the sides of your salad bowl before mixing your salad. There are hundreds of varieties of garlic grown worldwide. Elephant garlic is not really a member of the garlic family, but is a form of leek with a milder flavor than most garlic.

♦ If you wish to store garlic for an extended period do not peel it, just leave the cloves intact, and it will store for 3 months in a cool, dark, dry location.
♦ When garlic sprouts, some of the garlic flavor will go into the sprouts, however, the sprouts can then be used for salads.
♦ Garlic should not be frozen. If garlic is damaged or nicked with a knife it must be used or it will develop mold very quickly.
♦ Garlic vinegar can be made by placing 2-3 fresh cloves in each pint of white vinegar, then allow to stand for at least 2 weeks before using.
♦ Garlic will have better flavor if it is at room temperature.
♦ If you have used too much garlic in your soup or stew, just simmer a sprig or small quantity of parsley in it for about 10 minutes.

Science of Garlic Odor

The cells of garlic contain an odorless molecule called "allin." The space between the cells contains another molecule called "allinase." When a chemical ends in "ase" it is an enzyme that will cause a reaction to occur, which is the case of garlic molecules throwing the two chemicals together causing the intense aroma and flavor. The more you chop and mince garlic, the more you bring the molecules together and the more intense the aroma and flavor becomes.

When garlic is heated the chemical that gives garlic its unique flavor is partially destroyed. The chemical is "diallyl disulfide" which is a sulfur compound. If garlic is allowed to sprout most of the chemical will enter the new sprouts and the garlic will become milder.

♦ To remove the garlic odor from your hands, try rubbing your hands with salt on a slice of lemon or rub your hands across the blade of a stainless steel knife.
♦ Read the label before you buy a garlic product. Garlic products should contain an antibacterial or acidifying agent such as phosphoric acid or citric acid. If this is not on the label the product must be sold and stored under refrigeration at all times.
♦ Garlic butter does not have a long shelf life and should be stored in the refrigerator for no more than 14 days. Most butter is not made with a preservative.
♦ Garlic, once processed, is more perishable than most other herbs.

- When cooking with whole garlic cloves and you don't want them in the dish when you serve it, just place a toothpick firmly into the garlic and it will be easy to retrieve. Another trick is to use a tea infuser for a number of herbs that fall apart easily.
- When a recipe calls for adding garlic, always add the garlic last. Garlic burns very easily and may taste bitter.
- If you place garlic cloves in the microwave for 15 seconds, the skins will come right off.
- If you have a large number of garlic cloves to peel, just drop them into a pot of boiling water and allow them to cook for about 30 seconds then place them into a colander and rinse with cold water. As soon as they are cool enough, peel them.
- If you are using a garlic press, you do not have to peel the garlic. The flesh will go through the press and the skin will stay in the press.
- If you chop garlic using a small amount of salt, the minced garlic will not stick to the knife as much.

When cooking with garlic, be careful not to over-brown it or it will turn bitter and too pungent. Garlic will cook very quickly, usually in less than minutes.

Flavor Booster

An easy way to add garlic flavor to soup is to remove the papery outer layer of a whole garlic head then cut off ½" off the top to expose the flesh of the cloves and keeping it intact drop the whole head into the soup. After the soup is done cooking, just remove and discard the garlic head or squeeze the garlic juice into the soup.

The Real Skinny

To peel the skin off garlic, try using an old fashioned rubber jar opener. Take the round flat piece of rubber and place one or two garlic cloves inside the center and roll the cloves around inside until the friction created by the rubber causes the paper-thin skin to fall off.

- If you would like garlic to retain its color when cooking the garlic with onions, just sauté the onions first, and then add the garlic.
- If garlic is cooked with onions, be sure and add the garlic toward the end of the cooking time. If added when you start cooking the onions, the garlic will be burned and bitter.
- Storing garlic is relatively simple; all you have to do is place the garlic in a cool, dry location as close to 50^0F as possible or even at room temperature and it will easily last for about 1-2 months. Garlic will retain its flavor better if it not stored in the refrigerator; however, there is no harm in storing it there. Storing garlic in a small jar of olive oil is the chef's way of keeping the flavor in the garlic for 2-3 months. Garlic should never be frozen or it will lose its flavor.
- Garlic vinegar is an excellent substitute for garlic clove. You can substitute 1 teaspoon of garlic vinegar for each small clove of garlic.

If you like garlic but hate the aftertaste and odor, just chew on fennel seed or a coffee bean. Fresh parsley will also help the problem.

Chefs love to use garlic and know just how to temper its pungency. The strength of the flavor is controlled by how you cut or cook the garlic. Here's how they do it:

Science of Cooking Garlic

Mildest Flavor
Cook long and slow, then chop coarsely and add to a liquid. You can also roast the whole head slowly.

Medium Flavor
Cut the garlic up fine and sauté just enough to soften, but don't allow the color to change or it will get sweet.

Strong Flavor
Crush the cloves with the flat side on a knife blade.

Very Strong Flavor
Just crush the cloves in a garlic press and use.

Strongest Flavor
Crush the cloves, unpeeled in a garlic press then sauté to a deep brown or use raw.

Garlic cooked in water will have a milder flavor than garlic that has been cooked in oil.

GARLIC, REPAIRING
If your soup or stew has been overpowered by garlic, just place some parsley in a tea ball and swirl it around for a minute or so. Garlic is attracted to parsley and you can then discard the garlic, laden parsley.

GELATIN
Gelatin can be acquired from a number of different sources, however, the most common source is animal hoofs, muscle, bones, and connective tissue. Other sources include seaweed from which agar-agar is produced and Irish moss from which carregeenan is made. Both of these are popular commercial thickeners, however, carregeenan is especially useful for thickening ice cream products.

Gelatin granules have the capability of trapping water molecules and then expanding to ten times their original size. The firmness of a product will depend on the gelatin/water ratio.

If the product becomes too firm, a small amount of heat is all that is needed to change the firmness closer to a liquid, if you chill the product it will become firm again.

Since gelatin is high in protein you can never use fresh figs, kiwi, papaya, or pineapple in the product since these contain an enzyme that breaks down protein thus ruining the product. The enzyme in pineapple (bromelain) can be neutralized, by simmering the pineapple for a few minutes. When using gelatin for a dish, be sure and moisten the gelatin first with a small amount of cold water, then use the hot water to completely dissolve the gelatin. When hot water is poured into the dry gelatin a number of the granules will lump and some will not totally dissolve which may cause your dish to be somewhat grainy. The hot water should never be over 180^0F for the best results. If your recipe calls for an equal amount of sugar to gelatin the cold, water step is not required since the sugar will stop the clumping.

However, you should never pour the hot water into the gelatin. Place the gelatin in the water.

Gelatin is sold in two forms, powdered gelatin, which is the most common and leaf gelatin, which is only sold in bakery supply stores and is produced in brittle sheets. Leaf gelatin is rarely called for in most American recipes and is usually only required in European recipes.

Leaf gelatin, however, does have a better flavor and produces a clearer gelatin. Both types are interchangeable in recipes. Gelatin dishes are only at their best for about 12 hours. They will keep for about 2-3 days when refrigerated then allow them to stand at room temperature for 30 minutes to soften them up before serving. Never freeze a gelatin dish since they will crystallize and separate.

- Gelatin needs to be really stiff for aspic. If you are curious as to whether the gelatin will be set up enough, just place a small amount in the freezer for 5 minutes. If it jells up in that period of time, it will make good aspic.
- To release the gelatin from a mold or pan, just place the bottom of the mold in very warm (not hot) water for a few seconds to loosen the sides.
- To resolve the problem of removing gelatin from a mold, try spraying the mold with a light coating of vegetable oil.
- After completing the gelatin and placing it in the mold, try putting the mold in the freezer for 20-30 minutes before placing it into the refrigerator. Remember gelatin will crystallize if frozen, so keep an eye on it occasionally.

As a rule of thumb, a 1¼-ounce package of gelatin is capable of gelling about 2 cups of liquid.

- Apple juice can be substituted for water in most Jell-O recipes.
- If you accidentally set gelatin to a stage that is not desired, just place the mold in a pan of very hot water and stir the gelatin until it melts. Place the gelatin into the refrigerator and keep an eye on it until it jells to the stage you desire.

- If you are having a problem with your ingredients that have been added sinking to the bottom and not staying put, they were probably added at the wrong time. When this occurs, try melting the gelatin until just syrupy, then stir the mixture until the fruits, etc., are back where they belong.
- If your gelatin set up is too solid and rubbery, you probably used too much gelatin. When this occurs, the only way to fix it is to melt it and add more liquid.
- Gelatin will last forever if stored in an airtight container and placed in a cool, dry location.

If you rinse a mold with cold water before adding any gelatin-based dish, it will be easier to remove after it sets up.

- Gelatin needs to be soaked in a cold liquid for 3-5 minutes before it is used in any recipe. This will soften and swell the gelatin granules causing them to dissolve more easily and smoothly.
- Never allow gelatin to boil or it will never set up.
- If you want to speed up the setting of a gelatin dish, just place the dish in a larger bowl of ice water with ice cubes. Keep stirring the mixture until it is the consistency you desire.
- Placing the mixture in the freezer for about 20 minutes will also speed up the setting.
- If you are placing pieces of fruit into the gelatin mixture, it is best to wait until the mixture is partially set up before adding the fruit. This will stop the fruit from going to the bottom.
- If you are going to prepare a layered gelatin mixture, be sure and wait until the bottom layer is sticky to the touch then spoon the second layer on very carefully.
- If you use too much gelatin, the food will be somewhat rubbery.

When using either powdered or leaf gelatin, it must first be softened in cold liquid. Water is usually the liquid of choice.

To soften powdered gelatin:
Place the gelatin in a dish and gently drop cold water on the gelatin. For every tablespoon of gelatin, use ¼ cup of cold water then allow it to stand for 5 minutes until rubbery.

To soften leaf gelatin:
Place the sheet in a bowl and cover with cold water. Allow the leaf to remain in the water for 5 minutes or until it is very soft. Remove the gelatin with your hand and squeeze out the excess water, then return it to a dry bowl. If the gelatin will be added to a hot liquid it will not have to be further melted in a hot water bath.

MELTING THE GELATIN
To melt either type of gelatin, just place the dish with the gelatin into a pan of hot water and heat over a burner.

You are allowed to shake the mixture gently, but never stir the gelatin or it will become stringy. To check the gelatin, just remove a small amount and there should be no visible crystals.

Gelatin should never be dissolved over direct heat since it will stick to the pan.

THE THREE STAGES OF GELATIN

Partially Set
The gelatin appears syrupy and has the texture of beaten egg whites. Add additional ingredients, such as nuts, fruits, beaten eggs or vegetables.

Almost Firmed-Up
It is almost set-up, but still able to flow when the pan is tipped. Able to add additional layers of gelatin: if so desired.

Firm
It should remain fairly solid when the pan is tipped and does not lose its shape when sliced. It is ready to serve.

TOO LOOSE

Many fruits and vegetables will affect the setting up of gelatin. They all have an enzyme that has the tendency to keep the protein in a liquid state and not allow it to become a semi-solid. These include pineapple, papaya, kiwi, ginger root, figs and mangoes. If you would like to use any of these fruits, just cook them for about 5 minutes to destroy the enzyme. However, some of these fruits tend to lose their color and flavor when heated. If you use too much sugar it will also stop the gelatin from setting up.

GELATIN, REMOVAL FROM MOLD

To easily remove a gelatin dish from its mold, just insert a knife between the mold and the food in several places. That should release the vacuum then dip the mold in very warm water up to its edge, keeping it in place for no more than 5-6 seconds. If you leave it in any longer you may start to melt the gelatin causing you to lose some of the detail.

Place a plate over the top of the mold, hold the plate and mold then turn them over and give the mold a firm shake. The food should drop onto the dish. If it doesn't fall immediately, give gravity a chance to work and it should fall out without much coaxing. If it won't release, just dip it in hot water for a few more seconds and try again.

It is best to return the food to the refrigerator for a few minutes to firm it up if necessary.

GLAZES

A common coating for desserts and confections is a "glaze." A glaze is usually brushed or poured on and is prepared by combining a jam or jelly with a liquid, such as water or liqueur.

The mixture is then strained to remove any pulp and warmed before being used. One of the more common glazes is a chocolate glaze, which is prepared from melted chocolate, cream, butter and corn syrup. Confectioner's sugar glaze is prepared by mixing confectioner's sugar with liquid, such as lemon juice or even water.

Glazes are actually just a stock that has been reduced to a point that it will coat the back of a spoon. They are used as flavorings in many sauces and used in moderation since they are a concentrated source of flavoring. Glazes are the original bases and are still thought of as a base. Even though the glaze has been reduced from a stock, it will not taste like the stock. The types of glazes are basically the same as the stock they were prepared from such as, chicken, meat or fish.

GUIDELINES FOR PREPARING A GLAZE

- The stock should be reduced over medium heat.
- The surface should be skimmed frequently to remove any debris or skin.
- When reducing by at least ½ a small saucepan should be used.
- Continue reducing over low heat until the glaze is syrupy and coats the back of the spoon.
- Glazes will store well in the refrigerator for at least 3-4 weeks if not contaminated and sealed well. Glazes may also be frozen for 2-3 months.

GRATERS

- If you are going to grate cheese or a citrus rind, be sure and spray the grater with vegetable oil or rub a small amount of oil on the side you will be grating on. Place the oil on the front as well as the inside.
- If you are grating several foods, be sure and start with the foods that won't leave too much residue.
- A grater can be cleaned using a toothbrush.

GRAVY

Gravy is always best if you use the pan drippings, which contain the flavor of the meat or poultry. Many people avoid using the drippings because of the high fat content; however, the fat content can easily be reduced by separating the fat from the flavorful liquid; using a separating cup to pour off the fat.

Other methods include placing ice cubes in a piece of cheesecloth and swirling that around to trap the fat, or if time allows, the drippings can be placed into the freezer for a few minutes until the fat rises and can easily be removed.

- High-fat gravy (which should only be eaten in moderation) will have a better consistency if you add ¼ teaspoon of baking soda to it. If it has high starch content, don't add baking powder or it will turn it black. Try a small amount first before going the distance.
- A method used in the 19th century was to add onionskins to the gravy while it is cooking to make it brown; just make sure you remove them after a few minutes and discard.

- When at all possible make your own sauces and gravies. Packaged products are lower quality convenience items that contain numerous additives, preservatives, and coloring agents.
- New studies from the Agricultural Research Service reported that E.coli bacteria are getting tougher and some strains cannot be killed with low heat. Gravy with E.coli was heated to 115^0F for 15 to 30 minutes and E.coli was still swimming around and enjoying the hot bath. To kill the E. coli it took a temperature of 140^0F.
- A common problem with gravy is that it almost always separates, especially as it cools down.
- You will never have lumpy gravy if you just add a pinch of salt to the flour and mix it in before adding any liquid.
- If your gravy is not brown enough and you need a quick fix, just add 1 teaspoon of hot instant coffee. There will not be any flavor of coffee in the gravy.
- To improve the taste of over-salted gravy, just add ¼ teaspoon of brown sugar to the gravy.
- If you would like your gravy to have a rich, dark brown color, just spread the flour on a cookie sheet and cook over a low heat, stirring occasionally until the flour browns. Just before serving the gravy, add a teaspoon of coffee to the gravy to firm up the color permanently.

ELIMINATE FATS FROM SOUP AND STEWS

A percentage of fat can be eliminated by placing 4 to 5 ice cubes in a piece of ordinary cheesecloth and swirling it around in the soup or stew. Another method is to place a few iceberg lettuce leaves in the food and stir them in for a few minutes, then remove them, and throw them away. Fat is attracted to both the ice cubes and iceberg lettuce leaves. Another method is to gently place a piece of paper towel on the top and absorb the fat (works great on pizzas). A piece of fresh white bread can also be used as a sponge and discarded before it breaks down.

LOW-FAT TURKEY GRAVY TIP

To prepare low-fat gravy using the turkey drippings, just place the drippings into a fat skimmer cup and allow the fat to stand for a few minutes then pour off the top layer of fat. Use the remaining liquid and add as much de-fatted turkey or chicken broth as you wish and any other ingredients you desire to thicken the gravy.

THICKENING SECRET

Add 1 teaspoon of cornstarch or arrowroot to 1 cup of cold water, mix thoroughly then add to gravy. Using cold water first will prevent lumps forming.

Chef's Gravy Recipe

The rule of thumb to remember is to use the same number of tablespoons of fat (need to use a little) drippings to flour.

- The pan drippings should be taken from the pan before you remove the fat.

- The following recipe is for about 2½ cups of gravy and should be adjusted depending on the number of people to be served. This amount usually serves 8 people comfortably.
- Unsalted butter may be used in place of the fat drippings and be sure to start with the butter at room temperature, do not microwave.
- In a medium saucepan over low heat, place 4 tablespoons of pan drippings and 4 tablespoons of all-purpose flour.
- Cook the mixture until brown stirring occasionally. Add 2 cups of de-fatted drippings and continue to cook over low heat until the desired thickness is achieved.

Science of Gravy

To eliminate the floury flavor in gravy, just place the flour you are going to use in a baking pan and bake at 350°F until the flour in a nice brown color. Onionskins added to gravy while it is cooking will give the gravy a nice brown color. Remove them before serving. One of the more frequent problems when cooking gravy is when the gravy decides to separate into fat globules. To solve the problem all you have to do is add a pinch or two of baking soda to emulsify the fat globules in a matter of seconds.

One of the most frequent problems with gravy is the temptation of the cook to use too much flour to thicken the gravy. When this is done it tends to detract from the gravy's flavor, which is dependent on the small amount of drippings used. Chefs rarely use flour and usually de-glazed the roasting pan with water to trap the drippings that have adhered to the bottom of the pan. Try adding a small amount of butter and reduce the mixture over heat, stirring frequently, until it is thick. Try not to prepare gravy too thick since it will thicken as it cools, and may be relatively solid by the time it is poured.

GRAVY, REPAIRING

Burnt gravy
If you accidentally burn the gravy, all you have to do is add a teaspoon of peanut butter to the gravy. You won't notice the taste of the peanut butter at all.

Lumpy
Place the gravy in a blender for a few seconds.

Not Brown Enough
Add 1 teaspoon of instant decaf coffee to the gravy and cook for a few minutes more.

Not Thick Enough
Use instant potato powder, arrowroot or cornstarch.

Too Salty
Place 3-4 slices of peeled raw potato into the gravy and stir while the gravy is heating. Salt has an affinity for raw potato then discard the potato. You can also add a few pinches of brown sugar.

230

GREASING PANS

- When you are greasing a pan, make sure you don't use too much grease or you may cause the food to over brown.
- Always use unsalted butter, vegetable spray or margarine.
- Salted butter will cause browning at temperatures over 400^{0}F, which is why chefs recommend unsalted butter.
- If you are having a problem getting baked goods out of a pan. Try greasing the pan then place waxed paper in the bottom then grease again before adding the dough. The waxed paper will easily peel off.

GRILLING

- Never use any type of barbecue grill indoors.
- Never place charcoal lighter fluid on the coals after they have started.
- Watch out for clothing with shirttails or any clothing that hangs down away from the body.
- If you have too big a fire, close the vents a little or place a few iceberg lettuce leaves over the coals.
- Line the drip pan with aluminum foil to stop fat from going through.
- If you want a more moist indirect grilling, try adding 1 cup of liquid, such as wine, beer or stock to the drip pan.
- Sprinkle herbs such as, oregano or rosemary on the coals just before you start grilling. It will add fragrance as well as some flavor to the food.
- Keep about ¾ of an inch between the coals for even heating.
- Remember to use medium heat for meats. High heat tends to dry out the meat.

Cover the grill with aluminum foil as soon as you remove the food and the grill will much easier to clean. Be sure it is shiny-side down and the heat will clean the grill.

- If you are going to grill poultry, bring it to room temperature first and it will cook more evenly.
- Roasts need to be cooked very slowly so that the outside does not get done before the insides.
- When basting, be sure and warm up the basting solution since a cold solution will slow down the cooking.
- If you are going to grill meat for a long period of time, it is best to baste only during the last 30 minutes.
- If the basting sauce is high in sugar, don't baste until the last 15 minutes of cooking time.
- Foods can be removed from the grill a few minutes before they are done. The residual heat will continue cooking the food.

HHHHH

HAM

Serving ham for a special festival predates Christianity.

When fresh meats were not available in the early spring months, pagans buried fresh pork buttes in the sand close to the ocean during the early winter months. The pork was cured by the "marinating" action of the salt water, which killed the harmful microbes. When spring arrived, the salt-preserved meat was dug up and cooked over wood fires.

♦ Frozen ham will last for 6-9 months in the freezer at 0^0F. Ham will last for 10 days in the refrigerator after heating providing it is wrapped well.
♦ Half bone-in ham   –   8-10 dinner servings
  Boneless whole ham –   16-20 dinner servings
  Whole bone-in ham –   28-32 dinner servings
♦ Removing a ham rind (bone) can be easy if you slit the ham above the rind lengthwise, down to the rind, before placing it into the pan. While it is baking the meat will pull away and the rind can easily be removed.
♦ I'm sure at one time or another you have purchased a ham that has shown some signs of a multicolored sheen that glistens and is somewhat greenish. This occasionally occurs from a ham when it is sliced and the surface exposed to the effects of oxidation. It is not a sign of spoilage, but is caused by the nitrite-modification of the iron content of the meat, which tends to undergo a biochemical change in the meat's pigmentation.
♦ After ham is cured it contains nitrite salt. This chemical reacts with the myoglobin in the meat and changes it into nitrosomyoglobin. This biochemical alteration forces the meat to remain reddish even if cooked to a high temperature.

Get Out the Hacksaw

Country hams are somewhat hard to cook because of their large size. The ham is usually placed into a stockpot to simmer before being roasted: however, it is difficult to fit it into most stockpots. Just use a hacksaw to remove the hock end to make it fit and then you can freeze the hock for beans or soup.

♦ If your ham slices are too salty, try placing them in a dish of low-fat milk for 20 minutes then rinse them off in cold water and dry with paper towels before you cook them. The ham will not pick up the taste of the milk.
♦ Since ham is naturally salty, try pouring a can of ginger ale over the ham and then rubbing the meaty side with salt at least 1 hour before placing the ham into the oven. This will cause the salt water in the pork to come to the surface and reduce the saltiness of the ham.
♦ Many times you will see hams placed on the shelves in the market and not under refrigeration.

- These hams are actually sterilized to retard bacterial growth for longer periods of time. This sterilization, however, tends to detract from the flavor, texture, and nutritional values of the ham. Best to purchase one that is under refrigeration.
- Country hams go through a special curing process, which tends to make them saltier than most other hams.
- Country hams need a lot of special preparation, such as scrubbing, skinning, soaking and simmering.
- To easily remove a ham from a metal can, just immerse the can in hot water for about 2 minutes before you open it.
- When you purchase a canned ham, make sure you refrigerate it if it says perishable, pasteurized or keep refrigerated on the label. If the ham says "shelf-stable" or "sterilized" they can be stored on the shelf for up to 1 year. If it is a "cured ham" then it will not freeze well and will lose texture and flavor.
- The flavor of a fully cooked ham can be improved by cooking. Cooking releases the juices.
- If you want thin ham slices, place the ham in the freezer for 20 minutes before you begin slicing.
- If you want a moist ham, place the contents of a 12-ounce can of cola in your pan and wrap the ham in tin foil. About 30 minutes before the ham is done, remove the tin foil and allow the ham juices to mix with the cola.
- If you're going to buy a canned ham, purchase the largest you can afford. Smaller canned hams are usually made from bits and pieces and glued together with gelatin.
- Cured hams are immersed in a solution of brine salts, sugar, and nitrites, which are injected into the ham. The ham will increase in weight due to these added solutions and if the total weight goes up by 8%, the label must read "ham, with natural juices." If the weight of the ham increases more than 8%, the label must now read "water added."

HAM, CANNED
CANNED YUK!
Chefs will never purchase a canned ham that needed to be stored at room temperature and always purchased one that has to be refrigerated.

Science of Canned Ham
Canned hams that are refrigerated will have a much better flavor than those that do not need refrigeration. In order to leave a ham out at room temperature the ham must be processed to a very high temperature, which changes the flavor, aroma, nutritive content and texture of the ham. The hams that are chosen for this high heat processing are also the poorest quality hams.

I'm sure at one time or another you have purchased a ham that has shown some signs of a multicolored sheen that glistens and is somewhat greenish. This occasionally occurs from a ham when it is sliced and the surface exposed to the effects of oxidation. It is not a sign of spoilage, but is caused by the nitrite-modification of the iron content of the meat, which tends to undergo a biochemical change in the meat's pigmentation.

HAM, REPAIRING

Too Salty

Place the ham in the oven and cook for ½ the time, remove and pour a can of ginger ale over the ham and then rub salt on the outside and finish cooking. The ginger ale and salt will draw salt water out of the ham and should de-salt the ham about 60%.

HAMBURGER

In 1885 Charles Nagreen, age 15, who lived in Seymour, Wisconsin, was selling meatballs from an ox-drawn cart outside the Outagamie County Fair.
Business was poor since people couldn't walk around carrying meatballs. He decided to flatten the meatballs and place them between two pieces of bread and called it a "hamburger." He sold the hamburgers at the fair until he died in 1951 and was known as "Hamburger Charlie."

- The most commonly purchased meat item in the United States is hamburger (which is no surprise).
- The maximum fat content is 30% (70% lean) by law.
- Fresh hamburger cannot have any phosphates, water added or binders. It is possible to find hamburger meat that is only 5% fat (85% lean).
- Remember, the leaner the meat, the redder the color.
- When hamburger meat is packaged, the exterior of the meat that is covered with plastic wrap still remains red since it is an contact with a certain degree of oxygen. When no oxygen is present the meat turns brown and is not able to retain its "bloom." Fresh hamburger meat will still be red on the inside since enough oxygen has been introduced during the grinding process.

If you would like a crispy surface on your burgers next time you are cooking them, try lightly dusting the surface with cornstarch just before you cook them.

- When preparing hamburger or meatloaf and having purchased very low-fat meat, try mixing in one well beaten egg white for every pound of meat. Also, adding a package of instant onion soup mix will really make a difference. A small amount of small curd cottage cheese or instant potatoes placed in the center of a meatloaf makes for a different taste treat while keeping the meat moist.

- If you are going to make hamburger patties or meatballs, place the meat in the refrigerator for 30 minutes before forming the patties or meatballs and they will form better and stay in shape when cooking. If you place a small piece of ice inside your meatballs before browning, they will be more moist.
- To make your burger juicy, try adding 1/3 cup of very cold water per pound of meat before mixing and putting it on the grill. Do this in a colander so that the excess water runs out.
- If you need to cook hamburgers really fast, try puncturing the burgers with a fork a few times to allow the heat to enter more easily.

Never press down with a metal spatula when cooking hamburgers. This causes more of the flavorful juices to be removed. Many restaurants do this, since it will cause the burger to cook a little faster and dry it out.

- If you would like all your burgers to be the same size, just use an ice cream scoop to measure the meat out.
- When you work with ground beef, try wetting your hands first and your hands won't stick to the meat.

Science of Hamburger and Oxygen

Any meat that has been ground up has had a large percentage of its surface exposed to the air and light. Oxygen and light cause a breakdown in the meat and tends to change the color as well as making the meat go bad in a very short period of time. Exposure to oxygen leads to deterioration known as "self-oxidation." Grinding meat also speeds up the loss of vital nutrients.

THE BETTER BURGER

The best hamburgers are never prepared from the expensive, low fat hamburger meat. You need a certain amount of fat to give a hamburger good flavor and keep it moist. If you prefer to use the low fat hamburger, just ask the butcher to grind it for you and add a small amount of fat. You will be surprised at the difference in taste.

There are many additions that can be added to help the hamburger meat retain moisture, such as breadcrumbs and eggs; however, chefs know that the flavor of a good hamburger has to have a certain percentage of fat.

If you broil hamburgers so that the excess fat drips down into the pan, the fat content will not be too high and the flavor will still be retained.

When preparing other meat dishes such as meatloaf, meatballs and meat stuffing, you can add the fillers, which will help retain the fat that is already there.

DANGERS IN RAW FOODS

The bacteria salmonella comes from the intestines of humans and animals and is often found in raw meats and eggs. Salmonella can be present after foods are dried, processed, or frozen for long periods. The bacteria can also be transferred to food by insects or human hands, especially infants and people with poor cleanliness habits. Salmonella is easily killed with high heat, which is why raw meats need to be cooked thoroughly.

Food preparation surfaces that are not cleaned adequately after preparing raw meats and egg dishes are usually the cause of most cases of salmonella related illnesses.

COOKING A SAFE BURGER

While undercooked burgers may pose a risk of E. coli, a well-done burger may pose a risk of a potentially harmful carcinogen called a heterocyclic aromatic amine (HAA). This compound is formed when meat is cooked to high temperatures.

- If you microwave the meat for a few minutes before cooking, this will make the meat safer and remove a large percentage of the HAA's.
- Choose a lean cut of beef. Have the butcher remove all the visible fat from around the edges and grind it through the meat grinder twice. That will break up the remaining fat.
- Place the hamburger in a microwave oven just before you are preparing to use it for 1-3 minutes on high power.
- Pour off the excess liquid, which will contain additional fat and the creatine and creatinine that form the HAA's.
- Reduce the meat content of the burgers by adding mashed black beans or cooked rice and you will have a safer and great tasting medium-well burger.

TAKING TEMPERATURE

When you take the temperature of a hamburger to be sure it is done, you should place the thermometer in at the top edge of the burger and push it toward the center. Most other methods will break apart the burger.

HERBS

Herbs are noted for their aroma more than for their taste in most instances. Chefs know how to appeal to your sense of smell when preparing a dish and will add either some or all of the herbs just before the dish is served, since many herbs lose some of their flavor during the cooking process.

Studies show that certain herbs can reduce the bacterial count in certain foods. Seasoning foods may even reduce the risk from E. coli in meats and other foods. Herbs such as cloves, cinnamon, garlic, oregano and sage were all good active herbs. The most effective herb, however, in the study was garlic. The addition of 7.5% garlic and clove herbal mixture killed 99% of the pathogen that was added to the food.

- When using oils to replace herbs, remember that oils are so concentrated that it is almost impossible to calculate the amount that you will need to replace the herb to acquire the same taste.
- A good example is cinnamon of which the oil is 50 times stronger than the ground cinnamon. If you did want to substitute the oil to replace the cinnamon extract, you would only need to use 1-2 drops of the oil to replace ½ teaspoon of the extract in candy or frostings.
- If you crush dried herbs before using them it will intensify their flavor. You can also intensify their flavor by soaking them for a few seconds in hot water, especially before adding them to a salad. When doubling a recipe, never double the seasoning until you taste the dish. This also works well if they have lost their flavor.
- Remove the fresh, undamaged leaves from the stems and lightly spray them with cold water. Place the leaves into small paper cups and fill the cup with fresh (filtered if possible) cool water, then freeze. To defrost the herbs, place the cup under cool running water until fully defrosted.
- All fresh herbs should be washed and patted dry before use.
- Depending on the season, the flavor and aroma intensity will vary and should be taken into consideration when using them.
- When you add chopped herbs to a cold dish; be sure and cover the dish and place it in the refrigerator for about 2 hours so that the flavors can mingle with the food.
- When you heat herbs, they lose a good percentage of their flavor.
- To prepare herb butter, just grind up your favorite herb as fine as you can and blend it with the butter after it has softened. Do not melt the butter; just allow it to soften before mixing in the herbs.

Storage

The best location to store spices is in a cool, dry spot where they will not be around heat. Storing spices near a microwave exhaust fan or over the range are two of the worst locations.

If you decide to store them in the refrigerator, make sure you remove them at least 30 minutes before you plan to use them. This will allow the herb to warm up enough to release its flavor and aroma. Herbs that contain oil readily oxidize and should always be stored in the refrigerator. The flavor of fresh herbs is milder than those from the supermarket that have been dried.

- ◆ Shake the leaves from the stems as soon as the leaves are dry and throw away the stems.
- ◆ The leaves can be crushed and stored; however, the whole leaf will retain its flavor longer.
- ◆ Be sure and store herbs in an airtight container.
- ◆ Store in a cool, dry location for longer life.
- ◆ To check to see if the herb is still potent, rub the herb in your hands and breath in the aroma. If no aroma, the herbs are bad.

OLD CO$_2$ TRICK TO PRESERVE HERBS

Place fresh herbs into a plastic baggie and blow air through your mouth into the bag. Then close the bag up as fast as you can so that the carbon dioxide will remain in the bag. Carbon dioxide will help preserve the freshness of the herbs for a week or more.

Release Those Flavors

For the best flavor from many herbs it is necessary to release the flavorful oils, especially thyme and oregano. They can be crushed between your fingers or placed in a mesh sieve and forced down with your fingers as you shake the sieve over a bowl.

Year-round summer herbs

If you would like summer herbs all year long and preserve them for winter soups and stews, just make herb cubes in the freezer. Chop up your herbs and place them in ice cube trays, then cover with water and freeze. To preserve the color and flavor, use boiling water to fill the tray (this blanches the herbs). Some herbs, like cilantro, keep better when frozen in oil. Mince the herb in a food processor then introduce olive oil until you produce a fine puree. Pour into ice cube trays or bags and freeze. When introducing the frozen herbs to recipes, remember that they contain water or oil. If this will throw off the recipe's consistency, thaw and drain the cubes first.

CHEF'S HERB & SPICE RECOMMENDATIONS

FOOD	HERBS
BAKED	
Apple pie	Cinnamon, cloves, nutmeg
Bread	Caraway, cinnamon, cloves, nutmeg, poppy seed, sesame seed
Cakes	Allspice, cardamom, cloves, coriander, cumin
Cookies	Anise, cinnamon, cloves, ginger, nutmeg, poppy seed
Custard pie	Nutmeg
Doughnuts	Mace, nutmeg
French toast, pancakes	Cinnamon, nutmeg
Fruit pies (general)	Allspice, cinnamon, ginger, nutmeg
Pumpkin pie	Allspice, cinnamon, cloves, ginger, nutmeg
CEREALS & GRAINS	
Oatmeal	Cinnamon
Rice	Chives, curry, saffron, thyme, turmeric
DESSERTS	
Chocolate pudding	Cinnamon
Custards	Cardamom, cinnamon, nutmeg
Rice pudding	Allspice, cinnamon, cloves, ginger, nutmeg
EGGS	
Omelet	Dill, cumin, curry, marjoram, parsley
Scrambled	Chili powder, dill, fennel, oregano, thyme
FRUIT	
Baked apples	Allspice, cardamom, cinnamon sticks, cloves, nutmeg
Jams & jellies	Mint
Preserves	Basil, cloves, ginger root, thyme
Stewed prunes	Allspice, cinnamon, ginger, nutmeg
MEAT	
Beef	Allspice, bay leaf, cayenne, curry, mustard, black pepper, rosemary, sage, thyme
Game (venison)	Rosemary, sage, savory, tarragon
Ham	Cloves, mustard, black pepper
Lamb	Basil, dill, mint, oregano, sage
VEGETABLES	
Beans, green	Marjoram, sage, savory
Beets	Parsley, rosemary
Carrots	Basil, cloves, nutmeg, savory, tarragon
Cauliflower	Chives, parsley, burnet
Corn	Sage
Potato, sweet	Cinnamon, cloves, nutmeg
Potato, white	Chives, dill
Tomatoes	Basil, cayenne, chives, parsley, sage, borage

HERBS, DRYING OF

DRIED HERBS

* Herbs can be dried in a microwave on paper towel for about 2-3 minutes depending on the amount of herbs to be dried.
* Dried herbs do best when stored in as airtight a container as possible and refrigerated.
* Dried herbs that are sold in the supermarket are usually more potent than fresh herbs; however, they do not retain their potency for a very long time.
* When storing herbs always date the package or container.
* Herbs will retain their potency for about 4-6 months before starting to lose it.

The rule of thumb when using dried herbs to replace fresh herbs is 1 teaspoon of dried herbs for 1 tablespoon of fresh herbs.

---

* If you are going to replace leaf herbs and use dried to replace them use ½ the amount of dried herbs.
* The potency of dried herbs can be intensified by crushing them with your fingers before using them.
* If you are planning to use dried herbs in a cold salad dressing or sauce, you can obtain better flavor by first mixing the herbs in hot water to moisten them and allowing them to remain for about 10 minutes before draining and drying them on paper towel.

DRYING FRESH HERBS

Preparation

♦ The stalks should be cut when the leaves are mature and the plants have just started to bloom.
♦ Only use the tender, leafy tops and flower clusters and discard all leaves below 6-inches from the top of the stalk.
♦ These will not be as pungent as the top leaves.
♦ Be sure and remove any dead or discolored leaves.
♦ Rinse the herbs with cold water and wash off any dust and dirt.
♦ Remove the excess moisture by blotting with paper towel.
♦ If you plan on drying dill, harvest the plant as soon as you see that the seeds are ripe.

Air Drying

To air dry herbs, just tie 6-8 stems together in a small bunch. Then you need to tie a large brown paper bag around the bunch to protect the herbs from too much light. Make sure that the leaves do not touch the sides of the bag or they may stick to the bag, which will affect the way they dry. You will need to make a few holes in the bag for ventilation and then hang the bag in a warm, dry location with good air circulation. It should take about 2 weeks to dry the herbs.

> **HERBS SHOULD NEVER BE SUN-DRIED: THE LIGHT WILL DESTROY THE NATURAL AROMA.**

Oven Drying

To oven dry herbs, just place the fresh leaves on racks in a single layer allowing about 1-inch around the racks as well as between them so air can circulate freely. The oven should be set on the lowest temperature setting so that the herbs will dry slowly. Be sure and keep the oven door propped open slightly for ventilation. It will take about 2-4 hours to dry the herbs.

Microwave Drying

You can dry herbs in a microwave, however, the herbs need to be placed between paper towels and placed on a rack. Use the medium setting and it should only take 2-3 minutes before the herbs are dry. The leaves should be crumbly and brittle, if not continue for another 30 seconds.

Using the Herbs

The herbs should be cut up, chopped or ground up into very fine bits before adding them to a food. Grinding with a mortar and pestle is an excellent method of powdering herbs. Herbs should be added to the liquid in a recipe for the best results. The amount of the herbs used depends on your taste preferences.

Remember if a recipe calls for fresh herbs, you can substitute dry herbs, but only use ¼th of the recommended amount. ¼ teaspoon of dried herbs equals 1 teaspoon of fresh.

Herb Use - Rules to Follow

- When using herbs in soups or stews add the herbs during the last ½ hour of cooking.
- When adding to uncooked foods you should add the herbs 3-4 hours before serving. You can also add the herbs and allow the dish to remain overnight to release the flavor.
- If you want to release the flavor faster for cooked dishes, just place the herbs in a small amount of liquid such as lemon juice, vegetable oil or other liquid that is being used in the recipe for 8-10 minutes before adding them to the dish.

HOLLANDAISE SAUCE

- If you would like a hollandaise sauce that can be prepared in 10 minutes or less, try Knorr® Hollandaise Sauce Mix. The ingredients include modified food starch, wheat flour, non-fat dry milk, hydrolyzed vegetable protein, partially hydrogenated peanut oil, lactose, salt, fructose, onion and garlic powder, citric acid, vegetable gum, yeast extract, soup stock, spices and a natural flavor. It really is not too bad tasting, but nothing like the "made-from-scratch" original.

Fake It!

To prepare a "mock" hollandaise sauce, just use 1 cup of white sauce and add 2 slightly beaten egg yolks and cook until just 2 bubbles (not 3 or 4) appear on the surface. Remove the pot from the hot burner and beat in 2 tablespoons of unsalted butter and 2 tablespoons of pure lemon juice. Voila, fake hollandaise sauce that will fool everyone but a chef.

Safe Eggs

Eggs may contain the salmonella bacteria even if they are in perfect condition. Because of this when making sauces that call for raw eggs and the sauce is not cooked thoroughly it may give you cause for concern. When preparing a hollandaise or béarnaise sauce it might be best to microwave the eggs before using them in your sauce. This can be accomplished without damaging the eggs too badly and still allowing them to react properly in your sauce.

First you need to separate the egg yolks completely from the white and the complete cord. Second place the yolks in a small glass bowl and beat them until they are well mixed. Third add 2 teaspoons of lemon juice and mix thoroughly again. Fourth cover the bowl and place into the microwave on high and observe the mixture until the surface begins to move then allow it to cook for 10 seconds past this point, remove the bowl and beat the mixture with a clean whisk until they appear smooth. Return the bowl to the microwave and allow it to cook again until the surface starts to move, allow it to remain another 10 seconds, remove and whisk again until it is smooth.

Finally, allow the bowl to stand for about 1 minute and the yolks should be free of any salmonella and still usable in your sauce.

Since eggs may be contaminated even if they are not cracked, it would be wise to microwave the eggs to be sure that there is no contamination before you make the sauce. The procedure will not harm the eggs and they will still be in good shape for the sauce. The procedure can only be done with 2 large yolks at a time and in a 600-watt microwave oven.

- The first step is to separate the egg yolks from the white and remove the cord then place the yolks in a small glass bowl and beat them until they are well mixed.
- Next, add 2 teaspoons of real lemon juice and mix thoroughly.
- The bowl should then be covered and placed into microwave on high and the surface observed.
- When the surface starts to move allow the mixture to cook for no more than 10 seconds.
- Remove the bowl and whisk with a **clean** whisk.
- Return the bowl to the microwave and cook until the surface moves again and then another 10 seconds.
- Remove and whisk again with a **clean** whisk.
- Allow the bowl to sit for one minute before you use it for the sauce and it will be salmonella free.

HOLLANDAISE SAUCE, REPAIRING

The secret to saving the hollandaise sauce is to catch the problem and nip it in the bud. As soon as the sauce starts to curdle, add 1-2 tablespoons of hot water to about ¾ of a cup of the sauce and beat it vigorously until it is smooth.

Repeat this for the balance of the sauce. If the sauce has already curdled, just beat a tablespoon of cold water into the sauce and it will bring back the smooth texture.

HOT DOG

Hot dogs are called a number of names such as Frankfurters and Weiners in Germany and Austria and even "Dachshund Sausages" in the United States. Hot dogs as we know them were first sold at Coney Island in Brooklyn, New York in 1880 by a German immigrant by the name of Charles Feltman, who called them Frankfurters.

The actual name "Hot Dog" was coined at a New York Giants baseball game in 1901 by concessionaire Harry Stevens.

The weather was too cold to sell his normal ice cream treats, so he started selling "Dachshund Sausages" and instructed his sales team to yell out "Get 'em while they're hot."

A newspaper cartoonist seeing this drew a cartoon showing the sales people selling the sausages, but since he didn't know how to spell "Dachshund" called the food a "Hot Dog." Hot dogs were sold at Coney Island from carts owned by Nathan Handwerker (Nathan's Hot Dogs). His employees sold the dogs dressed in white coats and wearing stethoscopes to denote cleanliness. In 1913 it was a dark year for hot dogs since they were banned at Coney Island when a rumor was started that they were made from ground dog meat.

The rumor was cleared up and they were sold again a few months later.

- In New York City, the Coney Island Chicken is actually the nickname for a "hot dog."
- When boiling hot dogs, try using the top of the double boiler to keep your buns warm.
- The United States consumes more hot dogs than the rest of the world put together. This amounts to almost 2 billion hot dogs per year almost enough to circle the globe.
- The American Culinary Institute and the American Tasting Institute in San Francisco have judged hot dogs and found that the number one hot dog based on taste, freshness and appearance was produced by Best Kosher Foods and sold as Shofar Kosher Hot Dogs. Over 1 million Shofar hot dogs are produced every day.

♦ If hot dogs are labeled "All Meat" or "All Beef" they must contain at least 85% meat or beef. The "All Meat" variety can contain a blend of beef, pork, chicken or turkey meat. It can also contain bone, water, etc. Kosher hot dogs are only pure beef muscle meat and are the better source of protein. However, they all still contain nitrites.

♦ One of the worst sources of protein is the hot dog.
They have less protein in a 3½oz serving than any other type of meat. Legally, they can contain up to 56% water, edible offal, and 3% powdered bone, which may even be listed on the list of ingredients. Sugar is a very popular ingredient in hot dogs and may show up on the label as corn syrup.

Safety First

The bacteria Listeria monocytogenes may be lurking in a number of foods, such as hot dogs, sausage, raw milk, chicken, and deli-prepared salads and sandwiches. Listeria first became noticed when 48 people died from eating a Mexican-style cheese in 1985. The number one food related risk in the United States is from bacterial food contamination not pesticides or fertilizers. The Listeria organism can survive refrigeration or freezing and over 1,900 cases of food poisoning are reported annually.

People with weak immune systems are more at risk. To avoid the problem the following should be adhered to:

- Be sure to cook all ready-to-eat hot dogs, sausage, and leftovers until good and hot.
- Chicken and turkey dogs should be cooked.
- Hot dogs should always be kept hot (above 140°F) until they are ready to eat.
- Be aware of "Sell by" and "Use by" dates on all processed food products.

HOT PEPPER NEUTRALIZER

Drinking malty, high alcohol content beer may neutralize capsaicin, the spice in hot peppers. The hot pepper chemical is literally dissolved by alcohol. Water will not do the trick, but dairy products will temporarily reduce the discomfort.

HYDROGENATED OILS

Hydrogenated oil has been partially converted from liquid polyunsaturated oil into a more solid saturated fat.

This process is done by adding hydrogen molecules from water to increase the solidity of the fat. Basically, it turns relatively good fat into bad fat, which has more "mouth feel."

Check the label of commercial baked goods to see if the word "hydrogenated oil" is on the list of ingredients. If so these products will be higher in saturated fat. Hydrogenation changes the texture of the product giving it added body. It also allows more of a "feel" to the food when it's in your mouth.

New oil processing techniques are being studied that will change oil and create an oil that is a high-saturate oil. This will eliminate the need to hydrogenate oil and eliminate the trans-fatty acid. This new fat science will create fat that will have the same desired properties of the hydrogenated oil.

IIIII

ICE CREAM, FREEZING
Ice cream never lasted long at grandma's house and that was a good thing since ice cream has a very short freezer life.

Science of Storing Ice Cream
When ice cream is stored for long periods even in the freezer, it may pick up refrigerator odors and even lose its creamy texture. Ice cream should not be stored more than about 10 days after being opened even in the freezer. Every time you open the carton to remove some ice cream you change a percentage of the ice cream and end up refreezing a coarser and icier ice cream than you had before.

Placing a piece of plastic wrap on top of the ice cream will slow the process of deterioration down but will not stop it for any length of time. After you place the plastic wrap on, you will still need to place the entire carton in a plastic bag and seal it up as airtight as you can. Ice cream cannot be refrozen once it does thaw to any degree or you may end up with bacterial contamination.

COLD FACTS
Jelly, salad dressing, and mayonnaise do not freeze well on bread products. The freezer in your refrigerator is not the same as a supermarket food freezer.

It is best used for storing foods for short periods only.

Foods should be frozen as quickly as possible and temperatures should be 0^0F or below. Potatoes become mushy when frozen in stews or casseroles. Their cells have high water content and break easily when frozen. However, mashed potatoes freeze well.

Any bakery item with a cream filling should not be frozen since they will become soggy. Custard and meringue pies do not freeze well. The custard tends to separate and the meringue becomes tough. Waffles and pancakes may be frozen, thawed and placed in the toaster.

THERE ARE ICICLES IN MY ICE CREAM
Icicles or ice crystals in ice cream are usually formed from opening the door to the

freezer too often. It doesn't take very much of a temperature drop to force the water molecules out of some of the ice cream cells and form the ice crystals. If the ice cream is stored for a prolonged period of time at 0^0F (-17.8^0C), the crystals will change their form again. Just scrape the crystals away since they are harmless.

ICING/FROSTING

While frosting is used to enhance the cake and add sweetness, it was originally used to prolong the life of the cake and help keep the moistness in. Most icing will also improve the flavor of the cake.

Science of Icing Consistency

When making icing with powdered sugar, just add a pinch of baking soda to the sugar and the icing will not lose its moisture or get crumbly as fast.

JUST THE RIGHT AMOUNT OF ICING

CAKE SIZE	ICING NEEDS
8" or 9" 2-layer round cake, top & sides only	1½-2½ cups
8" or 9" 2-layer round cake, top, sides & filling	2½-3½ cups
8" or 9" 3-layer round cake, top, sides & filling	4 cups

FONDANT ICING

Fondant icing is produced from glucose, sucrose, and water that is cooked to 240^0F **then quickly cooled off to** 110^0F and rapidly worked until it is a white, creamy smooth texture. To ice with the mixture, cool it down to 100^0F and it will flow smoothly. Normally, it is used as a base for butter-cream icing.

- ♦ Icing tends to become thick and difficult to work with after a short period of time. If this happens just add 2-3 drops of lemon juice and re-mix the icing.
- ♦ Next time you make icing try adding 1 teaspoon of butter to the chocolate while it is melting to improve the consistency.
- ♦ To produce a unique design with two different icing colors, just use two icing bags, then place the two bags into a larger bag and wrap them around each other. Squeeze them both at the same time to produce a swirled two-color effect.

THROW OUT THE ANCHOR

It is best to frost a cake on a cardboard round for the best results. Be sure that the cardboard round is just larger than the cake making it easy to turn the cake while you are working. You can anchor the cake to the cardboard with a dab of frosting placed in the center of the cardboard.

- To keep boiled icing from hardening, just add a small amount of white vinegar to the water while it is cooking.
- If you are in a hurry to make a frosting, try mashing a small boiled potato, then beat in 1/3 cup of confectioners' sugar and a small amount of vanilla.
- If you sprinkle a thin layer of cornstarch on top of a cake before you ice it the icing won't run down the sides.
- If you add a pinch of baking powder to the powdered sugar you are using to make icing, it will remain creamy and not harden.
- To eliminate the problem of icing sticking to your knife, just dip your knife in cold water frequently.
- If you are having a problem with icing getting crumbly, just add a pinch of baking soda to the powdered sugar. The icing won't get crumbly and this will also help to retain some moisture so that the icing will not dry out as fast.
- Best to sift confectioners' sugar before using it to prevent lumpy frosting. If you don't have a sifter, try placing the sugar in a sieve and push it through with a spoon.
- Confectioners' sugar can be moistened with milk, coffee, fruit juice, honey, maple syrup and even jam or jelly.
- If you do use sugar that is not sifted, use warm milk or warm fruit juice to moisten it.
- Confectioners' sugar frosting tends to have a "raw" flavor, allow it to remain in the top of a double boiler over water that is just simmering for 8-10 minutes. Stir occasionally and allow it to cool before frosting.
- If you want to keep the surface of the icing soft, just beat 2 tablespoons of soft unsalted butter into the confectioners' sugar. That will stop the sugar from becoming dry and cracking.
- If you want to lower the calories and get rid of some fat, just stir ¼ teaspoon of baking powder into the confectioners' sugar before adding any liquid and don't use the butter. The icing will remain creamy and be moist.

Icing will last frozen for up to 6 months

- Never add chopped nuts, raisins or chocolate until icing is finished or it may thin it.
- If the cake is very soft, try placing a crumb coating on it by first spreading a very thin layer of icing over the whole cake, which will seal the surface. Set crumbs and fill in any areas that are bad. Allow the coating to fully dry before applying the remaining icing.
- If the cake is too crumbly, place it in the freezer and when it is solid, frost it.
- Be sure that the icing is not too thick or it may tear the cake.

Placing Layers on Frosting
Always use the piece of round cardboard to place the layers on top of the frosted layer. Using your hands is risky and may break the layer.

The tines of a dinner fork can make waves in the icing. You can use the back of a soupspoon to make swirls or the tip of a thin, metal spatula to stipple the top and sides. You can also use a hair dryer lightly on the top to give the icing a smooth appearance.

ICING, BOILED

A commonly use icing is called "boiled icing." The icing is prepared by cooking sugar with whipped egg whites then beating the mixture until it is smooth, syrupy and glossy. It may also be called Italian meringue.

JJJJJ

JELLIES & JAMS

When preparing jams and jellies, honey can be substituted for sugar. If the recipe calls for 4 cups of sugar, just use 2 cups of honey and cook the jelly just a little longer. Always use liquid honey and powdered pectin for the best results.

When jelly is poured into the jars from the pot, the pot must be close to the top of the jar or as the jelly is poured slowly, air becomes trapped in the hot jelly and bubbles will form.

Always hold the pot close to the top of the jars and pour the jelly as fast as you can. Bubbles may also indicate that the jelly has spoiled. When there are bubbles that move, throw out the jelly.

CHEF'S JELLY SECRET

When cooking fruits for preserves and jellies, add a small pat of butter and there will be no foam to skim off the top. The fat tends to act as a sealant, which does not allow the air to rise and accumulate on top as foam. The air just dissipates harmlessly in the product.

COMMON PROBLEMS

One of the most common problems when preparing jelly is that of the jelly being too soft. There are a number of reasons for this problem. The following are six of the most common ones:

- One of the more common problems is overcooking the fruit to extract the juice. Overcooking tends to lower the pectin level and thus reducing the capacity of the jelly to thicken properly.
- The use of too much water when extracting the juice will produce a jelly that is too runny. Follow instructions as to the proper amount to be used.
- The wrong proportions of sugar and juice will also cause the jelly to be too soft.
- When the jelly is undercooked, it tends to be soft due to insufficient concentrations.
- Too little acid can cause the jelly to become soft. If the fruit is low in acid, try adding a small amount of lemon juice.
- Making too large a batch can also cause the jelly to have difficulty setting up properly. Never use any more than 4-6 cups of juice for each batch.

When grandma made jelly and jam she would always try to purchase fruit that is not fully ripened. Grandma would prefer to pick the fruit at farms that had *"U-Pick"* sign and would never pick the best looking ripened fruit.

Science of Under-Ripe Fruit

When preparing jelly and jams, there are a number of factors that must be considered. The pectin content must be perfect and the acid and sugar have to in the right proportions. The acid content is very important to a good end product and the almost ripe fruit has a higher acid content than does a ripe fruit. If you do use a ripe fruit and add in pectin, you can add the necessary acid by adding about 1 tablespoon of lemon juice per 1 cup of fruit juice.

Jelly making was different than jam making and grandma knew all the secrets to preparing the perfect jelly.

She knew how to avoid crystallization by not using too much sugar and making sure that there were no crystals stuck to the sides of the pan. She also knew that if she cooked it too slowly or too long crystals could form. She always cooked the juice at a rapid boil and when it reached the jelling stage, she immediately removed it from the heat.

CRYSTALS IN JELLY

There are a number of reasons why crystals form in jellies. The following are four of the more common reasons:

- The crystals may form if too much sugar is used. Test the fruit juice with a Jelmeter (sweetness tester) to be sure that you have the proper proportions of sugar.
- Crystals can form if there is sugar that has not been dissolved and is stuck to the sides of the saucepan. Make sure you wipe the sides of the pan clean and free of crystals with a damp rag before you fill the jars.
- The grape juice you are using may have tartrate crystals in it. To resolve this, just extract the grape juice and allow the tartrate crystals to settle down, which can be done by refrigerating the juice overnight and then straining the juice to remove the crystals.
- Crystals can also form from cooking the mixture too slowly or too long. The juice should be cooked at a rapid boil, when it reaches the jellying point, remove it from the heat immediately.

OVERCOOKING

When you overcook jelly some of the sugar and juice tend to burn and cause a darker color than you may be used to. Boiling too long is usually the cause of the darkness and making too large a batch. If the jelly is stored for too long a period at too high a temperature it may also cause jelly to darken.

WEEPING

There are a number of reasons that cause jelly to "weep." Too much acid will cause a tear or two or the pectin used is unstable and old.

Proper acidity levels is very important if the jelly is stored in too warm a location, or if the temperature fluctuates too much it may shed a tear as well. Jelly should always be stored in a dry, cool location.

- If the fruit you are using is green or not ripe enough, the jelly may be cloudy. Other reasons for cloudiness may be poor straining, which means that you may have forced the fruit through the strainer instead of allowing it to drip naturally or not allowing the juice to stand before it was poured into the jars.

- The reason that jellies tend to get tough and stiff is usually cause by overcooking. Jelly should be cooked to a temperature that is 8^0F (-13.3^0C) higher than the boiling point of water or until it flows from a spoon in a "sheet."

- Too much pectin or too little sugar in the juice will also contribute to the problem. When pectin is added, you should only use 3/4 cup of sugar to every 1 cup of juice for the majority of the fruits.

- Jellies should never be placed in the freezer. They tend to lose their consistency and turn very granular.

- Always remember to never prepare jellies or preserves on a day while the humidity is over 50%. High humidity causes the gelatin or pectin to absorb excess moisture leaving the product too watery.

- If you place jelly in a plastic squeeze bottle it will be easier to use.

- It is always best to prepare jellies in small batches. Large batches use large quantities of juices and it is necessary to boil it longer resulting in a loss of flavor. The jelly may also darken and become somewhat tough.

- Always boil jelly rapidly and as fast as possible. When jellies are boiled slowly, the pectin in the fruit juice may be destroyed.

- Jellied fruit may ferment because yeast is allowed to multiply. This usually occurs only when the product is poorly processed and the jar poorly sealed. It may also occur if the sugar content is too low. If this occurs don't try and save the batch, best to throw it away.

- If you think that a fruit jam or jelly will have vitamin C. Think again! The processing kills almost all the vitamin C.

- Jams and jellies are now being produced from a number of artificial ingredients. Best to read the label and make sure that the product you purchase is made from the "real fruit." If they are and are labeled "lite" that would be even better since the sugar content has been reduced.

- If you have problems with fruit jelly setting-up, try placing the jars in a shallow pan half-filled with cold water, then bake in a moderate oven for 30 minutes. This will reduce the moisture content of the jelly enough to set them up.

JERUSALEM ARTICHOKE (SUNROOT)

These are members of the sunflower family and also known as the "sunchoke." The sunroot contains a number of indigestible carbohydrates that cause flatulence in susceptible individuals.

These annoying carbohydrates can be almost entirely eliminated naturally from the vegetable by a month of cold storage in the refrigerator before being used.

About half of the remaining carbohydrates can be eliminated through cooking, providing the sunroot is sliced and boiled for 15 minutes.

- Do not buy them if they are tinged with green or have any soft spots.
- They should be firm and look fresh.
- They will stay fresh under refrigeration for about a week and are easily peeled with a vegetable peeler; however, they do contain a fair amount of nutrition in the skin.
- It has a somewhat nutty, sweet flavor, and should be crunchy. It can be boiled, sautéed, or even breaded and fried.
- Sunchokes contain no fat or sodium and is a good source of trace minerals.
- The only way to eliminate all the problem carbohydrates is to cook the whole root for about 24-hours, which will break carbohydrates down to fructose.
- Sunroot is very high in iron, which may cause it to turn gray while cooking. If you add ¼ of a teaspoon of cream of tartar to the boiling water 5 minutes before it is done, it will prevent the gray discoloration.
- If you add 1 tablespoon of lemon juice to the boiling water when you first start cooking, it will keep the root crisp and eliminate the color change.

JICAMA

Originated in Mexico and is becoming very popular in the United States. It is a root vegetable that can weigh up to 5 pounds or more. The skin is brown and the flesh is white.

- It can be used in salads either diced or in small sticks.
- Choose only unblemished jicama with no soft spots.
- Jicama is excellent for stir-fries and an excellent source of vitamin C.
- It has a slightly sweet flavor and can be substituted for potatoes.
- One pound equals about 3 cups.
- The texture is similar to a water chestnut.
- To peel jicama, use a sharp knife and use it to peel the skin back and remove in sheets. If you have a good vegetable peeler, it may work as well.

KKKKK

KNIVES

When grandma was working in the kitchen she kept washing the knives off to avoid contamination. She never worried about the knives getting rusted or staining. I found out that she actually brought the knives she used frequently from Germany. It was one of her possessions she brought with her. The only thing I can remember is that the metal part of the knife went all the way through the handle.

KOSHER FOODS

While kosher foods do not contain any animal-based additives such as lard, or edible offal they still may contain tropical oils (palm and coconut), which are high in saturated fats. Kosher meats usually have higher sodium content than any other type of meat or meat product due to the heavy salting in their special type of processing.

Kosher products for the most part are no more healthful than any other product and the additional cost is just not worth it unless you adhere to the religious restrictions.

LLLLL

LAMB

Lamb is meat that comes from sheep that are less than one year old. The younger, the lamb is butchered, the more tender the meat. If the animal is over 2 years old, the meat is called mutton. Domestic lamb fed on grain will have a milder flavor.

- ♦ Lamb is graded Prime, Choice, Good, Utility, or Cull. Prime is only sold to better restaurants. Most supermarket lamb is good grade.
- ♦ Coffee tends to bring out the flavor in lamb. Next time you prepare lamb stew, add a cup of black coffee to the stew as it is cooking. It will enhance the flavor and give the sauce a richer color.

- If you are a Texan you will know the phrase "wool-on-a-stick." It refers to lamb, and in Texas that's a nasty word. However, there are 100,000 sheep farms in the United States producing 347 million pounds of lamb. New Zealand and Australia are always thought of as large exporters at about 44 million pounds per year. In Colorado sheep ranchers are using llamas to protect the sheep, which are more effective than dogs.

If you rub lemon juice on the surface of lamb, it will help tenderize it. If it's older lamb mix the lemon juice with olive oil, rub it on and refrigerate for 2 hours before cooking.

- When purchasing a lamb shank, be sure that it weighs at least 4 pounds, any smaller and it will contain too high a percentage of bone. The plumper, the better.
- If you're buying lamb be sure it comes from New Zealand, since they do not allow the lamb to be injected with hormones. When buying leg of lamb, always buy a small one (two if need be) since the larger legs are from older animals and have a stronger flavor.
- Lamb stew will have a great flavor if you cook it in black coffee. The meat will come out dark and more flavorful.
- The darker the color of lamb, the older the animal. The more tender lamb will be light colored.

LAMB CHOPS

- The blade-end chops have a higher fat content than loin-end chops. However, the loin-end chops are more tender.
- A thin layer of fat is desirable on lamb chops.
- The darker the meat, the stronger the taste and the older the animal.
- Cuts of lamb that have the bone in will be more flavorful.
- Should be served hot for the best flavor.
- The lamb chop rack will cook in about 30 minutes at 450^{0}F.
- Rack of lamb is usually roasted medium or medium-rare.
- As much fat as possible should be removed from lamb chops before cooking.

LARD

During the 1800's California lighthouses used "sperm oil" from whales to light their lights. By the late 1860's the sperm oil became too expensive as the sperm whales became an endangered species and the lighthouses switched to lard oil.

- Lard can be stored at room temperature for 6-8 months. If you substitute lard for butter or shortening, reduce the amount you use by 25%.
- Lard is derived from the abdomen of pigs and is used in chewing gum bases, shaving creams, soaps, and cosmetics.

- Future studies may implicate lard in shortened life span as well as a factor in osteoporosis.
- Leaf lard is derived from the kidney area of the pig and is a higher quality than all other types of lard. It makes piecrust and biscuits flakier than any other type of fat.

LARDING

It is used to make lean cuts of meat more juicy by adding a layer of fat. Larding is done by inserting long, thin strips of fat every few inches throughout the meat. The fat will melt while the meat is cooking and will moisten the meat.

- The fat of choice used for larding is pork and is called a "lardon." Some butcher shops will sell lardons.
- If you decide to lard meat, it would be best to purchase a larding needle to make the job easier.
- You can also do larding by piercing the meat with a long, thin knife and forcing the fat strips through the holes.
- Lardons are always inserted across the grain of the meat.

LEMONS/LIMES

Lemons and limes were probably brought to this country by one of the early explorers and were grown in Florida around the sixteenth century.

The ladies of King Louis XII's court used fresh lemons to redden their lips.

The commercial industry was started around 1880 for lemons and around 1912 for limes. California is now the largest producer of lemons. There are two types of lemons, the very tart and the sweet. We are more use to the tart, however, the sweet, are grown mostly by home gardeners.

Limes originated on Tahiti. Key limes are a smaller variety of limes with a higher acid content. The California variety of limes, are known as the "Bears" and is a seedless lime. If sprinkled with water and refrigerated in plastic bags, lemons and limes will last for 1-2 months. If frozen, both their juices and grated peels will last about 4 months. Look for lemons and limes with the smoothest skin and the smallest points on each end. They have more juice and a better flavor.
- Submerging a lemon or lime in hot water for 15 minutes before squeezing will produce almost twice the amount of juice.
- Warming the lemon or lime in the oven for a few minutes will help release the juice.
- If you only need a few drops of juice, slightly puncture one end with a skewer before squeezing out the desired amount. Return the lemon to the refrigerator and the hole will seal up and the balance of the fruit will still be usable.
- Lemons and limes will keep longer in the refrigerator if you place them in a clean jar, cover them with cold water and seal the jar well.

- After using ½ of the fruit, store the other half in the freezer in a plastic bag. This reduces the loss of moisture and retards bacterial growth.
- When lemon is used as a flavoring, it tends to mask the craving for the addition of salt.
- Lemon and lime peelings may cause skin irritation on susceptible people. They contain the oil "limonene."

 When chefs want to use lemons, they know that rough skinned, bumpy lemons are best for grating and zesting. The smooth skinned lemons are best for getting the most juice, especially if they are at room temperature and rolled on the counter before juicing.

Science of Lemons

Good source of vitamin C; however, they should not be eaten raw, since they may cause excess erosion of tooth enamel. Their high citric acid content can cause stomach upsets as well.

Ouch!

Grandma would stab a lemon with a toothpick and squeeze out just the amount of juice she needed. The lemon was then stored in the refrigerator and used over and over.

Saves Time

When grandma wanted just one lemon slice she didn't bother with a whole lemon. She kept lemon slices in the freezer and just sliced up a whole lemon and froze the slices in one layer on a piece of parchment paper in a plastic bag.

The Mixer Reamer

If you don't have a citrus reamer and need to ream out a lemon, just use a hand-held mixer blade to do a great job.

LETTUCE

Lettuce was brought to the America's by Christopher Columbus in the 1490's and was not a commercial produce product until the 20th century. Romaine lettuce originated on the Greek Island of Cos. The plant was named for the way its leaves looked like a Roman tablespoon of the day.

Chefs know how to serve salad so that the salad dressing remains on the lettuce and doesn't end up in the bottom of the salad bowl mixed with water to dilute it. They know that wet lettuce will not hold salad dressing and always make sure that the lettuce was dry after being washed and placed into a plastic baggie.

The lettuce is then placed into the refrigerator and chilled for 1 hour before serving. Also, place an inverted saucer on the bottom of the salad bowl so that if there is any water left, it will run under the saucer.

- Lettuce is second only to potatoes in popularity in the United States. It is mainly used in salads and as garnish.
- It is available year round and should be heavy and solid, depending on the variety.
- The greener the leaves: the higher the nutrient content.
- Never add salt to lettuce prior to serving as this may cause the lettuce to wilt.
- All types of lettuce love the cold and the closer the temperature gets to 32^0F without going below that, the longer it will last and the crispier the lettuce will be.
- Most refrigerators range between 35^0-40^0F, which is good and not the ideal temperature for lettuce.
- The lettuce should be stored without washing in a sealed plastic bag with a small hole or two for ventilation.
- Lettuce will turn brown easily if allowed to remain near other fruits or vegetables due to the level of ethylene gas given off by most fruits and vegetables.

Science of Lettuce
Lettuce leaves as well as many plants have a waxy cuticle, which is a water-repelling mixture of various chemicals that are all related to repelling water and assisting the leaves from becoming waterlogged. This cuticle also protects the leaves from losing too much of their internal moisture. The oils in salad dressing are related to the chemicals that keep the water out and to at least allow the oils to stick to the surface. Water molecules also tend to bead up and fall off the leaf, while the oil spreads out and coats the surface. Always place the oil on the salad first then vinegar, and the vinegar will remain on the lettuce. If you place the vinegar on first, the oil will slip off.

- Americans consume approximately 11 pounds of lettuce per person, per year. Romaine lettuce has 6 times as much vitamin C and 8 times as much vitamin A as iceberg lettuce.
- Over 60 chemical agents can be applied to lettuce. Most can be removed by washing with a good organic cleaner or by placing the head stem side up in a sink with 6-8 inches of cold, lightly salted water for a minute while shaking and swirling it around.

Science of Storing Lettuce

When you wash lettuce and place it back in the refrigerator you are adding surface water, which can promote the growth of bacteria. There are two schools of thought about the lettuce core, one is to bang the head on the counter and twist the core out before storing it to slow down the moisture leaving the lettuce and then there is the chefs theory about leaving the core in. You can also leave the lettuce in a plastic bag to help the lettuce retain its natural moisture.

- Iceberg lettuce will remain fresher than any other type of lettuce due to its higher water content and will store for 7-14 days, romaine lasts for 6-10 days, and butterhead for only 3-4 days.
- If you need to crisp lettuce leaves, place them in the freezer for no more than 2-3 minutes, any more and you may have to discard them.
- If the head of lettuce you are going to use is a little droopy, just place the head into a large pan or bowl of very hot water for a few seconds then plunge it into ice, cold water.

Check the bottoms of lettuce to be sure that the ring is white, not brown!

SCRUB-A-DUB-DUB

Greens need to be thoroughly washed before using them in a salad and they are not always as dry as they should be if you are in a hurry to prepare the salad. When this happens, just put the greens in a clean pillowcase and place them in the washing machine on the fast spin cycle for no more than 2 minutes.

Recently, I watched two different cooking shows on television and watched one chefs tear the lettuce and the other cut the lettuce with a knife. The chef that tore the lettuce mentioned that tearing it would extend the life of the lettuce before it would turn brown. After trying this, I found out that it makes no difference at all whether you tear or cut lettuce. It will brown and oxidize in the same amount of time.

Lettuce Replacement

Certain herbs can be used to replace lettuce on a sandwich for a unique flavor experience. Try using basil or parsley in small amounts.

LIMES

Limes should have a bright outer covering and be smooth, skinned and heavy for its size. Do not purchase if the skin is shriveled.

- The most popular lime in the United States is called the Persian lime. The key lime is used in pies are not very available.

- Whole limes will store for about 10 days under refrigeration. If sliced, they will only last from 4-5 days in the refrigerator.
- Be sure and wash the limes before cutting them.
- You can substitute lime for lemons in most recipes.

LIVER

The liver acts as a filtration plant for the body and may concentrate toxins in its cells. These may include pesticides and heavy metals, depending on what the animals diet consists of.

The liver is also extremely high in cholesterol, more than any beef product. A 3½ oz serving of beef liver contains 390mg of cholesterol compared to 3½ oz of grilled hamburger at 95mg.

Science of Liver

Calf liver is more tender and the best to use for liver and onions. Beef liver is less expensive but has a stronger flavor and usually has more veins. Liver is best when used within 24 hours after being purchased and best when not frozen. Calf liver needs to be cooked quickly and on high heat, usually no more than 1 minute on each side. If calf liver is overcooked it can become tough. Beef liver needs more work and should be braised. The old fashioned method of making onions to go with liver was to slow cook the onions in bacon grease.

- The acidic nature of tomato juice will tenderize liver.
- Just soak it for 1-2 hours in the refrigerator before cooking.
- Milk will also tenderize young calves liver.
- If you overcook live, it will become very tough.
- The older the animal, the more contaminants may be in the liver. It is recommended to only purchase calf liver to be on the safe side.

GETTING YOUR VITAMIN A

We were only served liver and onions once a month, but I really enjoyed the way grandma made it. She only used calf liver and never beef liver since she thought it was too tough and harder to cook.

LOBSTER

During the 1700's and early 1800's lobsters were so plentiful on the beaches of New England that they could be easily picked up. They were once the food of the poor and even ground up and used for fertilizer. Lobsters can grow to 3 feet and weigh up to 40 pounds off the coast of Maine.

Female lobsters are more tender and flavorful than male lobsters. To tell the difference, just turn them on their back and look at the place where the head meets the body.

You can see 2 tiny spiny appendages and if they are soft to the touch, it is a female. If they are hard to the touch it is a male. The two most common species of lobster consumed in the United States are Maine and Spiny. Maine lobsters are the most prized and are mainly harvested off the northeastern seaboard.

It is an excellent flavored lobster and the meat when cooked is a snow-white color. A smaller lobster but still a popular one is the Spiny lobster, which can be identified by the smaller claws. Never purchase a lobster unless you see movement in the claws or if their tail turns under them when carefully touched.

- Rubber bands are placed on lobster's claws to protect the lobsters from hurting each other. When lobsters are placed in close areas, they tend to fight and since they are very carnivorous will eat each other.
- Female lobsters have more meat than male lobsters and their meat is sweeter.
- Females also have the coral roe, which is sought after by many lobster lovers.
- Before you start to tear a lobster apart, make sure you cover it with a towel, so that the juices don't squirt out.
- High tech lobster traps are getting so efficient that by 2009 lobsters may end up on the endangered species list. In Maine 40 million pounds of lobsters were captured and sent to market, the biggest season haul ever. This over-fishing may cause Maine to issue licenses that limit the number of lobsters a person can catch in a season.
- Lobster should be added to dishes just before serving in order to retain their flavor.
- Overcooking is the biggest problem in retaining the taste of lobster.
- Lobster tails have the tendency to curl up when they are cooked. To avoid this problem, just place a bamboo skewer through the back of the tail and out the front. When the skewer is removed the tail will stay straight.
- The "Newburg" is any seafood dish means that the recipe contains a special cream sauce that includes sherry. The name "Newburg" *refers to a Scottish fishing village called "Newburgh."* The dish was first introduced in the early 1900's in the United States and has remained a popular way of serving lobster. Most restaurants tend to purchase the Spiny lobster for these types of dishes since they are the least expensive.
- Fresh lobsters will be more tender than those kept live for a week or more.

- When broiling lobster, be sure and baste the surface with butter several times.
- If you are going to serve lobster cold, it would be better to just undercook it and it will be more flavorful. If you can cool them in the cooking liquid, it will help as well.

GET OUT THE LOBSTER BOOS

Lobsters must be cooked alive or they will release an enzyme into the meat and ruin the flavor making the meat somewhat bitter. Grandma hated to plop the lobster into the boiling water and had her own method of making a happy lobster.

- Believe it or not Maine lobsters may be either right or left-handed. They are not symmetrical with identical sides. The two claws are different and are used differently, one is larger with very coarse teeth for crushing, and the other has fine teeth for ripping or tearing.

- Depending on which side the larger, coarse-teethed claw is on will determine whether the lobster is right or left-handed. However, the flesh found in the smaller fine-toothed claw is sweeter and more tender.

GRANDMA AND THE DRUNK LOBSTER

It was only a once or twice a year treat when grandma would splurge and buy lobster. She couldn't just plop them into boiling water and watch them suffer for the few seconds it took to kill them, nor could she sever the spinal cord. What she did was a little more humane and dunked the lobsters in a pot of cheap beer for about a minute. This relaxed their muscles and made for more tender meat and made grandma feel better.

Lobster must still be cooked live due to the enzymatic breakdown action problem, which occurs immediately upon their death.

- If you are bothered by the lobster movements when cooking, which is just reflex, then place the lobster in the freezer for 10 minutes to dull its senses and it will only have a reflex reaction for about 20 seconds.
- The red coloring was always there, however, it is not visible until the lobster is boiled. The lobster along with other shellfish and some insects, have an external skeleton, which is made up of "chitin." Chitin contains a bright red pigment called "astaxanthin" which is bonded to several proteins. While the "chitin" is bonded it remains a brownish-red color, however, when the protein is heated by the boiling water the bonds are broken releasing the "astaxanthin" and the exo-skeleton turns a bright red color.

BIGGER IS STILL NOT BETTER

When grandma served the lobster claws she always gave us kids the biggest claws. I thought that this was really nice of her, however, after investigating, which lobster meat was better in which claw I was surprised to find out that there is a difference.

- Shellfish lovers seem to think that a special treat is to consume the green "tomalley" or liver found in lobsters or the "mustard" found in crabs. These organs are similar to our livers and are involved in detoxifying and filtering toxins out of the shellfish. Many of these organs do retain a percentage of the toxins and possibly even some PCB's or heavy metal contaminants.

Science of Lobster Claws

The smaller claw has the more tender and the sweetest flesh. The larger claw tends to contain more meat and even has a somewhat different taste. It makes no difference if the lobster is left-handed or right-handed as to which lobster will be sweeter and more flavorful. The side the larger claw is on will determine whether the lobster is right or left-handed.

- Since in most instances you are not aware of the areas these crustaceans are found, you should never eat these organs. However, the roe (coral) found in female lobsters is safe to eat. Lobster roe (eggs) are a delicacy in many countries.
- To keep a lobster alive for up to 1 week, just soak a few pieces of newspaper in cool water; then wrap the lobster up by rolling it in the newspaper. Make sure that the lobster is completely enclosed and refrigerate it.

BITTER LOBSTER

Lobsters and crabs have very potent digestive enzymes, which will immediately start to decompose their flesh when they die. Both should be kept alive until they are to be cooked. The complexity and location of their digestive organs make it too difficult to remove them.

Lobsters should never be placed into boiling water as a method of killing them. The best way is to sever the spinal cord at the base of the neck with the end of a knife; then place them into the water.

MICROWAVE

Microwave lobster is actually the preferred method in many of the better restaurants. The taste and texture are far superior to boiled or steamed lobster. Microwave allows all the natural juices to be retained. The color of the lobster is better as well. The problem some restaurants have is that it takes too many microwave ovens to handle a large volume of business.

To microwave a lobster you need to place the lobster in a large microwave plastic bag and knot it loosely.

A 1½-pound lobster should take about 5-6 minutes on high power providing you have a 600 to 700 watt oven. If you have a lower wattage oven allow about 8 minutes. To be sure that the lobster is fully cooked, just separate the tail from the body and if the tomalley (mushy stuff in cavity) has turned green the lobster is fully cooked.

MMMMM

MACARONI & CHEESE

The word "macaroni" actually came from the exclamation made by the Italians when they saw the price of pasta the Germans were trying to sell them in the 1700's. The Italians were upset at the price and said "ma caroni," which meant "but it's too dear" so the Germans reduced the prices.

Macaroni was brought to the United States by Thomas Jefferson. When Jefferson was the ambassador to France he developed a liking for macaroni. When he returned from France he brought a machine back that made pasta. He is credited with making the first macaroni and cheese dish.

CHEF'S MACARONI & CHEESE

- ◆ Use small elbow macaroni for the best results.
- ◆ The butter should be melted in a saucepan, but be sure that you let it soften at room temperature.
- ◆ Your recipe should call for about ¼ cup of unsalted butter.
- ◆ Whatever cheese you prefer, always remember to shred it before adding it for a topping or in a recipe.
- ◆ After the butter has softened (at room temperature), add the ¼ cup of flour, salt and pepper to taste.
- ◆ Most recipes call for 2½ cups of milk. Low fat or nonfat milk can be used but will detract from the original richness.
- ◆ Continue heating until the mixture starts to thicken, then remove from the heat and stir in 2 cups of shredded yellow cheddar cheese just until it melts.
- ◆ At this point add the cooked macaroni and place into a casserole dish and crumble bread slices (about 3-4) on top before sprinkling on ¼ cup of shredded yellow cheddar.
- ◆ Bake the dish for 30 minutes at 375⁰F until it bubbles.
- ◆ Make sure that you add a small amount of olive oil to the cooking water so that the pasta will not stick together.
- ◆ Another method is to place a layer of macaroni in the casserole dish then sprinkle a layer of cheese on top, crumbled bacon bits and finely chopped scallions.
- ◆ The macaroni should only be boiled for 5 minutes then drained.
- ◆ The casserole should hold 3 layers with a topping of breadcrumbs.

```
┌─────────────────────────────────────────────────────────────────┐
│                   Science of Macaroni & Cheese                   │
│ The milk should be added to the butter, flour mixture very slowly, while stirring │
│ continually. This is extremely important to obtain the perfect consistency. The pasta │
│ used should be the best quality you can purchase. Low fat cheese does not work well │
│ in this recipe.                                                   │
└─────────────────────────────────────────────────────────────────┘
```

The Dryer, the Better

Draining macaroni in a colander does not get all the water out of the curved pieces. After you drain in the colander and shake it well, it would be best to place a piece of paper towel on a cookie sheet and pour the macaroni on the paper towel and roll it a few times to dry it thoroughly before placing it into a bowl.

MARINADE

Marinades are usually prepared with one or more acidic foods, which are used to soften the food and allowing the flavors to be more easily absorbed. They are usually thin liquids; however, most utilize oil as a carrier of the flavorings into the food. Marinades may be used for as little as 30 minutes and as much as 2-3 days depending on the type of food and the recipe.

Large pieces of meat should be placed into a large tightly sealed plastic bag to conserve the amount of marinade needed. Smaller foods can be marinated in a glass container with excellent results. The acidic nature of the marinades may react with metals and give the food a poor flavor. Never baste the food with marinade that the food was in.

Bacteria from the food may contaminate the cooking food and the food may not cook long enough to kill the new bacteria. Always cover the food that is marinating, and keep it refrigerated. Also, make sure the food that is in the marinade is fully covered with the marinade.

- ◆ Most marinades are used to both flavor the food as well as tenderize it. The more common tenderizing acids are papaya (papain), pineapple (bromelain), kiwi, lemon or lime juice, apple cider vinegar and wine.
- ◆ The number of seasonings used in marinades is endless and really depends on a person's taste. The most common seasonings used are black or red pepper, garlic and onion.
- ◆ Marinades will provide a small amount of moisture to a piece of meat; however, one of the major components of a marinade is acid. Acid will reduce the ability of the meat to retain its natural moisture when the meat is cooked. In some meat, the addition of the marinade will balance off this process and you will not notice any dryness. Always remember to allow your roast to rest for 10 minutes after you remove it from the oven so that the liquids that are left can return to the surface of the roast.

Science of Marinade

If you ever wondered why meats turn brown too quickly when they are cooked on a shish kebab or similar method of cooking, it's the marinade. Marinade has a high acid content that tends to react with the myoglobin (muscle pigment) and turns it brown very quickly.

The lower the temperatures the slower the marinade will react, turn brown, and tenderize the meat. If you marinade at room temperature it will take less time than if you do it in the refrigerator. However, it's safer under refrigeration. The acid in most marinades may reduce the moisture retaining properties of the meat, and the meat may not be as moist as you would expect. This problem is usually countered by the fact that the meat will have a better flavor and may contain some of the marinade. Marinades may be a product that contains papain, bromelain, tomato juice, lemon or lime juice, white vinegar, etc.

CHEF'S SECRETS

Many chefs use a plastic bag to apply the marinade to meats and fish, just pour the marinade into the bag, add the food and seal it up well with a rubber band, plastic strap or metal tie. The bag can easily be turned occasionally to be sure that all areas of the food are well marinated. Sometimes a chef will boil the marinade after removing the food, thus reducing it and concentrating the flavors making it safe to use as a sauce.

Marinade Times under Refrigeration

Fish .... 20-40 minutes
Poultry .... 3-4 hours
Meat .... 1-2 days

Chefs are very careful not to marinade too long. The action of the acid will sometimes start to cook the exterior of the meat or poultry causing the whole piece of meat or poultry to dry out when cooked and get somewhat tough.

Chicken should never be marinated very long.

Most cookbooks tell you throw out the liquid used in the marinating process because of possible contamination from bacteria that may be present in the meat. However, the flavor of the marinade is excellent, especially served on grilled meats. Just boil the marinade for 3-4 minutes to kill any bacteria that may be present. The majority of the flavor will be retained.

Marinated meats should be at room temperature when they start cooking.

MAYONNAISE

Mayonnaise may be made using any type of vegetable oil. The preferred oil would be one that is low in saturated fat and ideally one that is high in monounsaturated fat, which would be olive or canola oil. If you wish to have a somewhat nutty flavor, you can use walnut or almond oil. Always use the highest quality of the oil you choose.

♦ When preparing mayonnaise, always remember to add the oil drop by drop, which gives the emulsification enough time to fully form up. As soon as the mixture begins to become more solid and looks somewhat white, you can then add the oil in a slow, thin, steady stream. Adding the oil too quickly will result in separation.

♦ If the oil that is being added does cause a separation, the problem can be solved by either adding ½ teaspoon of prepared mustard or 1 teaspoon of vinegar to the mixture. If this doesn't work, try using an egg yolk that has been beaten well. Whisk the egg yolk into the mixture a small amount at a time just until the mixture is emulsified again. The balance of the oil then needs to be added in a small amount at a time.

♦ Once all the oil has been added to the mayonnaise, flavorings can be added if desired. If you would like a more tart sauce, just add 1 teaspoon of lemon juice. Additional mustard may be added or any other condiment that appeals to your taste. Always serve mayonnaise at room temperature for the best flavor.

♦ Emulsions, such as mayonnaise do not freeze well. The water in the products tends to freeze into ice crystals and separates from the oil. This causes the sauce to break up when thawed and cannot be put back into suspension easily.

Drizzling Good Idea
Trying to whisk and pour oil slowly at the same time can be difficult. Grandma, however, used to place a small hole in the bottom of a paper cup and holding the cup in one hand whisked with the other hand. The oil just dribbles out of the bottom of the cup.

When the temperature or humidity is high, it will cause the mayonnaise to come out heavier and greasier than normal.

- Fresh mayonnaise will only remain fresh for about 3 days under refrigeration and should not be frozen. After 3-4 days the mayonnaise will start to separate and there is no method to bring it back into a separation.
- Mayonnaise will stay fresh in the refrigerator after it is opened for about 2 months, but does not freeze well.
- Food processors' make making mayonnaise much easier.
- Mayonnaise can be made with only egg whites, but it will not be as rich.
- If the recipe calls for mayonnaise, you can use ½ mayonnaise and ½ sour cream. You can use the low fat of each if you desire.

MEASURING

PEEK-A-BOO

If you have ever poured ingredients into a measuring cup and peered over the top to see if it was at the level you desired, you have probably made an error. Chefs always look at the measuring cup at eye level.

Science of Measuring

If you look over the rim of a measuring cup, you will be reading the measurement at the cup's thick glass angle and will probably get a false reading. Refraction from the glass will make the reading look farther up than it really is. Always read the marks on the near side of the cup and keep your eyes level with the surface of the ingredient.

- Accurate measurements are more important when preparing baked goods.
- Do not measure ingredients over a mixing bowl. Spillage may ruin the dish.
- You can purchase two different types of measuring cups, dry and liquid.
- Dash is $1/16^{th}$ of a teaspoon. Use the $1/8^{th}$ teaspoon and just use half of it.
- Best to sift flour and confectioners' sugar before using for an accurate measurement.
- Always place a sheet of waxed paper under the measuring cup when measuring flour or similar product so that you can save the spills and return them to the box.
- Shortening, softened butter or soft margarine should be packed into the measuring cup or spoon and then leveled off with a knife.
- Before measuring a sweet syrupy product, be sure and spray the measuring unit with vegetable oil so that they will slip right off.
- Kitchen scales are very handy. Purchase one that is easy to read.

Certain measurements in old cookbooks may stump you, such as "butter the size of a walnut," which is 2 tablespoons.

A heaping teaspoon = just a little less than 2 teaspoons.
A heaping cup = 1 cup plus 1 tablespoon.
A heaping tablespoon = just under 2 tablespoons.
Butter, the size of an egg = ¼ cup

266

1/3 tablespoon = 1 teaspoon
2/3 tablespoons = 2 teaspoons

MEASUREMENTS

½ Tbsp.	= 1½ Tsp.
1 Tsp.	= 60 drops or 5ml
3 Tsp.	= 1 Tbsp.
2 Tbsp.	= 30 ml. or 1 fl. oz.
8 Tbsp.	= ½ cup
5 Lg. Eggs	= 1 cup
2 Tbsp butter	= 1 oz.
1 oz.	= 30 grams
Orange	= 5-6 Tsp juice
8 Fluid Oz	= 1 Cup
16 Fluid Oz	= 2 Cups (1 pint)
32 Fluid Oz	= 4 Cups (1 quart)
4 Quarts	= 6 Cups (1 gallon)

U.S. WEIGHTS AND MEASURES

1 pinch = less than 1/8 teaspoon
1 tbls. = 3 tsp. = ½ ounce liquid
2 tbls. = 1 ounce, liquid or dry
8 ounces = 1 cup = 16 tbls. = ½ Lb.
2 cups = 16 ounces = 1 pint
1 quart = 2 pints

8 tbls. = 4 ounces = ½ cup = 1 stick butter
1 cup pre-sifted all-purpose flour = 5 ounces
1 cup granulated sugar = 8 ounces
1 cup brown sugar = 6 ounces
1 large egg = 2 ounces = ¼ cup =4 tbls.

MEAT

There are a number of factors that relate to the tenderness of a piece of meat, such as the actual location the meat is cut from, the activity level of the animal, and the age of the animal. The areas of the animal that are the least exercised are the areas that will be the most, tender. However, even if a steak is labeled sirloin and expected to be tender, it will still depend on which end it is cut from. If it is cut from the short loin end it will be more tender than if cut from the area near where the round steaks are cut. Activity levels in most beef, is kept to a minimum so that they will develop only minimum levels of connective tissue.

♦ Kobe beef from Japan actually are massaged by "beef masseurs" to relax them since stress and tension may cause muscles to flex thus resulting in exercise that would increase the level of connective tissue.

- Small cuts of meat will spoil more rapidly and should not be kept in the refrigerator, without freezing for more than 2-3 days. Liver, sweetbreads, cubed meats, and marinated meats should be used within 1 day or frozen.
- Meat products that are "ready-to-eat" usually contain more fat than fresh meat. When these products are manufactured more of the meat by-products can be added which increases the fat content.
- When meat cools on your plate it will get tougher because the collagen, which has turned to a tender gelatin, thickens and becomes tougher. The best way to counter this problem is to be sure you are served steak on a warmed plate. After carving a roast it would be best to keep it in a warmer or back in the oven with the door ajar.
- Meats may turn a grayish color if they are cooked in a pot where there is insufficient room for them. Overcrowding tends to generate excess steam, give them some room to breathe for better results.
- If the meat has been cut from near the head or the hoof, the meat will be tougher, than if it is cut from other locations. The most, tender cut of beef is the "filet mignon," which means "dainty ribbon." The toughest cut is the "chuck."

The mental state of the animal hours before they are slaughtered is important to the storage life of the meat. When you slaughter an animal that is stressed out, tense, or afraid, its body gears up for the flight or fight reflex and starts to convert glycogen (carbohydrate) into glucose for quick energy needs. This will provide the animal with greater strength but when it is slaughtered the excess glucose shortens the storage life of the meat. The glycogen is needed to remain in the muscles to convert to lactic acid and help retard bacterial growth.

When you are hunting, the meat will be better if the animal is killed instantly instead of wounding it and allowing it to live and convert the glycogen. Most slaughterhouses are aware of this problem and see to it that the animal is well relaxed, most of the time by playing soothing music before they kill it.

The process of rigor mortis occurs in all animals and is characterized by the stiffening of the meat and occurs a few hours after slaughtering. If meat is not consumed immediately after it is slaughtered then you should wait at least 15-36 hours, which gives the enzymes a chance to soften the connective tissue.

When thawing meats and poultry, always thaw them slowly in the refrigerator. When you try and rush it with a microwave or place it in a pan to heat partially frozen you will lose a large percentage of the juice and the quality of the meat will not be as good.

COOKING MEATS THAT HAVE BEEN FROZEN
Meat and fish may be cooked directly from the freezer, but should be cooked slowly. This is not a preferred method!

TAKING THE TEMPERATURE

When taking the temperature of a piece of meat, hold the meat with a pair of tongs and insert the thermometer in the side of the meat, making sure you do not touch the bone.

USDA MEAT GRADING

PRIME
Very tender due to higher fat (well marbled) content and comes from young, cattle that are well fed. Prime is the most expensive cut of beef. Not widely available to the general public since most prime is sold to better restaurants.

Calories from fat = 50%.

CHOICE
It is relatively tender still fairly expensive and becoming harder to find in supermarkets.

Calories from fat = 39%.

GOOD
Due to its present pricing has become the most common grade in supermarkets. Has less fat and may need some tenderizing. Common meat used to prepare hamburgers.

Calories from fat = 30%.

COMMERCIAL
Tougher beef from older animals used mainly in TV dinners, hot dogs, cold cuts, sausage, and canned meat products.

UTILITY, CUTTER AND CANNER
These are usually leftover bits and pieces used in processed meat products. It may be very tough and includes neck bones and lower shanks.

MEAT, AGING OF

Aging meat causes the enzymes in the meat to soften the connective tissue and the meat to become more tender. When aging beef, the temperature is very important, and must be kept between 34^0 and 38^0F.

The meat should not be frozen since the enzymes will become inactivated also too high a temperature will cause bacterial growth.

MEAT, COOKING OF

If you are having a problem with meats sticking to the pan, just allow the meat to stand at room temperature 1 hour before cooking: It will cook more quickly, brown more evenly, and stick less when pan-fried. (Do not do this with highly perishable meats like ground beef and organ meats.)

MEAT, SEASONING

The rule is never to use a seasoning that contains salt or pepper before cooking. The salt tends to draw liquid from the meat, the liquid then boils in the pan and the surface of the meat may not have the desired texture or brown color you desire. The salt does not work its way into the meat to flavor it unless you puncture the meat, which is not recommended. If you wish the flavor of a seasoned salt, the best method is to season both sides of the meat just before serving. Ground pepper should never be placed on any meat that is cooked in a pan using dry heat. Pepper tends to become bitter when scorched.

MEAT, TENDERIZING

Since the main problem with tough cuts of beef is the level of collagen (protein substance) in the connective tissue it is necessary to use a moist heat to break down the collagen and soften the connective tissue. A slow moist heat will solve the problem, however, if you cook the meat too long it will actually cause the meat to get tough again due to another constituent in the connective tissue called elastin, which does not soften and become tender. The best method of slow cooking meat is to cook it at 180^0F for about 2-3 hours using a moist heat. Boiling is not effective nor is slow cooking at 140^0F for an extended period. Baking soda is the preferred product to use when tenderizing beef, since all you have to do is rub it on the meat and allow it to stand for 3-5 hours before you rinse and cook it.

Some of the best tenderizers for meats have an alcohol base such as beer and hard cider. The fermentation chemical process gives these products the tenderizing quality.

Other meat tenderizers are made from papaya (papain), pineapple (bromelain), and kiwi.

Tomatoes or tomato sauce will act as a natural tenderizer for all types of beef. Meat should always be cut across the grain whenever possible, the meat will be more tender and have a better appearance.

MEAT, THAWING

When thawing meat there are two considerations to be aware of. First, you want to reduce any damage from the freezing process and second, you need to be cautious of bacterial contamination. Rapid thawing may cause excessive juices to be lost since some of the flavor is in the juices, which is now combined with water and ice crystals.

To thaw the meat and avoid excessive loss of flavor and reduce the risk of bacterial contamination it is best to thaw the meat in the refrigerator once it is removed from the freezer. This means that you will have to plan ahead. Placing the meat in the microwave to quick defrost will cause a loss of flavor and possibly cause drying out of the meat as it is cooked.

All meat should be thawed as quickly as possible, preferably under refrigeration, then cooked immediately. The color of fresh beef should be a bright red color, which is from the muscle pigment. The darker the red color, the older the cow. Beef fat, if fresh, is always white not yellow.

MEATLOAF

When you are preparing meatloaf, try rubbing a small amount of water on top and on the sides instead of tomato sauce. This will stop the meatloaf from cracking as it cooks and dries out. The tomato sauce can be added 15 minutes before it is fully cooked.

To mix meatloaf easier, try using a potato masher.

Science of Meatloaf

By rubbing water around the meatloaf, it keeps the meatloaf moist and stops it from cracking. Tomato sauce does not have the same affect but can be added about 15 minutes before the end of the cooking time to flavor the meatloaf. Never place aluminum foil on top of tomato sauce or the acid in the tomato will breakdown the foil and place aluminum into the food.

- Chefs prefer ground chuck for making meatloaf since it has good fat flavor, but if you want it more lean use ground round.
- The meat should be coarsely ground and finely ground if you like a moist meatloaf.
- To keep your hands clean, just use a large plastic bag when mixing the meatloaf.
- Adding a cup of grated cheddar cheese adds a real treat to any meatloaf.
- If you want a richer flavor add 1/3 cup of wine or beer to your recipe.
- Best to use soft breadcrumbs instead of dry breadcrumbs to produce a more moist meatloaf.
- Be sure and rub the top of the meatloaf with water to stop cracking.
- Use a meat thermometer and be sure it hits 170^{0}F and the meatloaf will be fully cooked.

- Solution of 2 cups of orange juice with sugar or honey for about two hours.

MERINGUE

> **NOTE:**
> If the weather outside is gloomy, rainy or the humidity is high, you will have droopy peaks no matter what you do.

PEEK-A-BOO

Lemon meringue pies are my favorite and I hate to see even one water droplet on a pie. This seems to be a common complaint, whenever people make this type of pie.

> ### Science of Eliminating Water Droplets
> When you open the oven door a crack it releases steam after the pie has cooked for half the cooking time. This will cause the temperature to drop about 50° and solve the problem.

Making the perfect meringue is an art! Chefs know just what to do to make the peaks really perk-up and not droop over. They only use 4-5 day old eggs and make sure that the whites are at room temperature before adding a small amount of baking powder and beating them while adding 2½ tablespoons of sugar for each egg. Beat until the peaks stand up and don't droop over.

> ### Science of Solid Peaks
> If you want your meringue to be world-class, you need to be sure you adhere to all the little tips. Make sure the egg whites are at room temperature, then add a small amount of baking powder to them and as you are beating them add 2-3 tablespoons of sugar for each egg used. Beat only until they stand up. If you want the peaks to stand up for a long period of time, add ¼ teaspoon of white vinegar for every three eggs (whites only) while beating. Adding 4-5 drops of lemon juice for every cup of cream also helps.

MICROWAVE OVEN

- If a child accidentally turns on the microwave, damage may occur. To avoid a problem, just keep a cup of water in the microwave when it is not in use.
- Microwave cooking usually results in short cooking times, which retains the nutrients. The water content of the vegetables will determine just how well they will cook.
- Microwave ovens should have a movable turntable so that the food will not have "cold spots." This can result in the food being undercooked. If you wish to brown foods in the microwave, be sure and use a special dish for that purpose. The dish should always be preheated first for the best results. If you don't have a browning dish, try brushing the meat with soy or teriyaki sauce.

- A steak will continue cooking after it is removed from the microwave and it is best to slightly undercook them.
- Microwave cooking is less expensive than most other methods of cooking; however, it is only desirable for certain types of foods. If you are baking a dish, it will rise higher in a microwave oven, however, meats do not seem to have the desired texture and seem a bit mushy.
- When it comes to placing something frozen in the microwave, it will take longer to cook since it is difficult to agitate the water molecules when they are frozen.
- When foods become hot, chemicals from plastic wrap may be released and migrate into the food.
- The wrap may also stick to the food, especially fatty or sugary foods. Waxed paper, paper towels, or a plate work best.
- If the meat has a bone, microwave cooking will send more energy to the bone than the meat and the meat may not cook evenly. If possible remove the bone and give it to the dog or cat (only if it's a really big one).
- Microwave doors may become misaligned, especially if you tend to lean on them occasionally. They will leak radiation and should be checked periodically with a small inexpensive detector that can be purchased in any hardware store.

Science of the Microwave

Microwave ovens work by emitting high-frequency electromagnetic waves from a tube called a "magnetron." This type of radiation is scattered throughout the inside of the oven by a "stirrer." The "stirrer" is a fanlike reflector, which causes the waves to penetrate the food, reversing the polarity of the water molecules billions of times per second, causing them to bombard each other and creating friction that heats the food. The liquid molecules vibrate so fast they collide with each other and create friction, causing heat cooking the food. The action will not penetrate plates since they do not have active water molecules available.

Plates become hot from the food being heated, not from the waves in the microwave.

Frozen foods do not do well since there are not enough free water molecules until the food thaws enough. Since browning is a problem in a microwave, some manufactures are now adding convection fans and electrical heating elements.

Paper plates make excellent covers when you microwave foods.

- Microwave ovens are just as safe as a regular oven. However, make sure you never place a sealed container in a microwave.
- The thicker, tougher areas of the food should always be placed toward the outer edge of the cooking pan to obtain the best results in a microwave oven.

- The majority of microwave oven cookbooks are written for 700-watt ovens. For a 650-watt oven, add about 10 seconds for each minute the recipe calls for.
- For a 600-watt oven add 20 seconds for each minute and for a 500-watt oven add 40 seconds to each minute of cooking time.
- If you don't have a turntable, the food must be turned regularly. However, inexpensive turntables are available in most kitchen shops.
- Waxed paper can be used to line the bottom of a microwave to avoid having to clean it.
- Round dishes work better in a microwave. Foods in the corners of square or rectangular dishes will cook faster and may burn since the microwaves tend to concentrate there.
- Microwave paper towels are now available to cover foods.
- Room temperature foods will cook much faster than cold or frozen foods.
- Frozen cheese chunks can be brought to room temperature in about 30 seconds on high.
- Only use 30% power when softening butter and no more than 20 seconds for the best results.
- If you want to caramelize sugar, place it in a measuring cup and microwave.
- When reheating leftovers, make sure that you just reheat and not cook or you may ruin the food or dish.
- When food splatters all over the inside of your microwave and cooks itself on after time, to easily remove this mess, place a sponge soaked in water or just a dish filled with ½ cup water in the microwave then cook on high heat for 2 minutes. The splatter is now ready to be wiped right off - no scrubbing!

MILK

Milk was first consumed about 4,000 years ago from dairy animals. Animal milk is not as easily digested as human milk due to the lower amount of protein in human milk, thus resulting in less curdling when the milk hits the stomach acid. When milk is heated, however, animal milk tends to form a looser curd making it easier to digest. The percentage of protein by weight of human milk is about 1% compared to cow milk protein at 3.5%. The fat in milk contains carotene, which give the milk its yellowish color. The non-fat milks are whiter since they do not have the fat content of whole milk.
Two proteins are found in milk called "curds" and "whey." Both react differently when they come into contact with acid and rennin. The casein (curds) forms a solid, while whey remains a liquid in suspension.

If you have ever purchased a quart of milk that had a cooked flavor, the milk was poorly pasteurized, which does happen occasionally. If the milk has a grassy or garlic-like flavor, it was because the cows were milked too close to their last meal.

REDUCING THE SKIN

When chefs have to cook milk for a recipe, they are very careful not to allow a thick skin to form on top of the milk. They have two ways of avoiding the problem.

274

One was to cover the pot and the second was to stir the milk rapidly causing just a small amount of foam to form.

- If milk is left at room temperature for 2-3 hours, the bacteria will multiply to over 300 million and the milk will go sour. Every ½ gallon of Grade A, pasteurized milk contains over 50 million bacteria, give or take a million bacteria and if not refrigerated will sour in a matter of hours.
- Milk should really be stored at 34^0F instead of the average refrigerator temperature of 40^0F. Milk should never be stored in light as the flavor and vitamin A are affected in 4 hours by a process known as "auotoxidation." The light actually energizes an oxygen atom that invades the carbon and hydrogen atoms in the fat.
- If you are going to heat milk in a pot, remember to spread a very thin layer of unsalted butter on the bottom of the pot. This will stop the milk from sticking. Salted butter will not work.
- After you remove the water, 3½ % whole milk contains 50% fat, 2% fat-reduced milk contains 34% fat and 1% low-fat milk contains 18% fat. This is meant to confuse you; if they placed the actual fat content on the package many people would not buy milk.

Science of Milk Skin

The skin that forms on top of milk is composed of the protein "casein," which is the result of the protein coagulating as well as the calcium being released from the water as the milk evaporates. Stirring the milk frequently and leaving the lid off the pot as well as watching the pot will lessen the risk of the film forming. Milk should always be cooked below 140^0F, above that the proteins tend to coagulate. Another problem may occur in that air bubbles may form between the film and the milk pushing the film up and possibly over the top of the pot. The skin contains a number of valuable nutrients and by covering the pot or the rapid stirring it will slow the evaporation and reduce the amount of skin formation.

Never cover any food that is cooked in milk, since it will boil over very easily.

- More milk is produced by California cows than any other cows in any state. California cows produce almost 20,000 pounds of milk annually or about 2,500 gallons. One cow can produce enough milk to provide 130 people a 10-ounce glass of milk every day. California has 800,001 cows producing milk.
- When purchasing milk, be sure and buy it in a container that is not clear plastic. If the milk is exposed to the ultraviolet rays emitted from florescent lights for 4 hours in the supermarket, the milk will lose 45% of the vitamin A content in 1% low-fat milk and 32% in 2% low-fat milk. Manufacturers are now starting to sell milk in yellow-tinted containers.

Milk should be purchased as your last purchase in the supermarket. The longer it is away from refrigeration, the shorter its lifespan and freshness.

♦ The substance in hot peppers "capsaicin" that causes discomfort and can even produce a burn in your mouth and hands can be neutralized by milk, which contains a protein that has an affinity for the capsaicin, binds to it and removes it from your tongue.

If you want your milk to have a longer shelf life, just add a pinch of baking soda to the carton. When you place a small amount of baking soda in milk, it will reduce the acidity level, just enough to add a few more days to the expiration date. However, milk will normally last for a week after the expiration date and still be useable if stored properly and no one drinks out of the carton. Another method is to transfer the milk from a carton to a screw-top glass jar to reduce the effects of oxidation.

♦ Milk is sold in many forms and consistencies, such as powdered, dried, dehydrated, whole, raw, 1% milk, 2% milk, buttermilk, chocolate milk, acidophilus milk, non-fat milk, evaporated milk, condensed milk, goat's milk, etc. Then we have all the products that are made from milk, such as butter, sour cream, cottage cheese, cheese, yogurt, etc.
♦ Fresh milk contains about 5% milk sugar (lactose), which gives milk a somewhat sweet taste. However, as the milk ages, bacteria feed on the sugar and convert the sugar into lactic acid (sour smell), which sours the milk.
♦ When heating milk, try spreading a small layer of unsalted butter on the bottom of the pot to keep the milk from sticking. Salted butter may cause the food to stick.

If you don't use all the milk you purchase, freeze the balance and use it for cooking or baking at a later date. It will take about 4 hours in the refrigerator to thaw. Chefs' also add a pinch of baking soda to milk if it was starting to go bad to give it a few more days by reducing the acidity level.

♦ If you're going to freeze milk be sure and pour a small amount off allowing for some expansion.
♦ Remember the quality of milk depends on the feeding habits of the cows. Poor quality grass produces lower nutritional quality milk.
♦ Milk will absorb refrigerator odors very easily and should always be kept tightly sealed.
♦ The colder the milk is when served, the better the flavor will be.
♦ Milk will scorch easily due to the whey protein than sinks and sticks to the bottom of the pot. Best to use a double boiler.
♦ If you warm milk before you combine it with flour or any other starch it will not have the tendency to clump as much.

MILK, CONDENSED

- Contains 980 calories in 8 ounces.
- Condensed milk can be stored at room temperature for up to 6 months.
- After opening a can it must be stored in a glass jar and as airtight as possible, then refrigerated.
- If heated condensed milk will turn into a thick, golden brown color and tastes a little like caramel.
- Never try and heat a can of condensed milk in an unopened can or it may end up in your neighbor's house. They tend to explode.
- Condensed milk cannot be substituted for evaporated milk in recipes.
- Sweetened condensed milk is not the same as evaporated milk. The sugar content is about 40%.

MILK, CURDLING

Science of Curdled Milk

When milk comes into contact with a mild acid such as vinegar, the acid actually "cooks" the protein and turns the milk into what looks like scrambled eggs. Heavy cream, however, will usually not curdle since the high fat content protects the small amount of protein. If you must make a dish with vinegar and milk, try adding a teaspoon of cornstarch to the cold milk and heat it before adding the vinegar.

MILK, DRY

There are a number of dry milks available at the supermarket, which can be used for several types of cooking purposes as well as drinking and in your cereal. Remember that after you reconstitute the milk to allow it to age for 4 hours in the refrigerator for the best taste. After dry milk is reconstituted it will last for about 3 days in the refrigerator.

All dry milk products should be fortified with vitamins A and D. If the label reads "Extra Grade," the product will be of the highest grade. Grade A is not the highest grade of dry milk. Powdered milk has a tendency to absorb odors and moisture from the air. Try and purchase small packages unless you use a large amount. When powdered milk is canned with nitrogen or carbon dioxide it will last for long periods of time.

MILK, DRY (NON-FAT)

Skim and non-fat powdered milk is the same product and is just milk that has been dehydrated to a powder form. There are two types of non-fat milk, regular and instant. A special spray-drying process is used; however, the instant is processed further so that it will dissolve faster. The regular non-fat milk is mainly used in the baking industry.

To prepare a cup of milk you will need to add 3 tablespoons of the instant to 8 ounces of water. Shaking the milk before you drink it will also add some air to the milk and make it more palatable.

The powder can be added to most dishes to increase the calcium level in foods. It can last for 6 months without refrigeration. Flavored non-fat is now appearing in supermarkets, especially in chocolate flavored drinks, such as cocoa and malted milk.

MILK, DRY (WHOLE)

This milk contains 100% of its fat content and has a shorter shelf life than non-fat dry milk. This milk is usually found in camping stores for hikers. It requires refrigeration to have a better shelf life.

MILK, EVAPORATED

Evaporated milk is made from fresh non-pasteurized whole milk that is then processed in its can at temperatures of over 200^0F (93.3^0C) to sterilize it.

This results in a somewhat burnt taste that can be eliminated by mixing it into a recipe. Condensed milk does not require high heat sterilization since it contains over 40% sugar, which acts as a preservative, thus reducing bacterial growth.

If you are going to substitute condensed milk for evaporated milk, it will only work well in baked goods, cream soups, custards and cream-based sauces. However, you may notice a somewhat off-flavor in dishes that are not heavily spiced and rely on the cream for some flavor. If you are going to substitute evaporated milk for heavy cream in foods that are not cooked, such as mousse or a whipped cream topping, it would be best to substitute with cottage cheese or a part-skim ricotta cheese.

EVAPORATED MILK FACTS

- 4 parts of evaporated milk + 4 parts of water = equal amount of milk.
- May be sold in whole, non-fat, or low-fat types.
- Labels should state "vitamin D added."
- Goat milk is available as evaporated milk.
- If you do not use the whole can, transfer the remainder into a well-sealed glass jar and refrigerate.
- If the milk is slightly frozen, it can be whipped and used as a low-fat ice cream topping. When whipped it will remain stable for about 45 minutes if refrigerated.
- The stability of evaporated milk can be improved by stirring in 1 tablespoon of lemon juice to 1 cup of milk.
- Evaporated milk can be sweetened by adding 3 tablespoons of sugar.

Evaporated milk is now available in whole, low fat, and nonfat, and is only sold in cans. It is heat-sterilized and will store at room temperature for 5-6 months. Partially frozen evaporated low-fat milk can be whipped and will make a low-fat whipped topping. If you need higher peaks, try adding a small amount of gelatin.

MILK, GOAT

Goat's milk has a better protein and mineral ratio that is closer to mother's milk than cow's milk. It also contains a higher level of niacin and thiamin. The protein is of a better quality and there is a lower incidence of allergic reactions than to cow's milk or soymilk. Goat's milk contains 13% more calcium, 25% more vitamin B6, 47% more vitamin A and 134% more potassium more than cow's milk. Supermarkets are starting to carry more goat milk products and if they do not have any in your favorite market, just have them call the Meyenberg Goat Milk Products Company. Evaporated goat milk is available that is pasteurized and homogenized.

Goat's milk is actually healthier than cow's milk for humans and especially infants. The protein and mineral ratio is closer to mother's milk and the milk contains a higher level of niacin and thiamin (B vitamins). The protein is even of a better quality and it less apt to cause an allergic reaction.

MILK, LOW FAT

Some is and some isn't, if that sounds confusing it is meant to be by the milk producers. A good example of this is 2% low-fat milk, which most people think is really low-fat, however, when the water weight is removed from the milk it is approximately 34% fat (not a low-fat product). Whole milk is actually 3.3% fat or about 50% fat, while 1% low-fat milk is about 18% fat. There is new milk ready to hit the supermarkets which is .5% milk and that will contain about 9% fat. Best to use skim, non-fat, or buttermilk, which is now made from a culture of skim milk.

MILK, SCALDING OF

Scalding milk is heating the milk to a point just below its boiling point. To prevent scorching, which is a common problem it would be best to use a double boiler. There are two reasons that a recipe calls for scalded milk; first is that it will kill any microorganisms that may be present and also to kill enzymes that would interfere with emulsifying agents in the milk and retard thickening. Scalding is only needed if you use raw milk. Since almost all milk is now pasteurized, it is not necessary to scald milk, even if the recipe calls for it.

Milk is easy to scorch if it is somewhat stale. Fresh milk is the best choice to avoid scorching as well as using a thick-bottomed pot instead of a thin-bottomed pot. The double boiler is still the best choice except some prefer a faster method. Never heat the milk for too long a time at a high temperature or too fast. The milk proteins tend to get very sticky as they break down and will almost glue themselves to the bottom of the pot when overheated.

MILK FILM, FORMATION OF

A common problem when cooking with milk is the formation of a film of milk protein that rises to the top, coating the surface. Stirring the milk frequently and watching the pot should lessen the risk of the film forming.

Milk should always be cooked below 140°F, above that the proteins tend to coagulate. If the film does form, another problem may occur in that air bubbles may form between the film and the milk pushing the film up and possibly over the top of the pot.

MUFFINS

EASY DOES IT

Muffins will actually be too dense and sticky if they are over-mixed; chef's muffins always come out perfect. The dry ingredients need to be mixed together and then the liquid ingredients need to be mixed together before they are incorporated into each other. Mix only enough to blend the ingredients.

Science of Muffin-Making

Using cake flour will result in less gluten formation and a tender muffin. Hard wheat flour will produce a muffin with the normal interior crumb texture. Mixing too much will result in a smoother textured muffin and will not have the normal muffin texture. When you lift the mixing spoon out of the batter, the batter should break and separate easily.

STUBBORN MUFFINS

Occasionally muffins will stick to the tin and are difficult to remove without breaking them. Next time it happens, try using a grapefruit knife. The curved end gets right underneath the muffins and loosens them.

- To remove muffins, rolls, or biscuits from a sectioned pan, try placing the pan on a damp towel for about 30 seconds. Use an old towel it might stick.
- Try substituting buttermilk for milk in a muffin recipe for the lightest muffins ever. When adding the liquid, be sure and add the liquid in steps with the least amount first.
- Muffin cups will be easy to grease if you use vegetable spray.
- Never grease muffin cups that will not be used or they will burn.
- Place 3 tablespoons of water in unused muffin cups to keep a pan from warping.

If you want perfectly rounded muffin tops, just grease the bottoms and halfway up on the sides of the muffin cup.

- To fill muffin tins, try using an ice cream scoop.
- Before beginning to bake muffins, you need to preheat the oven for 10-15 minutes.
- Never stir muffin batter too vigorously or the muffins will be tough. Lumps will disappear during the cooking process.
- When you fill a muffin cup more than ¾ full, you will get tops that look like flying saucers.

- Muffins can be checked, by inserting a toothpick in the center. If it comes out clean the muffins are done.
- The easiest method of removing muffins from the cups is to run a knife around the edges then under the muffin and tilt it out of the pan.
- Muffins need to be cooked on a rack, not in the pan.
- Muffins should be stored at room temperature in a plastic bag and should last for about 3-4 days.
- Muffins can be frozen in a single layer on very heavy aluminum foil or in a sturdy plastic freezer bag.

MUFFINS, REPAIRING

Moist Bottoms

Muffins were allowed to remain in the pan too long and moisture from condensation occurred. Muffins should be removed from the pan and cooled on a wire rack.

Stuck to Pan

Place the pan on a wet towel for 2-3 minutes to cool the pan and release the muffins.

Too Tough

It is caused by beating the dough instead of folding it. They can't be fixed, just slice them up and toast them.

MUSHROOMS

Mushrooms can be traced back to the Egyptian pharaohs. They are an excellent source of nutrients and are a fungus without any roots or leaves.

- There are approximately 38,000 varieties of mushrooms, many toxic, and a few varieties that are edible. It is best **never** to pick and eat a wild mushroom.
- Mushrooms contain the chemical substance "hydrazine," which is found mainly in the stems. Cooking tends to neutralize this chemical, therefore mushrooms should be cooked. However, most of the "hydrazine" is found in the stems.
- An egg slicer will easily slice fresh mushrooms.
- Grandma used dried mushrooms frequently since they were always available to her.
- These are readily available in most supermarkets today and all you have to do is wash them to remove any sand residue then soak them in warm water, covered for about 30 minutes.
- Save the liquid from the soaking and strain it through a coffee filter or piece of cheesecloth to remove the sand and add the liquid to your dish for additional flavor.
- Chefs may soak dried mushrooms for 2 hours to remove the flavor and then filter the liquid and discard the mushrooms, which have lost its flavor.
- Mushroom juice is used in many dishes to add to the flavor of the dish.
- Studies from the University of Nebraska showed that mice developed malignant tumors from ingesting large quantities of mushrooms.

Science of Mushrooms

Mushrooms have the ability to intensify the flavors of many foods since it contains glutamic acid. They are therefore a natural type of monosodium glutamate (MSG). Mushrooms respire very actively after they are picked and need to be used within a very short time after harvest. After 4 days of storage, mushrooms will lose 50% of their sugar and starch. Refrigeration will slow the process down and give you an extra day or two.

Stems should be discarded or at least $\frac{1}{4}$ inch cut from the bottom of each stem before using since they contain "hydrazine," which in large quantities is not healthy. Spraying the surface of mushroom caps with a solution of vitamin C (ascorbic acid) and water will keep the mushrooms white.

- They are available year round but are best November through March.
- Be sure that the caps are closed around the stem and refrigerate soon after purchasing.
- Mushrooms can be kept white and firm when sautéing if you just add a teaspoon of lemon juice to each quarter pound of butter or olive oil.

MUSHROOMS NEED ROOM TO BREATH

Fresh mushrooms have a very short shelf life of only 2-3 days and need to be stored in an open container in the refrigerator. Plastic containers should never be used since they tend to retain moisture. It is best to use the original container or a paper product to store them in. Never clean them before storing them, they will retain moisture and become soggy.

If you need to keep them stored for a few days place a piece of single-layer cheesecloth on top of the container. If they do become shriveled, they can be sliced and used in dishes.

When freezing mushrooms, just wipe them off with a piece of damp paper towel, slice them, sauté, them in a small amount of butter until they are almost done, allow them to cool, then place them in an airtight plastic bag and freeze. They should keep for 1 year.

THE FLAVOR OF MUSHROOMS AND MSG

The unique flavor of fresh mushrooms is caused by glutamic acid, the natural version of the same flavor enhancer used in the flavor enhancer, Monosodium Glutamate (MSG). Mushrooms, however, do not have any sodium.

VARIETIES

Button

The standard mushroom that is widely cultivated throughout the world. A large majority of the production goes into jars and is canned and dried. They are a short, stubby mushroom with a round cap and gills on the underneath side. Sizes can vary from 1-10 inches.

Cepe

Have a stout stem and a spongy surface instead of gills on the underneath, it has a solid brown cap. It is also known as the Bolete, Cep and Porcino mushroom. They range in size from 1-10 inches and are one of the best tasting mushrooms.

Chanterelle

These are shaped like trumpets. They are large with frilly caps and range in color from gold to yellow-orange.

Enoki

These are sprout-like and have very small caps on a long thin stem. Their color is creamy white and they have a mild flavor. Best served raw in salads or soups and are occasionally called "enokitake" mushrooms.

Italian Brown

These are less expensive mushrooms and are similar in appearance to the standard button mushroom. They have a good flavor and are not as tender as button mushrooms.

Kombucha

They are also known as Japanese tea fungus. Claims have been made recently that it is a cure-all for numerous diseases and recommended for the prevention of hair-loss, arthritis, psoriasis, and cancer. According to recent information from the FDA, scientific evidence is lacking. Cornell University is studying the mushroom and has found it to have properties that may have an anti-tumor effect.

Morel

These are one of the more high-priced mushrooms. Morels are a dark brown mushroom with conical shaped spongy caps and have a honeycombed surface.

Oyster

A wild variety, ranging in color from off-white to a gray-brown, they grow in clusters and have a very dense chewy texture. More flavorful when fully cooked!

Portobello

Also known as Roma mushrooms, they have a hearty flavor, circular caps and long, thick stems. Cut off the woody part. Never wash or soak a Portobello since their caps are like a sponge and will become waterlogged. Clean them with a damp cloth or soft vegetable brush. If they are real dirty, just give them a quick rinse.

Shiitake

At one time these were only grown in Japan, but are now grown and are available in the United States. They are grown on artificial logs and are umbrella-shaped, and brown-black in color. They have a rich flavor and are excellent in salads. They may also be called golden oak, forest, oriental black, or Chinese black mushrooms. Remove stems.

Wood Ear

May have anti-coagulant properties and health claims are presently showing up in the literature. There are no conclusive studies at present in relation to the avoidance of heart attacks. They are mostly sold dried and have flattened caps that tend to vary in size with a crunchy texture. They have also been known as tree ear and black tree fungus.

STUFFED MUSHROOMS

Stuffed mushrooms are great and grandma only stuffed them with spinach. Sauté the mushroom caps in butter and brown just slightly. Save the stems and freeze them to be used in soups or other dish. Drain the spinach as well as you can, pressing out all the water. Place the spinach is a sauté pan on low heat to dry out the remaining liquid without burning the spinach.

Add enough heavy cream to just moisten the spinach and continue cooking it on very low heat until the cream thickens slightly. Add a small amount of salt, white pepper, nutmeg and onion powder. Pile the creamed spinach high on the mushroom caps and add a small buttered crouton or piece of pimento.

MUSSELS

Aquaculture mussel farming has become big business in the United States. Mussels are raised on rope ladders, which keep them away from any debris on the bottom. This produces a cleaner, healthier mussel, and reduces the likelihood of disease. When grown in this manner, they are also much larger.
- ♦ Be sure that the mussels are alive when purchased. Try tapping their shell, if they are open, the shell should snap closed, if not, they're probably a goner.
- ♦ When mussels are shucked, the liquid that comes out should be clear.
- ♦ When you are cooking mussels, they will be done when their shell opens. If the shells remain closed they should not be forced open and eaten.
- ♦ Prepared from mussels, white wine and cream and named for a regular patron of Maxim's Restaurant.
- ♦ Live mussels, covered with a damp towel may be stored for about 2-3 days on a tray in the refrigerator. Never place one on top of the other.
- ♦ Mussels are a common shellfish that is enclosed in a bluish shell and are for the most part aquafarm raised. They should always be purchased live and should be cleaned with a stiff brush under cold water.
- ♦ The visible "beard" needs to be removed; however, once they are de-bearded they will die.

MUSTARD

Mustard is mentioned as far back as 3000 BC in Indian and Sumarian literature. The mustard seed was a symbol of faith and Hippocrates often prescribed mustard to his patients. He produced the mustard by grinding up mustard seeds and mixing other ingredients with the powder.

The mustard we know today can be traced back to 1726, and was produced by Adam Bernhard Bergrath in Dusseldorf. He combined strong brown mustard seeds with a milder yellow seed and added vinegar, water and salt. One of the finest quality mustard's produced in the world is made by Appel & Frenzel under the name Lowensenf Mustard.

Yellow or white seeds will produce mild mustard, while the brown seeds produce the more spicy variety. Powdered mustard has almost no aroma until mixed with a liquid. Mustard has hundreds of uses and is one of the popular spices worldwide. Most mustard will last about 2 years if kept under refrigeration. If a recipe calls for a particular type of mustard, it would be best to use that one.

Using the wrong mustard will make a difference in the taste desired. Mustard oil, which is pressed from brown mustard seeds, is extremely hot and sometimes used in Chinese or other oriental dishes.

TYPES OF MUSTARDS

American Mustard

The typical hot dog mustard is produced from a mild yellow mustard seed, sweetener, vinegar, and usually colored with the herb turmeric. It has a fairly smooth texture.

Chinese Mustard

Found in small ceramic dishes in all Chinese restaurants. It is produced from powdered mustard, water, and strong vinegar. The sweetener is left out and the mustard will only retain its bite for 1-2 hours.

Dijon Mustard

It originated in Dijon, France and is produced from brown mustard seeds, white wine, unfermented grape juice and a variety of seasonings. It has a smooth texture and is usually a grayish-yellow color.

English Mustard

This mustard is produced from white and black mustard seeds, a small amount of flour, and turmeric for coloring. This is one of the hottest mustards sold.

German Mustard

It is produced from a variety of mustard seeds. The color varies and the flavor is somewhat mild due to a small amount of sugar used in the production.

NNNNN

NUTMEG

A relatively sweet spice that is available in ground form and imported from the East and West Indies. Commonly used in sauces, puddings, as a topping for custards, creamed foods, eggnogs, whipped cream, sausages, frankfurters, and ravioli. The most pungent is the freshly ground nutmeg. Special nutmeg graters are sold in kitchen specialty shops.

- ♦ Nutmeg can be found in the supermarket and is sold either ground or whole.
- ♦ Freshly grated nutmeg is very pungent and should be used sparingly in breads, stews and vegetable dishes.
- ♦ Use a toothbrush to clean nutmeg grinders.

♦ Mace is the dried, ground outer membrane of the nutmeg seed.

OOOOO

ODORS

If odors are a problem with a particular dish, try placing a cloth that has been dampened with ½-water and ½-vinegar over the pot. Be sure and make sure that the edges are not near the flame or intense heat.

OIL, FRYING

To use butter, margarine, or lard for frying or sautéing add a small amount of canola oil to them to raise the smoke point. This will allow you to cook with them without their breaking down for a longer period of time.

OILS

Bad Oil

Grandma always saved the used containers from half-and-half or heavy cream and washed them out. She would pour the used fat in the containers and allow them to cool before disposing of them. Never pour hot fat down the drain or it may clog it up.

Avoiding a Mess

Next time you need to spray oil on a muffin tin, just place the tin on the inside of the dishwasher door. Open the door flat and spray away then it will clean off the next time you run the dishwasher.

If you need to place a thin layer of oil on food, try using a spray bottle with oil in it or PAM™. Beats using a brush!

Mixing Oil and Vinegar

When you shake oil and vinegar together, the oil breaks into smaller particles, which allows the two to mix together temporarily. As soon as you stop shaking the mixture, the fat droplets start to combine again and come out of suspension rising back to the surface. However, if you use an emulsifying agent, such as lecithin it will hold the oil and vinegar in permanent suspension.

USING THE RIGHT OIL FOR THE JOB

Knowing which oil to use and for what purpose is very important. Chefs know just which oil to use that they will be able to cook with without the oil smoking and breaking down. They also know what oil to use for flavoring the food.

The best substance to keep oil and vinegar together is lecithin (obtain from health food store). Just break open two lecithin ampoules and mix the liquid into the oil and vinegar. The shaking will break down the fat globules again into very small particles and the lecithin will grab them, encircle them and keep them from combining again. Lecithin is the emulsifying agent in egg yolks, which keeps Hollandaise sauce in suspension.

The majority of oils sold in supermarkets are refined oils and have very little, if any, flavor. Unrefined oils can be found in health food stores and have a much richer flavor. Just add 1-2 tablespoons to replace the refined oil in a recipe and you will be able to tell the difference.

OILS, BREAKDOWN

Oil has the tendency to breakdown when used for prolonged periods or if heated to very high temperatures. This problem will be to a great degree solved with the increase of the oleic fatty acid content. The process of producing high-oleic oil has been too costly; however, scientists feel that the problem can be solved. This will provide oil for frying that will be a healthier oil and not breakdown to trans-fatty acids as easily.

OILS, COLD-PRESSED

The best quality oil is "cold-pressed" extra virgin olive oil. It is made from the plumpest, "Grade A" olives, has the best flavor, and is processed by pressing the oil from the olives with as little heat and friction as possible. The next best is virgin olive oil then pure olive oil, which is a blend of both. Many companies are using "cold processed" instead of "cold-pressed." Cold processed usually means that the olive oil is produced, by using a chemical solvent to extract the oil. Chemical residues are not uncommon. Read the labels and watch for this intentional use of a similar phrase, which does not denote a quality processing.

OILS, CONTAINERS

Only purchase oils in containers if you cannot see the oil. Oil is very sensitive to light and will become rancid. All oils with the exception of cold-pressed olive oil starts oxidizing as soon as it is heat processed then continue to breaks down until it becomes rancid.

OILS, REFRIGERATION OF

When oils are refrigerated and become cloudy, it is due to the buildup of harmless crystals. Manufacturers will sometimes pre-chill the oils and remove the crystals in a process known as "winterization." These oils will remain clear when refrigerated. Lard has larger fat crystals than butter, which has a lot to do with the texture of these fats and is controlled during processing.

The large fat crystals in lard will make it the choice for a number of baked goods where a flakier crust is preferred, especially pies. Moderation in eating these lard products, however, is the key word.

Oxygen has been found to be eight times more soluble in fat that in water, which is why fats tend to oxidize so easily and turn rancid. Every time you open a bottle of oil, more oil leaves and is replaced by oxygen.

OILS, SMOKEPOINT

The smokepoint of oil is the point at which the oil starts deteriorating. All oils have different smoke points; canola oil having one of the highest makes it the best oil for frying. Flavor would be another determining factor in using oil with a lower smoke point. The smoke point is the point at which the oil is starting to convert a percentage of the oil into Trans-fatty acids.

The flash point is the point that the oil starts to show a small amount of flame emanating from the surface of the oil this usually occurs at about 600^{0}F and should tell you that the oil has reached a dangerous level. The fire point is about 700^{0}F, which is the point that you had better have a fire extinguisher ready and remember never to use water on a grease fire. The fire needs to be smothered to extinguish it.

SMOKEPOINTS OF COMMON OILS

Canola Oil	525^{0}F (273.9^{0}C)
Safflower Oil	510^{0}F (265.6^{0}C)
Soybean Oil	495^{0}F (257.2^{0}C)
Corn Oil	475^{0}F (246.1^{0}C)
Peanut Oil	440^{0}F (226.7^{0}C)
Sesame Oil	420^{0}F (215.6^{0}C)
Olive Oil (blend)	375^{0}F (190.6^{0}C)
Vegetable shortening	375^{0}F (190.6^{0}C)
Clarified Butter	350^{0}F (176.7^{0}C)
Butter	250^{0}F (121.1^{0}C)

WHOOOOSH, THERE GOES MY EYEBROWS

A good test to tell whether hot oil is still usable and not high in trans-fatty acids is to drop a piece of white bread into the pan. If the bread develops dark specs, the oil has reached an unsafe level of deterioration. Never allow oil to heat to the smoke point, as it may ignite. It will also make the food taste bitter and may even irritate your eyes. The oils with the highest smoke points are canola, safflower and corn.

OILS, SPRAY

For many years the only spray oil that was sold was Pam. The markets now are selling many different brands as well as different oils available in spray containers.

The latest to hit the shelves has been olive oil.

If you find these products too pricey, all you have to do is stop by a kitchen supply store and purchase an oil spray bottle. These are small pump action spray bottles that you can easily fill. Use any oil and an equal amount of lecithin to keep the oil in suspension. Lecithin may be found in the vitamin section of your market or any health food store.

Most of the market brands contain lecithin, which helps keep the propellant and the oil from separating, however, it is best to purchase the pump-type sprays to protect the ozone layer.

Never spray the oils on too hot a surface or an open flame since they are flammable. Also, be careful of inhaling the oil spray as it is capable of coating the lungs and could be fatal.

OILS, STORAGE OF

One of the first things chefs learn is how to store oils. Saving money is very important and oils are expensive. Not only that but if they were not stored properly, they would deteriorate, get rancid and go bad too fast.

PEEK-A-BOO

The oil that chefs purchase is almost always in a tin, which will keep the oil fresher longer.

Science of Storing Oils

All oils should be resealed as tightly as possible and stored in a cool, dry location, preferably the refrigerator. Cloudiness is common when oil is refrigerated and the oil will return to normal if allowed to remain at room temperature for about 15-20 minutes. If a container of oil is left out of the refrigerator for even a short period of time on a hot, humid day, the oil will start to become rancid very quickly. Oil that has been opened is only fresh for about 4 months and should be discarded after that. It would be wise to date the oil container when it is purchased. Rancidity will usually begin about 4 months after the oil is purchased regardless of the method of storage. Exposure to light for long periods will cause almost any oil to turn brown.

Oil that is in a sealed, unopened bottle will stay fresh for 1 year. When oil is poured out of the bottle into any other container for any reason, it should never be returned to the original container and mixed with the clean oil. Contamination is possible and may ruin the balance of the oil left in the container. Unrefined oils high in essential fatty acids only have a high quality shelf life of 3-6 weeks and must be refrigerated. If you wish to freeze the quality oil, it will be good for about 12 months.

OILS, VEGETABLE

The best vegetable oils to use for cooking are those that are lowest in saturated fat. However, some dishes require that certain oils or fats be used to produce the desired flavor of the dish.

In those instances, the recommended oil should be used. In all other instances, olive oil is highly recommended since it is high in monounsaturated fat, which is fat the body prefers over other types of fats. Throughout the book, when recipes call for cooking with olive oil you should note that a small amount of canola oil is usually recommended along with it. The canola oil raises the smoke point of olive oil just enough so that it slows down the breakdown of the olive oil.

OKRA

- ♦ When you purchase fresh okra, be sure that the pods are a fresh, bright color, are very firm and are under 4 inches long.
- ♦ If the pods are damaged in any way, do not purchase them.
- ♦ Before you cook okra, be sure and remove the stem ends.
- ♦ Okra is best, boiled and used in soups or stews but can also be sautéed or cooked in the microwave.
- ♦ Okra goes great with tomatoes, corn and onions.
- ♦ The taste is a cross between eggplant and asparagus.
- ♦ Because of its sticky juice has been mainly used in soups and stews.
- ♦ It is a good source of vitamins and minerals.
- ♦ Okra tends to spoil rapidly and should be refrigerated soon after purchasing. It is usually best between May and October.
- ♦ Never wash okra until you are ready to use it or the protective coating will be removed that keeps the pods from becoming slimy.
- ♦ Try grilling okra with a small amount of olive oil brushed on.
- ♦ Okra has the tendency to become stringy and tough, which is called "roping." To avoid the problem (roping), just add 1 teaspoon of white vinegar to the cooking water.

EXCELLENT THICKENER

Okra is actually a vegetable that consists of numerous unripe seed capsules. It is a very high carbohydrate food that is high in fiber and starch and contains a good amount of pectin and gums. The combination of these food elements provide an excellent thickener for soups and stews.

As okra is heated the starch granules absorb water and increase in size. The starch granules soon rupture and release "amylose" and "amylopectin" molecules, as well as, some of its gums and pectin. These then attract additional water molecules and increase the volume, thus thickening the food.

GET OUT THE HAMMER AND CHISEL

Okra seeds have a very hard outer coat, which can hamper germination resulting in an uneven patchy garden. There a number of ways to avoid the potential problem:

- Barely nick the seed coating with a sharp knife.
- Place seeds on a piece of fine sandpaper and rub them with another sheet.
- The seeds can be soaked in tepid water at room temperature for 24 hours.
- The seeds can be placed in the freezer for about 12 hours, and then soaked in hot tap water for 30 minutes just before planting.

OLIVE

Olives were originally a native of Iran, Syria and Israel and spread to all surrounding Mediterranean countries almost 5,000 years ago. The olive tree is one of the oldest cultivated tree crops in the world. Olive trees are presently grown in hundreds of countries worldwide. There are thousands of varieties of olives.

In 3½ ounces of olive pulp, it will contain 165 calories, 71% water, 1.2gr protein, 18.7gr of fat, 80mg of calcium, 760mg of sodium, 200IU of vitamin A, a few mg of B vitamins and 3mg of vitamin C, as well as assorted minerals including iron and potassium.

- ♦ If olives have been sitting around for too long a period and are getting bitter, chefs just simmer them in water for about 10 minutes to reduce the bitterness.

To pit large olives, chefs may place them on a piece of paper towel and roll them gently with a wooden rolling pin. They will then press them gently with the heel of their hand and the pits will pop right out.

- ♦ An unopened jar of olives will last and be fresh for about 12 months. Once opened it needs to be refrigerated and will remain fresh for about 1 month.
- ♦ Canned olives that are in brine need to be placed into a glass container with the brine and refrigerated.

291

> If you place a thin layer of vegetable oil on top of the brine, the olives will last longer.

- Bulk olives can be stored for up to 2 months if placed in a jar with fresh vegetable oil and refrigerated.
- When olives get soft, it is best to discard them.
- The white film that tends to develop on top of olives can be skimmed off then wash the olives and they will still be good.

OLIVE OIL

Olive oil is high in monounsaturated fat (77%) and is gluten-free. One tablespoon contains 8% of your daily requirement of vitamin E. Greece is one of the largest producers of olive oil with an annual output of 300,000 tons. The oil produced is of the highest quality, which is the low acid, extra virgin variety. Most of the Mediterranean countries produce olive oil of such poor quality that it must be refined to produce an acceptable flavored product. Look for oil from Greece or California that states "cold-pressed, first-pressing, extra virgin, pure organic."

- Law has set the standards for olive oil and the saturated fat levels it contains. Extra virgin olive oil must not contain more than 1% unsaturated fatty acid and virgin olive oil must not contain more than 3.3%.
- Pure olive oil is a combination of both oils.
- Olive oil is one of the healthiest oils to use in salads or for low temperature cooking. It has a low smoke point, which means that it will break down easily and start smoking. You can extend the usable life of olive oil and slow its breakdown by adding a small amount of canola oil to the olive oil. Canola has a very high smoke point. This will also work well with butter when you are sautéing.
- The most popular oil is olive oil with soy oil coming in second. Olive oil will stay fresh longer than most oils while soy oil tends to lose its flavor the longer it is stored due to the linolenic acid it contains.

Science of Olive Oil

Olive oil has a high level of vitamin E since it is cold processed and will stay longer at room temperature than any other oil before going rancid. The oil can last up to one year; however, the flavor will mellow over time.

Olive oil is high in monounsaturated fat (77%) and is gluten-free. Extra virgin, cold processed olive oil from Italy is the choice of most gourmet executive chefs worldwide. One tablespoon of olive oil contains 8% of your daily requirement of vitamin E. Greece is one of the largest producers of olive oil with an annual output of 300,000 tons.

The oil produced is of the highest quality, which is the low acid, extra virgin variety. Most of the Mediterranean countries produce olive oil of such poor quality that it must be refined to produce an acceptable flavored product.

Look for oil from Greece or California that states "cold-pressed, extra virgin, pure organic." The color of the best extra virgin olive oil should be emerald green. If the oil is a deep green then it is young oil and has not had time to mellow with aging and lose a percentage of its flavor.

This oil is still expeller-pressed: however, the process is not allowed to reach the high temperatures that are produced from the full extraction processing. Only three oils: olive oil, peanut oil and sesame oil, can be processed by this method and obtain enough oil to sell commercially. The low heat processing reduces the quantity of oil obtained significantly. Cold-pressed oils are the highest quality oils and contain the highest levels of nutrients.

ONIONS

Onions probably originated in prehistoric times and was a popular favorite in ancient Egypt and Rome. Onions are a member of a family that has over 500 varieties. They are low in calories and some are an excellent source of vitamin A.

- ♦ Try burying an onion wrapped in aluminum foil in the coals for 1 hour. Try it! You will like it!
- ♦ Onions should only be purchased hard, and dry avoid onions with wet necks, this indicates decay. Also, avoid onions that have sprouted. They can easily be stored at room temperature or refrigerated.
- ♦ If you are only going to need half an onion, use the top half since the root half will store longer in the refrigerator.
- ♦ An onion that has become pithy and has started to sprout can be placed in a pot on a windowsill, as it continues to sprout snip off the sprouts for salad seasoning.

IT'S A LITTLE CHILLY IN HERE
If you store onions or shallots in the refrigerator they won't last long and may sprout.

COOKING ONIONS AND GARLIC TOGETHER
When you are sautéing onions and garlic together, be sure and sauté the onions first for at least ½ their cooking time. If the garlic is placed in at the same time, it will over cook and possibly burn and release a chemical that will make the dish bitter.

RETAINING THE SWEETNESS IN RAW WHITE AND RED ONIONS
Place the raw chopped onions in a medium strainer, then dip the strainer into a bowl of cold water that contains a small amount of white vinegar (about ½ teaspoon to 1 quart of water). The slight acidity from the vinegar is just enough to stop the onions from turning bitter.

STORING ONIONS

Onions should be stored ideally in hanging bags, which will allow the air to circulate around them. Never purchase an onion if it has the slightest hint of decay since it will spread rapidly to healthy onions.

The location should be cool and dry. If the weather is hot and humid it will cut the storage time in half otherwise they should last about 2-3 weeks.

♦ If you refrigerate onions they will last for about 2 months but may pass their aroma on to other foods in the refrigerator, even eggs.
♦ Sprouted onions are still good to use as well as the sprouts. To freeze onions, just slice then (do not blanch them) and place them into a sealed plastic bag.
♦ They will freeze well for about 1 year.
♦ The smell of onions can be removed with a strong solution of salt water or a small amount of white vinegar.
♦ Chives need to be refrigerated and used within 3-4 days after purchase for the best flavor. If frozen, they can be added to any dish while still frozen. Chives can be stored in the refrigerator wrapped in paper towels in a plastic bag. They should last for about 1 week.

If the onion you are working with tastes too hot, just soak the cut onion in ice water with 2 tablespoons of white vinegar to 4 cups of water for 25 minutes. When grandma paints a room, she places a cut onion in room and closes the door. The onion will neutralize the paint fumes and odor overnight.

ONIONS, BOILING

Occasionally, chefs like to boil onions whole, however, whenever I tried it, the insides would always pop out.

Science of Popping Insides

When onions are cooked, the steam from the high water content tends to build up and cause the insides to pop out to release the pressure. To avoid this problem, just cut an "X" into the bottom of the onion before you start cooking it to allow the steam to escape. You should only have to boil the onions for 1 minute.

ONIONS, COOKING WHOLE

Have you ever cooked a whole onion only to have the insides pop out and ruin the appearance of the dish you are preparing?

This is a very common occurrence and happens almost every time unless you pierce the onion with a thin skewer once or twice allowing the steam to escape.

Another method, similar to one that is done to chestnuts so they won't explode, is to cut an "X" on the root end which will allow the steam to be released without damaging the onion.

Cooking an onion will actually turn the sulfurs in the onion into sugars, which is why onions tend to have a sweeter flavor after they are cooked. As onions brown, the sugars and proteins change and become a deep brown color and caramelize; which also intensifies the flavor. The reaction is called the "Maillard Reaction." Onions also change color when cooked and turn a creamy white color caused by the chemical "anthocyanin." This chemical should not come into contact with metal ions from aluminum or iron pots or it will turn the pot brown. When onions are sliced with a carbon-steel knife the same reaction takes place and may change the color of the onion.

When a recipe calls for onions, remember that it always means a round, yellow onion. If the onion is too strong for a dish you can reduce the pungency. To control the pungency chefs use the following methods:

Strong Onion Flavor – Grate or chop very fine and sauté in a small amount of butter just until a deep gold color or use raw.

Medium Onion Flavor – Slice or chop the onions into small pieces and sauté just enough to soften them. Do not cook until golden brown.

Mildest Onion Flavor – Use the whole onion and cook or roast very slowly for a long time. After cooking, chop in medium pieces and cook in a liquid.

If you want to serve raw onions and want to make them a little milder, just soak them for 1 hour in water that has been sweetened with 1 teaspoon of sugar per cup of water. Drain and dry off well with paper towel before using.

One of the funniest things I ever saw grandma do was to wear plastic goggles when she cut onions. She wore glasses and placed the goggles over her glasses to stop the onion fumes from getting in her eyes. She also chewed on a piece of parsley.

Science of Crying & Onions

When you slice into an onion, a gas is released that affects the lachrymal glands in the eyes and causes a defensive reaction by the body against the chemical "propanethiol S-oxide" which reacts with the fluid in your eyes forming sulfuric acid. The body protects itself from the acid by tearing action, which washes out the eyes ridding itself of the irritant. One of the best methods to avoid tearing is to wear solid plastic goggles.

Other methods if you prefer not to shed tears is to cut the root off last, freeze the onion for 10 minutes, or refrigerate for 1 hour before slicing. Other tricks that have worked are to ball up a piece of white bread and place it on the tip of the knife or hold it between your teeth to absorb the fumes. Chewing gum may also help. Another method that works well is to light a candle to absorb the fumes.

ONIONS, SAUTEED

Science of Sauteing Onions

Onions are often sautéed so that they will blend better into a dish or soup. If they are not sautéed first, they will not combine well with other foods, especially if the other foods contain acid, such as tomatoes. If the onions are not softened first, the acids in the other foods will keep the onions from remaining soft and the onions will remain firm. When combining onions with foods that contain a dairy product such as milk, the onions may curdle the milk if they are not sautéed first releasing some of their acids.

ORANGES

♦ Before oranges are squeezed they are inspected for damage and contamination. The oranges are then kept chilled to help retain the vitamin C content. All fruit is then washed with a neutral detergent, sanitized and rinsed with pure water. The orange is then squeezed from the outside in which eliminates the bitter taste from the peel. As soon as it is squeezed it is cold chilled to below zero temperatures and placed in cold storage.

♦ Florida oranges are thin-skinned which means that they will have more juice than all other oranges grown outside of Florida. The climatic changes in other growing states cause the oranges to develop a thicker, more protective skin and less juice.

♦ For citrus fruit to be "seriously" damaged by freezing, the dryness caused by the freezing temperatures must cause the fruit to appear dry more than ½ inch from the stem and. If the dryness extends only ¼ inch then the fruit is considered only "damaged."

♦ Never store oranges in sealed plastic bags. If they are stored in airtight container small drops of moisture will form and cause mold to grow. The best temperature to store any citrus is around 45^0F (7.2^0C). Refrigerators are the recommended location.

♦ The best oranges for juicing are the Hamlin and Valencia. Both will be found to have thin-skins either no seeds or very few seeds and will produce the most juice.

♦ A tasty dressing for fruits can be prepared by grating an orange rind and adding it to orange juice and low-fat sour cream.

- The color of an orange does not necessarily indicate its quality, since oranges are usually dyed to improve their appearance.
- Brown spots on the skin indicates a good quality orange. Pick a sweet orange by examining the navel. Ones with the largest navel will usually be the best.
- If you place an orange into a hot oven for 2-3 minutes before peeling, no white fibers will be visible and the pectin will melt into the flesh.
- Mandarins are a very close relative to the orange, are more easily peeled, and the sections are more pronounced. They come in a number of varieties.
- The rinds of oranges and grapefruits should be stored in a tightly sealed jar and refrigerated. They may be grated and used for flavoring cakes, frostings and cookies.

THE NO WASTE ORANGE

The orange juice industry uses every bit of every orange it processes. The residue from the production of orange juice is a multi-million dollar industry.

Everything, including the pulp, seeds, and peel are used in food products such as candy, cake mixes, soft drinks, paints, and even perfumes. Over 100 million pounds of "peel oil" is sold for cooking uses and is also made into a synthetic spearmint base for the Coca Cola Company to be used as a flavoring agent.

Science of an Orange

Oranges that look green have undergone a natural process called "re-greening." This is due to a ripe orange absorbing chlorophyll pigment from the leaves. Florida oranges normally have more of green tint than oranges from California or Arizona. This occurs due to the warm days and nights allowing the orange to retain more of the chlorophyll. A number of companies that sell Florida oranges may dye the oranges since we are not used to purchasing green oranges and think that they are not ripe.

When oranges are dyed they must be labeled "Color Added" on the shipping container. The cooler nights in California and Arizona remove the green, however, both states have laws prohibiting adding any color to citrus fruits. Over 100 million pounds of "peel oil" is sold for cooking uses and is also made into a synthetic spearmint base for the Coca Cola Company to be used as a flavoring agent.

OREGANO

A relative of the mint family, and may be found by the names origanum and Mexican sage. It is commonly sold in leaf or ground forms. It is a common herb used on Italian specialties such as pizza (gives it its unique flavor) and spaghetti sauces. Try oregano on a grilled cheese sandwich and you will never eat another one without it.

Chefs only use oregano sparingly and in certain foods. Their favorites are as follows:

➢ **Chicken**
   Rub the inside and outside with 1-2 teaspoons of oregano before roasting.
➢ **Fish**
   Rub the inside of fish with ¼ teaspoon of crushed dried oregano.
➢ **Veal**
   Rub the meat gently with some of the dried herb before roasting. Use about 1 teaspoon.

OVEN, TEMPERATURE

Place about 1 tablespoon of flour on the bottom of a cookie sheet and place it into a preheated oven for about 5 minutes. When the flour turns a light tan color, the temperature is between 250^0 to 325^0F.

If the flour turns a golden brown, the oven is at 325^0 to 400^0F. When it turns a dark brown, the temperature is 400^0 to 450^0F and almost a black color the oven will be 450^0 to 525^0F.

If anyone has ever driven you crazy because you opened the oven door when something was cooking, this is your chance to explain why you did it and that it was no "big deal." When the door is opened or left ajar for a few minutes, it only takes 40-50 seconds for the temperature to return to the preset temperature. It is not really a big deal and will not affect the food.

♦ You need to check your oven temperature regularly and adjust recipes accordingly.
♦ Always preheat ovens for 15 minutes before doing any baking.

> **Pouring salt on oven spills immediately will make them easier to clean up.**

PPPPP

pH

This refers to the scale to measure acidity and alkalinity. The pH is actually the hydrogen "H" ion concentration of a solution. The small "p" is for the power of the hydrogen ion. The scale used to determine the level of acidity or alkalinity of a product or solution is measured with the number 14 as the highest level and 7 as a neutral point where the acidity and alkalinity are balanced. Water is 7, and if the number goes above 7 the solution is considered to be alkaline. If the number falls below 7 then the solution is considered to be acidic. Human blood has a pH of 7.3, Vinegar and lemon juices are 2.3, and common lye is 13.

PAN BROILING

Chefs love to pan-broil meats and will only use large cast iron skillets that had ridges in the bottom. Pan-broiling is similar to frying except that you use very little fat. They normally do this with bacon, hamburgers or small pieces of meat.

The pan would leave grill marks and would make you think that they had grilled the burgers.

PANCAKES

Grandma's secret to the greatest pancakes is never to mix the batter too much and refrigerate it before using it. She knows exactly how to blend everything together to make the perfect pancake.

Science of Perfect Pancake Batter

By mixing pancake batter for too long a period, you will overwork the batter and make the pancakes tougher since the gluten in the flour will overdevelop. This will create a tough pancake and the premature formation and escape of carbon dioxide, thus affecting the leavening of the pancake. If you stop mixing before all the tiny lumps of flour dissolve and allow the batter to complete the process in the refrigerator, you will have a better batter. The batter will be smoother and the refrigeration will slow bacterial growth, slow gluten development and also slow the baking powder activity.

Science of Flipping Pancakes

To make the lightest pancakes, they must be flipped at exactly the right moment. Flip the pancakes as soon as the bubbles start appearing on the upper surface and before they start breaking to release the gas otherwise you will have a flat pancake instead of a puffy one.

Make sure you turn pancakes as soon as the air pockets form on the top for the best results.

THE HOT GRIDDLE BOUNCING-WATER TEST

Pancakes should be cooked on a griddle that is approximately 325^0F for the best results. To be sure of having the proper temperature, just dribble a drop or two of cold water on the hot griddle. The water should bounce around on the top of the griddle close to the spot you drop it because of steam being generated and gravity forcing the water back down to the griddle.

- ♦ If the griddle is too hot, the water drops will be propelled off the griddle, this usually occurs at about 425^0F. Instead, stop mixing before this occurs and place the batter in the refrigerator slowing the development of the gluten and the activity level of baking powder or yeast.

◆ Adding sugar to your recipe causes the sugar to caramelize, producing a golden brown outside. The more sugar, the more caramelizing that takes place and the more brown the pancake becomes. Using a meat baster works great for squeezing the batter onto the griddle in just the right amount.
◆ Pancakes will never stick to the cooking surface if you clean the surface after every batch with coarse salt wrapped up in a piece of cheesecloth. The salt will provide a light abrasive cleaning and won't harm the surface if you're gentle.

UP, UP & AWAY
When chefs make pancakes, they never use milk or water they just substitute club soda or seltzer to make the pancakes so light they will float around the house and you will have a problem finding them. You can also substitute fruit juice in place of the milk or water.

◆ To make pancakes light and tender, try separating the egg yolks then beat the whites until stiff. Stir the yolk along with the other liquid ingredients into the dry ingredients before folding in the egg whites.
◆ The batter should always be mixed between batches of pancakes, waffles, and latkas (potato pancakes). This will assure that settling of ingredients does not take place as well as keeping it aerated. The quality of the product will be excellent.
◆ If you over-mix the batter, it will cause the gluten to overdevelop resulting in a tougher pancake. Over-mixing can also force out more of the trapped carbon dioxide that assists in the leavening. Most people tend to mix the batter until all the small lumps of flour are dissolved; this is overkill.
◆ A meat baster can be used to squeeze your pancake batter out onto the hot grill for perfect pancakes every time. However, you may need to have a baster just for pancakes since you will need to cut the opening up a little more.
◆ Lighter pancakes can be made by replacing milk with apple cider for a different flavor treat.
◆ A tablespoon of **REAL** maple syrup added to your pancake batter will really improve the taste.

Nice and Cozy
It is always best to eat pancakes right from the hot griddle; however, if that is not possible you can keep them warm for a few minutes by placing them on a platter lined with a cloth napkin. Pull the napkin over the pancakes and cover them with an inverted colander. Do not use a metal bowl or they will get soggy.

PANS, GREASING & FLOURING

ONE OF CHEF'S BEST TRICKS
Many recipes call for you to "grease & flour" the pan before using it.

The standard method is to grease the pan with oil then sprinkle the flour in and tap the pan allowing the flour to move around and distribute evenly. However, sticking may occur and it may be a bit messy.

Science of Greasing & Flouring

The trick to doing this is to prepare a mixture of $\frac{1}{2}$ cup of vegetable oil, $\frac{1}{2}$ cup of room temperature vegetable shortening mixed with $\frac{1}{2}$ cup of all-purpose flour. Blend the mixture well and use it to grease and flour a pan. Make sure you store the leftover in an airtight container and it will last for about 6 months.

PAPAYAS

The papaya is also known as the "pawpaw." However, this is really a different fruit. Papaya originated in South America and is now extensively grown in Hawaii and Mexico.

- The fruit can weigh from ½-pound up to 20 pounds and can be in any number of shapes, from pear to oblong.
- Ripe papaya is better if consumed raw.
- Papaya will ripen in a brown paper bag with an apple or green tomato.
- The papaya seeds are edible and can be used as a garnish similar to capers. They may also be dried and ground, then used like pepper.
- The Hawaiian papayas are the sweetest and the most common in the markets.
- Scoop out the seeds with a spoon before you eat papaya.
- The Mexican papayas are much larger and not as sweet. It is an excellent meat tenderizer utilizing an enzyme called "papain."
- Only papayas that are not fully ripe have sufficient papain to be useful as a meat tenderizer. The more ripe a papaya is the less papain content.
- The papaya leaves also contain the tenderizer and meat is commonly wrapped in these leaves when it is cooked in Hawaii. When ripe, they will be completely yellow. They will take 3-5 days to ripen at room temperature.
- Gelatin will not set if you put papaya in it. However, heat does kill the enzyme that stops the gelatin from setting up.

PAPRIKA

The best paprika is imported from Hungary in the form of ground pods. The milder variety, red sweet, is grown in the United States. It is commonly used in a wide variety of dishes such as cream sauces, vegetables, mustards, salad dressings, ketchup, sausages, and fish dishes. It makes an excellent powdered garnish.

- Paprika can be purchased in the hot as well as the mild forms.
- Paprika is made from grinding aromatic sweet red peppers.
- The flavor can be intensified by roasting in a dry pan for just a few minutes.

PARBOILING

- Parboiling is performed by partially cooking foods in boiling water then immediately plunging them into ice cold water to stop the cooking process.
- When using carrots in a dish with other softer vegetables, parboiling can be very useful because of the hardness and density of the carrot.
- Before you place a food in to parboil it, be sure that the water is rapidly boiling.
- Be sure and test food to be sure that it has softened using a fork.
- Always have the bowl of ice water with ice cubes ready to place the food in the second you take it out.
- After you parboil food it can be refrigerated for 2 days before you use it.

PASTA

When it comes to which sauce to serve with which pasta, the rule is: the longer the strand, the thinner the sauce should be. Noodle-shaped pastas like creamy sauces, while capellini likes a thin sauce.

Cook pasta only until it becomes slightly chewy (al dente). The more you cook it, the less nutrients it will retain. When preparing pasta, always cover the pot as soon as you place the pasta into the rapidly boiling water. Keep the water boiling and **DO NOT** allow it to cool down to obtain the best results. When draining pasta, make sure you warm the colander; a cold colander will cause the pasta to stick together. Adding a small amount of vegetable oil to the water as it is cooking will also help.

- If you see the chemical "disodium phosphate" on a package of pasta it is only used to help the pasta cook faster by softening it up.
- The finest pasta in the world is produced in Russia and is called "Amber Durham."
- If you're making pasta dough, don't make it on rainy or high humidity days, it will be very difficult to knead.
- A large pasta meal may help you relax by increasing a chemical called Serotonin. However, if you eat pasta without a protein dish, you may feel somewhat sluggish 1-2 hours later. This is related to a blood sugar level change in some individuals.

> **When serving pasta, be sure and serve it in a warm bowl.**

- Most pasta is easily digested and has a low fiber content making this a good food for children and the elderly. Also, pasta is normally made with hardly any salt and is excellent for a low sodium diet.
- If you are purchasing pasta with a clear plastic window or in a see through package you will have a nutrient loss due to the lights in the supermarket. Purchase pasta in boxes without a window.

302

- The ratio of cooked pasta to uncooked pasta is 2:1. For every cup of uncooked pasta you will end up with two cups of cooked pasta. Uncooked pasta contains 3.4 grams of protein per ¾ cup.
- When eating pasta, which is a high carbohydrate food, it would be wise to have some protein with the meal to balance off all that carbohydrate. This will allow the blood sugar levels to be normalized in susceptible individuals.
- Dried pasta will last for years if stored in a cool, dry location.
- The amount of pasta to purchase for each person will depend on the type of pasta you purchase: dried or fresh. Fresh pasta is heavier since it contains more moisture. If dried pasta will be a side dish 2 ounces person is sufficient, however, if it is the main dish you will need 4 ounces per person. Fresh pasta will require 3 ounces per side dish and 5 ounces for the main dish.
- If pasta will be used in a salad it would be best to rinse it under cold water to get rid of the excess starch. This will stop the pasta from sticking together.
- You will need 2 cups of sauce for every pound of pasta.
- When boiling pasta, be sure to rub vegetable oil around the inside top of the pot to avoid boil over.

Science of Pasta

Pasta is composed of two main ingredients, water and either standard flour or the coarsest part of the wheat called semolina. Pasta dough needs to be very stiff and is therefore only 25% water compared to bread dough, which is about 40% water. Durum wheat 100% semolina is the choice for most of the better quality pasta and contains a very low percentage of starch and a high percentage of protein. When cooked properly it will not get mushy or sticky. The gluten matrix is very strong since the protein does not have to compete with the starch for the moisture. Because the protein is strong it can be extruded by machine without falling apart. Standard flour pasta is easily broken and is the poorer quality product.

PASTA, COMPOSITION OF

Pasta is composed of two main ingredients, water and either standard flour or the coarsest part of the wheat called "semolina." Pasta dough needs to be very stiff and is therefore only 25% water compared to bread dough, which is about 40% water. Durum Wheat Semolina is the choice for most of the better quality pastas and contains a very low percentage of starch and a high percentage of protein. The gluten matrix is very strong since the protein does not have to compete with the starch for the moisture. Because the protein is strong it can be extruded by machine without falling apart. Standard flour pasta is easily broken and is the poorer quality product.

PASTA, COOKING OF

Some chefs' will tell you that to tell if pasta is ready, you need to throw a piece at the wall. If the pasta sticks to the wall it is ready to eat.

When you add pasta or other food to boiling water the foods will contain a percentage of organic matter, especially proteins, which are released into the cooking water. These elements that are released accumulate on the surface and disrupt the surface tension that has been created by the boiling water. When this occurs, foam is formed and mixes with the water causing the bubbles to be somewhat stronger and not burst as easily, thus flowing over the top of the pot.

To avoid this problem, just add a **small** amount of oil to the water, which does not mix well with the water causing tiny oil droplets to form on the surface. The oil acts as "bubble-breakers," does not allow the bubbles to become large and the pot will not boil-over. The majority of dried pasta will double in volume when cooked. In order to be accurate, try measuring pasta by weight rather than by the cup. Four ounces of uncooked pasta (1 cup dried pasta) equals 2½ cups of cooked elbow macaroni, shells, penne or ziti.

Science of Cooking Pasta

Always use a pot big enough that you can have plenty of boiling water so that it will remain at a rolling boil without spilling over. The pasta needs to move around when it is cooking to prevent it from sticking together. Pasta is a starchy food and is prepared from egg and wheat. It contains strong starch molecules and when these molecules are placed into boiling water, they start to absorb the water and swell up. However, some of the starch molecules leak out of the pasta into the water and will thicken the water. If there is not enough water, the water becomes too thick with these molecules and causes the pasta to stick together.

Pasta placed in water that is not boiling rapidly will not "set" properly and the pasta may stick together. Also NEVER add too much oil to the pasta water or it will coat the pasta and keep the sauce from sticking to the pasta. Pasta should be stirred with a wooden spoon since certain metals in utensils may cause a slight discoloring of the pasta by reacting with the starch.

PASTA, DOUGH (preparation of)

PROPER DRYING OR CONTAMINATED PASTA

When chefs make pasta dough they try and dry the dough at a fast even rate. If the pasta dough is dried too fast, the outer layer tend to shrink faster than the inner layers and cause cracking. If it is dried too slowly, bacteria from the air and mold may spoil the dough.

PASTRY

The ingredients for baking should always be warm or at room temperature, never chilled or cold to start.

For pastry it is just the opposite, the ingredients should be chilled or cold.

If you use some sugar in the pastry recipe, it will tenderize the dough. Pastry dough should look like coarse crumbs.

- ➤ Rub the fat into flour before adding any ingredients.
- ➤ The mixture always has a fine texture that had all the small pieces of flour bound up with fat.

Science of Pastry

When you rub the fat in the flour it provides a hydrophobic layer around the starch granules, which helps to prevent water from enlarging the protein around them. Hydration is the initial step in the formation of gluten, which is important in keeping the flour dry until you have rubbed all the fat in. The cold water is less likely to hydrate the proteins and will help you avoid forming tough gluten resulting in a poor-textured product. When the pastry rests it will allow any elastic deformation to return to normal and the pastry will keep its shape when baked as well as allowing any proteins that did become stretched to relax. If the pastry dough is too dry and breaks when you roll it, you did not use enough water. If it is damp and sticky then you used too much water.

- ➤ The flour mixture should always be kept cool and only use cold water when preparing raised pie pastry.
- ➤ After the dough is kneaded, always allow it to rest for 15 minutes before using it.

PASTRY BAGS

- ♦ Pastry bags can be purchased almost anywhere food is sold. Best to purchase the plastic ones that are disposable. They can be purchased in a number of different materials; however, they are a mess to clean.

305

- You can use a small plastic bag if you need one and don't have one available. Fill it and snip off a corner and squeeze away.
- Be sure and give the bag a good shake after you fill it to be sure to compact the contents before you use it.
- Apply pressure from the top then continue squeezing it as you use it.

PASTRY BRUSHES

- If you don't have a pastry brush handy, you can use a NEW untreated natural-bristle paintbrush.
- If the pastry brush you are going to use has an odor of any type, do not use it!
- To easily grease a pan, try using a pastry brush dipped in vegetable oil or shortening.
- Wash pastry brushes as soon after they are used in hot, soapy water. Oil tends to get rancid very quickly and ruin the brush.

PEANUT OIL

Peanut oil is one of the more popular oils and one of the easiest to extract oil from since peanuts are about 50% fat. They tend to maintain their nutty flavor in recipes and especially stir-fried foods. Many chefs tend to mix the oil with unrefined sesame oil, which will complement each other's flavors and aromas. Peanut oil has a high smoke point and is common oil for most cooking purposes, especially frying. However, 90% of peanut oil is saturated fat, which is higher than almost every other vegetable or nut oil.

Peanut oil has very little flavor when used for cooking purposes. It has a relatively high smoke point, which makes it a good choice for frying, especially turkey. The mild nut flavor is popular with Asian cooks; however, it is not flavorful enough for most American dishes. The oil will remain fresh for about a year under refrigeration and if it becomes cloudy will clear up if allowed to remain at room temperature in a short period of time.

PEPPER

This one of the most popular spices in the world and is commonly sold in both black and white varieties. It is imported from India, Indonesia, and Borneo, is sold in whole or ground forms and used in almost any dish. After pepper has been ground, it tends to lose its flavor rather quickly.

- Best to use a pepper grinder so that your pepper will be fresh and flavorful.
- Grind white pepper and you won't change the color of your dish.
- Szechwan pepper berries are harvested from the prickly ash tree and have a very tiny seed and a somewhat hot taste.
- Cayenne pepper is produced from chili peppers.

PEPPERCORNS

Green, white and black peppercorns are basically all the same with the only differences being that they are harvested at different times of maturity and the method processing.

- **Green peppercorns** are picked before they are fully ripe and are preserved and used mainly in the pickling industry and in dishes that do not require a strong pepper flavor.
- **Black peppercorns** are picked when they are only just slightly immature and are the wrinkled peppercorns we use in our household pepper, shakers or in the fresh pepper grinders.
- **White peppercorns** are harvested when the peppercorn is fully ripe and have a smooth surface. These are used in dishes where the color of the black peppercorns would detract from the color of the dish, such as a white cream sauce.
- **Pink peppercorns** are harvested from the Baies rose plant and have a very pungent odor and a somewhat sweet flavor.

PEPPERS, HOT

Some of the hotter peppers will cause eye irritation and it is recommended that you wear rubber gloves so that your hands will not touch the pepper and accidentally touch your eyes. Once you get hot pepper juice in your eyes you will remember the experience for some time to come. If you do not have any rubber gloves and must work with the peppers, just coat your hands with vegetable oil. The vegetable oil will protect your skin from being burned.

The chemical in hot peppers is called "capsaicin" and can be very irritating to your skin and especially your eyes. The same chemical is used in police pepper sprays. To reduce the hotness, remove the seeds and the ribs then wash the peppers in cold water.

THE COLOR AND HOTNESS OF CHILI PEPPERS

The color of chilies is only an indication of the level of ripeness of the vegetable. If the chili is picked before full maturity it will be green and contain more chlorophyll than a red chili that has matured and lost its chlorophyll. The highest concentration of capsaicin (hot stuff) is located in the white ribs that the seeds are attached to. If you remove the ribs and seeds and wash the insides a few times in cold water, you will eliminate 70-80% of the hotness. When the chili is then fried or boiled it will lose even more.

People that consume chilies frequently are less susceptible to the hot effects and tend to become immune to the bite. Remember there are two liquids that will neutralize the hot bite; they are whole milk (most dairy products will work) and beer.

THE HOTTEST OF THE HOT

The hotness of chili peppers is attributed to the chemical "capsaicinoid" which acts directly on the pain receptors in the mucosal lining of the mouth and the throat. A single drop of this pure chemical diluted in 100,000 drops of water will still cause a blister to form on a person's tongue.

This chemical is measured in parts per million which are converted into heat units called Scoville units. This is how the degree of hotness of a chili pepper is measured. One part per million of "capsaicinoid" is equal to 15 Scoville units.

BLACK OLIVES ABSORB HOTTNESS

If you add sliced black olives to a dish that has been over-spiced toward the end of the cooking cycle they will absorb a large percentage of the hot spice. It is best to discard the peppers by straining them out before serving unless you want to light up your guests.

PEPPERS, PEELING OF

When recipe books tell you to peel peppers, they never tell you why and just tell you to do it, however, chefs knew the secret. When you remove the outer skin of a pepper whether it is a hot or sweet one, it allows the pepper to absorb the seasoning better.

Science of Peeling Peppers

Peeling peppers is a pain in the neck unless you place them on a cookie sheet under the broiler at 450^0F and turn them as they char (about 15 minutes). When the skins look black, they are ready. Remove them and place them into a sealed plastic bag for about 10 minutes before removing them and slipping off the skins, stems and seeds. Do not rinse the peppers while removing the skins and wear rubber gloves if working with hot peppers.

PEPPERS, SWEET (Bell Peppers)

When purchasing peppers, be sure the sides of the pepper are firm. Do not purchase if the colors are dull. Refrigerate and use within 3 days. They are a good source of vitamin A and C, in fact studies have shown that eating hot peppers does not cause stomach ulcers and may even speed the healing process by increasing circulation. Sweet red peppers contain more vitamin C than an orange.

Grandma had trouble digesting green bell peppers; however, she used the sweeter red, yellow or orange ones without a problem.

♦ When making stuffed bell peppers, coat the outside of the pepper with vegetable oil and it will retain its color.
♦ Next time you plant peppers, try wrapping each plant stem in 6X6-inch square of newspaper. Dip the newspaper in cool tap water before wrapping each pepper plant. When the roots are kept moist it keeps away the cutworms.

SWEET PEPPER VARIETIES

Bell

Sweet bell peppers are available in four colors, green, red, orange or yellow. They are all relatively sweet but each has its own distinctive flavor difference. When the four are mixed in a salad it is a real taste treat. Bell peppers contain a recessive gene, which neutralizes capsaicin, which is why they are not spicy.

♦ Bell peppers should be stored in the refrigerator in a plastic bag; they will stay fresh about a week.
♦ They can be frozen for 6 months and retain a good amount of their nutrients.
♦ To seed a bell pepper is to hold on to it tight and hit the stem end on the counter hard. This will loosen the seed core and it should pull out easily.
♦ Every sweet pepper starts out as a green pepper and as it ripens, changes to the final color of that variety, which may be yellow, red, green, purple, brown, white or orange. The purple peppers will turn back to green when they are heated.

You can roast your own peppers by holding them over a gas flame on the range with a pair of tongs. As the skin blackens turn the pepper. If you wish to roast a large quantity of peppers, just slice them in half and place them on a cookie sheet in the broiler oven, about 4 inches from the flame or heat source. After they have blackened, place the peppers in a plastic bag, seal it and allow it to stand for 15 minutes. The steam that builds up will loosen the skin and make it easy to remove.

♦ These peppers are long, skinny peppers that range in color from red to orange and even yellow. They are smaller than the American bell pepper and can replace bell peppers in any dish.
♦ One of the largest peppers grown is the Italian Bull Horn Pepper. These peppers can grow to one foot in length and can be purchased in red or yellow when fully ripe. It is an excellent pepper for sautéing and is very mild.

If you would like to keep peppers crisp when canning, just add a grape leaf or two to the jar.

Science of Removing the Burp
To eliminate the "burp" factor related to sweet bell peppers, just use a vegetable peeler to remove the skin before using the pepper. The complex sugar is more concentrated in the skin, which is the main cause of people burping.

PESTO

Pesto sauce tends to turns brown in a very short period of time instead of remaining the pleasant medium green we are used to seeing. The browning, which is almost black at times is caused by enzymes in one of the herbal ingredients, basil. Both the stems and the leaves of basil will cause the pasta to quickly be discolored with brown spots as well as turning the sauce brown. When nuts are added such as walnuts, sunflower seeds, or pine nuts the sauce will turn almost black. There is little to be done unless the pesto and pasta are prepared and served as soon as possible.

One method of keeping the pasta yellow is to add ¼ cup of lemon juice or 1½ tablespoons of cream of tartar to each quart of cooking water. You may have to stir your noodles more frequently and keep the water boiling rapidly to keep the noodles from sticking together since the acid tends to cause excess attraction between the noodles.

Ouch!
Pesto is easily made using a food processor; however, the grinding action of the blades will not produce the richest sauce. To get the richest flavor you will need to bruise the basil leaves before placing them into a food processor.

You can also use chef's method of placing the basil leaves into a plastic baggie and bruising them with a meat mallet or rolling pin.

PHYLLO DOUGH
Very thin pastry dough usually sold in one-pound cartons. Sold fresh in the Middle East and sold frozen in the United States. Must be kept wrapped, otherwise the dough will dry out rapidly.

Don't Get Me Too Cold
Once you thaw Phyllo sheets, never re-freeze them. The texture will never be the same.
- If Phyllo dough is kept tightly wrapped, it will last for about a month in the refrigerator.
- You can freeze Phyllo dough for 1 year at 0^0F.
- When working with Phyllo sheets, always keep them moist. Cover them with waxed paper and place a damp cloth over the paper.

PICKLING

It all starts with a fresh cucumber arriving at the pickle factory. There are three processes to control their fermentation. The first is a type of processing that begins with the "curing" stage, where the cucumbers are stored for up to 3 years in large tanks filled with a salt-brine mixture. Next they are washed and placed in a vat of fresh water, then heated to remove any excess salt residues. After being cleaned and heated they are packed in a final "liquor" solution, which turns them into the dark green color we are used to purchasing.

The second type of processing is for "fresh pack" pickles, which eliminates the holding tanks and speeds the cucumber into a flavored "brine" or "syrup" then immediately into pasteurization. The pickles emerge less salty than the cured pickles and are a lighter green in color. The third method of processing is done totally under refrigeration. These special pickles are known as "deli dills."

They are then cleaned and graded and proceed right to the flavored brine without any further stages. They are never cooked or pasteurized and remain very cucumber-like in flavor and texture. These pickles are always found in the refrigerated section of the market and must be stored under refrigeration. Sour pickles are completed in a solution of vinegar and special spices. Sweet pickles are just sour pickles that have been drained of all traces of brine and bathed in a mixture of vinegar, sugar, and spices. The most popular are the small gherkins.

- ♦ Pickled dill cucumbers have 3 calories per ounce compared to sweet pickles at 30 calories per ounce.
- ♦ Table salt should never be used when pickling. Use only kosher salt, pickling salt or any other salt that is not iodized. Never use salt that is used on highways.
- ♦ When cucumbers are stored below 50^0F they tend to deteriorate and cannot be used for pickling.
- ♦ Burpless cucumbers do not remain crisp during pickling. They are best used for bread and butter pickles or relishes.
- ♦ When making pickles, remove ¼ inch from each end. The ends contain an enzyme that may cause the pickles to soften prematurely.
- ♦ A number of metals will react with the acid in the vinegar when pickling. Never use brass, copper, iron, or even any galvanized utensils. Glass or ceramic pots and plastic or wooden spoons are best.

CHEF'S TRICK

If you add a small piece of horseradish to the pickle jar, it will keep the vinegar active while keeping the pickles from becoming soft.

- ♦ For the best flavor in pickles, make sure you pickle them within 24 hours of harvest. If this is not possible, ask your produce manager to notify you when a fresh shipment arrives. Farmer's markets are best for fresh cucumbers.

- Before using a cucumber for pickling, make sure you remove a small piece of the blossom end. The blossom end contains an enzyme that can make the pickle become soft and mushy.
- The longer you boil vinegar, the more acid will be released weakening the vinegar. Boiling vinegar for long periods will result in a poor quality pickle and the preservation qualities will be lost.
- Never use a cucumber that has been waxed when preparing pickles. The wax coating will not allow the liquids to be absorbed.
- The best pickling cucumber is the **Kirby.** The smallest is the gherkin.

Science of Brining
The temperature of the pickling brine needs to be at 70^0-75^0F at all times otherwise the lactic acid will lose the battle over other bacteria and the pickles will not turn out as good. Chefs know that adding just the right amount of salt will help stabilize the lactic acid. Be sure and follow your recipe to the letter.

PIECRUST
Leaf lard has large fat crystals, which will produce a flakier piecrust. The lard is derived from the kidney area of pigs instead of the abdomen, which is where lard is usually derived from. When substituting lard for butter or shortening in a recipe, reduce the amount of lard used by 25%.

Science of Flaky Pie Crusts
When the dough is prepared with the above method (hand mixed) and baked, the fat melts and the steam that is generated separates the layers. This results in layers of dough separated by the fat. Lard has large fat crystals making the end product excellent.

Most recipes tell you to make sure that pastry and pie dough is chilled before placing it into the tin or dish. The reason for this is that the cold will help to firm up the fat or shortening and relax the gluten in the flour. This will cause it to retain its shape and reduce shrinkage.

- Pies with graham cracker crusts are difficult to remove from the pan. However, if you just place the pan in warm water for 5-10 seconds, it will come right out without any damage.
- Never stretch pie dough when you are placing it in the pan. Stretched dough will usually shrink away from the sides.
- If you place a few slices of fresh white bread on top of your pie while it is baking this will eliminate blistering. Remove the bread about 5 minutes before the pie is finished to allow the top crust to brown.

A chef's secret when using measuring cups and you have to measure both eggs and oil is to measure the eggs before the oil. The egg will coat the cup and allow the oil to flow out more easily.

♦ All-purpose flour is best for piecrust; cake flour is too soft and won't give the crust the body it needs, while bread flour contains too high a gluten content to make a tender crust.
♦ Never add water to pie dough unless it is ice water. However, ice-cold sour cream added to your recipe instead of ice water will result in a more flaky piecrust.
♦ The juices from pies will not spread when you dish it out if you blend 1 egg white, which has been beaten until stiff, with 2 tablespoons of sugar and add it to the filling before baking. Adding tapioca helps as well.
♦ To stop your dough from crumbling when worked and to make thinner dough for pie shells, try coating the surface you are rolling on with olive oil.

There are a number of ways to make a flakier piecrust. The following are just a few: (1) adding a teaspoon of vinegar to the pie dough; (2) substituting sour cream or whipping cream for any water; (3) replacing the shortening or butter with lard. Lard has larger fat crystals and 3 times the polyunsaturated fat as butter.

GUARANTEEING A DRY BOTTOM

If you have a problem with fruit or fruit juices soaking the bottom of your piecrust and making them soggy, try brushing the bottom with egg whites.

This will seal the piecrust and solve the problem. Other methods include, spreading a thin layer of butter on the pie-plate bottom before placing the dough in, warming the pan before placing in the under-crust, and making sure that the crust is fully thawed out if it was frozen.

♦ When making a piecrust, be sure and have the kitchen cool. A hot kitchen will affect the results. All pie ingredients should be cold when preparing a crust.
♦ When using a cream filling in a pie, coat the crust with granulated sugar before adding the cream. This usually eliminates a soggy crust.

BUBBLE, BUBBLE, TOIL AND TROUBLE

Chefs like to prepare bottom piecrusts ahead of time and keep them in the freezer until they need them. They hate blisters or small bubbles in the crust and will always make some holes (called docking) in the crust. However, their favorite method of avoiding the blisters is to double-pan the dough. They will place a pan on top of the piecrust as it bakes to hold the crust in place.

A Crumby Situation

If you need to press crumbs into a pie plate it can be a bit messy especially if the crumbs are buttered. If you want to avoid the mess and keep the crumbs where they belong, place your hand in a plastic baggie and then press the crumbs into place.

Convenient Ice Water

Since most piecrust recipes call for using ice water to bring the dough together you have to be careful of using too much water or the dough will become mushy. If you fill a small plastic spray bottle halfway up with water and place it on its side in the freezer it will be ready when you need ice water. Just remove the bottle and fill it with cold tap water, which will turn into ice cold water. While you are making the pastry you can easily spray ice water over the dough as you are mixing it as needed. The water will then be evenly distributed and you won't use too much.

Time to Move

After the dough has been rolled out it has to be transferred to the pie plate, which is a very delicate task. Use a thin metal spatula under the dough to raise it then gently roll the dough onto the rolling pin. Move the pin to the pie plate and unroll the dough over the filling.

Just A Trim around the Sides, Please

The best tool for trimming off the excess dough so that you can make a neat edge is a pair of kitchen shears. If you leave about ½" around the edge you will have enough to make a fluted edge. To create the fluted edge, just fold the excess dough under the edge and press firmly to seal it up. This will make it thick enough to work with and can be easily fluted.

Foiled Again!

Since the fluted edges of a pie will easily burn, just use a larger piece of aluminum foil and make a hole in the center the size of the opening of the pie only. Be sure that the hole is only open over the center of the pie and not the fluted edge. By covering the fluted edge it will not burn and bake normally.

There is an old saying that says "you have pastry hands." This refers to someone who has cold hands, which are excellent if you want to make a tender, flaky piecrust.

PIE PANS

- If you want a deep-golden crust you will need to use a glass, dark-metal or dull-metal pan, which absorbs heat better and will give you the crisp crust. The shiny aluminum pans will result in a much lighter colored crust.
- If you are going to use glass, reduce the oven heat by 25^0F.
- Pie pans normally do not have to be greased.

PIES

APPLE PIES

Only certain apples can be used for cooking and to prepare pies. These include Rome Beauty, Northern Spy, Granny Smith and York Imperial. It depends on whether you prefer a tart or sweet flavor. Rome Beauty will give you a sweeter flavor than the other three apples. Granny Smith is usually chef's favorite for pies since it will be just sweet enough and not be too sweet.

For apple pies you should not need a thickener, for all other fruit pies the best thickening agent is a combination of 2 tablespoons each of cornstarch and tapioca. Just mix them with the sugar before adding to the fruit. When baking, remember that cornstarch has twice the thickening power of flour.

Dried fruits tend to go to the bottom of the baked goods when cooked because they lose some moisture and become more solid. If you coat them with the same flour that you are using in the recipe they will stay put.

- Glass baking dishes will conduct heat more efficiently than metal pans. When you use a glass, baking dish remember to lower the temperature by 25^0F, which will reduce the risk of burning the bottom of your cake.
- A pastry chef's trick to add flavor to a lemon tart or pie is to rub a few sugar cubes over the surface of an orange or lemon then include the cubes in the recipe as part of the total sugar. The sugar tends to extract just enough of the natural oils from these fruits to add some excellent flavor.
- Spray a small amount of vegetable oil on your knife before cutting a pie with a soft filling. This will stop the filling from sticking to the knife.
- The acidic (ascorbic acid) nature of fruit pies and tarts may cause a reaction with a metal pan and discolor the food. Always use a glass dish when baking a fruit pie or tart for the best results. Remember to reduce your baking time or lower the temperature of the oven.

CUSTARD PIES

The reason a custard pie shrinks away from the crust is that you have cooked it too long in an oven that was too hot.

FRUIT PIES

If you have a problem with juices bubbling out or oozing out when baking a pie, try adding a tablespoon of tapioca to the filling. This will thicken the filling just enough. Another method is to insert a tube wide macaroni in the center of the top allowing steam to escape.

MERINGUE PIES

ELIMINATING TEARSDROPS

The nature of meringue is to develop small droplets of water on the surface shortly after it is removed from the oven. This is a common problem with tarts and pies and can easily be eliminated by just allowing the tart or pie to remain in the oven until it cools off somewhat. Turn the oven off a few minutes before the dish has completed cooking to avoid over cooking it. This will also eliminate the problem of cracking.

CUTTING MERINGUE

If you lightly butter the knife you use to cut meringue pies, they will cut more easily.

PERK UP YOUR PEAKS

There are a number of methods for making world-class meringue and high peaks.

(1) Make sure that your egg whites are at room temperature before adding a small amount of baking powder then as you beat them add 2-3 tablespoons of a quality granulated sugar for each egg used. Keep beating until the peaks stand up without drooping.

(2) To keep the peaks firmer for a longer period of time, try adding ¼ teaspoon of white, vinegar for each 3 eggs (whites), while beating. Also, add 4-5 drops of lemon juice for each cup of cream.

Remember: if the weather is bad, rainy, or even damp out, the meringue peaks will not remain upright.

MINCEMEAT PIES

The filling should contain pears, dried fruit, dried cranberries, orange juice, orange zest and one jar (27 ounces) of mincemeat. Be sure and brush the lattice strips with low-fat milk.

PUMPKIN PIE

Manufacturers may be placing smaller amounts of "real" pumpkin into the cans that say "pumpkin pie filling." The reason for this is that they are finding out that "real" pumpkin does not retain its flavor well, so they are adding a large percentage of banana squash to the cans.

For a unique pumpkin pie, try placing small marshmallows on the bottom of the piecrust. The marshmallows will rise to the top as the pie bakes and looks great. This feat is accomplished by the air expanding inside the marshmallows.

♦ Frozen pumpkin pies should be baked without thawing at 400°F for just under 2-hours then reducing the heat to 325°F until done.

- The cracking in the pumpkin pie custard filling is caused by over-baking.
- Pumpkin pie should always be stored in the refrigerator.

PINEAPPLE

Pineapples originated in South America and were brought to the Hawaiian Islands in the 1700's for cultivation. It became the main crop of Hawaii and was canned there for the first time. Pineapples are similar to melons in that the starch, which converts to sugar as the fruit ripens, is found only in the stem until just before the fruit reaches maturity. The starch then converts to sugar and enters the fruit. The fruit will not become any sweeter after it is picked, so it must be picked ripe.

- To check for ripeness, gently pull at a leaf anywhere on the stem. If the leaf comes out easily, the pineapple is ripe. The leaf should be dark green. It should also smell sweet.
- It is available year round, but is best March through June. Buy as large and heavy as possible and be sure the leaves are deep green. Do not purchase if soft spots are present and refrigerate as soon as possible for 3-5 days.

POOR GELATIN

Fresh pineapple contains the enzyme "bromelain" that will prevent gelatin from setting up. This enzyme may also be used as a meat tenderizer. Studies in the future may also show that bromelain may be effective in reducing the plaque in arterial walls.

The easiest method of ripening a pineapple is to cut off the top, remove the skin, and slice. Place the pineapple in a pot and cover with water, add sugar and sweeten to taste then boil for 5 minutes, cool and refrigerate.

Del Monte Golden Ripe Pineapple is the sweetest pineapple you can purchase. The rind should be a golden color when fully ripe. There will be a tag attached to every pineapple.

Science of the Pineapple

Pineapples are picked when they are ripe. The color of the outside will not determine whether the pineapple will be sweet or not. If the crown leaves are a fresh, deep-green color that is a good sign. If the pineapple looks brown or dry it will probably be too sweet. Some pineapples have a very high acid content and may irritate your system. Del Monte® pineapples are one of the best, since they contain less acid and are sweeter than most other brands.

Pineapples should have a somewhat sweet smell when ripe. It is named for its resemblance to a pinecone.

PIZZA

Pizza was not invented in Italy or America! It actually originated in Greece and the original idea was to make an edible plate.

The Greeks made a bread trencher so that the toppings would not fall off. They took this food to southern Italy where it really took hold and became popular.

Pepperoni is at the top of the list. Americans consume 300 million pounds on pizza every year. If you placed all the pepperoni pizzas eaten in the United States next to each other they would take up an area the size of 13,000 football fields. The favorite pizza topping in Japan is squid.

One of the easiest methods of cutting a pizza is to use a scissors with long blades. Make sure it is sharp and only use it for that purpose. Pizza cutters do work fairly well providing they are always kept very sharp. However, they tend to dull quickly since most are produced from poor quality metal.

Science of Shaping Pizza Dough
- Dough should be lightly floured after it has rested for 15 minutes. The surface you are working on should be dusted with flour.
- When working the dough, use your fingertips and heel of your hand and work in a circular motion, continually flattening the dough. Flip it and continue to stretch it out until it is the size you want.
- If the dough is relaxed it will be easier to work.
- The pan that you place the dough on should be lightly dusted with cornmeal.

Homemade pizza usually comes out a bit soggy unless you are very adept at preparing pizza crust. It might be wise to add the cheese before the tomato sauce. This will keep the crust from becoming soggy.

Flavor-Savor
If you want the best tasting pizza never add the spices to the tomato sauce, only salt and pepper as desired. Spices should be added last on top of the ingredients after the pizza is complete. The acid in tomato sauce tends to reduce the potency of many spices, especially as the tomato sauce heats up.

How Dry I Am
Brushing olive oil on top of the dough before adding toppings is another pizza parlor secret in order to stop the ingredients from making the dough soggy.

I'm Getting Dizzy
Never place tomatoes slices on pizza unless you place them into a salad spinner first to release the liquid. Tomatoes will cause pizza to become too soggy.

Science of Making Pizza Crust
- To prevent a soggy crust on a homemade pizza, just place the cheese on before the tomato sauce.

- If you add a small amount of olive oil to the dough while you are working it, it will produce a crispy crust with a soft interior.
- When the pizza is done, try brushing a small amount of olive oil around the outer crust to keep the crust from getting too hard.
- Some of the best pizzas in the United States sprinkle some extra virgin olive oil on top of the pizza just before placing it into the oven to keep it from becoming too crispy.
- Another trick to preventing a soggy crust is to sauté vegetables that have high water content, such as peppers, onions and mushrooms to decrease their water content before placing them on top of the pizza.
- Pizza crust is easily cut with large kitchen scissors.
- You should never use all-purpose flour for making pizza crust or the texture will not be the same as using the Gold medal flour.
- Pizza dough should be allowed to rise for at least one hour to double in size.
- After pizza dough rises it should be "punched" down and divided into balls, then allowed to rest for 15 minutes before being used.
- If you add a small amount of whole-wheat flour the crust will have a nuttier taste.
- If you add semolina flour it will produce a very crispy crust.
- If you use a food processor to mix the dough, the dough will be thoroughly kneaded when the dough forms one or two balls on the top of the blade.

Science of Freezing Pizza Dough

Allow the batch to rise only once then punch it down and separate it into separate balls enough for one crust. Flatten the balls into discs and then wrap them separately with plastic freezer wrap or freezer bags that have had oil sprayed on the inside first. This will allow you to remove the dough without it sticking to the bag. Frozen pizza discs will stay fresh for 3-4 months. Thawing is best done by placing the disc in the refrigerator overnight. Frozen pizza dough should not be shaped until it is at room temperature.

Bakers know their cheeses, especially when it comes to making the perfect pizza and always purchase the "real" Parmesan cheese, which is called Parmigiano-Reggiano and stamped on the rind, and is grated fresh.

CHEF'S TOMATO SAUCE RECIPE

- It takes 1½ cups of tomato sauce for a 12" pizza.
- The basic pizza parlor recipe for tomato sauce is one can of Italian style tomato puree, one large crushed garlic clove, one teaspoon of dried oregano, four fresh basil leaves, salt and fresh pepper to taste.

♦ This is the basic recipe but not recommended if you want the best tasting pizza.

Science of Cheese for Pizza

Mozzarella is the cheese of choice for most pizza since it melts easily and does not become tough. It also doesn't cost as much as Parmigiano-Reggiano. Mozzarella originated in Italy and was made with the milk from water buffalo, which is where the term "buffalo mozzarella" came from. Romano cheese is also used with excellent results. Imported provolone will add a somewhat sharper flavor. New England style pizza uses white cheddar as the cheese of choice.

Science of Baking Pizza

- The oven should be at the highest temperature possible.
- The pizza should be placed directly on a special pizza screen, which looks similar to the screen on your screen door so that the heat can easily get to the bottom of the crust.
- If you have ordered a delivered pizza and the crust is usually soggy, just make sure that your oven has been pre-heated to 400°F before it arrives, then place it in for 5 minutes.
- Pizza will always taste better when prepared in a coal-fired or wood-burning brick oven or at least directly on the heat source, which must be at least 550°F. Home ovens usually will not go over 500°F.
- Unglazed quarry tiles can be placed on the bottom of the oven, which does help. They must be at least ½ inch thick or they will crack from the intense heat.
- If you are going to use the tiles, be sure that the dough is at room temperature for the best results.

Toppings

♦ If you use meats they are best if pre-cooked, such as salami, pepperoni, sausage, ham or hamburger.
♦ Tuna is an excellent topping, but should be a good quality and placed on in chunks.
♦ Meats high in fat such as sausage need pre-cooking.
♦ Vegetables other than tomatoes should also be pre-cooked since they may not cook through if they are thick or the water content is too high.
♦ Grilling vegetables is recommended, however, they can be sautéed or just blanched.
♦ Sautéing vegetables, allows you to add additional flavors, which enhance the taste of the pizza.

320

Pizza crust is best made with Gold Medal, high-gluten bread flour. The crust will be more tender and crisp.

PLASTIC CONTAINERS

To remove onion & garlic odors from plastic containers and to deodorize a plastic storage container in which onions or garlic were stored, wash thoroughly then stuff a crumpled piece of newspaper in the container and snap on the lid. In a few days the smell will disappear. To stop tomato products from staining plastic containers, just spray vegetable oil lightly on the inside before adding the sauce.

POACHING

Both poaching and simmering are methods of cooking which require a large amount of water or stock. The liquid should be very hot, but not to the point of boiling. If the food is accidentally allowed to boil it may fall apart. The cooking pot may be covered or uncovered and are mainly used for softer foods such as fruits, eggs, fish and shellfish.

- Tougher cuts of meats and stewing chickens can also be tenderized using this method.
- Poaching is commonly used to cook and tenderize corned beef in delicatessens.
- When chefs wish to poach fish they will frequently place the fish in the cold water and bring the water up to a gentle simmer, remove the pot from the heat and allow the fish to cook off the heat.
- Use only just enough liquid to barely cover the food.
- Only use a pan that is just big enough for the food and the liquid you are using.
- If you were going to poach a whole fish, it would be best if you wrapped the fish in cheesecloth first so that it will hold its shape better.

When poaching fruits, the best method is to use sugary syrup with a spiced wine to poach in. If you are going to poach a whole fish the recommended technique is to wrap the fish in a small towel and lightly tied so that it will not fall apart.

This will also make it easier to handle when removing the fish from the pot.

POPCORN

Popcorn is composed of a complex carbohydrate (starch), and includes insoluble fiber (cellulose), which may help prevent constipation. It is always best, however, to drink plenty of fluids when consuming any large amount of insoluble fiber. Insoluble fiber tends to absorb water from the intestinal tract and will add bulk. The only risk that might exist would be if you ate a large tub of popcorn without drinking any liquids, then you may have a major traffic jam.

Science of Popcorn

When the popcorn kernel is heated, the moisture inside turns to steam and as the pressure builds it has to vent and bursts the kernel. The explosion forms a fluffy white starch. Normal corn will not explode because it does not have as high moisture content as special popcorn. As soon as the popcorn is popped it is best to open the bag or remove the lid as soon as possible to avoid the popcorn absorbing the steam and becoming soggy. Popcorn should always be stored in a well-sealed container so that it will retain as much of its moisture as possible.

SIZE DOES MAKE A DIFFERENCE

Raw corn for popping is sold in many different grades. Most of the corn products sold in the supermarkets to produce popcorn have an expansion ratio of only 28:1, while those sold to movie theatres have an expansion ratio of 42:1. The oil to corn ratio of quality popcorn should be about 3 parts of corn to 1 part of oil.

Grandma's favorite snack food was popcorn, which she always stored in the freezer and never had "old maids."

- Salt should never be included in packaged popcorn or placed in a popcorn popper. Salt should only be added after the popcorn has fully popped to keep the popcorn tender. Salt will cause the popcorn to become tough.
- Popcorn that is purchased with oil in the container should not be kept more than 3 months at room temperature or the oil may start to become rancid.
- One tablespoon of oil + ½ cup popcorn = 4 cups of popped corn. Be sure and use a 4-quart pot.
- When popping popcorn, be sure and leave the lid cracked just a little to allow the steam to escape. This will eliminate having soggy popcorn.
- Salt will stick better to air-popped corn if you spray the corn very lightly before salting it.

It may be healthier to air pop your popcorn; however, all this does is to make larger blossoms that are tougher and not as crispy.

SAVING AN OLD MAID

Old maids are kernels of corn that are too pooped to pop. The kernels usually have lost sufficient moisture and can be revived by placing a handful of them into a sealed container with 1-2 tablespoons of water, shake for at least 3-4 minutes. The container should then be placed in a cool (not cold) location for about 3 days. This should revive them, and you should have no problem popping them.

- Nutritionally, regular popcorn and gourmet popcorn is equal. The only difference is that gourmet popcorn pops into larger blossoms.
- It would be wise to read the label on air-popped popcorn packages before you buy the product if you're trying to cut down on fats. Some products are now sprayed with oil.

PORK

Recent studies have shown that a typical piece of pork found in a supermarket may only have a few hundred bacteria per square centimeter, compared to over 100,000 bacteria in the same area of a piece of chicken. This is one of the reasons it is so important to clean up well after handling poultry.

- Pork can be frozen for 3-6 months. However, the larger the cut, the longer the storage time.
- To keep pork tender, you can cook it to only 150^0-165^0F and be safe.
- If you do cook it to the recommended temperature of 170^0-185^0F the meat will probably be overcooked and dry. The trinchinae is killed at 137^0F if any exists at all.

Pigs require about 8 pounds of grain to produce 1 pound of meat. It requires 16 pounds of grain to produce 1 pound of beef while chickens only require 3 pounds to bring them to market size. The latest statistics are that there are 1.6 billion cattle worldwide. These cattle consume $\frac{1}{3}^{rd}$ of the world's grain, which is not a very efficient use of a natural resource.

MUST BE CLEAN LIVING

The USDA has now published information stating that only 1 in 1,000 pigs are now found to contain the trichinosis parasite. My recommendation, however, is to still cook pork until the internal temperature is 160^0F. The trichinosis parasite is killed at 137^0F.

PORK CHOPS

CHEF'S PORK CHOP SECRETS

- Just to be safe, even though there is rarely a health problem with rare pork, cook pork chops only to an internal temperature of 155^0-165^0F.
- Pork chops should be purchased about 1" thick to maintain the juices when they are cooked.
- If you prefer thin pork chops, cook then with the lid on the pan for a short period of time since they dry out very quickly.

- Pork chops that are to be stuffed should be at least 1½" thick and should be rib or loin chops.

- Always cut the pork chops to be stuffed from the fat side and make the slit almost to the bone. After you stuff the chop use small metal skewers to close the opening while they are cooking.
- Pork should never be left at room temperature for more than 1 hour before being refrigerated.

POTATO PANCAKES (LATKAS)

Jewish pancake originally used to commemorate the biblical story of the Jewish Maccabees' defeat of the Syrians in 165 B.C. The oil used for frying the latkas symbolizes the oil that was found in the Temple of Jerusalem and was only enough for one night but lasted for eight nights.

Science of Potato Pancakes

Some people tend to get indigestion from potato pancakes, probably not being able to tolerate the frying oil. This can be solved by adding 1 teaspoon of baking soda to the batter. If you don't have the problem, don't add it. You should use Idaho or russet potatoes that are very fresh. Be sure and stir the batter before making each batch since some of the ingredients tend to settle.

Potato pancakes should be crispy, not overly greasy from the frying and flavored just right. The following is my grandmother's recipe:

To keep pancakes warm, place the pancakes on a platter lined with a tea towel then pull the towel over the pancakes. Cover the platter with a large inverted colander and they will stay warm. The oven can keep them warm as well if it is heated then the heat turned off at around 200^0F. However, they may dry out.

WORLD'S GREATEST POTATO PANCAKES (LATKAS)

Ingredients:

5 Large, fresh potatoes
2 Large eggs (well beaten)
½ Cup of all-purpose flour
¼ Teaspoon of freshly grated black pepper (powdered) (optional)

1 Large onion (grated)
¼ Teaspoon of baking powder (fresh)
½ Teaspoon of table salt

Peel and grate potatoes in a large bowl, cover with cold water and refrigerate. This needs to be done 2-3 hours before you plan on using the potatoes to allow the water to soak some of the starch out of the potatoes.

The water should be changed every hour. When you are ready to prepare the latkas, drain the potatoes and squeeze out as much water as possible. Peel and grate the onion and add it to the potatoes, then stir in the eggs, flour, salt, pepper (optional) and baking powder.

Heat enough vegetable oil in a heavy pan to cover the bottom (about ¼ inch deep). Drop the potato mixture into the hot oil by the tablespoonful and form 3-inch patties. They should be fried over moderate heat, turning to brown each side.

POTATO SALAD
Only use one type of potato to make potato salad. Always use a "new red potato" and never use any other for the best potato salad ever.

Science of New Potatoes
New potatoes have a higher moisture and lower starch content allowing them to absorb less water when cooked. They will also absorb less mayonnaise or other dressing.

Because of these facts the new potato is sturdier than other potatoes and will not breakdown when you are mixing it with the other ingredients. New potatoes need to be used within a week after harvest for the best taste, however, they will store for 2 months.

POTATOES
The earliest mention of the potato goes as far back as 500 B.C. when remains of potatoes were found in Chile. They were grown by the Inca Indians and even worshiped by them. In recent times during the 16th century potatoes were brought to Europe and were looked down upon at first thinking that they caused a number of diseases. In the Unites States they were first cultivated in Virginia around 1610.

White potatoes originated in South America and were introduced to Europe in the 16th century. They are one of the most nutritious vegetables and a member of the "nightshade" family. Americans consume approximately 125 pounds of potatoes per person annually with the United States producing 35 billion pounds per year. In the last 30 years Americans have reduced their consumption of fresh potatoes by 40%.

There are over 5,000 varieties of potatoes worldwide and only 4 varieties are sold and used in U.S. markets. The potato is the number one vegetable in the world with potato chips ranking number one snack food.

It is best to purchase potatoes in bulk bins and not in bags. It is too difficult to determine which ones are bruised. If ginger root is stored with potatoes it will help them stay fresh longer. If half an apple is stored with potatoes it will stop the sprouting by absorbing any moisture before the potato does.

If you place ½-apple or a piece of ginger root in a bag of potatoes, they will not sprout.

REFRIGERATER POTATO

The only potato that can be stored in the refrigerator is the new potato. They will retain a good quality for 7-10 days.

OLD POTATO, NEW POTATO, BEST POTATO?

A new potato will have more moisture than an old potato; however, both can be used for different dishes. A new potato should be used for dishes such as potato salad since they will absorb less water when boiled and less mayonnaise when prepared, thus adding less fat to the dish. They are stronger and won't break as easily when the salad is stirred. Idaho and other varieties of older potatoes are best for baking and French fries. They are drier, meatier, and have more starch. Because of this they will bake fluffier and have a lighter texture.

When French fries are made with an older potato, the frying fat will splatter less because of the potatoes low water content. When baking a potato make sure you pierce the potato to allow steam to escape otherwise it may become soggy.

- ◆ Onions should never be stored with potatoes in the same bag. Onions tends to release gases that will alter the flavor of a potato. Cooking the two together is not a problem unless you overdo the quantity of onions and it takes over the flavor and aroma of the potato.
- ◆ To re-harden potatoes, try placing soft raw potatoes in ice water for ½ hour or until they become hard. Brown areas on potatoes are the result of oxidation and vitamin C losses.

Science of Stored Potatoes

Chefs know **not** to store potatoes in the refrigerator, but if this ever occurs, just allow the potato to remain at room temperature and the sugar will convert back to starch. The starch to sugar conversion happens below 45°F (7°C). The perfect temperature to store potatoes is 50°F (10°C). They also know **never** to store onions and potato close to each other since they both give off a gas that ruins flavor and rots them.

THE REAL SKINNY

When chefs make potatoes they rarely serve them with the skins on or use skins in mashed potatoes.

Science of Potato Skins

There are a number of facts regarding potatoes and potato skins that are interesting. Potatoes do not digest very quickly and it takes 2 hours for a medium potato to be digested. If you cook the potato with the skin intact it will retain the majority of its nutrients.

Potato skins are the only vegetable skin that will retain traces of pesticides and fertilizers even after extensive washing and cooking. The EPA has registered 90 pesticides that can be used on potatoes, with only 55% of these detectable.

A Little Jab Will Do Ya

When peeling a raw potato, try holding the potato with a corkscrew that has a handle. If you are trying to peel a hot potato, just hold it with a fork.

Idaho became the main potato growing state in the early 1800's. Potatoes; were planted by a Presbyterian missionary, Henry Harmon Spaulding to prove to the local Indians that he could provide food.

Even though grandma didn't know how the chemical reaction occurred making potatoes sweet when stored, she knew how to convert a sugary potato back to a starchy one. Cold storage will change the starch in a potato to sugar and will give the potato a strange sweet flavor.

Science of Buying Potatoes

It seems that even one bad potato is like having one bad apple in a barrel in that it can spoil the whole batch and contaminate all of them. Potatoes need to be free of any blemishes, smooth with no bumps and gullies, which may hide bacteria. Check for signs of rot, such as soft areas, slight stickiness, cracks or a green tinge. If the eyes are black it means that the potato has been frozen and is not as fresh.

POTATOES, BAKED

Baked potatoes are one of my favorites, but I like the skin to be crisp and not soggy. Chefs will prick the skin of the potato 3-4 times and place a few drops of olive oil on the potato then rub it in. The potato gets a massage before being baked. They will then rub some crushed sea salt on the skin.

When baking a potato, many people tend to wrap the potato in aluminum foil thinking that it will speed up the cooking time. After trying to bake potatoes a number of different ways to see which method was the fastest, I was surprised to find that by oiling the skin with vegetable oil, the skin reached a higher temperature faster and baked the potato in a shorter period of time than when it was wrapped in aluminum foil.

- One method that will speed up the cooking time is to insert an aluminum nail into the center of the potato, thereby transferring heat inside.
- You can place the potato in the microwave for 7-8 minutes before placing it into the oven, but be sure and make a few short cuts in the potato first.
- Another method is to allow the potato to stand in boiling water for 15 minutes before placing the potato in the oven.

- Baked potatoes that are leftover can be re-baked if you dip them in water and bake them in a 350°F oven for 15-20 minutes.
- When baking potatoes, try piercing the skin with a fork to allow the steam to escape. This will stop the skin from cracking.

Open Wide

To open a baked potato the correct way, just make an "**X**" on top of the potato with the tines of a fork then push the ends in and pop out the middle.

Science of Baked Potato Skins

Salt is very anhydrous, which means that it loves water and will readily absorb it. Rubbing salt on the potato draws excess liquid out of the potato, making the skin crispy as the potato bakes in the oven.

POTATOES, BEST FOR COOKING

The most popular potato is the Idaho or russet. They are starchy and mealy and best for baking mashed potatoes and French fries. The "new potatoes" are thin-skinned potatoes that are somewhat waxy and young and are called red or white potatoes. These are best for boiling and make great potato salad, used in stews and soups and to prepare scalloped potatoes since they hold their shape better than russets.

POTATOES, BOILING OF

To boil potatoes in less time, remove a small strip of skin from one side. After they are cooked the balance of the skin will be more easily removed.

- To keep peeled potatoes white, place them in a bowl of cold water, add a few drops of white vinegar then refrigerate.
- White potatoes should have a small amount of sugar added to the cooking water, which will revive a percentage of the lost flavor.
- Potatoes prefer to be stored in pantyhose. Just cut a leg off and drop the potatoes in, then hang it up in a cool, dry location.
- If you want to keep potatoes firm while you are boiling them, just cook them in 2 parts of water to 1 part of white vinegar and a small amount of kosher salt. Leave the skins on and peel after they are finished cooking to retain the nutrients.
- If you store a boiled or baked potato in the refrigerator for 3-4 days, it will lose approximately 90% of its nutrient value. Potatoes should only be stored for 1-2 days. When boiling potatoes, place them into a mesh, frying basket to make them easier to remove and drain since they may get somewhat mushy.

Shake 'em Up

While many people shake just-boiled potatoes to dry them after the water has been removed from the pot it may break some of the potatoes. The better method is to cover the pot with a kitchen towel after pouring the water off then replacing the lid over the towel for 1-2 minutes to allow the excess moisture to be absorbed into the towel.

POTATOES, FRENCH FRIES

The following is the step-by-step commercial production of French fries:
Peeling the potato
Large hot pressurized tanks are used that increase the pressure to such a point that when the pressure is released the skins actually fly off. They are then sprayed with high-power jets of water to clean any skin residues off.

The assembly line
The potato then travels by inspectors on conveyer belt, who remove the bad ones and any small bad spots and send the potato on to the next station.

The slicing station
The potato flies through a centrifugal pump and is shot into the cutting blades at 50mph to be cut into "strips."

The strips are inspected again and rejects sent to the hash brown, dehydrated potatoes, or tater tot department, for further processing.

Blanching is coming up next
The real processing is now beginning with the blanching process. A conveyer belt carries the potato through a vat filled with very hot water, which removes excess sugars and cooks them just enough so that they are all a uniform color. Occasionally, sugar is added in this stage so that the potato will brown more uniformly as well.

Drying out the strips
The strips are placed on a belt and go through a machine, which sends out blasts of hot air partially drying the strip. The amount of drying depends on the water content of the potato strip and they need to be left a little damp and not completely dry. The water content must be regulated at about 73% if the potato strip is to be fried, while oven fries must be 68% and microwave fries only 57%.

Now the fries are par-fried
A process, which partially fries the French fry for about 1½-minutes. This will add some fat to the fry but will make them faster to fry when they are fried just before being served. The final fry at the restaurant site basically finishes cooking the already cooked fry, then browns and crisps it.

The chilling ending
The fries now go through a process called blast freezing, where the fries travel down a conveyer belt on which the air is cooled to -40^0F and only very small ice crystals form, which will not allow the fries to stick together.

This method protects the flavor. French fries prepared in this manner must be served within 10 minutes of leaving the frying vat or they will become soggy and limp.

- ♦ When frying French fries never allow the oil to go above 380^{0}F or the fry will burn on the outside before cooking the insides.
- ♦ For the crispiest French fries sprinkle them with all-purpose flour before frying.

WHY SOAK FRIES IN WATER?

The surface of a cut potato deteriorates very quickly when exposed to air. When this occurs a layer of sticky starch is formed as soon as the potatoes are placed into the frying vat. The potatoes may stick to each other as well as the pan and it will be almost impossible to serve them.

For the greatest gourmet French fries, try allowing crinkle-cut potatoes to stand in ice cold water and refrigerate for 1 hour before frying. It will also wash off a large percentage of the surface starch. They should be drained on a paper towel and be good and dry when you fry them otherwise you will have hot oil splatter.

SKINNY FRENCH FRIES, IS THERE A REASON?

A number of the fast food chains like McDonald's serve their French fried potatoes thinner than most other restaurants. When raw potatoes are thin pre-cut exposing the surface, a percentage of the complex carbohydrates have time to convert to sugar. The extra sugar causes the French fries to brown faster and the thinner fry will cook faster. If they tried to serve normal size fries they would be too brown or undercooked.

MAKING GRANDMA'S FRENCH FRIES

1. Crinkle-cut the potatoes to allow more of the potato surface to come into contact with the fat.
2. Heat the oil to only 330^0F and par-fry the potatoes for only 2 minutes.
3. Drain the potatoes and dry thoroughly and place into the refrigerator for 30 minutes. Remove and allow them to come to room temperature for 20 minutes.
4. Toss them in seasoned flour and place them into 365^0F oil for 3 minutes. Drain and dry on paper towel before serving.

POTATOES, MASHED

There are number of hints to follow when preparing mashed potatoes:

First: Never pour cold milk into the potatoes, it has a tendency to mix with the starch that has been released through the mashing process and may make the potatoes heavy, soggy, and even create lumps. The milk should be warmed in a pan with a small amount of chives for flavor before being added. Buttermilk will give the potatoes a great flavor. A pinch or two of baking powder will give them extra fluff.

Second: Never over-mix or overcook the potatoes; both of these will cause the cell walls to rupture releasing an excess of starch and produce a soggy, sticky product. Potatoes should be stirred with a vertical motion and never circular stirred. This will lessen the damage, which occurs by crushing the cells on the wall of the bowl. Never put baking soda, in potatoes it will turn them black. Instead of adding liquid milk to the potatoes when making mashed, try adding powdered milk or instant potato flakes for extra fluffy mashed potatoes.

Mashed potatoes that sit out on a buffet will lose up to 100% of all their nutrients after 1 hour. The loss is due to the constant heat, lights, mashing, exposing more of the surface to oxidation, and cooking in boiling water.

When preparing mashed potatoes, add 1 teaspoon of white vinegar to the potatoes for every pound of potatoes. The vinegar should be added after the milk has been mixed in well.

Jolly Good Idea

Since it is best to boil potatoes to be used for mashed potatoes with their skins on so that they won't become mushy, just mash them in a "ricer" half a potato at a time with their skins on. You don't have to peel the potatoes and the skin will remain in the ricer.

CHEF'S MASHED POTATOES

Rice the potatoes into a pot, which has melted butter in it.

Use heated milk brought to a boil, stop boiling and add only 3 tablespoons of milk to the potatoes as you whisk continually. Only add enough milk to give you a good consistency and do not let the mashed potatoes get thin and watery.

If it accidentally gets too thin, place the potatoes back on the heat and heat until they thicken up. Use Yukon Gold potatoes if available. Some chefs also add a small amount of chopped raw onions to the potatoes. The heat of the potatoes calms the onions down providing a great flavor.

Science of Mashed Potatoes

If you overcook or overwork mashed potatoes you will break too many of the cell walls and allow too many starch granules to escape. When this occurs the potatoes will become gummy rather than light and fluffy. Never stir the potatoes in a circular motion; stir only with an easy vertical motion to lessen the damage.

POTATOES, PAN-FRIED

Pan-fried potatoes are a favorite for breakfast, but my friend the chef never makes them unless he has leftover potatoes from the day before. I never really understood why until now.

If you try and pan-fry raw potatoes at a high temperature, you would burn the outside of the potato before the inside was cooked. However, if you have leftover potatoes, the potato is already cooked and it is easy to pan-fry them. When you cook pan-fried potatoes, they cook up fast and a sticky starch will not build up on the outside and cause the potatoes to stick together.

POTATOES, PEELING TIP

If you have problems peeling the potato, drop it into a bowl of ice water for a few seconds to loosen the skin. To keep peeled potatoes white during cooking add a small amount of white vinegar to the water.

POTATOES, ROASTED

The best potatoes for roasting are russets, long whites and new. Just slice the potatoes into medium-sized pieces and place into baking pan. Be sure and coat the potatoes with oil on all sides then bake at 375^0F for about 1-1½ hours or until the outside is crispy and nicely browned. They will be great if you turn them regularly, about every 10-15 minutes. Baking the potatoes in pan drippings is what the chefs do to make them taste great.

POTATOES, STORAGE OF

Sweet potatoes, yams, and white potatoes are actually an enlarged stem called a "tuber" that extends from the plant underground and is the storage depot for the plants excess carbohydrates. The potato plant bears a vegetable similar to a small mini tomato and is not that good to eat. If potatoes are stored below 40^0F they tend to release more sugar and turn sweet.

Potatoes will last longer and remain solid longer if they are stored in a cool, dry location, preferably at 45^0-50^0F. Air must be allowed to circulate around potatoes since moisture will cause them to decay. Potatoes do not freeze well, since a large majority of the cells tend to burst causing the potato to become mushy and watery when thawed. Commercially processed potatoes will freeze.

POTATOES, SWEET

They are usually only available around Thanksgiving. However, yams are available year round. Sweet potato skins are normally a light copper color while yams are more reddish.

- They should not be purchased if they have any soft spots, visible mold, or white areas.
- Sweet potatoes and yams tend to decay faster than white potatoes due to their high sugar content.
- Yams originated in Asia and are a close relative to the sweet potato but are less sweet and contain 10-20% less nutrients.

- Sweet potatoes have 10 calories per ounce less than yams.
- Sweet potatoes cook somewhat different than regular white potatoes in that they tend to become sweeter the more you cook them.
- A percentage of the starch in sweet potato converts to sugar when the potato is heated.
- The cells in a sweet potato are not as strong as those in a white potato and when it is boiled it will easily absorb water and swell up.
- Sweet potatoes unlike white potatoes will freeze without becoming mushy if fully cooked, either boiled or baked.
- They need to be placed in a well-sealed plastic container and as much air as possible bled out.
- The container then needs to be placed into a large sealed plastic bag. They will keep for 10-12 months.

Sweet potatoes have been my favorite all my life and when chefs pick them from the market they examine them thoroughly. I am surprised some chefs don't bring a magnifying glass when they're picking out sweet potatoes.

If the potato had the slightest hint of bruising or a soft spot they will never purchase it. Never purchase them if they are bagged under any circumstances.

Science of Buying Sweet Potatoes

Sweet potatoes have a very short life and are not as hardy as white potatoes. They are very injury-prone and if bruised in the slightest may be invaded by decay organisms. One bad spot on a sweet potato can affect the flavor of the entire potato. When my grandmother handled and stored sweet potatoes you would think that she was handling eggs. At room temperature sweet potatoes will only last for up to two weeks.

SWEET POTATOES VS YAMS

The best way to tell the difference between sweet potatoes and yams is to look at the flesh, which should be orange in a sweet potato and reddish in a yam. Supermarkets commonly label yams as sweet potatoes. Sweet potatoes contain the same number of calories as white potatoes; however, they contain more vitamin C and 3 times the beta-carotene. The best sweet potato is called a "boniato" or "Cuban" sweet potato and has a very light yellow flesh.

The sweet potato crop in Africa is one of the more important crops but is damaged almost every season by the feathery mottle virus. The African sweet potato crop is now protected by biotechnology and is able to fight off the virus without the heavy use of chemicals.

A chemical in sweet potatoes is activated by temperatures below 40°F and tend to make a sweet potato taste bitter. It would be best not to refrigerate that poor sweet potato.

To peel a sweet potato easily, take them from the boiling water and immediately immerse them in a bowl of ice cold water for about 20-30 seconds. The skins should almost fall off by themselves.

♦ After peeling raw sweet potatoes they should be placed in a large bowl of acidulated water until you are ready to use them or they will turn brown very quickly.

♦ If you are going to fry sweet potatoes, be sure they are very dry first.

♦ The flavor of sweet potatoes will be more intense if they are served with maple syrup and freshly grated nutmeg. They seem to like brown sugar as well with a little cinnamon butter.

POT LID, STICKING

GET OUT THE CROWBAR

I never heard grandma swear, but I think she came pretty close once when a pot lid would not budge off the pot she was cooking with. She finally got the lid off but the food was not exactly the way she wanted to cook it.

POTS, CLEANING OF

To loosen caked-on food from a pan, just place a fresh dryer sheet in the bottom of a dirty pan or pot then fill it with lukewarm tap water and allow it to sit in the sink overnight. The chemicals in the dryer sheet will make the pan easier to clean in the morning.

PUMPKIN

When your pumpkins or squash start to mature, try placing a small board under each fruit. This will protect the fruit from soil-borne bacteria and fungus.

One of the biggest problems every Halloween is that the pumpkin will get soft and mushy a few hours after it has been carved. The problem is the result of the air coming in contact with inside flesh, thus allowing bacteria to grow at a rapid pace. Spraying the inside of the pumpkin with an antiseptic spray will retard the bacterial growth and reduce the time of deterioration. Make sure you do not eat the pumpkin or the seeds, after it has been sprayed.

- When choosing pumpkins, be sure they are brightly colored and heavy for their size.
- Pumpkins will store at room temperature for about 1 month if not opened.
- Smaller pumpkins will be sweeter and more tender.
- If you are going to eat the pumpkin, be sure and only purchase the "sugar" variety.
- To get rid of the strings when cooking with pumpkin, use a hand mixer and the strings will wind around the blades and be easy to remove.

QQQQQ

QUICHE

Quiche is of French origins, especially of Lorraine. The first popular quiche dish in the United States was "Quiche Lorraine" and prepared from egg, onion and bacon.

Quiches should be served right from the oven to the table and never allowed to cool.

Science of Serving Quiche

Quiche is usually made with onions and mushrooms, both of which have high water content. Because of this fact, the quiche will lose a large amount of moisture as it cools causing the crust to become soggy. If you want to serve a quiche with a flaky, dry crust you will need to serve it as soon as it finishes cooking.

RRRRR

REFREEZING FOODS

Meat & Poultry

May be re-frozen if freezer temperature was maintained at 40^0F (4.4^0C) or below and the meat has no odor and is not discolored.

Vegetables

May be re-frozen only if ice crystals are present or if the freezer temperature was 40^0F (4.4^0C) or below.

Fruits

They may be re-frozen providing they do not show any signs of spoilage. If they have fully thawed it would be best to use them in cooking or preserves.

Cooked foods

May be re-frozen only if ice crystals are present or the freezer was 40^0F (4.4^0C) or below. If questionable the food should be discarded.

Ice cream

If even partially thawed, discard it. If temperature was above 40^0F (4.4^0C) the ice cream could be dangerous.

RHUBARB

Grandma's favorite vegetable for making pies! She never added strawberries to it and left it somewhat tart, which is how everyone liked it best. She also grew rhubarb in her garden every year.

> ➢ To stew rhubarb, place the cut up rhubarb in a large saucepan with just enough water to cover. Bring to a boil then lower the heat to simmer and cook gently until tender.
> ➢ After rhubarb has cooked sweeten to taste and cook for about 5 minutes more to be sure that all the sugar has been dissolved.

Science of Rhubarb

Its origins can be traced back to Southern Siberia. The plant has edible stalks with heart-shaped large leaves, which are poisonous (NEVER USE THE LEAVES). Rhubarb is occasionally referred to as a fruit since it is a common pie ingredient, but it is a true vegetable. Two varieties can be purchased, the hothouse, and the outdoor types. Rhubarb does contain oxalic acid, which may reduce the absorption of calcium and is not recommended in large quantities, especially for women who are close to or going through menopause.

When cooking rhubarb, never use aluminum or cast iron cookware. The chemicals in rhubarb will react with the metal.

> ➢ To sweeten rhubarb it usually takes about ½ cup of granulated sugar per pound of rhubarb.
> ➢ Stewed rhubarb is excellent cold and if served cold it would be best to taste it just before serving to be sure the sweetness is correct. The total time to stew rhubarb is 6-8 minutes.

Use Less Sugar in Rhubarb

If you add a pinch of baking soda to the cooking water you will need less sugar in your recipe to achieve a somewhat sweet taste. Rhubarb should be a little tart and the baking soda will help.

The outer layer of rhubarb stalks is very stringy and needs to be removed before cooking. To accomplish this trim off both ends of the stalk then place a knife just under the skin and peel it away. Continue doing this until all the skin has been removed.

RIBS, BARBECUE

One of the key secrets to making tender spareribs is to place them in a pot and cover with boiling water, then simmer for 30 minutes before baking or barbecuing. Very slow-cooking ribs works well too, however, if time is a problem, the boiling method may be preferred.

- ◆ Baby back ribs can be made in a roasting pan on a rack cooked at 400°F for about 1¼ hour.

RICE

Rice is the most common grain consumed in the United States at about 17 pounds per person annually. This is very low compared to the 300 pounds consumed per capita in Japan and China.

History records the first cultivation of rice to be in Thailand in 3500BC; however, China produces more rice than any other country, almost 90 percent of all the rice grown worldwide. It is an excellent source of the B complex vitamins as well as a number of minerals. Brown rice is more nutritious and higher in the B vitamins and fiber than white rice.

If you accidentally burn rice, just remove the good rice and place it into a clean pot. Place a fresh piece of white bread or a thin layer of onionskins on top of the rice and continue cooking for about 10-15 minutes before removing the bread or onionskins and discarding them.

Vitamin E is only found in brown rice. Instant brown rice is now becoming available. It is really hard to tell the difference between white rice and brown rice after it is cooked. The brown rice, however, will have a much higher nutritional content.

The only difference between brown and white rice is the removal of the husk. It is only sold in small boxes because the bran portion is higher in fat, which may cause the rice to go rancid if not used up in a short period of time. If you allow brown rice to soak for about 1 hour before cooking it will be more tender. There are more varieties of rice grown than any other food. Worldwide there are over 7,000 varieties of long, short, or medium grain rice.

For a different, taste try soaking 1 cup of rice in cider for 5 minutes before cooking.

Rice, unlike other processed products does not have the number of nutrients replaced that are lost. Even though rice may be sold as "enriched" the number of nutrients replaced is minimal. When the rice is then cooked in boiling water additional nutrients are lost. Brown rice is always best.

- The rice with the lowest nutritional content is Minute Rice and any instant rice.
- Salt should never be added to any food while it is cooking since it tends to toughen the food.
- Rice is very susceptible to toughening from salted water. Rice will retain its white color if you add a few drops of lemon juice to the water.
- If you accidentally burn rice, just remove the good rice and place it into a clean pot. Place a fresh piece of white bread or a thin layer of onionskins on top of the rice and continue cooking for about 10-15 minutes before removing the bread or onionskins and discarding them.
- Always store rice at cool room temperature and make sure that you wash the rice before using it to clean out the hulls.
- Rice is mainly composed of starch similar to pasta, but needs to be cooked in a small amount of water.
- The liquid that the rice absorbs needs to be just enough to be completely absorbed by the rice and should make the rice "fluffy."

COOKING RICE

The easiest method determining the amount of water to cook rice in is to place the rice in a pot, shake it to settle the rice then pour enough water in up to your fist knuckle of your index finger that has been placed gently on top of the rice. The rice should be covered with about 1 inch of water.

Cook the rice by bringing the water to a boil then cover and simmer on low heat for 35 minutes. The heat should then be turned off and the rice allowed standing for 8-10 minutes. If you want your rice to always be dry and fluffy, try placing a few folded paper towels under the lid to absorb the steam and excess moisture for the last 2-3 minutes of cooking time.

- When rice is cooking in boiling water, the heat is transferred by the water molecules, which are moving by convection. If you don't stop the cooking and allow the rice to rest at this point, the heat may now be transferred through the bottom of the pan (conduction) and ruin the rice.

Do not stir rice while it is cooking unless the recipe calls for it.

- Covering the pot and allowing the rice to finish cooking uses steam and continues convection cooking. When you cover the pot, place a kitchen towel between the lid and the pot to absorb excess moisture.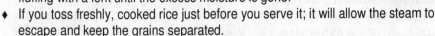
- When the rice is done and there is still some moisture left, just remove the cover and cook the rice over low heat while fluffing with a fork until the excess moisture is gone.
- If you toss freshly, cooked rice just before you serve it; it will allow the steam to escape and keep the grains separated.
- Best not to rinse rice after it has cooked or you will lose nutrients.
- Leftover rice should not be added to soups or stews until the very last minute or the rice will get soft and mushy.

Grandma had another method of cooking rice that was different from most methods. She placed 1 cup of rice in a saucepan and covered the rice with 2 cups of cold lightly, salted water.

The rice was then brought to a boil over very high heat and then simmered uncovered over medium heat just until the water evaporated to just above the level of the rice. She then covered the pan and turned the heat to the lowest setting for about 20 minutes.

RICE, BROWN

Science of Brown Rice

Vitamin E is only found in brown rice. Instant brown rice is now becoming available. It is really hard to tell the difference between white rice and brown rice after it is cooked. The brown rice, however, will have a much higher nutritional content. The only difference between brown and white rice is the removal of the husk. It is only sold in small boxes because the bran portion is higher in fat, which may cause the rice to go rancid if not used up in a short period of time. If you allow brown rice to soak for about 1 hour before cooking it will be more tender. There are more varieties of rice grown than any other food. Worldwide there are over 7,000 varieties of long, short, or medium grain rice.

RISOTTO

- To prepare creamy, Italian style risotto, use short-grained rice; which is high in starch. The best one to use is called "Arborio."
- Rice is never rinsed or you will wash off some of the starch, which you need to make the risotto creamy.
- Before cooking the rice, be sure and sauté the rice in about 2 tablespoons of olive oil for 2 minutes or until the rice looks opaque.

- The chef's secret to making risotto is to add hot broth to the rice ½ cup at a time and be sure to stir constantly until all the liquid is absorbed before adding the next ½ cup.
- Make sure you keep the broth hot over low heat as you are preparing the dish.

ROAST

A roast should never be carved until it has had a chance to rest and allow juices to dissipate evenly throughout the roast. When you cook a roast the juices tend to be forced to the center as the juices near the surface evaporate from the heat. A roast should be left to stand for about 15 minutes before carving. This will also allow the meat to firm up a bit making it easier to carve thinner slices.

- After a few days the exterior of a roast will start to change color when refrigerated due to oxidation. The roast is still good but try not to refrigerate meats for more than 2-3 days before cooking them.
- When you burn or scorch a roast, remove it from the pan and cover it with a hot water dampened towel for about 5 minutes to stop the cooking.
- Remove or scrape off any burnt areas with a sharp instrument and finish cooking.
- When purchasing roasts you should figure the cost per pound and realize that boneless cuts usually cost less per serving. The bone weight contributes considerable cost to the meat making the cost per serving higher in most instances.

> When preparing fatty-looking roasts, refrigerate the roast after it is partially cooked. The fat will then solidify and can easily be removed. Then return the roast to the oven and complete the cooking time. To stop fat from entering a roast, just sprinkle dry mustard on top of the fat. The dry mustard will allow seasonings to enter the roast but will stop the fat.

TREASURE HUNT

When purchasing a chuck roast look for the white cartilage near the top of the roast. If you can spot a roast with this showing you have found the first cut, which will be the most tender. When purchasing an eye of the round roast, look for one that is the same size on either end this will be the more tender one. However, with round steaks purchase ones that have uneven cuts and you have found the one closest to the sirloin.

- Sealing in the juices by lightly flouring the surface of meats works very well. When storing a roast, always place the roast back into its own juices whenever possible. When re-heating meats, try placing the slices in a casserole dish with lettuce leaves between the slices. This will provide just the right amount of moisture to keep the slices from drying out.

ROAST, COOKING SECRETS

When cooking a roast, there are two methods that are normally used either using dry heat (without liquid) or moist heat (with liquid).

When the meat is covered it is cooked with steam that is trapped in the pan. Many cooks use this method to prevent the roast from drying out.

Dry heat with the lid off will keep the outside of the roast crisp instead of mushy and if you wish the roast can be basted every 15 minutes to provide the desired moisture. This is the preferred method by most chefs. However, if you do roast with a lid on and in liquid, you must lower the temperature by 25^{0}F.

Chefs will occasionally roast with the lid off the pot. They will baste the roast about every 20 minutes, which seems like a lot of work instead of just covering the pot. They obviously know something that I don't since their roasts are always juicier.

Science of Dry Roasting

A good roast should have moist, tender meat and a deep brown crust on the outside. When a roast is covered, the outside will be a pale brown and not that appealing. By basting the roast instead of covering it and allowing the roast to be steamed, chefs know how to produce the greatest looking and best tasting roast ever. Even though they use dry heat instead of steam, the basting made all the difference. Also, never allow the roast to sit on the bottom of the pan or the bottom will be cooked by moist heat and not the dry heat preferred.

The deep brown crust is caused by the Maillard reaction. The juices come to the surface and the sugar and amino acids (proteins) react and browning takes place. This causes an intense flavor and crusty texture in a dark brown pigmentation and unbelievable flavor. Some of the pigmentation falls off in the bottom of the pan and are used for gravy.

♦ Roasts should always be cooked on a rack or stalks of celery and never allowed standing in the liquid on the bottom of the pan; this gives a mushy bottom to the roast. This can be done with meatloaf as well.

If you purchase a tough cut of beef to save money, just roast the meat in a covered pot with water in the bottom to create steam.

Some cooks tend to use this method and slow cook the roast for many hours at a low temperature, but most chefs do not like this method and prefer to cook the roast in about 3 hours at the most.

Science of Moist Roasting

Prolonged cooking in moist heat may actually ruin a piece of meat. It may soften the connective tissue but at the same time actually harden the muscle fibers defeating the process.

Slow cooking involves about 6 hours and a temperature of 140°F, while mama's slow cooking, which softened the connective tissue, and did not harden the muscle tissue took 3 hours at 180°F. A temperature of about 212°F may cook the meat faster but will cause the meat collagen to gelatinize, kill the muscle fiber and make the meat tough.

A Crusty Situation

If you want to keep a crust on your roast and do not want the juices to ruin it, just place the roast on a rack set in the roasting pan and place a piece of aluminum foil gently over the top.

Steady Now

When chefs need to carve a roast they never place a big fork in it and move it as they carve. They hold the roast with a long-handled pair of kitchen tongs otherwise some of the juices will be lost.

DON'T COMMIT A CRIME

Even though the body may prefer roast beef to be well done, it would be a crime to ruin a good roast and never ask a chef to prepare a well-done roast. I can just imagine what they would say.

The only time I have ever had anything close to a roast well done is when we make a brisket. Chefs always leave the roast in the oven until it is at a medium temperature then they remove the roast before it is fully cooked.

Science of Allowing the Roast to Rest

When the roast is removed from the oven, the meat that is near the surface has very little of its juices left. The juices that were at the surface either evaporated or went to the center to hide. If you carve the roast as soon as it leaves the oven, the juices will not be distributed evenly throughout the roast. Allowing the roast to rest will let the juices to redistribute throughout the roast and make the roast more juicy.

Ding-A-Ling

It's dinnertime and everyone is sitting around the table waiting anxiously for the family chef to take the roast out of the oven. However, when he removes it, he won't allow us to have any or even cut the roast until it has a chance to rest for at least 15 minutes. Looking at that beautiful roast and having to wait 15 minutes is really hard.

Science of Removing a Roast Before It Is Full Cooked

Since many people prefer their roast to be medium-rare you cannot cook the roast fully; you need to remove the roast before it is fully cooked to achieve this level of doneness.

If you want to cook your roast to 140°F and the roast is left in the oven until the thermometer reaches 140°F, the surface meat will probably be 160°F to 180°F. If the roast is about 8" thick, the internal temperature will increase about 10° and if the roast is about 12" thick the internal temperature will increase about 15° as it is resting before you start carving it. Remove a roast just before it reaches the internal temperature you desire and allow the roast to increase slightly as it rests before you carve it.

- When a roast is brought to room temperature or at least near room temperature it will cook more quickly than one that is placed into the oven directly from the refrigerator. Also, it will protect the roast from the exterior becoming overcooked and dried out before the inside is cooked. The only caution is that if the roast is very thick (over 6 inches in diameter) there may be a problem with bacterial contamination from spores in the air.
- Leaving a refrigerated roast out for about 1 hour should be sufficient to warm it without risking contamination. However, this should not be done in a warm, humid climate.
- Lightly coat the roast with seasoned flour.
- Slowly brown the roast on all sides in a pan with a small amount of oil.
- Add about 1-2 cups of broth to the pan and bring to a boil, reduce heat.
- Cover the pan and simmer gently in a pre-heated 325°F oven.
- Always use a shallow pot for cooking roasts, this will allow air to circulate more efficiently.

ROAST, SIRLOIN TIP

YUMMY FOR THE TUMMY

Grandma rarely spent the extra money buying a prime cut of beef, but occasionally she would for special guests. When these roasts are prepared properly you don't even need a knife to cut them.

If you really want a luxurious roast, you have to follow these steps:

1. Buy the best cut of meat. Prime beef will give you the best flavor but is hard to find unless you go to a butcher shop.
2. Always roast fat side up so that the fat can baste the meat and provide flavor.
3. If you are going to roast a quality piece of meat, you will need to roast it at a high temperature. Be sure that the roast had not been previously frozen and be sure it is at room temperature when you start.
4. Preheat the oven to 500°F and place the roast in the oven for 15 minutes then reduce the temperature to 350°F and continue roasting.

RARE	Roast for 15 minutes per pound + 15 minutes
MEDIUM	**20 minutes per pound + 20 minutes**
WELL DONE	25 minutes per pound + 25 minutes

> **Cooking the roast well done will dry out the roast and is not recommended.**

SSSSS

SAFFRON

This is one of the more difficult herbs to acquire as well as one of the most expensive. It is extracted from the stigma of a flowering crocus and is only imported from Spain. It is used in moderation in poultry, baked goods and rice dishes. Saffron color strength will determine the level of flavor and aroma.

Each flower only provides 3 stigmas, which can only be handpicked and then dried. It takes 14,000 of the tiny threads to produce one ounce of saffron. Saffron can be purchased in either powder or in the stigmas (whole threads).

- The best quality saffron is sold in saffron threads and not the powder. When working with saffron, it is best never to use a whisk, since the threads will become entwined in the whisk.
- Always crush saffron threads before you use them.
- Heat will release the flavor of saffron and if you mix it with one tablespoon of very hot water and let it stand for about 10 minutes before you use it; you will notice the difference.

> **Wooden utensils will absorb saffron and should be avoided.**

- Saffron quality is measured in "coloring strength" with the best strength between; 246-256. It is possible to purchase saffron with strength of only 110 but this will be an inferior product.
- Saffron should never be purchased with a level below 190 degrees. To use saffron properly the threads should be soaked to infuse the saffron before adding it to a recipe.
- Saffron threads should never be added to boiling water or directly into a dish.

SALAD DRESSING

Lettuce leaves as well as many plants have a waxy cuticle, which is a water-repelling mixture of various chemicals that are all related to repelling water and assisting the leaves from becoming waterlogged. This cuticle also protects the leaves from losing too much of their internal moisture.

The oils in salad dressing are related to the chemicals that keep the water out and to at least allow the oils to stick to the surface. Water molecules also tend to bead up and fall off the leaf, while the oil spreads out and coats the surface.

Always place the oil on the salad first then vinegar; the vinegar will remain on the lettuce. If you place the vinegar on first, the oil will slip off.

SALADS

You will never have another soggy salad if you just place an inverted saucer in the bottom of a salad bowl. The excess water left after washing the vegetables and greens will drain off under the saucer and the salad greens will be high and dry.

Any salad bar item that incorporates dairy products into a dressing should be kept cold. The easiest method is to place a larger bowl with ice or dry ice under the food dish. This will keep the temperature cold enough so that bacteria will not be a problem before it is refrigerated.

After you tear or chop up your lettuce, place a pinch of salt in the bowl and shake it. This will keep the lettuce crisp and prevent premature wilting.

- Always try and balance colors of vegetables when making a salad.
- Never use too much salad dressing or the salad will become soggy.
- When adding pasta to a salad, be sure and leave the pasta al dente and not cook it too much or when it absorbs the salad dressing it will become soggy.
- Be sure and always chill salad plates when serving salad.

SALT (SODIUM CHLORIDE)
While salt contains important minerals that are beneficial to the body, in excess it may be detrimental. Body fluids and their distribution in the body depend on the location and concentrations of sodium and potassium ions.

Our kidneys regulate the blood sodium levels and provide the bloodstream with the exact amount as needed. When blood levels rise due to excess sodium ingestion, the body's thirst receptors are stimulated and fluid intake increases to balance the sodium to water ratio. The excess sodium and water is then excreted by the kidneys.

When this balance cannot be maintained the result may be higher blood pressure and an increased deposition of atherosclerotic plaque material. When salt is processed the native minerals are stripped away and it is then enriched with iodine and dextrose to stabilize it, sodium bicarbonate to keep it white and anti-caking agents to keep it "free-flowing." Morton's Special Salt is one of the only salts that have no additives.

Salt is used in almost every food that is processed and is one of the best preservatives.

It is estimated by the National Institute of Health that over 10 million people over the age of 65 have some degree of high blood pressure problems. Since sodium is found in thousands of food items, it is recommended that "added salt" be avoided to help control your total sodium intake. When preparing food and seasoning with salt the recommended amounts for certain dishes is:

1 teaspoon for Soups and Sauces
1 teaspoon for raw meat dishes
1 teaspoon for every 4 cups of flour (dough)
1 teaspoon for every 2 cups of liquid used in cooked cereals

40% of regular table salt is sodium: Lite salt has only 20% sodium content.

If you eat a piece of bacon and it doesn't taste salty you are consuming too much salt. Excess sodium intake builds up in the bloodstream, kidneys are unable to clear the excess water it retains, an increase in blood volume occurs and the heart has to work harder causing higher blood pressure.

The most popular salt chefs ever use is kosher salt. Kosher salt has large irregular crystals and is half as salty as regular table salt. Depending on the dish you will need to use a little more salt but kosher salt tends to give a salty flavor using less salt in most dishes.

Science of Coarse Salt

Try buying coarse salt and using it on corn on the cob for a big surprise. Coarse salt has little jagged edges and will cling to the kernels as well as not melting too fast. This is the popular salt for pretzels since it won't melt too quickly when you use it for baking. Coarse salt is the salt of choice, however, for most chefs, since it is easier to pick up and measure by hand.

- Salt tends to draw moisture from foods. If a food is salted before placing it in the fryer, it will draw moisture to the surface and cause spattering when the food is placed into the heated oil.
- If you add 1 teaspoon of salt to your cooking water, it will raise the temperature $1\text{-}2^0$F. Sugar and many other ingredients will also raise the temperature of the water. Unless the recipe calls for this raise, it is best not to add salt because salt has the tendency to cause many foods to become tough.

Rice to the Rescue

If you live in a hot humid climate you know that the saltshaker will not shake the salt out easily. The salt will absorb moisture from the air, however, if you add a few grains of raw rice to the shaker, the salt will flow more easily.

SALT, THE MICROBE INHIBITOR

For thousands of years salt has been used to preserve foods by inhibiting microbial growth. Salt has the ability to draw liquids from tissues and freeing water that is bound by breaking down proteins. The mechanism involves salt's ability to create a concentration of "ions" (electrically charged particles) outside of the bacteria and mold cells encompassing the microbe drawing out its water and either drying it up and killing it or slowing down its replication. It is the drying out feature of salt that makes it such a good preservative.

- ♦ Never salt a sauce that is going to be reduced.
- ♦ You may want to use a little more salt in a cold dish than a hot one since chilling reduces the flavor of most foods.

SAUCES

Sauces are never served hot, always warm. High heat will melt the butter too fast and ruin the emulsification and cause separation. You want the butter to turn into a foamy mixture, not a liquid. Start with cold butter, which will keep the mixture cool and reduces the risk of the butter melting instead of foaming. It is best to keep the pan moving on and off the heat if necessary while beating the butter with a whisk. You can also use a double boiler, which is easier for the person who is not used to making a white sauce.

Most sauces and custards that are thickened with flour or cornstarch do not freeze well. The starch, amylase, which is commonly found in grain starches such as wheat flour and cornstarch tend to freeze into a very firm, spongy-texture and allows the liquid to drain out. If the food is thickened with a root starch, such as arrowroot or tapioca they can be frozen and thawed without any problem.

If you accidentally burn your dessert sauce don't fret just add a small amount of pure vanilla or almond extract in the sauce to cover up the burnt taste.

Sauces are only meant to complement the flavor or provide moisture for the dish. Sauces should never detract from the original flavor of the food.

French cooking schools classify sauces in five categories: Espagnole, which is a brown, stock-based sauce, Velote, which is a light, stock-based sauce, Béchamel, which is a white sauce and usually milk-based, Hollandaise or mayonnaise is an emulsified sauce and Vinaigrette is an oil and vinegar sauce. However, we place mayonnaise in the condiment class because it is usually always purchased as a commercial product and vinaigrette as a salad dressing.

HOW TO DE-FAT A SAUCE

Chefs have a wild trick using a wine bottle to de-fat sauces. They pour the sauce into a wine bottle with a long neck and wait until the fat rises to the top then pour it off.

CHEF'S SAUCE SECRETS

♦ If your egg-based sauce separates, remove the pan from the heat and beat in two tablespoons of crushed ice to reduce the heat and place the eggs back into suspension, thus saving the emulsion.

♦ You can also change pans and add one tablespoons of ice water to a small amount of the sauce while slowly whisking back the balance of the separated sauce. Additional ice water can be added slowly, but only as needed.

♦ If your recipe calls for egg yolks, never add them to a sauce that is too hot. The instant change in temperature, resulting from placing the cool egg into the hot liquid is just enough of a change to curdle the egg yolk and may ruin the sauce. To eliminate the possible problem, remove a small amount of the sauce and allow it to cool for a few minutes before mixing the egg yolk in. The cooled sauce can then be added to the hot mixture.

♦ Cornstarch, arrowroot and potato starch should only be used just before you are finishing the sauce, since they have twice the thickening power of flour and can only be cooked for a few minutes before losing their thickening power.

♦ Flour will not lump if you add the flour to any fat that is already hot. In fact, you can add flour to any hot liquid without the flour lumping. Regular flour tends to turn into a form of gelatin when it comes into contact with hot water; that tends to block the water from entering. Instant flour contains smaller irregular-shaped granules that allow space for the water to enter.

♦ One easy method of reducing the salt level in sauces and soups is to dip a sugar cube into the dish and run it back and forth covering the surface only once and before the cube melts. Salt is attracted to sugar and a percentage of the salt will adhere to the cube; then discard the cube.

♦ Sauces are never served hot, always warm. High heat will melt the butter too fast and ruin the emulsification and cause separation. You want the butter to turn into a foamy mixture, not a liquid. Start with cold butter, which will keep the mixture cool and reduces the risk of the butter melting instead of foaming.

♦ It is best to keep the pan moving on and off the heat if necessary while beating the butter with a whisk. You can also use a double boiler, which is easier for the person who is not used to making a white sauce.

♦ Most sauces and custards that are thickened with flour or cornstarch do not freeze well. The starch, amylase, which is commonly found in grain starches such as wheat flour and cornstarch tend to freeze into a very firm, spongy-texture and allows the liquid to drain out. If the food is thickened with a root starch, such as arrowroot or tapioca they can be frozen and thawed without any problem.

♦ If you accidentally burn your dessert sauce, just add a small amount of pure vanilla or almond extract in the sauce to cover up the burnt taste.

◆ Occasionally, sauces tend to taste a bit bitter and the reason escapes you. It may be from a tomato seed or two that ended up not being strained out. A crushed tomato seed will cause a sauce to become bitter.

When sauce is finished cooking, it should fall from the whisk in a wide ribbon or sheet. This should take about 5 minutes of cooking.

SOY SAUCE

Soy sauce is one of the most popular condiments in the world. It is prepared from roasted soybeans and wheat (or barley), which have been fermented.

The Chinese claim that ketchup was originally produced from a Chinese soy sauce recipe. There are four varieties of soy sauce:

- Light soy sauce that we normally see in the supermarkets.
- Dark soy sauce, which is not as salty but has a very strong flavor.
- Chinese black soy sauce, which is very thick and the color of blackstrap molasses.
- Japanese tamari soy sauce which is very dark, thick and has a lower salt content that the Chinese variety.

Kikkoman International, Inc. is the largest producer of soy sauce in the world. Their latest product is a clear soy sauce that can be used in recipes without altering the color of the food. The company also produces soy sauce that is preservative-free and reduced-sodium, both available in powered or liquid forms.

STEAK SAUCE

The ingredients are: tomato puree, high fructose corn syrup, distilled vinegar, corn syrup, salt, raisins, spices, orange base (combination of orange, lemon and grapefruit juices), orange peel, dried onion and garlic, xanthan gum and caramel color.

SAUCES, ADDING EGG YOLKS

If your recipe calls for egg yolks, never add them to a sauce that is too hot. The instant change in temperature, resulting from placing the cool egg into the hot liquid is just enough of a change to curdle the egg yolk and may ruin the sauce. To eliminate the possible problem, remove a small amount of the sauce and allow it to cool for a few minutes before mixing the egg yolk in. The cooled sauce can then be added to the hot mixture.

When sauce is finished cooking, it should fall from the whisk in a wide ribbon or sheet. This should take about 5 minutes of cooking.

SAUCES, REPAIRING

One easy method of reducing the salt level in sauces and soups is to dip a sugar cube into the dish and run it back and forth covering the surface only once and before the cube melts. Salt is attracted to sugar and a percentage of the salt will adhere to the cube then discard the cube.

Occasionally, sauces tend to taste a bit bitter and the reason escapes you. It may be from a tomato seed or two that ended up not being strained out. A crushed tomato seed will cause a sauce to become bitter.

If your egg-based sauce separates, remove the pan from the heat and beat in two tablespoons of crushed ice to reduce the heat and place the eggs back into suspension, thus saving the emulsion.

You can also change pans and add one tablespoons of ice water to a small amount of the sauce while slowly whisking back the balance of the separated sauce. Additional ice water can be added slowly, but only as needed.

SAUTÉING

♦ When sautéing, make sure that you only use a small amount of oil. If you wish to have the food turn out crisp you need to heat the oil to a high temperature before adding the food. To test the temperature of the oil, try dropping a small piece of food into the pan, if it sizzles, it is ready for you to sauté.

Remember to always have the food at room temperature if you wish the food to brown faster and more evenly. Cold foods tend to stick to the pan. During the sautéing process, the pan should be moved gently back and forth a number of times to assure even browning.

♦ Before sautéing carrots, potatoes or any dense food, try parboiling them first. This will assure that all the food will be done at the same time.
♦ Foods that are to be sautéed should be dry. Never salt any food that is to be sautéed; salt tends to retard the browning of foods.
♦ Before sautéing meats, try sprinkling a small amount of sugar on the surface of the meat. The sugar will react with the juices, caramelize, and cause a deeper browning as well as improving the flavor.
♦ Never overcrowd a pan that you are sautéing in. Overcrowding causes poor heat distribution resulting in food that is not evenly browned.
♦ If the fat builds up from the foods that are being sautéed, remove the excess with a bulb baster.

♦ Never cover a pan when sautéing. Steam tends to build up and the food may become mushy.

Chefs will never use salted butter when they are sautéing. The salt in butter may separate from the butter and impart a somewhat bitter taste to the food being sautéed. Always use unsalted butter.

♦ Always use a small amount of oil and heat the oil to a high temperature before adding the food. Try placing a small sample of the food (at room temperature) into the pan, if it sizzles, the fat is hot enough.
♦ If the food is cold it will stick to the pan.
♦ Move the pan gently back and forth while sautéing.
♦ Parboil any dense foods such as carrots or potatoes first. This will assure that all the food will be done at the same time
♦ Never salt food that is to be sautéed; that will retard the browning.
♦ Before sautéing meat, sprinkle a small amount of sugar on the meat. The sugar will help the browning and caramelize and will also improve the taste.
♦ Never overcrowd the pan.
♦ Remove any excess fat with a bulb baster.
♦ Never cover the pan or the food will become mushy.
♦ To prevent spattering and burns while sautéing, tilt the pan away from you to pool the oil every time you add more food, then place the pan flat again. You can also add a few sprinkles of salt to the pan to prevent spattering.

SAUTE-AWAY
When sautéing, be sure and keep the heat low if the meat is thick. The thicker the meat is the lower the temperature. When the meat is thick it takes longer for the heat to reach the insides.

SEASONINGS, GENERAL INFORMATION

The difference between herbs and spices is that herbs are the fragrant leaves of plants that do not have a woody stem and spices are barks of trees, berries, roots and fruits. Spices may also be the stems of certain trees, plants and vines. Pre-ground herbs and spices will not have the full rich aroma or flavor of the fresh ones.

When you need to increase the amount of food in a recipe and are not sure if you should increase the seasonings in the same proportion as the original recipe called for, the answer is never increase the seasonings to the full degree. If you double the recipe, increase the seasonings only by 1½, if you increase by three times, only increase two times the original. When the recipe is complicated, it would be best to make two batches. Never increase sugar in tomato sauce dishes. Never increase salt more than a pinch or two at the most.

It's very handy to keep a shaker of ¾ salt and ¼ pepper next to the range or food preparation area.

Chefs rarely have to taste food to tell if the flavor is what they want it to be. Many chefs just use their nose to sniff out the flavors and to make sure they are just right.

Science of Food Sniffing
I didn't understand how they did this until I found out that a lot of the taste sensations are in the nose not the tongue. The tongue only deciphers sweet, sour, salty and bitter flavors.

Certain herbs lose their flavor when cooked too long (over 1½-hours) and need to be added toward the end of the cooking time. These include garlic, most ground spices, chili powder and bay leaf. The one herb that doesn't lose its flavor during cooking is paprika.

Science of Substituting Herbs
Substituting oil for dried herbs is never a good idea; however, it is tried all the time. Oils are so concentrated that it is almost impossible to calculate the amount that you will need to replace the herb to acquire the same taste. A good example is cinnamon of which the oil is 50 times stronger than the ground cinnamon. If you did want to substitute the oil to replace the cinnamon extract, you would only need to use 1-2 drops of the oil to replace ½ teaspoon of the extract in candy or frostings.

CHEF'S HERB & SPICE SECRETS

- ❖ Try to always use freshly dried herbs
- ❖ Use spices sparingly
- ❖ Use less of dried herbs than you would of fresh
- ❖ Fresh herbs can replace dried herbs in any recipe
- ❖ If you want the herb to be more aromatic, try warming it in hot butter before using it
- ❖ Never use the same herbs for different dishes at the same meal
- ❖ Crushing fresh herbs before you add them to a dish will bring out their aromatic oils and flavors

---

Try tying dried or fresh herbs in a small cheesecloth bag and place them into stews or soups.

I once saw a chef blowing into a plastic bag that had what looked like different herbs in it and thought for a minute that he had lost it and had gone over the deep end.

I have heard of glue sniffing but never herb sniffing. When I asked him about it he explained that they were fresh herbs and he wanted to preserve them for a few more days.

Science of Preserving Fresh Herbs
By blowing into a plastic bag with fresh herbs and then sealing it as fast as you can, you place carbon dioxide from your breath into the bag. Carbon dioxide is an herbal preservative and will keep the herbs fresh for about a week longer.

SHELLFISH, COOKING
When you cook shellfish, try not and overdo it or they may become very tough. Clams, crab, and lobster only need to be steamed for 5-10 minutes. Crayfish and mussels only need 4-8 minutes. Always remember to turn all shellfish except lobsters. Grilling an 8-ounce lobster tail only takes 10-12 minutes.

SHRIMP

BLACK TUBE ON A SHRIMP'S BACK
The intestinal tract of the shrimp can be found running the length of its back. It would be best to remove it since it does harbor bacteria but is safe to eat if the shrimp is cooked, which will kill any bacteria. If you do eat it and you notice that the shrimp is somewhat gritty, it is because the intestinal tube remained intact containing sand granules. De-veining the shrimp is relatively simple, all you have to do is run a small ice pick down the back and the tube will fall out.

➢ Do not fry more than 4-5 shrimp at a time so that the oil does not cool.
➢ The oil should be at 375⁰F.
➢ As the shrimp are fried, place them in a pre-heated 250⁰F oven on a baking sheet that has been lined with paper towels. Turn the oven off before you place the baking sheet in.

Shrimp have high water content and therefore will reduce down from one pound to about ¾ of a pound or less after cooking. Worldwide there are over 250 species of shrimp of which the largest are called "prawns." Depending on where the shrimp feed and are caught they may be found in a variety of colors from white, the more desirable color, to brown which mainly feed on algae and have a stronger flavor.

DECAPITATION
Shrimp with heads are more perishable than those without heads. The head contains almost all its vital organs and the majority of the digestive system.

IS A PRAWN A SHRIMP?

Biologically a prawn is different from a shrimp in that it has pincer claws similar to a lobster. A relative of the prawn is the scampi, both of which are considerably larger than the average shrimp. Restaurants in the United States rarely serve real prawns, they are just jumbo shrimp. Jumbo shrimp costs less than the giant prawns but are not as tasty. If you do eat a "real" prawn you will know the difference.

♦ If shrimp develops a strong odor, it is probably ammonia, which means that the shrimp has started to deteriorate and if not cooked immediately should be discarded.

♦ Shrimp cannot be re-frozen and remember almost all shrimp you buy has been frozen. This means that if you don't eat the shrimp that same day or possibly the next day it should be thrown out.

♦ A common problem with purchasing shrimp that has already been breaded is that a number of firms have been over-breading to increase the weight of the packages. The FDA has taken action against some companies for this practice.

♦ The cholesterol content of shrimp may be higher than most other fish; however, it is lower than any other type of meat product and does not contain a high level of saturated fat.

♦ If you purchase canned shrimp, always place the can into a pan of ice-cold water for about 1-2 hours before opening. This will usually eliminate the "off flavor" from the can. If canned taste still exists, try soaking the shrimp for 15 minutes in a mixture of lemon juice and cold water.

Shrimp will always cook up nice and tender if you cool them down before cooking them. Either, place the shrimp into the freezer for 10-15 minutes or in a bowl of ice cubes and water for about 5 minutes.

They should then be prepared by placing them into a warm pot (not over a hot burner), sprinkle with a small amount of sea salt, then pour boiling water over them and cover the pot.

The larger shrimp cook in about 6 minutes, the average size ones are cooked in about 4 minutes and the small shrimp in about 2 minutes. The size of the shrimp should not affect their quality.

SIEVES

♦ Sieves should be purchased with strong handles and a solid frame. Be sure that it has a hook or other type of extension so that it can be rested on top of a bowl or pan.

♦ Buy one that is dishwasher safe.

♦ Always use a wooden spoon when forcing foods through a sieve so that you won't damage the sieve.

- Be sure that the bottom of the sieve does not touch the liquid or food being put through it.

> If you find that you need a sieve but don't have one, just use a colander with a few layers of cheesecloth that have been moistened with water and squeezed out. You can also use the leg of an old pair of CLEAN pantyhose.

- Best to wash a sieve immediately after using it or the food will stick in the small holes and you may have to poke the food out with a fine needle.

SOUFFLÉ

When preparing a soufflé, be sure and use a soufflé dish with straight sides, which will force the expanding soufflé upwards. Also, always use the exact size dish called for in the recipe.

- A soufflé dish should always be buttered unless the recipe says not to use any type of fat on the sides of the dish.
- If more egg whites than yolks are used, the soufflé will be lighter.
- A soufflé must be served as soon as it is removed from the oven. When an item is steam-baked, it has a tendency to collapse as soon as it starts to cool down. Best to serve it in its baking dish or on a very warm plate.

> **Science of Soufflé**
> The perfect soufflé is very delicate and rises because of air bubbles that are trapped in the egg whites when they are beaten. When the soufflé is placed in the oven the air in the bubbles expand causing the soufflé to rise. If the soufflé is punctured or shaken, the air will be released prematurely and the soufflé will collapse. The greasing of the dishes will assure you that the egg proteins will not stick to the sides of the dish.

- The egg whites should be beaten in such a way as to insure the highest amount of air will be trapped. Never over beat or they will become too dry and cause a collapse.

> If you want to prepare a soufflé at the last minute, it would be best to have all the ingredients ready beforehand. Just butter and sugar the soufflé dish and set aside the unbeaten egg whites in a covered dish. Prepare and cover the base mixture. The egg whites and base should be allowed to remain at room temperature for about 30 minutes before you use them. Always preheat the oven and at the last minute, just beat the egg whites and fold them into the base mixture then bake and enjoy the soufflé.

- The oven door should never be opened when the soufflé is cooking for at least ¾ of the cooking time.
- European soufflés are usually served a little underdone with a custard-textured center. This is the preferred method in the finer restaurants.
- The oven needs to be preheated and the dishes are always greased. The yolks are always separated at room temperature.
- Soufflé must be served as soon as it is taken from the oven or the crown may collapse as it cools.

SOUP

Laboratory testing has shown that if a spoonful of very hot soup is held at room temperature for 45 seconds before it is consumed it will cool down to an acceptable temperature, one that will not burn the mouth. If the same spoonful is blown on to speed-up the cooling it will cool to the same acceptable temperature in 20 seconds. The fast moving air when blowing on the hot soup will carry heat away from the soup more efficiently by forcing evaporation from the surface.

- When preparing vegetable soup only pour enough water into the pot to cover the vegetables by two inches. Too much water makes the soup too watery.
- If you have a problem with over-salting your soup or stew, just add a can of peeled tomatoes. Other methods include, adding a small amount of brown sugar or placing a slice or two of apple or raw potato in, mixing it up, and then discarding them.
- Instead of sugar to give your soup or stew a sweeter taste, try adding a small amount of pureed carrots.
- Dark-colored bones should never be used for cooking. They are probably too old and have deteriorated.
- To help a semi-solid soup slide right out of the can, try shaking the can first and then open it from the bottom.
- Soups and stews can be refrigerated for 3-4 days safely and can be frozen with little or no problem for 2-3 months. A texture change can easily be corrected, however, it is advised to whisk in any dairy product after thawing to avoid curdling. That goes for egg yolks as well.
- The best soups for canning are vegetable, dried bean, dried pea, meat-based and seafood-based. Meats should be cooked in a liquid until tender; then strained to remove all debris.
- Vegetables should be fully cooked to the consistency desired. Cover the meat and vegetables with water and boil for 5 minutes. Never thicken soups to be canned; however, you can add some salt to taste.
- Fill your jars halfway with the solid mixture then add the remaining liquid, allowing 1-inch headroom for expansion.
- If you wish to blend the flavors in the soup, be sure and cook the soup with the cover on.

- Always use salt and pepper toward the end of the cooking time. Both of these seasonings will intensify the more they are heated. If too much salt is added, just place a piece of raw potato in and mix it around to absorb the salt then discard it.
- Chefs usually prepare soup the day before they serve it to allow the flavors to blend.
- Always use a warmed bowl for hot soups.
- If the soup becomes lumpy, just place it into the blender for a few seconds and then re-heat it.

THE PARSLEY MAGNET

When you overdo the garlic, just place a few parsley flakes in a tea ball to soak up the excess garlic. Garlic tends to be attracted to parsley.

- To make clear noodle soup, cook the noodles, then drain before adding them to the soup. When noodles are cooked in the soup, the excess starch will turn the soup cloudy.
- Next time you make cream soup, try adding a little flour to the milk. It will make it smoother and it will work even with 1% milk.
- Always make soup at least a day ahead of time, so that the seasonings will have time to improve the flavor. Never use salt or pepper to season soups until you are almost finished with the cooking process. Both of these seasonings will intensify and may give the soup too strong a flavor. When cooking soup, always cook with the lid on to help the flavors become better absorbed.
- When you make cold soup, remember that cold soup needs more seasoning than hot soup. The heat tends to drive the flavors into the product more efficiently.
- Grandmother used to freeze leftover soup in ice cube tray and then use the cubes in soups and stews at another time.
- Wire whisks work better than any other kitchen tool for removing lumps in soups and sauces.
- To make soup go further, just add pasta, rice or barley to it.
- When preparing cold soups you will need to add additional seasonings, since heat will increase the release of flavors in vegetables, seasonings and herbs.
- To avoid scorching your soup when simmering for long periods, try placing two or three bricks under the pot. This slight elevation will prevent a boil-over from occurring.
- The best floaters to use to top off soups are croutons, small pieces of bacon, broccoli, small celery chunks, mushrooms, crushed hard-boiled egg, parsley, Parmesan cheese; miniature onions, a dollop of sour cream or yogurt or chives.

MILK CURDLING

There is always the risk of curdling, especially if you are preparing cream soups and sauces.

To avoid the problem you should always wait until you have thickened the mixture with flour or cornstarch before adding any ingredients that are acidic, such as wine, any type of citrus, or tomatoes. Remember heavy whipping cream won't curdle when you boil it.

Next time you make soup or stew, try using a metal pasta cooker basket. Just place the basket into your pot and cook all your ingredients. When you remove the basket it will contain all the veggies or bones you may not want.

SOUR CREAM

Sour cream should never be added to a recipe if the dish is still hot. The sour cream will usually separate and ruin the dish and should be added just before serving. If it is necessary to reheat a dish containing sour cream, reheat it slowly or the sour cream will separate.

- If your sour cream is starting to have an off odor but is not really bad, just add 1/3rd teaspoon of baking soda to neutralize the lactic acid that is starting to build up. However, if the odor persists, throw it out!
- Sour cream can be made from heavy cream by just placing 4 drops of lemon juice concentrate into ½ cup of heavy cream. Allow the mixture to stand at room temperature for about 20 minutes before refrigerating.
- Sour cream is easily made by adding 4 drops of pure lemon juice to ¾ cup of heavy cream. Allow the mixture to stand at room temperature for about 40 minutes.
- Sour cream will usually last for about a week after the expiration date if you have not eaten out of the container.
- Be sure to bring sour cream to room temperature before you add it to any mixture.

SPAGHETTI

In Italy, a spoon is not used to twirl spaghetti only a fork is used. However, they do serve spaghetti in a large round bowl allowing the fork to twirl the spaghetti on the sides of the bowl. The better Italian restaurants serve spaghetti in these bowls.

Give Spaghetti a Break

Smaller pieces of spaghetti are needed for some dishes and it is difficult to break spaghetti neatly without making a mess. Next time you need to break long strands of spaghetti, just roll the bundle of spaghetti in a kitchen towel making sure that it overlaps the pasta by at least 3 inches on either end.

Holding on to both ends you can then roll the bundle over the edge of the kitchen counter and push down slightly to break it up neatly. You can then hold the bundle by one end and drop the spaghetti in boiling water without any mess.

SPAGHETTI SAUCE

Spaghetti sauces that contain meat may not really have much of the actual muscle protein. By law, companies only need to include 6% actual meat. It would be best to add your own meat and you will know what you are eating.

SPICES

Place the spices in a 350°F oven spread out on a cookie sheet for 3-5 minutes or until they release their aroma. Remove from the oven and use as is or grind them up.

There are certain spices that must be refrigerated during the summer months. Chefs know just which spices will not make it through the summer heat and humidity without refrigeration.

Science of Storing Spices

A number of herbs and spices will lose their potency if not stored properly over the summer months. These include cayenne, paprika, chili powder and red pepper. Seeds with oils also need to be refrigerated all the time such as sesame seeds and poppy seeds. Saffron needs to be stored in a lightproof container.

The best location to store spices is in a cool, dry spot where they will not be around heat. Storing spices near a microwave exhaust fan or over the range are two of the worst locations. If you decide to store them in the refrigerator, make sure you remove them at least 30 minutes before you plan to use them. This will allow the herb to warm up enough to release its flavor and aroma. Herbs that contain oil readily oxidize and should always be stored in the refrigerator. The flavor of fresh herbs is milder than those from the supermarket that have been dried.

It's A Bit Chilly in Here

If you want to store sage or thyme in the refrigerator, they will handle the cold very well. Store them in a plastic container and use parchment paper or paper towel between the layers. Allow room for airflow; so don't pack them tightly.

Labeling Trick

When you purchase small bottles of spices and place them on a rack that is below eye level, it is difficult to see the labels without moving all the bottles around. Just use stick-on dots with the name of the spice on the top of each bottle.

Spice Removal

Certain spices need to be removed after they have seasoned the soup or stew. Try placing these spices into a mesh tea ball and place that into the soup or stew. This will make it easy to retrieve the spent spices.

- ♦ Ground spices lose their flavor and aroma very quickly, so it is best to purchase them in small quantities.
- ♦ When spices are ground fresh they will be more potent than pre-ground spices.

STEAK

The experienced chef rarely uses a thermometer when cooking a steak.

Meat has a certain resiliency that after testing thousands of steaks the chef will just place their finger on the steak and exert a small amount of pressure, telling them if the meat is rare, medium-rare, medium, medium-well, or well done. When meat cooks it tends to lose water and loses some of the flabbiness, the more it cooks the firmer it becomes.

White streaks running through the steak and all beef, is fat! It is a storage depot for energy and for the meat to be well marbled the animal must be fed a diet high in rich grains such as corn, which is where the old saying that corn-fed beef was the best.

The fat imparts a flavor to the meat and provides a level of moisture, which helps tenderize the meat. The presence of fat means that the animal did not exercise a lot and the meat will be more tender.

FAT = FLAVOR

Chefs always leave the fat around a steak and slashed the fat about every ¾ inches. They say that the fat provides extra flavor for the steak and helps the steak cook more evenly.

Science of Slashing Fat

The fat strip shrinks relatively fast and if left on the steak will actually warp the steak while it is cooking. If the steak curls in different areas along its flat surface it will cook unevenly. Also a steak that has buckled is not very nice to serve and you end up having to make a slit in the steak to flatten it out.

THIN IS NOT IN

When it came to broiling, barbecuing or grilling a steak, chefs will never cook one that is too thin. The steak had to be at least between 1 inch and 3 inches thick. This is the ideal thickness for a steak to cook properly.

Science of Steak Thickness

If you cook a steak that is less than 1-inches thick by broiling, barbecuing or grilling, the steak will come out too dry and tough. The surface will not have the time needed to become brown properly before the insides are cooked. A thin steak needs to be pan-broiled for the best results.

SMART IDEA

When cooking a T-bone or porterhouse steak, be sure and place the small tenderloin area of the steak over the coolest coals or lean that area on the side of the pan.

This are will cook faster and get very well done before the rest of the steak cooks to the doneness you desire.

Science of Cooking Steak

Steak when you first buy it is a slimy, red mass of muscle protein. It is mainly coiled-up animal protein. Heating the muscle makes the protein uncoil and become drier as it loses water. One of the proteins is called myoglobin, which has the capacity to store oxygen and makes the meat red. When you heat the muscle over 140°F the myoglobin loses its ability to store oxygen and changes the color of the meat to brown. Cooking meat causes it to lose its ability to store oxygen.

The blood in meats is drained at the slaughterhouses and hardly any ever remains in the meat. The pigment, called myoglobin, in all meat contributes to the reddish color of the meat. Myoglobin is found in the muscles not the arteries. Blood obtains its color from hemoglobin. Those red juices are for the most part colored by myoglobin (and water) not hemoglobin.

Beef will have a more reddish color than pork since it contains more myoglobin in the meat.

Searing a piece of steak does not help in any way to retain the juices (many chefs won't agree), in fact the steak dries out faster because of the more rapid higher temperature cooking. The investigation found out, that if steak is cooked at lower heat and more slowly it would be more tender and retain more of its juices.

The color of fat that surrounds a steak can give you some insight as to what the cow ate and the quality of the beef. If the fat has a yellowish tint it indicates that the cow was grass-fed, and if the fat is white the cow was fed a corn and cereal grain diet. The meat with the white fat will be more tender and probably more expensive.

The one thing that chefs never do is to use a thermometer or cut into a piece of steak to see how well done it was. What they do is to touch the meat and put pressure on it. The following is how you tell the doneness of a steak without cutting into it:

RARE
Touch your thumb and forefinger together around the middle of the steak or at a thick area and press on the fleshy area that you want to test. The meat should feel a little bouncy and soft to the touch. Rare is 135°F (57°C).

MEDIUM
Touch your thumb and middle finger together around the middle of the steak or a thick area and press them together. There should be some give and be a little springy to the touch.

The rare will have a lot of give compared to the medium. Medium-rare is 145°F (62.8°C). Medium is 155°F (68.3°C).

WELL DONE

Touch you thumb and little finger around the middle of the steak or a thick area and press the flesh. There should hardly any give and it will be very firm. Well done is about 170°F (76.7°C)

♦ Never salt steak until close to the time when it will be removed from the heat or you will cause juices to be released.

♦ If you want the steak to have a golden brown top then be sure and keep the steak dry by wiping the surface with paper towel.

STEAMING

This is the most nutritious method of cooking since it hardly washes any of the nutrients from the foods.

♦ Foods to be steamed should be placed on a rack and should be at least 1 inch above the boiling water. Water should never touch the food.
♦ Best to use a vegetable steamer if you steam vegetables regularly.
♦ Steam must be allowed to circulate around the food freely to be sure that the food will cook evenly.
♦ Be sure that the steamer has a good-fitting top.
♦ Stir the vegetables once or twice to make sure they all get cooked.
♦ Check the liquid to make sure that it does not boil away.

STEW

Stew should be cooked at a medium heat and not allowed to boil. The turbulence causes all the ingredients to be blended with each other and flavors intermingle instead of picking up the flavor of the base. Stew meat or chicken should not be too lean or the taste will suffer since the taste for the most part comes from the fat. Fish stew is made with some olive oil and needs to be boiled somewhat vigorously to blend the oil in with the ingredients. Bouillabaisse is a good example.

♦ Stews are usually best if prepared the day before allowing the flavors to be incorporated throughout the stew.
♦ Stews are basically prepared from almost any combination of meats, vegetables and seasonings you enjoy. Stew should always be relatively thick and not watery.
♦ Basil is a common spice used in stews; however, it does not hold its flavor very long when subjected to heat for as little as 15 minutes. Basil should be added during the last 10 minutes of cooking.

TOUGH STEW MEAT

If you have a problem with tough stew meat, you may have added hot water when water was needed instead of cold water. Studies have shown that hot water added to boiling or simmering stew may cause the meat to become tough. Cold water does not have the same effect.

THE TENDERIZING TREE

In grandma's backyard she had a fig tree and I acquired a liking for raw figs. However, she used the figs to tenderize a tough piece of meat, usually in a stew. She would add 2-3 fresh figs to the stew. You could never taste the fig flavor but the meat was very tender.

Science of Figs as a Tenderizer

Figs contain the chemical "ficin," which is a proteolytic enzyme, one that is capable of breaking down protein structures. It has a similar action to that of "papain" from papaya and "bromelain" found in pineapples. Ficin is best when it comes from raw figs and effective in the heat ranges of 140^{0}to160^{0}F (60^{0}to71^{0}C), which is the temperature at which stews simmer the best. If the temperature rises above this level, the ficin will be inactive. Canned figs will not work since they have been heat processed and the ficin destroyed.

CHEF'S BEEF STEW SECRETS

- Stew should be cooked at a medium heat and not allowed to boil. The turbulence causes all the ingredients to be blended with each other and flavors intermingle instead of picking up the flavor of the base. Only add cold water when adding water or the beef will become tough.
- Stew meat or chicken should not be too lean or the taste will suffer since the taste for the most part comes from the fat.
- Fish stew on the other hand is made with some olive oil and needs to be boiled somewhat vigorously to blend the oil in with the ingredients. Bouillabaisse is a good example.

Science of Tea in Stew

Tea contains tannic acid, which can be used as a tenderizer for meat. Grandma was probably out of figs or did not bother to tenderize the meat using another method and used one of the oldest methods; that of using very strong tea (containing tannic acid) to tenderize the beef in beef stew.

- An easy method of thickening stews is to add a small amount of quick-cooking oats, a grated potato, or some instant potatoes or onions.

363

- If you need to thicken a stew or sauce, try mixing 2 tablespoons of cornstarch, potato flour, or arrowroot in 3 tablespoons of water, then adding the mixture to the food. Do this for every cup of liquid in the product.
- If you just wish a medium amount of thickening, reduce it to 1 tablespoon of cornstarch mixed with 2 tablespoons of water for every cup.
- To change your stew just a little, try taking a stack of tortillas and cut them into long thin pieces. Add them to the stew during the last 15 minutes of cooking. If you don't want the extra fat, use corn tortillas instead of flour.
- For the best results and to keep the flavors intact, soups and stews should only be allowed to simmer, never boil.
- Make your own TV dinner by just placing leftover stews into individual baking dishes or small casserole dishes, cover with pie crust or dumpling mix and bake.

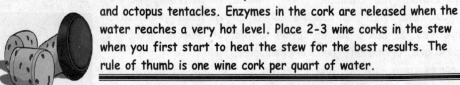

Science of Wine Cork Tenderizing
Wine corks have been used for hundreds of years in France to tenderize beef stew and octopus tentacles. Enzymes in the cork are released when the water reaches a very hot level. Place 2-3 wine corks in the stew when you first start to heat the stew for the best results. The rule of thumb is one wine cork per quart of water.

STOCKS
Stocks are the basis of many soups and sauces. There are four basic stocks: brown, white, poultry and seafood. Stocks are prepared from a liquid that fish, meat or poultry are cooked in. The liquid is then seasoned and usually cooked for 8-10 hours to assure that the flavors are adequately incorporated into the stock. The liquid is then removed leaving the flavored residue or stock. Stocks may be frozen and used as needed.

Brown Stock
It is usually prepared with beef and veal bones. The bones are grilled, producing a rich brown color and should be included in the initial stages of preparation whenever possible.

Chicken Stock
This is a clear liquid stock prepared from chicken or other poultry parts and usually simmered with vegetables, herbs and spices.

Fish Stock
It is prepared from fish bones and poached fish or shellfish.

Vegetable Stock
Usually prepared from onions, carrots and celery and flavored with garlic and other herbs. The formula for making the stock is 60-20-20 with 60% onions and 20% celery and carrots. Strong-flavored vegetables such as broccoli and cabbage should be avoided.

Poultry Stock
It is prepared from any kind of poultry but usually chicken. Vegetables are used and include onions, carrots and celery.

White or Veal Stock

Originally prepared with only veal bones, providing a clear stock that contains very little flavor of its own. The stock, however, is now made with veal, beef or poultry bones or a combination.

- Never use salt, since salt will concentrate and ruin the stock as the liquid reduces. Salt may be added later, if desired.
- Always simmer with the pot uncovered. Condensation may affect the final result. Stock should never be boiled or it may become cloudy.
- Gelatin from the bones is important, since the stock should become completely gelled when cooled down. The stock can be spooned as needed.
- Stocks should be kept frozen until needed, especially if they contain an animal product. If refrigerated for storage, stock can be kept for about 6 days. For more than 6 days in the refrigerator the stock should be boiled for 8-10 minutes before using.
- Brown stock can be reduced until it is syrupy or even very dark, if desired. Brown stock is usually very concentrated and very little is needed to flavor sauce. It is easy to overpower with a brown sauce and detract from the flavor of the dish.
- Any stock can be more concentrated the more you boil it down.
- All fat should be trimmed off before placing the meat and bones into the stockpot. The stock should only be stirred 3 times during the first hour or the stock may become cloudy.
- When dissolving dry gelatin, never pour hot water directly on the gelatin. This causes clumping and reduces the ability of the gelatin to dissolve properly. Try using a small amount of cold water until it ise dissolved then add the additional hot water.
- For the best results the hot water added to gelatin should never be over 180^0F $(82.2^0$C$)$.
- If your recipe calls for an equal amount of sugar to gelatin: the cold water step is not required since the sugar will stop the clumping. However, you still should never pour hot water into gelatin; place the gelatin into the water.

PURE SALT, A MUST FOR A QUALITY STOCK

Kosher salt is the preferred salt that most chefs use when preparing a stock. Kosher salt contains no additives, which may cause the stock to become cloudy. Also, salt should not be added at the start of the cooking since it is impossible to estimate the amount needed. Salt is important to stock but should be added after it has cooked for 10 minutes. Salt will help draw the albumin (a protein) from the bones to keep the stock clear.

Next time you prepare soup or stock, try placing a pasta basket into the pot, or just use a large pasta pot. The basket can be removed and will contain many of the ingredients you may wish to dispose of or keep.

- When you simmer bones to extract the flavor, it may create foam on the surface, which is composed of a protein (albumin) and a number of impurities (mineral residues) that are released from the bone. This foam is usually bitter and needs to be completely removed.
- Even leaving a hint of the foam may alter the desired taste.
- If you are really in a hurry and need a stock that can easily be prepared in about 30 minutes, the following should solve your problem:

CLARIFICATION PLEASE!

All stocks need some degree of clarification. You need to first strain the stock through a piece of cheesecloth or very fine sieve, then for each quart of stock add 1 slightly beaten egg and a crumpled up eggshell. Stir the eggs and shell into the stock and bring to a slow simmer (do not stir). Foam will form on the surface as the heat rises. Allow the stock to simmer for 15 minutes, remove from the heat and allow the stock to rest for 30 minutes. Gently move the crusty foam aside and spoon the stock into a sieve lined with 3 layers of lightly moistened cheesecloth.

- The bones and meat from older cows will have more flavor for stock and their bones will have 8 times more gelatin than their meat.
- The bones are more important to making stock than the meat.
- When the stock is finished, you should strain it once only through a fine mesh strainer before refrigerating for 2-3 hours. Remove the stock and skim off the fat that has risen to the top, producing an almost fat-free broth with the flavor intact. Stock that will remain refrigerated for more than 3 days should be re-boiled or they will spoil.
- If you prefer to purchase stock in the supermarket, it may be sold under a number of different names such as bouillon, broth or consommés. There are two types of canned broth to choose from: ready-to-serve, which has liquid added and condensed, which requires that you add the liquid. Canned broth should be placed into the refrigerator overnight to allow the fat to rise. Remove the fat before using for a low-fat broth.
- An excellent poultry stock can be made using the turkey carcass from thanksgiving dinner. If you don't have the time right away, just freeze the carcass, well wrapped in freezer paper. Try to use it within 2 months for the best results.

ALUMINUM POTS AND STOCK ARE ENEMIES

Preparing stocks in aluminum pots should be avoided. The aluminum tends to impart a bitter taste to stocks and will stain the pot if the stock is stored in it.

- If your gelatin develops a thick rubbery skin it is probably because it sat out in the air too long without being covered. The only other reason is that it has aged too long before being used.
- Cold water is usually more pure than hot water. Hot water tends to leach more impurities from water pipes.
- Chefs always prefer veal bones when preparing stocks since they tend to provide a more delicate flavor than beef bones. Veal bones contain more collagen and therefore have a better thickening ability.
- The best method of cooling soup or stock is to place the pot in an ice bath that reaches at least halfway up the pot. Stir the soup or stock continually since it will cool faster by allowing all areas to come into contact with the sides of the pot.

  As soon as it is cool, the soup or stock should be refrigerated until you are ready to use it.
- The stock called for in pea or onion soup recipes can be replaced with the same amount of apple cider.

STUFFING

Stuffing should be reheated to 165^{0}F even after cooking and refrigerated within 45 minutes after the bird has been removed from the oven. If it contains the giblets, eggs, broth or juices from the bird, the temperature when re-cooked should be 175^{0}F.

DON'T USE A RAMROD

When I see people stuffing a turkey, I cannot believe how much stuffing they try and place into that poor bird. If grandma ever saw me stuffing a bird and forcing the stuffing into the cavity she would probably stop me and give me a stuffing lesson, if there is such a thing.

A common problem with stuffing is that it tends to get too moist and watery. A chef will never jam stuffing into the bird's cavity. Stuffing will always expand during cooking.

- The bread used for stuffing should be very dry and even lightly toasted in the oven the night before you are going to use it. Place the bread in last after mixing in any cooked meats or vegetables you use.
- Poultry seasoning is the one ingredient that really makes stuffing, stuffing. All *"poultry seasonings"* are not the same; there is a big difference in the freshness of the herbs and the methods of blending and storage before shipping. The finest poultry seasoning is produced by Brady Enterprises of East Weymouth, Massachusetts.
- Poultry seasoning was created around 1864 by William Bell. Bell's Poultry seasoning is more potent than what you may be used to so if you do use it remember that a little goes a long way.

The best temperature for cooking turkey is 325°F since a lower temperature will allow bacteria in the stuffing to multiply for too long a period.
Higher temperatures may shorten the cooking time, causing undercooked stuffing. Slow overnight cooking with the dressing in the bird has been the cause of numerous cases of food poisoning. The stuffing temperature when the bird has completed cooking should be 165°F.

- Stuffing or cooked poultry should never be allowed to remain at room temperature for more than 40 minutes before refrigerating. Salmonella thrives at temperatures of 60°F to 125°F. All stuffing should be removed when the bird is ready for carving, never leave even a small amount of stuffing in the bird.
- A warm bird will keep the stuffing warm and make the temperature perfect for bacterial growth.
- Supermarkets are now selling stuffing bags to be placed in the cavity of the bird before you place the stuffing in. This is an excellent idea since all the stuffing can be removed all at once. However, it is less expensive to just use any piece of cheesecloth.
- When stuffing a bird the opening may be sealed with a piece of raw potato.
- The giblets are the neck, gizzard, heart and liver. They can be boiled, chopped up and added to the stuffing or you can do as I do and give them to the dog since most of the organs are high in cholesterol.

Science of Stuffing
All ingredients that will be used for stuffing must be cooked before using them in the stuffing. Cool all the ingredients before combining. Stuffing causes the bird to cook longer and may dry out the meat. Over-mixing bread stuffing causes the stuffing to become too pasty. All ingredients should be lightly tossed for the best results.

SUBSTITUTIONS, GENERAL INFORMATION
If you're using a cookbook and it was published in England, the following information will be very useful since many of the common cooking ingredients are called by different names.

ACTIVE DRY YEAST (One Package)
1 cake compressed yeast

AGAR-AGAR
Use gelatin

ALLSPICE
¼ teaspoon cinnamon & ½ teaspoon ground cloves or
¼ teaspoon nutmeg for baking only or black pepper other than baking

ANISE (use equivalent amount)
Fennel or dill or cumin

APPLES .
One cup of firm chopped pears and one tablespoon of lemon juice.
1 pound of apples = 4 small, 3 medium, or 2 large or 2¾ cups sliced or 2 cups chopped

ARROWROOT
Flour, just enough to thicken, should take a few tablespoons.

BAKING POWDER (one teaspoon, double - acting)
½ teaspoon cream of tartar plus ¼ teaspoon of baking soda or
¼ teaspoon baking soda: plus ½ cup of sour milk, cream, or buttermilk.
Must take the place of other liquid or 4 teaspoons of quick-cooking tapioca

BAKING POWDER (one teaspoon, single - acting)
¾ teaspoon double-acting baking powder

BASIL (dried)
Tarragon or Summer savory of equal amounts or
Thyme or Oregano

BAY LEAF
Thyme of equal amounts

BLACK PEPPER
Allspice in cooking providing salt is also used in the dish

BORAGE
Cucumber

BRANDY
Cognac or rum

BREAD CRUMBS (¼ cup, dry)
¼ cup cracker crumbs or
½ slice of bread, may be toasted or crumbled or
¼ cup rolled oats or
¼ cup of matzo meal or
¼ cup of sifted flour or
¼ cup of corn flakes

BULGUR
Use equal amounts of: Cracked wheat, kasha, brown rice, couscous, millet or quinoa

BUTTER (in baking)
Hard margarine or shortening

DO NOT USE OIL IN BAKED PRODUCTS
1 pound = 2 cups
1 cup = 2 sticks

2 tablespoons = ¼ stick or 1 ounce
4 tablespoons = ½ stick or 2 ounces
8 tablespoons = 1 stick or 4 ounces

BUTTERMILK
One cup of milk plus 1¾ tablespoons of cream of tartar or equivalent of sour cream

CAKE FLOUR
Use 1 cup of all-purpose flour minus 2 tablespoons

CAPERS
Chopped green olives

CARAWAY SEED
Fennel seed or cumin seed

CARDAMOM
Cinnamon or mace

CAYENNE PEPPER
Ground hot red pepper or chili powder

CHERVIL
Parsley or tarragon (use less) or anise (use less)

CHIVES
Onion powder (small amount) or leeks or shallots (small amount)

CHOCOLATE, BAKING, UNSWEETENED (one ounce or square)
3 tablespoons of unsweetened cocoa plus 1 tablespoon of butter or
3 tablespoons of carob powder plus 2 tablespoons of water

CHOCOLATE, BAKING, UNSWEETENED (one ounce pre-melted)
3 tablespoons of unsweetened cocoa plus 1 tablespoon of corn oil or melted Crisco

CHOCOLATE, SEMI-SWEET (6 ounces of chips or squares)
Nine tablespoons of cocoa plus 7 tablespoons of sugar plus 3 tablespoons of butter

CILANTRO
Parsley and lemon juice or orange peel and a small amount of sage or lemon grass with a small amount of mint

CINNAMON
Allspice (use a small amount) or cardamom

CLOVES (ground)
Allspice or nutmeg or mace

CLUB SODA
Mineral water or seltzer

CORN SYRUP (one cup, light)
1¼ cups granulated sugar or
1 cup granulated sugar plus ¼ cup of liquid

CORNMEAL
Grits (corn) or polenta

CORNSTARCH
Flour, a few tablespoons for thickening, usually no more than two

CREAM CHEESE
Cottage cheese mixed with cream or cream with a small amount of butter or milk

CREME FRAICHÉ
Sour cream in a recipe or ½ sour cream and ½ heavy cream in sauces

CUMIN
1/3 anise plus 2/3 caraway or fennel

DILL SEED
Caraway or celery seed

EDIBLE FLOWERS (garnish)
Bachelor buttons, blue borage, calendula petals, chive blossoms, mini carnations, nasturtiums, pansies, rose petals, snap dragon, or violets.

EGGS, WHOLE (one)
2 tablespoons water plus 2 tablespoons of flour plus ½ tablespoons of Crisco plus ½ teaspoon of baking powder or;
2 yolks plus 1 tablespoon of water or;
2 tablespoons of corn oil plus 1 tablespoon of water or;
1 teaspoon of cornstarch plus 3 tablespoons of water if part of a recipe or;
1 banana (best for cakes and pancakes) or;
2 tablespoons of cornstarch or arrowroot starch;
¼ cup of tofu (blend with liquid ingredients before adding to any dry ingredients)

EVAPORATED MILK
Light cream or half and half or heavy cream.

FLOUR (thickeners, use up to 2-3 tablespoons only)
Bisquick, tapioca (quick cooking), cornstarch, arrowroot (use small amount), potato starch, mashed potato flakes, or pancake mix

GARLIC (equivalent of 1 clove)
¼ teaspoon of minced, dried garlic or
1/3 teaspoon of garlic powder or
¼ teaspoon of garlic juice or
½ teaspoon of garlic salt (omit ½ tsp salt from recipe)

GHEE
Clarified butter

HONEY (one cup in baked goods)
1¼ cups granulated sugar plus ¼ cup water

JUNIPER BERRIES
A small amount of gin

LEMON JUICE
Use ½ teaspoon of white vinegar for each teaspoon of lemon juice, unless the flavor is required.

LEMONGRASS
Lemon or lemon rind or verbena or lime rind

LOVAGE
Celery leaves

MARJORAM
Oregano (use small amount) or thyme or savory

MASA HARINA
Corn flour

MASCARPONE
Cream cheese, whipped with a small amount of butter

MEAT
Tempeh (cultured soybeans provides a chewy texture)
Tofu (after it has been frozen)
Wheat gluten

MILK, EVAPORATED
Light cream or half and half or heavy cream

MILK (in baked goods)
Fruit juice plus ½ teaspoon of baking soda mixed in with the flour

MILK (one cup)
½ cup evaporated milk plus ½ cup of water or
3 tablespoons of powdered milk: plus 1 cup of water. If whole milk is called for add 2 tablespoons of butter

MOLASSES (one cup)
1 cup of honey

NUTMEG
Allspice or cloves or mace

NUTS (in baked goods only)
Bran

OREGANO
Marjoram or rosemary or thyme (fresh only)

PANCETTA
Lean bacon (cooked) or very thin sliced ham

PARSLEY
Chervil or cilantro

POLENTA
Cornmeal or grits (corn)

POULTRY SEASONING
Sage plus a blend of any of these: thyme, marjoram, savory, black pepper, and rosemary

ROSEMARY
Thyme or tarragon or savory

SAFFRON (1/3rd teaspoon)
1 teaspoon dried yellow marigold petals or
1 teaspoon azafran or
1 teaspoon safflower or
½ to 1-teaspoon turmeric (adds color)

SAGE
Poultry seasoning or savory or marjoram or rosemary

SELF-RISING FLOUR (one cup)
1-cup all-purpose flour plus 1 teaspoon of baking powder, ½ teaspoon of salt, and ¼ teaspoon of baking soda

SHALLOTS
Small green onions or leeks or standard onions (use small amount) or scallions (use more than is called for)

SHORTENING (one cup in baked goods only)
1 cup butter or
1 cup hard margarine

SOUR CREAM (one cup)
1 tablespoon of white vinegar: plus sufficient milk to make 1 cup. Allow the mixture to stand for 5 minutes before using or
1 tablespoon of lemon juice plus enough evaporated milk to make 1 cup or
1 cup of plain yogurt if it is being used in a dip or cold soup or
6 ounces of cream cheese plus 3 tablespoons of milk or
1/3 cup of melted butter plus 3/4 cup of sour milk for baked goods

TAHINI
Finely ground sesame seeds

TARRAGON
Anise (use small amount) or chervil (use larger amount) or parsley (use larger amount) or a dash of fennel seed

TOMATO PASTE (one tablespoon)
1 tablespoon of ketchup or
½ cup of tomato sauce providing you reduce some of the other liquid

TURMERIC
Mustard powder

VANILLA EXTRACT (in baked goods only)
Almond extract or other extracts that will alter the flavor

VINEGAR
Lemon juice in cooking and salads only or grapefruit juice, in salads or wine, in marinades

YOGURT
Sour cream or creme fraiche or buttermilk or heavy cream or mayonnaise (use in small amounts)

SUBSTITUTIONS, LIQUID

The following substitution may be used for liquids that are not available at the time the recipe is being prepared. However, it is always better to use the ingredients called for in the recipe for the best results.

LIQUID INGREDIENT	ADEQUATE SUBSTITUTION
1 cup barbecue sauce	1 cup ketchup + 2 tsp. Worcestershire sauce
1 cup broth	1 bouillon cube dissolved in 1 cup of water
1 cup butter	1 cup vegetable shortening + 2 Tbsp. water
1 cup buttermilk	1 Tbsp. lemon juice + balance of cup in milk, then allow it to stand for 5 minutes before using or add 1 Tbsp. of vinegar to 1 cup of evaporated milk and allow to stand for 5 minutes before using.
1 cup chili sauce	1 cup tomato sauce + 1/2 cup sugar + 2 Tbsp. vinegar
1 cup corn syrup	¾ cup sugar + ¼ cup water
1 cup creme fraiche	½ cup sour cream + ½ cup heavy cream
1 egg	1 banana or 2 Tbsp. cornstarch or arrowroot starch or 1/4 cup tofu blended into liquid ingredients well
1 cup evaporated milk	Equal amount of light or cream or half and half
1 cup heavy cream	¾ cup whole milk + 1/3rd cup of butter
1 cup light cream	1 cup milk + 3 Tbsp. butter
1 cup ketchup	1 cup tomato sauce + 4 Tbsp. sugar + 2 Tbsp. vinegar + ¼ tsp. ground cloves
1 cup honey	1 ¼ cups granulated sugar + ¼ cup water
1 tsp. lemon juice	1 tsp. of vinegar
1 cup molasses	1 cup honey

1 cup whole milk	4 Tbsp. dry whole milk + 1 cup water or 1 cup buttermilk + ½ tsp. baking soda
1 cup non-fat milk (skim)	4 Tbsp. nonfat dry milk + 1 cup water
1 cup sour milk	1 Tbsp. lemon juice or vinegar + additional milk to fill 1 cup, allow it to stand for 5 minutes
2 drps hot pepper sauce	A dash of cayenne or red pepper
2 tsp. tapioca	1 Tbsp. all-purpose flour (more if desired)
1 cup tomato juice	½ cup tomato sauce + ½ cup water
1 Tbsp. tomato paste	1 Tbsp. tomato ketchup
1 cup tomato puree	6 ounce can of tomato paste + 6 ounces of water
1 cup wine	1 cup apple juice or apple cider or 1 part of vinegar, diluted in 3 parts of water
1 cup yogurt	1 cup buttermilk or sour cream

A Little Bit Will Do Ya

Small amounts of extracts and food colorings are difficult to measure, however, a medicine dropper can make all the difference. Just slowly squeeze the extract or food coloring from the dropper into the bowl letting the drops fall at different spots on the surface of the batter or food.

VINEGAR SUBSTITUTES

Apple Cider Vinegar ------- Wine Vinegar
Balsamic Vinegar ---------- Sherry Vinegar
Champagne Vinegar ------ Apple Cider Vinegar
Raspberry Vinegar --------- Red Wine Vinegar
Red Wine Vinegar --------- Balsamic Vinegar
Rice Vinegar ---------------- Apple Cider Vinegar
White Vinegar -------------- Apple Cider Vinegar (canning with at least 5% acidity)

SUGAR

Pretty Colors

To make your own colored sugar for holiday decorations is easy and you only need to make the amount you will need. You can make almost any color you want by sprinkling ½ cup of sugar evenly over the bottom of a pie plate or small metal bowl. Add 5-6 drops of food coloring and mix well. If you want to be sure that the color is distributed evenly, push the sugar through a fine sieve then place the sugar back on the pie plate and allow it to dry thoroughly.

TYPES & USES OF SUGARS

Brown Sugar

It is made by adding molasses to white sugar, sold in dark or light brown colors.

♦ When a recipe asks for brown sugar, make sure that when you measure it, it is packed down very well in the measuring cup.

- If brown sugar gets hard, place ¼-apple into the bag.
- Soften hard brown sugar in the microwave on high for 40 seconds.
- If the sugar gets lumpy, use a food processor to break them up.

Softening Brown Sugar

Brown sugar has a tendency to lose moisture rather quickly and develop lumps. To soften brown sugar, try placing the sugar in the microwave with a slice of fresh white bread or ½ an apple; then cover the dish tightly and heat for about 15 seconds. The moisture from the bread or apple will produce just enough steam to soften the sugar without melting it. If you

---

Store brown sugar in the freezer and it won't clump up. It is best to place it in a plastic baggie and remove it from the box.

- To remove hardened brown sugar from a box, wrap it tightly in a towel and hit it on the counter a few good whacks. If that doesn't do it just add a few drops of water to the box and microwave on full power for a few seconds. If neither one works, run over it with your car or throw it out and buy some more. Other than a touch of molasses, brown sugar is chemically identical to white sugar.

Granulated Sugars

Ultrafine
Excellent for cakes, dessert powders and coating confectionary pan goods.
Very Fine
Best for dry mixing in cake mixes, puddings and gelatin dessert powders.
Fine or Extrafine
Standard granulated sugar used for all-purposes in foods and beverages. It is typically used as table sugar.
Medium or Coarse
It is mainly used to produce crystallizing syrups in candy. Very strong sugar that will resist color changes in high-temperature cooking.

Powdered Sugars

Ultrafine (confectioner's 10X)
It produces the smoothest texture for frostings and icings.

- May be called icing sugar in recipes.
- If a recipe calls for sifting, it must be done to get an accurate measurement.
- If you don't have a flour-sifter, use a food processor.
- Place the sugar in a fine sieve and shake over a cake or other baked goods.
- Never shake confectioners' sugar over a moist or warm cake or it will melt into a gray mess.

Very Fine (confectioner's 6X)
Used in cream fillings and biscuits. Also used for sprinkling on buns, pies and pastries. Can be used for icings and combined with melted fats to produce confectioner's coatings.

Fine (confectioner's 4X)
Used in the production of chewing gum and lozenges as well as added to the packing material of marshmallows. It is used in chocolate manufacturing.

Medium Coarse
It is used to dust doughnuts.

Sugar will never cake-up if you just place a few salt-free crackers in the canister to absorb the moisture. Crackers should be replaced every week.

Science of Sugar

The right sugar can really make a difference in the recipe. Sugar has a lot of uses in baked goods. It provides sweetness, assists in the creaming process, creates a spreading action of the batter, gives the crust its color, helps retain moisture, prolongs freshness, and assists in the fermentation of the yeast. In most baking recipes sugar serves as food for yeast as well as splitting up to produce carbon dioxide gas, which assists in the leavening of the dough. The majority of the sugar we use is produced from sugar beets and sugar cane. It is able to blend other flavors and increase the level of aromas in products.

SUNFLOWER SEEDS

Beware

Sunflower seeds should never be combined with baking soda in any baked good product since a chemical reaction will take place and the product will have a blue-green color. It is not toxic and just a reaction between the baking soda and the trace minerals in the seeds.

- ♦ Sunflower seeds are sold either shelled or unshelled. They can also be purchased roasted or raw and salted or unsalted.
- ♦ They are 47% fat and should not be part of a diet program.
- ♦ Since they are high fat, you should store them in the refrigerator for longer life.

SUPERMARKET, MEATS
Supermarkets are using their own wording on meat packages to make you think that you are buying a better grade than it really is.

Most of the major chains are buying more "Good Grade" beef and may call it by a number of fancy names such as "Top Premium Beef," "Prime Quality Cut," "Select Choice," "Markets Choice," or "Premium Cut." Since the public does not want to pay the higher price for USDA Choice they have found a way to make the "Good Grade" sound better.

SYRUP, STOPPING CRYSTALLIZATION

When boiling syrup one of the more frequent and annoying problems is that of the syrup crystallizing when you are cooking it. The easiest method of avoiding this problem is to put a pinch of baking soda in the syrup while it is cooking. This will prevent the syrup from crystallizing by adding just a small amount of acidity.

SIZING UP THE BUBBLE

When making sugary syrup grandma's little secret to tell when the syrup is starting to thicken just right was to watch the size of the bubbles. The smaller the bubbles get, the thicker the syrup.

TTTTT

TAPIOCA

Tapioca is extracted from cassava root and is a starch that can be found in three forms: pearl tapioca, which is available in small and large sizes; quick-cooking tapioca and just plain old tapioca flour or starch. Tapioca flour is usually only found in health food stores. Tapioca is usually sold as a pudding mix and is sold in three forms.

TEA

BREWING METHODS

The following are temperatures that tea should be brewed at according to tea experts on two continents.

- **Green tea should be brewed between 180^0F to 200^0F (82.2^0C to 93.3^0C)**
- **Oolong tea should be brewed between 185^0F to 205^0F (85^0C to 96^0C)**
- **Black tea should be brewed between 190^0F to 210^0F (87.8^0C – 98.9^0C)**

The better quality teas should be brewed at a lower temperature since they will release their flavor more readily. The higher temperatures used in the lower quality teas tends to stimulate the release of the flavors.

The following steps will lead you through the process of making the perfect cup of tea:
1. Use the best grade of tea that you enjoy.
2. Use pure quality cold water and bring it to a boil. Only use the water when it is bubbling rapidly. Never use water from a hot water under sink unit.

3. Rinse the teapot with the hottest water possible or use boiling water. The teapot should be warm before you add the tea.
4. When pouring the boiling water into the teapot, take the kettle to the teapot to assure that the water will be as hot as possible.
5. Brew the tea for 3-5 minutes depending on your taste and the type of tea. Most teas should never be brewed for more than 5 minutes.
6. Make sure that the brewing tea is kept as hot as possible as it is brewing.
7. Always have a removable tealeaf strainer that is easily removable to eliminate the tealeaf residues. Always stir the tea after removing the infusion.
8. If the tea cools after you pour it, it would be best to brew another batch and not try to re-heat it.

HOW TO MAKE A STRONG TEA

The problem most people have when trying to make a strong tea is that it usually turns out bitter. Never increase the steeping period, always add more tea leaves. The longer the leaves remain in the hot water, the more polyphenols are released, thus producing a bitter tea.

THE STEAMING LEAVES

The reason why you would keep a cover on a cup or pot of steeping tea may seem simply that it keeps the heat in. However, another very important reason is that it traps the steam and dampens any tea leaves that are floating on the top, thus extracting their flavor.

STORAGE

ENEMIES ARE LIGHT AND HUMIDITY

Loose tea should always be stored in a cool, dry location. Humidity and heat will reduce the quality of the tea significantly. A sealed container works well allowing as little oxygen to come into contact with the loose tea. Containers should only be large enough to hold the tea and be opaque since the light can have a negative effect as well. A large container will retain too much oxygen and may cause undue oxidation to take place. Teabags should be stored in the container they are purchased in and also stored in a cool, dry location.

THAWING

- Thawing is best done in the refrigerator at about 41^0F (5^0C). This will not expose foods to the temperature danger zone.
- Many foods can be thawed under warm water at about 70^0F (21.1^0C) providing it takes less than 2 hours. This method is reserved for poultry.
- If you thaw in the microwave, the food should be cooked immediately to be on the safe side.
- Room temperature thawing should never be done since it allows the food to reach a temperature that may cause bacterial growth.

THERMOMETERS

There are many different types of food thermometers that can be used depending on the type of food you are preparing.

DIAL, INSTANT READ

These are not safe to leave in the food during cooking. Just insert the probe, making sure that the sensor area is inserted at least 2-2½ inches into the food for the best results. If you need to measure the temperature of a thin food, such as a hamburger or piece of chicken, insert the probe sideways with the sensing device as close to the center as possible.

Be sure to allow the sensor to remain about 15-20 seconds to be accurate.

  ➢ Normally used in roasts, casseroles and soups
  ➢ Best used to check the internal temperature of foods at the end of their cooking time
  ➢ The better models can be calibrated
  ➢ Should be easy to find in most kitchen stores and supermarkets

DIAL, OVEN-SAFE

This type can be inserted 2-2½ inches into the food. Be sure and insert the thermometer into the thickest part of the food and at the beginning of the cooking time. These thermometers can remain in the food for the entire cooking time without harming the thermometer.

  ➢ Easy to use in roasts, casseroles and soups
  ➢ Cannot be used in thin foods
  ➢ Some models can be calibrated
  ➢ Occasional false high readings caused by metal stem

DIGITAL, INSTANT READ

These are not designed to stay in the food while it is cooking. The tip of the probe is a heat-sensing device and should be placed into the thickest part of the food. It should be placed at least ½ inch into the food for the best results and be sure and leave it in for about 10 seconds.

  ➢ Provides fast readings
  ➢ Can be used in thick as well as thin foods
  ➢ Best if used toward the end of the cooking time
  ➢ Some models can be calibrated
  ➢ Easily found in kitchen stores and supermarkets

POP UP THERMOMETERS

These are almost always found in turkeys and chicken and will pop up when the desired internal temperature is reached. It is best to check the other parts of the food with another thermometer to be 100% safe. Occasionally they do not pop up at all.

Deep-Fat/Candy

The bulb should be fully immersed in the candy or food and should never be allowed to touch the bottom of the cooking container. To check the accuracy of the thermometer, place it in boiling water for 3-4 minutes. The temperature should read 212^0F or 100^0C.

Meat

Insert the thermometer into the center or thickest part of the meat making sure that it is not resting on a bone.

THE SMALLER, THE BETTER

If you are not sure that your roast is done, it is best to use a meat thermometer. Chefs have one they use that is very thin and make a very small puncture hole.

Science of Meat Thermometers

One of the best ways to see if a roast is cooked to the degree you are looking for is to use a meat thermometer. The standard thick ones make too big a puncture in the roast and allow too much of the juices to escape if you remove it. If you leave the larger thermometer in the meat, heat will be conducted to the meat around the thermometer and cooks the meat causing uneven roasting. It is best to purchase a thin, instant thermometer that makes a very small hole and checks the internal temperature and is then immediately withdrawn. The small puncture hole will seal up where the larger holes do not.

Oven

It is wise to check your oven temperature accuracy at least once a month. If the temperature is not accurate, it can affect the results of the food being prepared, especially baked goods. The thermometer should be placed in the middle of the center rack.

THICKENERS

To thicken any sauce, you will need to increase the solids and reduce the amount of liquid. This can be accomplished by boiling away some of the liquid, however, this will reduce the amount of useable sauce and may concentrate the flavors too much.

If the sauce is high in water content, cooling it causes the water molecules to lose energy and relax, thus thickening the sauce. There are, however, a number of good substances that will thicken sauces and depending on the type of sauce you are preparing one will surely be just right for the job. These include pureed vegetables, egg yolk, flours, gelatins, tapioca, pectin, okra, cornstarch, arrowroot, potato starch, kneaded butter, emulsified butter, cream, peanut butter, etc.

Cornstarch, arrowroot and potato starch should only be used just before you are finishing the sauce, since they have twice the thickening power of flour and can only be cooked for a few minutes before losing their thickening power.

OLD THICKENING TRICK

There are numerous methods of thickening sauces, but grandma had one that is different from all the rest. She would remove the crusts from one slice of bread and spread butter and some herbs or garlic butter on the bread and place it into the sauce. She then allowed it to remain for about 10 minutes until it softened then stirred it into the sauce.

KNEADED BUTTER

This is an excellent thickener, especially at the last minute. If you wish to make a sauce from leftover liquids that have remained in the pan, just place an equal amount of butter (unsalted) and flour in another pan and then mix them together to make a thick paste. Use small amounts of the paste adding it gradually to the leftover liquid.

Starch granules are a solid, which just by being there will cause a certain degree of thickening. However, the small starch granules tend to trap water molecules, thus reducing the percentage of free-flowing water that is in the sauce or soup. When you heat the starch it has the ability to expand and is capable of absorbing even more water.

One of the better commercial thickeners is Textra™. Textra™ is a modified tapioca starch that has been designed to improve mouth-feel and texture of foods.

It does not impart any taste to the product while providing thickening for drinks, sauces and syrups. It is one of the more stable thickeners and will assist particles, such as fruit pulp to remain in suspension.

There are two "jel" products that will do a great thickening job. These are ClearJel-310® and Rice Gel®. ClearJel-310® will thicken as soon as it is added to either water or milk and will provide a smooth, fully hydrated texture as well as being heat and acid resistant.

Rice gel is produced from pre-cooked rice flour with no noticeable taste of its own. It has a high water capacity and blends well with dry foods and is non-allergenic.

THICKENING A SAUCE OR MAKING GLUE FOR THE KIDS

The easiest method to thicken a sauce is to prepare a small amount of "paste." The paste should be prepared separate from the sauce. Never try and add the paste ingredients to the sauce to hasten the procedure. The paste needs to be smooth and the consistency will vary depending on the level of thickening needed. If the sauce is very thin, you will need a thick paste, etc.

Add the paste gradually, allow the sauce to boil and stir until the desired texture is obtained.

These pastes will work especially well with gravy and most other sauces.

Thin Paste ... Use 1 tablespoon flour + 1 cup of liquid
Medium Paste Use 2 tablespoons flour + 1 cup of liquid
Thick Paste.....Use 3 tablespoons flour + 1 cup of liquid

Use whatever liquid is compatible with the sauce you are preparing.

A FEW OF THE COMMON THICKENING AGENTS

All-Purpose Flour
Made from the endosperm of wheat and tends to turn opaque when cooked and somewhat pasty when set: very effective in thickening gravies.

Arrowroot
Purchased as a fine powder that is derived from the root stalks of a tropical tuber. It is prepared by dissolving a small amount in water. These stems are mainly composed of complex carbohydrates, which have the tendency to thicken at a lower cooking temperature than most other starches. The advantage of arrowroot is that there is less likely the chance of burning the thickener due to its low protein content.

Cornstarch
Produced from the endosperm of a kernel of corn and should always be dissolved in cold water before using for the best results. May become cloudy when cooked and satiny when fully set. When used in place of flour the sauce will be clearer.

Science of Cornstarch Vs Flour

All-purpose flour contains proteins and starch. Proteins has no ability to swell and is not active in the thickening process but does reflect the light and make the sauce appear to be cloudy. Cornstarch, however, is pure starch and when water and heat is applied to it, the granules absorb water and swell. When this occurs they become transparent. Cornstarch has double the thickening power than that of flour and less is used therefore cornstarch will not give sauces a pasty taste.

Tapioca
Extracted from the tropical cassava root and best used as a thickener if it is diluted with water before being added to a dish just before serving.

The roots are finely grated, left to ferment. Then pressed into cakes and baked. The baked cakes are then powdered into a pure starch. Tapioca is best when it is moistened, then heated and immediately used.

Vegetable Puree

Vegetable puree is a healthier method of thickening gravies and sauces. Purees may be made with any assortment of vegetables that compliments the dish it is to be used in. Vegetables need to be cooked first some need to be sautéed first then pureed in a blender or food processor. Once the vegetables are pureed, they should be put through a sieve or fine mesh before using.

TOMATO SAUCES

The French were the first to utilize tomato sauce in recipes after the tomato was discovered in Peru and brought to France by the Spanish Moors in the 1500's. There are over 4,000 varieties of tomatoes worldwide.

The largest is the ponderosa, which weighs in at about 3 pounds. Ketchup was sold as medicine in the 1830's.

- ♦ If you are going to use fresh tomatoes in a recipe, be sure they are at room temperature for the best results.
- ♦ Tomatoes can be refrigerated for storage; however, they lose almost all of their aroma and flavor when cold. Allow the tomatoes to remain at room temperature for 30 minutes before using them. This will re-activate the aroma and flavor.

Tomato sauce never came out of a can at grandma's house. She always made her own and always used a large pan and never a small pot. The tomato sauce always came out with great flavor and was a deep red color.

CHEF'S SECRETS

Since most recipes call for removing the skin and seeds of tomatoes, there is an easy method of accomplishing this. Just place the tomatoes in a large pot of boiling water for 2-3 minutes. This will loosen the skin then remove them with a slotted spoon. To remove the seeds, cut the tomato in half and squeeze the halves into a fine strainer. This will catch the seeds and allow the juice to be saved. Homemade tomato sauce can be stored in the refrigerator for 2 days and will freeze for 3-4 months.

Science of Tomato Sauce

To prepare homemade tomato sauce you will first need to use a tomato that will provide the best aroma and flavor. To release all of the aroma and flavor possible, you will first need to freeze the tomato and change its molecular structure. Ice crystals that form in the tomato form from the outside in and ice takes up more space than water. This liquid inside of the frozen tomato will crystallize and somewhat expand, so that after the tomato is defrosted, the crystals have already expanded and the tomatoes are more easily liquefied releasing maximum aroma and flavor.

Tomato sauce needs to be cooked as fast as possible and in a wide pan that will allow the liquids to evaporate quickly. The slower the process, the more flavor will be diluted by the liquid. However, meat-based tomato sauce can cook longer. The addition of tomato paste will enhance the flavor and a small amount of sugar will help reduce the acidity level.

TOMATOES

It is available year round and should be well formed and free of blemishes.
- Green tomatoes will eventually turn red, but will not have a good flavor. Green tomatoes will ripen faster if you store them with apples.
- A vine-ripened tomato is best. Refrigerate, but do not allow it to freeze.
- To peel tomatoes easily, place them in boiling water and remove from heat, allow them to stand for 1 minute before plunging them into cold water.
- Tomatoes will store longer if you store them stem down.
- Never allow tomatoes to ripen in direct sunlight, they will lose most of their vitamin C.
- Americans consume approximately 25 pounds of tomatoes per person, per year. If you are expecting a frost and have tomatoes on the vine, pull them up by the roots and hang them upside down in a cool basement until the fruit ripens.

Science of Picking the Best Tomato

The only way you will find a vine-ripened tomato is if you purchase your produce in a high-quality produce market. Don't be fooled by greenhouse tomatoes, they will only have about 50% of the vitamin C that a tomato has that has been grown in the full sunlight. Fresh looking leaves will also tell you that the tomato was not stored very long. When you store a tomato in the refrigerator it also deactivates the acid in the tomato causing an almost complete loss of flavor and aroma. Refrigerator temperature is about 40°F and tomatoes cannot take more than 50°F.

Tomatoes that chefs purchase have to say "vine ripened" or they will not purchase them. This is the best-flavored tomato and really tastes like a tomato should taste.

To quickly ripen most fruit, place the fruit in a brown paper bag then make holes in the bag to allow the ethylene gas to escape.

AROMA ONLY LASTS FOR THREE MINUTES

If you like the aroma of fresh tomatoes in your salad, don't refrigerate them. Tomatoes should be left at room temperature if they are going to be used within 2-3 days after purchase. They should never be sliced or peeled until just before you are going to serve them. The aroma is produced by the chemical z-3-hexenal, which is released when the tomato is sliced open. The aroma chemical only lasts at the "maximum aroma" level for three minutes before it starts to lose its scent. If you do refrigerate a tomato the chemical becomes dormant, but if you allow it to return to room temperature before you slice it the aroma will still be active. If the storage temperature is below 50^0F it will interfere with the ripening process and stop it cold. Even if the tomato does turn from green to red it will still not be ripe.

REDUCING ACIDITY IN TOMATO PRODUCTS

Some people are unable to eat spaghetti sauces and other tomato based foods due to their higher acidic content. When chopped or grated and carrots are added to any of these dishes it will reduce the acidity without affecting the taste. The high fiber content of the carrot seems to do the job.

♦ The easiest method of removing skin from a tomato is to first remove the core; cut an "X" on the bottom of the and place the tomato in a pot of boiling water for 10-12 seconds, quickly remove and place into a bowl of ice cold water (with ice cubes). Remove the tomato, in 25-30 seconds and the skin will peel right off.

♦ If you would like early tomatoes, purchase plants with flowers. Don't be upset if the flowers fall off while you are planting them. They are in their reproductive stage and more flowers will appear shortly. If the plants are young and without flowers they will bear fruit later but will give a better harvest.

♦ The easiest method of planting tomato plants is to use a bulb planter. It will result in a deep hole and will not take a lot of work.

♦ Dry cow manure is the best fertilizer for tomato plants. It will give you a higher yield. Use about 100 pounds per square feet in plants that are spaced about 3 feet apart.

♦ One ounce of tomato puree has twice the vitamin C and 20% more beta-carotene than one ounce of fresh tomato.

♦ Never place a whole tomato in the microwave; it will explode.

Tomato Paste

It is prepared from tomatoes that have been cooked for several hours then strained and reduced to concentrate the flavor and sold in cans or tubes.

Tomato Puree

It is prepared from tomatoes that have only been cooked briefly then strained and made into a thick liquid.

Tomato Sauce

A thinner tomato puree and sometimes sold seasoned. It is ready to use in soups, stews, etc. If you want to prepare tomato sauce from tomato paste, just combine 3/8th cup of tomato paste with ½ cup of water.

TUNA

When purchasing tuna, make sure you purchase the best grade, which is the "albacore white." The other classes of tuna are darker in color and have a stronger flavor and aroma. They may be labeled light, dark, or blended. These tuna are also very oily and usually higher in calories even if water-packed. Some brands use other types of fish in a related family and sell them as just "tuna." These fish include bonita, bluefin tuna, and skipjack. Bluefin tuna may weigh up to 1,000 pounds. When tuna is packed in oil it is sometimes called "Tonno Tuna."

- Contact with the ice tends to bleed out the color, nutrients and the flavor. Frozen tuna is fine and is usually frozen when it is caught retaining the flavor. Yellowfin is best!
- You probably think that if you purchase tuna in water it will have fewer calories than the type that is packed in oil. Well the truth is that albacore tuna may have a fat content that will vary by as much as 500%.
- Tuna manufacturers always try to use low-fat tuna in their product with about 1-gram of fat per serving. However, when the demand for the product gets extremely high, they have to resort to packaging the higher fat albacore, which contains 4-5 grams of fat per serving. Best to check the label.
- Solid-pack is tuna composed of the loins with the addition of a few flakes. Chunk tuna may have parts of the tougher muscle structure, while flake tuna has mostly muscle structure and smaller bits all under ½ inch.
- Choosing tuna for tuna salad is more a matter of taste than the type of tuna. If you have noticed that tuna in cans is darker than it used to be, you're right, the reason being is that smaller nets are being used so that the porpoises won't be netted. This means that the larger tuna won't be netted either. The smaller tuna has the darker meat.
- In 2012 tuna was still ranked as the most popular fish sold in the United States. Shrimp came in an easy second, while cod was third and Alaskan pollack next due to its use in imitation shrimp and crabmeat. Americans consume about 4.6 pounds of tuna per person annually.

TURKEY

- A 15-pound turkey has about 70% white meat and 30% dark meat, which has a higher fat content then white meat.
- Turkeys lived almost 10 million years ago.
- Wild turkey breasts are dark meat since they use their breast muscles more.
- Domesticated "tom turkeys" have been bred to have large breasts for the white meat that they are now unable to mate.
- Turkeys are given antibiotics (only if necessary) but no steroids or hormones.

Young turkey that are between 4-6 pounds of either sex will be the most tender and can be prepared the same as chicken. The larger turkey we get during the holidays can run up to 40 pounds and have more muscle and less fat, but will not be as juicy as the little guys, unless you cook them upside down.

- Before placing the turkey in the oven, be sure and allow the bird to rest at room temperature for 25 minutes before placing it in the oven.
- Cold meat tends to be tougher.
- If you cover the skin with a piece of cheesecloth that has been buttered you will have the greatest-looking skin you have ever had. Be sure and remove the cheesecloth 30 minutes before the bird is done.
- Plastic bags have the tendency to burst when in the oven. If you place some dry flour in the bag and shake it around to coat the inside of the bag, then make a few slits in the bag it will not burst.
- Figure about 1 pound of turkey weight per person. If you have hearty eaters, figure about 1½-pounds per person. If you want a lot of leftovers figure 2 pounds per person.
- Rub seasonings on the inside of the bird and the essences will be throughout most of the meat for a great taste treat.
- Since I have done this myself it is very embarrassing to start carving the bird and find the giblet bag inside. The bag is made of a special plastic and will not melt or catch fire, so just act as if you left it in there to cook for the pet.

BREAST-SIDE DOWN AND LOW SIDES

If you place your turkey breast-side down on a "V" rack that has been placed in a low-sided cooking pan and allow it to cook for ½ the cooking time, some the juices will go to the breast and moisten the meat. Purchasing a bird with basting solution injected into the breast just adds calories and fat to the lean white meat.

Turn the bird right side up after the first hour and continue cooking for the balance of the time. The low-sided pan is now recommended since it was found that a high-sided pan tends to steam the bird too much.

A cooking bag can be used to create a small amount of steam and keep the bird from drying out. When using the plastic cooking bag, be sure and preheat the oven to 350°F and continue cooking at 350°F. The flour that you shake on the inside of the bag, and the slits in the bag allow steam to escape.

♦ Make sure that your oven temperature is correct and use a thermometer placed into the thickest part of the thigh. The temperature should read 180°F when the bird is done. The bird can be removed from the oven when the temperature reaches 175°F since the temperature will keep going up about 5° while the bird is resting for 20 minutes.
♦ Be sure that the juices run clear (not pink) when the bird is sliced.
♦ Brush or apply a thin layer of white vermouth to the skin of a turkey about 15 minutes before you are ready to remove it from the oven. The skin will develop a nice rich brown tone and the turkey should really enjoy it.

COOKING THE TURKEY OVERNIGHT

This is not a recommended method of cooking a turkey. Lower temperatures and longer periods have proven dangerous in many instances. This method recommends that the turkey be cooked at 190°-200°F overnight for about 12 hours. Poultry must be thoroughly cooked and at a temperature of no less than 325°F to avoid food poisoning as recommended by the USDA. Use a meat thermometer and be sure the internal temperature is at 180°F.

♦ Raw turkey breasts should only be cooked to 175°F or they will tend to be dry. Then allow the breast to rest for 10 minutes before carving and the temperature will be 180°F.
♦ Basting does not really make the bird moist; all it does is produce a golden crispy, great-tasting skin that is high fat. Oven heat loss will increase cooking time; so don't baste too often.

LET THE BIRD RELAX!

Once the turkey has finished cooking it should be allowed to rest for about 20 minutes before carving it. This will allow the steam to dissipate and the meat will not fall apart. It also allows the juices to saturate the meat evenly.

♦ If you see pink around a fully cooked bird (180°F), it just means that a reddish pigment called hemoglobin was released from the bones. Usually seen in very young birds.

THE COLLAPSABLE PAN

Don't use a disposable aluminum pan for birds over 22 pounds or the pan may collapse too easily even if it has handles when removing the bird from the oven.

TURKEY, BRINING

Brining pre-treats the turkey and results in a more moist, well-seasoned bird. The whole turkey is placed into a saltwater bath solution called "brine."

The process is done in a large stockpot in the refrigerator or a cooler chest filled with ice. The brine should be done at 40^0F or below for the best results. The smaller the turkey the easier it is to brine it. Crystal kosher salt is recommended for brining. Table salt is never recommended since it contains anti-caking agents or additives.

1. Always start the brine the day before you plan on cooking the bird. Always use a fresh or fully thawed bird and wash out the inside. Remove the giblet bag.
2. Dissolve 2 cups of kosher salt and 1 cup of granulated sugar in 2 gallons of cold filtered or bottled water. Stir until the salt and sugar are fully dissolved.
3. Add any seasonings or spices you desire to improve the flavor. Bay leaves, dried thyme work great.
4. Place the turkey into the stockpot with the brine solution, breast-side down then cover and allow it to chill for 6-8 hours or overnight. If you allow it to remain overnight then reduce the salt and sugar by ½. If you do not reduce the salt, the turkey will absorb too much of the salt.
5. Remove the turkey from the brine solution and rinse the bird well both inside and out. Dry off with paper towels and place on a pan in the refrigerator overnight. This will allow the skin to dry out and cause it to become very crispy during the roasting process.
6. The oven should be pre-heated to 350^0F and the turkey placed on a shallow pan with the legs tied together loosely and the wings tucked under the bird. The skin should be lightly coated with extra virgin olive oil and the breast covered loosely with foil. Be sure and add 1 cup of water to the bottom of the pan.
7. Cook until the innermost area of the bird reaches 180^0F or when the thigh juices run clear.
8. Remove the foil during the last hour of cooking time and baste with pan juices to enhance browning.
9. Allow the bird to rest for 20 minutes before carving.

TURKEY, FRESH VS FROZEN

Turkeys, especially around the holidays, are very fresh. The decision to purchase a fresh turkey over a frozen turkey is more of a personal choice than the flavor or quality differences. There is no taste difference in a frozen turkey that was just purchased or a fresh one. The fresh turkeys are usually more expensive since they have a shorter shelf life and must be sold. Always buy only USDA Grade "A" turkeys.

Fresh turkeys must be kept at 26^0F or above while *frozen turkeys* must be kept at 0^0F. If the word "natural" is on the package then the turkey has not been injected with an artificial moistening solution. *Free range* means that the bird was allowed to run around outdoors. *Organic* means that the bird is free from antibiotics.

TURKEY, FRIED

This method of cooking takes special equipment and knowing what you are doing for the best results.

- Purchase a special deep-fat frying pot to fry the bird in. Use a 60-quart pot and a candy thermometer to check the oil temperature.
- Read the instructions well before starting.
- Be sure and place the bird in the pot and add water. Remove the bird and make a line so that you will know how much fat to use.
- Use peanut oil for the best results.
- Always cook the turkey outside, never in the house.
- Use caution when placing the bird into the hot oil, the bird must be at room temperature. However, it will still splatter.
- Never stuff the bird.
- The oil must be 350°F for the best results. The turkey cooks at about 3-4 minutes a pound. Don't overcook.
- Do not re-use the oil.

TURKEY, LEFTOVERS

Science of Leftovers

Never wrap warm meat or poultry in aluminum foil and place it in the refrigerator. Foil is an excellent insulator and the meat will remain warm for too long a period allowing bacteria to thrive. Wrap the food in plastic wrap or place in a well-sealed plastic container. Meat, poultry and stuffing should last 3-4 days if stored separately. Stuffing should be reheated to 165°F even after cooking and refrigerated within 45 minutes after the bird has been removed from the oven. If it contains the giblets, eggs, broth or juices from the bird, the temperature when re-cooked should be 175°F. Always refrigerate leftover turkey meat within 1 hour after the bird leaves the oven. When placing warm leftovers in small plastic containers, allow space between them so that they can cool off faster and avoid bacterial growth.

TURKEY, THAWING

Poultry thaws at approximately 5 pounds every 24 hours under refrigeration. You can submerse the turkey in cold water and allow 30 minutes per pound. If you add salt to the water it will improve the flavor of the poultry as well as providing additional cleaning. The water should be changed every 30 minutes to remove any residues and to keep it cold. Once the turkey is thawed it should be cooked or refrigerated at 400°F.

VVVVV

VANILLA

The vanilla pod is the only food produced by a plant member of the orchid family. The reason "real" vanilla is so expensive is that is hand pollinated when grown commercially. In the wild it is pollinated by only one species of hummingbird. Since they are very expensive to grow over 75% of the bean is grown in Madagascar where the pods are actually branded with the growers brand because of "vanilla bean rustlers" stealing the crop. Pure vanilla extract can only be made by percolating the bean similar to making coffee. Imitation vanilla is produced from the chemical vanillin, which is a by-product of the wood pulp industry.

The FDA has established guidelines for vanilla extract and if you use vanilla extract in your cooking you should know the differences in the various ones that are sold. To be called a "pure vanilla extract" the list of ingredients must read "extractives of vanilla beans in water, alcohol "(35%)." This will probably be the more expensive brand. Other labels may read "water, alcohol (35%), vanilla bean extractives and corn solids." The better brands may still use a small amount of corn solids; however, they will always have the vanilla bean as the first ingredient on the list of ingredients.

- To produce one gallon of pure vanilla extract it takes 13.6 ounces of vanilla beans, 35% alcohol and water. The alcohol evaporates when you bake or cook with the vanilla extract.
- Sugar should never be listed on the label and may affect the product. Time (aging) will improve the flavor of pure vanilla extract.
- Vanilla extract sold in Mexico has been implicated in numerous studies as containing contaminants from the harvesting of the bean and the processing procedures. Since there is no way of telling which are good and which are bad, it is recommended not to purchase any Mexican vanilla extract.
- The United States purchases more vanilla beans than any other country in the world, about 1,500 tons annually.

They are grown on trees and look like long, thin dark brown beans. They are expensive and not as easy to use as the extract. In order to use the bean you need to split it, then scrape out the powder-fine seeds. Seeds from a single vanilla bean are equal to about 2-3 teaspoons of extract. The beans need to be stored in a sealed plastic baggie then refrigerated.

PURE EXTRACT

If it says "pure" then it must come from the vanilla bean, however, the taste will be less intense. It still has an excellent flavor similar to the real bean.

IMITATION EXTRACT

Imitation means just that: Imitation. It is produced from artificial flavorings and has a stronger, harsher taste than pure vanilla. It should only be used in recipes when the vanilla flavor will not overpower the dish.

While grandma was very thrifty, she would never compromise on buying vanilla extract. If the bottle didn't say "pure vanilla extract" she would not buy it. She used the extract in many of her baked dishes as well as ice cream and was convinced that only the "real" thing would provide the flavor she wanted. She knew that if it didn't say "pure" the flavor would be too weak.

There are four types of vanilla available, the pods grow between 4" to 8" long and must be picked as they begin to turn from green to a golden brown color. After they are harvested the bean must go through fermentation and drying periods, which can take 4-6 months.

VEAL

Veal is from a calf that has been fed a special diet from the day they complete their weaning to the time of slaughtering which is usually at about 3 months old. Their diet lacks iron, which normally turns meat red; this is an undesirable color for veal. The animal is placed into a stall and not allowed to even lick a pail or anything else, which might contain the slightest amount of iron. They are not allowed to exercise and fed a formula of either special milk (milk-fed veal) or a formula consisting of water, milk solids, fats, and special nutrients for growth.

When the calf is about 3-4 months old the texture of the meat is perfect for tender veal. The most desirable is the milk-fed at 3 months old. However, the second formula is being used more since the calf will be larger at 4 months resulting in more salable meat.

The source of veal is from young milk-fed calves. Veal is very low fat, tender, and more costly, but contains less hormones than most beef. It contains 1/10th the fat of lean beef and the cholesterol content is lower. Breading veal will seal in the moisture.

VEGETABLES

The following are hints and chef's secrets to cooking and preparing the more common vegetables. Some general suggestions, however, are necessary that apply to all vegetables and these include washing the skins with a good quality organic vegetable cleaner before you peel them or even slice them. Also, always discard the skins, since many contain pesticide or fertilizer residues and be sure and inspect the vegetables for insects and insect damage.

To keep white vegetables white, try adding a small amount of cream of tartar to the water when they are cooking.

Peeling thin-skinned fruits and vegetables can be an easy task if you just place them in a bowl and cover them with boiling water then allow them to stand for 1-2 minutes. The skin can easily be removed with a sharp paring knife. You can also spear the food with a fork and hold it about 6 inches over a gas flame until the skin cracks. Peeling thick-skinned fruits or vegetables is much easier if you cut a small portion of the peel from the top and bottom of the fruit. Then set the food on an acrylic cutting board and remove the balance of the peel in strips from top to bottom.

When you cook a cruciferous vegetable such as cauliflower, never use an aluminum or iron pot. The sulfur compounds will react with the aluminum turning the cauliflower yellow. If cooked in an iron pot, it will turn the cauliflower brown or a bluish-green.

TO COVER OR NOT TO COVER VEGETABLES
Never When Frying...............Never When Roasting.............Never When Reducing

---

- Unless you really like the smell, try placing a few unshelled pecans in your saucepan when cooking kale, cabbage, or collard greens to reduce the odor.
- When cooking onions or cabbage, boil a small amount of vinegar in a pan to remove the odor.
- Next time you cook a fibrous vegetable such as cabbage, celery or beets, try adding 2 teaspoons of white vinegar to the cooking water. Vinegar is a mild acid and is able to breakdown the cellulose, which makes the vegetables stringy and somewhat tough.
- When washing your vegetables, place a small amount of salt in a sink full of cold water to draw out any sand and insects.
- Adding a small amount of sugar to vegetables when they are cooking will bring out the flavor; this is especially true with corn.
- If your frozen vegetables become lifeless, remember that these are an important staple; don't be embarrassed to use them. No need to cook before adding to dishes; simply pour boiling water over them in a colander and then add them to your casserole or stove-top dish to finish cooking.

Science of Dark Green Vegetables
All plants manufacture vitamin C from sugars, which are derived from the leaves and produced by photosynthesis. The more light a plant gets, the more sugars are produced and the more vitamin C the plant can produce. Another factor is that the more light a plant receives, the more chlorophyll and carotenoids the plant needs to handle its energy input, which causes the leaves to be darker. The darker the leaves of a vegetable the more precursor it contains to produce vitamins A and C.

VEGETABLES, BLANCHING

BLANCHING IN A MICROWAVE

Placing vegetables in boiling water or exposing them to steam for 2-5 minutes was the accepted method of blanching for hundreds of years. The heat would inactivate the enzymes that tend to destroy the vegetable in a short period of time and allow them to be stored for longer periods. Science has now found that if you microwave the vegetables in a 700-watt microwave for 4 minutes with a few teaspoons of water, seal them in a plastic bag and freeze them it will work better than boiling water or steam. The microwave provides just enough heat to inactivate the enzymes and retain the vitamin C content.

I DIDN'T BLANCH AT ALL

Vegetables that are frozen and not blanched are still good to eat, however, the quality, color, texture and flavor will be considerably lower than those that have been blanched before freezing.

After partially cooking vegetables (blanching) chefs shock vegetables by draining them into a strainer and then placing them immediately into a bowl of ice water. This stops the cooking process and sets the color of the vegetables. After you place the vegetables in the ice cold water (with ice cubes), remove after a few seconds and allow the excess water to drain off back into the bowl.

VEGETABLES, BOILING OF

When boiling vegetables or meats, allow the water to boil for about 2 minutes before adding the food. This will allow a percentage of the oxygen in the water to be released. Oxygen has the ability to reduce the percentage of available nutrients found in the food. Also the shorter the cooking time for vegetables, the more nutrients that will be retained and leaving the skins on also helps.

SAVING TIME

Grandmother used to put together a meal in no time and I never understood how she did it until I realized that she par-boiled the larger vegetables and then just finished the cooking just before she served them.

- Vegetables should be cooked right from the freezer for the best results. The only exception is corn-on-the-cob and leafy greens.
- When cooking vegetables in a pot of hot water, always add the hottest water you can if the water level gets too low.
- Adding cold water may affect the cell wall and cause the vegetable to become tough.

- Next time you are cooking greens, either stir constantly or rub a small film of butter or vegetable oil on the sides of the pan to prevent boiling over. The butter tends to stop the buildup of air bubbles.
- Adding a small amount of sugar to vegetables when they are cooking will bring out the flavor; this is especially true with corn.
- Vegetables should always be placed in the water after it has started to boil. The shorter the time in the water, the more nutrients that will be retained. Vitamin C is lost very quickly.
- The water should be allowed to boil for 2 minutes to release a percentage of the oxygen, which will also cause a reduction in nutrients.
- Leave the skins on and the vegetables in large pieces. The more surface you expose, the more nutrients will be lost.

Chef's Rule for Boiling Vegetables
(The rule applies for all vegetables except potatoes)

Cover any vegetables that grows below the ground

Don't cover any vegetable that grows above the ground

Science of Where Vegetables Grow

There is a simple scientific reason for this: vegetables that grow above the ground give off more acids than those grown below ground. The cover traps the acids and may turn the vegetables gray. This is truer for green vegetables than for other colored vegetables, but it is a rule chefs followed.

VEGTABLES, CRISPER DRAWER
THE MAGICAL CRISPER DRAWER

Vegetables always had to be placed in the crisper drawer in grandma's refrigerator. She knew that they would stay fresher and last longer if they were stored properly and she hated to waste food if it spoiled. If you place a sponge in the drawer, it will absorb excess moisture.

VEGETABLES, REFRIGERATION OF

BRRRRRRRRRRRRRRRR

Refrigerating fruits and vegetables and keeping them in top condition take an expert's knowledge. You need to know which fruits and vegetable to place in the refrigerator and which to never place in the refrigerator.

```
Science of Refrigeration
While most fruits and vegetables can handle the cold in a refrigerator fairly well,
there are exceptions, especially when it comes to tropical fruits whose cells are not
used to the cold. Bananas will suffer cell damage and turn the skin brown (but will
keep them ripe a little longer), avocados will never ripen when stored below 45°F
(7.2°C) and oranges will develop brown spots on the skin. The best temperature for
almost all other fruits and vegetables is about 50°F (10°C). The exceptions are
lettuce, carrots and cabbage; they prefer the cold at 32°F (0°C). Always use a
refrigerator storage drawer to keep the humidity up and reduce the chances of
drying out the fruits and vegetables.
```

VEGETABLES, RETAINING COLOR

When vegetables lose their color, it is the result of the loss of pigment by a chemical reaction to the pigment with the acid that is being released by the cooking process. A variety of colors may actually appear in the same vegetable depending on the length of time it is cooked. After a period of cooking the liquid may deplete the acid and turn alkali changing the color of the vegetable again.

In green vegetables the acid that is released reacts with the chlorophyll lightening the color. In cabbage, the pigment chemical "anthocyanin" may be changed from red to purple depending on the acid or alkali nature of the liquid.

Baking soda may reduce and neutralize the effects of the acid and keep some vegetables close to their natural color but will destroy a number of vitamins especially C and thiamin. The best method of retaining color is to steam your vegetables.

VEGETABLES, STORAGE OF

Try placing a few sponges in your vegetable drawer to absorb moisture. You can also add a piece of paper towel to the bottom of the drawer.

The best method of storing vegetables that have been cooked is to store them in a well-sealed plastic container in the refrigerator. They will last about 3-5 days.

If you wish to freeze them, then seal them in an airtight bag or a container in which most of the air can be removed. Since cells will burst releasing some of their liquid, they will be somewhat soggy but can be used in soups and stews. They will last from 8-12 months and still be edible.

VEGETABLES, WASHING OF
When washing your vegetables, place a small amount of salt in a sink full of cold water to draw out any sand and insects.

VINEGAR
The earliest record of vinegar use dates back almost 7,000 years ago to ancient Babylonia when dates were made into wine and vinegar. Vinegar was used as a medicinal as well as a flavoring for a number of dishes. Other fruits became popular around the same period and these included grapes and figs.

Laborers in ancient times were given small amounts of wine vinegar and water with a dash of salt to pep them up and work more hours. The Roman army was given vinegar rations to give them more stamina. In World War I vinegar was used to treat wounds. Vinegar does have certain antibacterial and antiseptic properties.

Vinegar is commonly produced from ethyl alcohol utilizing the bacteria, acetobacter, which feeds on the alcohol, converting it into acetic acid (vinegar). Vinegar, however, can be made from a number of other foods, which is the preferred variety to use such as, apples or grains. The distilled vinegars are best used for cleaning purposes and not as a food additive. Vinegar tends to stimulate the taste buds and make them more receptive to other flavors. The varieties of vinegar are endless depending on the food that is used to produce it. It is a mild acid called "acetic acid."

The actual amount of acid in vinegar varies from 4-7% with the average being 5%. Common types include apple cider vinegar, plain white distilled, red and white wine, barley, malt, rice, and balsamic. The acetic acid content of vinegar is referred to by "grains."

- Vinegar with 5% acetic acid content is known as 50-grain vinegar. The 50-grain means that the product is 50% water and 50% vinegar.
- Vinegar with 6-7% vinegar will keep foods fresher longer because of the higher acid content.
- Vinegar has a shelf life and will retain its effectiveness for 18 months.
- Studies have found that excessive use of vinegar, which contains a mild acid, may cause digestive problems, liver disorders, ulcers and destroy red blood cells prematurely.
- In moderation there should be no problem, however, if you can substitute apple cider vinegar in a recipe it would be healthier. Apple cider vinegar contains malic acid, which is actually friendly to the human digestive process.
- One cup of vinegar is composed of 98.8% water, hardly any protein, no fat, 14.2 grams of carbohydrate, 14 mg. of calcium, 22 mg. of phosphorus, 1.4 mg. of iron, 2 mg. of sodium and 34 calories.

Certain types of vinegar were grandmother's favorites. She used apple cider vinegar for salads if they had cabbage in them and she loved to use balsamic vinegar in stews and for a salad dressing.

The only time grandma used distilled white vinegar was for pickling. When she made chutney she used malt vinegar and when she marinated she used wine vinegar the most.

WWWWW

WAFFLES

SMOKE SIGNALS
To tell whether the waffle iron was hot enough, some chefs will place a spoonful of water in the iron, close it and turn it on. As soon as the water stops steaming, the iron is ready with a perfect temperature.

Science of Making Waffles
Waffle batter should be a little lumpy since it should never be over-mixed. Cook the waffles only until there is no more steam coming out of the waffle iron. Use a fork to remove the waffles and never stack them. If you need to keep them warm while making other batches, place them on a cookie sheet in the oven at 200°F. If you are having a sticking problem, just brush the iron between batches.

Waffle irons should be seasoned by brushing vegetable oil on the iron when it is cold. Turn the iron on and after it heats up turn it off and allow it to cool before wiping off the excess oil. Never eat the first waffle after you season the iron. Just wipe the iron clean after each use without washing it.

To prevent waffles from sticking to the waffle iron, just add a teaspoon of wine to the batter. The alcohol will dissipate and will not affect the taste.

WATER, COOKING WITH

Simmer at sea level at a normal barometric pressure is around 195^0F (90.6^0C). A high simmer is 210^0F (99^0C) and a low simmer is about 180^0F (82.2^0C). The simmer temperature can be important when the recipe asks for a specific type of simmer. Keeping a thermometer handy in the kitchen will improve the quality of your cooking.

♦ When water turns to steam, it must expand to 1,600 times its original volume. Steam is an important leavening agent for baked goods. This is especially important for piecrust and puff pastry. The more rapidly the steam develops, the better the product will turn out, therefore the higher the starting baking temperature, the better.

♦ When a recipe calls for water, the water should be between 60^0-80^0F (15.6^0C - 26.7^0C;) for the best results be sure that the temperature is correct and allow the water to stand at room temperature for about 30 minutes before using it.

♦ When water is called for in a recipe, it should be between 60-80^0F for the results. Allow water you are going to use stand at room temperature for about 30 minutes before using.

♦ Rinsing vegetables in a sink filled with water (instead of under running water) will save about 200 gallons of water per month for the average family.

♦ You will waste another 200 gallons waiting for the tap water to warm up. Best to save the cold water for the plants.

♦ There is a higher level of contaminants in hot tap water than cold tap water. The heat tends to hold the contaminants better. Boiling hot tap water, however, tends to release contaminants.

♦ Tap water should always be allowed to run for 2-3 minutes first thing in the morning in case contaminants have seeped in during the night.

♦ Just a bit of interesting trivia! Water is capable of absorbing a large quantity of energy to raise its temperature. For example: it takes 10 times the energy to raise one ounce of water 1^0F than to heat one ounce of iron 1^0F. A pot of water will take twice as long to heat up than the same pot of oil to the same temperature.

When water boils the bubbles that come to the surface are just pockets of water vapor that originate on the bottom of the pot. As soon as the bubble absorbs enough energy to overcome the weight of the liquid and the atmospheric pressure they rise to the surface.

WATER WEIGHT

Sometimes a recipe mentions the weight of water. The weight of 1 tablespoon of water = ½ ounce and the weight of 2 cups = 1 pound of water.

WHIPPED CREAM

The number of fat globules in cream is why cream whips. The cream as it is whipped causes the fat globules to be encompassed by air bubbles, which causes the foam and produces a solid reinforcement to the mixture. The fat globules actually cluster together in the bubble walls.

If a small amount of gelatin is added to the mixture it will help stabilize the bubble walls and the mixture will hold up better. Sugar should never be added in the beginning, since it will decrease the total volume by interfering with the proteins that will also clump on the bubble. Always stop beating whipped cream at the point when it becomes the stiffest so that it won't turn soft and have a glossy appearance. If small lumps appear in your whipping cream, this is a sign of butter formation and there is nothing that can be done to alter the situation. You will never obtain a good volume once this occurs.

- ♦ If you sweeten whipped cream with confectioners' sugar instead of granulated sugar, the whipped cream will hold its shape better.
- ♦ Light cream can be whipped just like heavy cream if you place a metal bowl and metal mixing utensils in the freezer before using them to beat the cream.
- ♦ Also, try adding 1 tablespoon of unflavored gelatin that has been dissolved in 1 tablespoon of hot water to 2 cups of light cream to help it whip up and keep its shape. After it whips up, refrigerate it for 2 hours. If you are using heavy cream and want it to set up faster, just add 7 drops of lemon juice to each pint of cream.

Chefs never have a problem whipping cream. Before they start they place everything including the bowl in the refrigerator.

Science of Whipped Cream

Have you ever wondered why cream will whip and milk will not? The reason is that cream has a higher fat content than milk. Heavy cream may be as high as 38% fat while even whole milk is only 3.3% fat. When the cream is whipped the fat globules break apart and the fat molecules stick together in clumps. This also causes the air that is being forced into the mixture to be trapped between the globules. The higher the temperature of the ingredients and the utensils used, the more difficult it will be to whip the cream. Fat globules are more active and tend to cluster more rapidly at low temperatures. The cream should actually be placed in the freezer for 10-15 minutes before whipping.

If a small amount of gelatin is added to the mixture it will help stabilize the bubble walls and the mixture will hold up better. Sugar should never be added in the beginning, since it will decrease the total volume by interfering with the proteins that will also clump on the bubble.

Always stop beating whipped cream at the point when it becomes the stiffest so that it won't turn soft and have a glossy appearance. If small lumps appear in your whipping cream, this is a sign of butter formation and there is nothing that can be done to alter the situation. You will never obtain a good volume once this occurs.

WINE, COOKING WITH

Most recipes that allow you to use a small amount of an alcoholic beverage will never mention bourbon since it is too sweet for most recipes.

- When figuring the total liquid in a recipe any wine that is added should be part of the total liquid figure.
- As a rule of thumb for almost all sauce and soup recipes, use 1 tablespoon of wine per cup of sauce or soup.
- When cooking with wine, it will reduce from 1 cup to ¼ cup in about 8-10 minutes.
- Keep wine stored for cooking in small bottles. The less space between the wine and the top, the longer the wine will retain its flavor.
- There are a number of foods that do not have an affinity with wine. Foods that have a high acid content such as vinegar and citrus fruits will give wine a bad flavor.
- Supermarket "cooking wines" are never used by chefs. These are usually inferior products that contain preservatives and additives and have poor flavor compared to the "real" thing. Cooking wines must be made undrinkable by the manufacturers with the addition of other ingredients that may include excess salt or even MSG.
- When cooking with wine, wine should be part of the total liquid suggested in that recipe. As a rule of thumb for almost all sauces and soup recipes, use 1 tablespoon of wine per cup of sauce or soup. When wine is heated, it will reduce from 1 cup to ¼ cup in about 8-10 minutes. Best to add wine close to the end of the cooking period.
- Cooking wine should also be stored in small bottles. The less space between the wine and the top, the longer the wine will retain its flavor and aroma.
- Cooking sherry usually has salt or a flavoring added so that people will not drink it.
- The more common fortified wines such as sherry, port and Madeira when added to soup should be added just before serving. You want the flavor of these wines to stand out just enough to be noticed. Remember 2 tablespoons of fortified wine is equal to ½ cup of table wine.
- Leftover wine can be saved and used in cooking. Best stored in a small bottle not the original large one and in the refrigerator or frozen in ice cube trays for future use.

- Wine has a tendency to cause curdling in recipes that contain dairy products. Since many recipes that have dairy products in them do call for wine to be included, it is best to add the wine and blend it in before you add the dairy product. This will prevent curdling. Another key to a successful dish is to keep the dish warm until you serve it. If it cools too much it may curdle. Another method is to reduce the wine slightly before adding the wine to the dairy products.
- Foods that have a high acid content do not get along well with wine. These include salad dressings with a vinegar base and citrus fruits. Some sulfur-containing foods such as egg yolks will also affect the flavor of wine. Other foods that may have a negative effect on the aroma and flavor are asparagus, onions, tomatoes, pineapples, and artichokes.

Science of Wine in Cooking

Wine is used by chefs to de-glaze pans since the flavor remain after the alcohol dissipates. Always add wine close to the end of the cooking period to retain the flavor and just lose the alcohol. Wine has the tendency to cause curdling in recipes that contain dairy products. Make sure you blend the wine in before adding the dairy product. Don't allow the dish to cool, always keep the dish warm.

When you add alcohol to any recipe it will lower the boiling point until it evaporates. The boiling point of alcohol is 175^0F (79.4^0C), which is much lower that the boiling point of water at 212^0F (100^0C). If you replace some of the water in a recipe with wine, you need to increase the cooking time by about 10%.

- When serving different wines at a dinner party, there are a few rules that will enhance the enjoyment of the wines. Always serve a young wine before an older one; serve a white wine before a red wine; a light-bodied wine before a hearty robust wine and a dry wine before a sweet dessert wine.
- Never overpower a recipe with wine. Wine should always be included to improve the flavor. Wine should be added 5-7 minutes before the completion of the dish for the maximum flavor and aroma to be enjoyed.
- Onions do not blend well with wine when wine is added to them while they are cooking. A good rule of thumb is to cook or sauté the onions first until they are somewhat transparent before adding the wine.

BRANDY

Will compliment most meat and poultry dishes, however, frequently used in compotes and puddings. Brandy is often used to flambé a dish.

If you have a problem igniting the brandy, warm it slightly (just slightly) before adding it to the food, then ignite.

Another method is to use a few sugar cubes that have been lightly dampened with a lemon or orange extract, placed on the dish and ignited.

DESSERT WINES

These sweeter wines are normally used in dessert dishes such as compotes, fancy fruit desserts, and sweet sauces. Try basting a ham at the beginning of the glazing period with port, sherry, any table wine or muscatel.

RED WINE

The richer body and stronger flavor make red wine the best choice to enjoy with chicken, beef, lamb, or pork dishes. When cooking with red wine, it will have a better flavor If used in marinades, meat sauces, stews, and hearty meat-based gravies.

Try basting chicken about every 10 minutes with red wine or vermouth. Game birds have an excellent flavor when basted with red wine. Dry red wine can be used on meat and lamb after they are braised. Dry red wine can be added to brown sauces or a tomato sauce if it is added with the liquid ingredients using a ratio of 2 tablespoons of wine per cup of liquid.

SHERRY

It is recommended for stews, soups and sauces. Poultry and seafood recipes seem to bring out the flavor of sherry the best. When adding sherry to cream soups add 1 tablespoon just before serving and always use a dry, white sherry.

If you add sherry to a meat or vegetable soup, it would be best to use a medium sherry or even a red wine and add then just before serving the dish. Dry or medium sherry can be added to cream sauces if it is added with the liquid ingredients using the ratio of 1 tablespoon of wine per cup of liquid.

ZINFANDEL/CHABLIS

Chefs normally recommend that these wines will compliment most poultry and seafood dishes. However, it is really your individual taste that counts. If you do use a white wine it should be a dry white wine or vermouth and added to a baked or pouched seafood dish when you begin baking the dish. The wine should be accompanied by equal amounts of butter or oil. Lamb or veal will have an excellent flavor if a small amount of white wine is added after the meat is browned. Dry white wine or sherry can be used for gravies that accompany meat or poultry dishes at a ratio of 2 tablespoons of wine to every cup of liquid. The wine should be added with the liquid and boiled.

Going Fishing

If you need to remove small bits of cork from inside a wine bottle, try using a straw placed over the cork crumb then place your finger over the end of the straw and the small amount of vacuum will trap the cork and you can remove it.

Cooking wine will stay fresher longer if you add a tablespoon of very fresh vegetable oil to the bottle.

WOK COOKING

This is a fast method providing the pan is well heated with a very small amount of vegetable oil first. The only problem that may occur is that if you cook the vegetables too long in oil some of the fat-soluble vitamins may be lost. The big difference in professional wok cooking is that a more intense heat develops. Your home gas range is only capable of producing less than 10,000 BTU's.

The BTU's produced in a professional wok is almost twice that high due to a larger gas feeder line and larger burner opening diameters. Also, the specially built wok has a series of burners, not just one.

The higher heat tends to seal the flavor and juices in and the amount of juice, which remains in the wok, is less, therefore, allowing the juices that are there to stick to the vegetables more readily. Beware of special woks built with flat bottoms for electric ranges. The flat bottoms make it very difficult to stir and cook the vegetables properly.

Cooking in a wok originated in China over 2,000 years ago during the Han Dynasty. It was prompted by the lack of cooking oil. It cooked the food fast and was an energy saver. There are a few things that every cook should be aware of when stir frying foods:

- You don't need a wok; just use any large skillet.
- If you have an electric range, buy a flat-bottomed wok.
- Gas ranges can use either a flat bottom or a round bottom wok.
- Before cooking beef, pork, or chicken, partially freeze the meat for about 1 hour so that it will be easy to slice thin, even-sized pieces.
- Place the meat in a marinade for great flavor for a few minutes while you are preparing the vegetables. Adding a small amount of cornstarch to the marinade will protect the meat from the high heat and make the meat more tender and juicy.

It's the Season

Steel woks need to be seasoned! Start by cleaning the wok and lid both inside and out in order to remove the rust-resistant coating. Rinse the wok very well and place 2 tablespoons of vegetable oil in the wok, rotating the wok to make sure that it is coated evenly. It is best to heat the wok over high heat until the oil gets very hot then allow it to cool and use a crumpled piece of paper towel to rub in the oil. Season the lid in the same manner after removing any handles that are not steel. After each use, be sure and re-season the wok by just rubbing 1 teaspoon of oil into the wok.

- Vegetables should be cut into uniform bite-size pieces to insure that they will cook evenly. If vegetables are preferred in different sizes, then they will have to be added at different times; which makes the cooking more difficult.
- Oil should be used very sparingly; approximately one tablespoon is all that is needed for four servings, which is just enough to place a thin coating on the bottom of the wok.

♦ Never stir-fry more than ½ pound at a time for the best results.

Most woks are made from steel, which is 98% iron. A study performed at the Texas Tech University found that if you stir-fry in a steel wok, it will increase the iron content in foods by as much as 200-500%. The amount of iron in a 3½-ounce portion of vegetables may rise from 0.4 mg. to 3.5 mg. when cooked in a wok.

If the wok is made of stainless steel it will only release an insignificant amount of iron.

Depending on the type of metal your wok is made of, it may rust. Always wipe off the inner surface with vegetable oil after each use.

XXXXXXXX'S ON SUGAR BAGS
The "X" symbol on sugar bags pertains to the fineness of the sugar. The more X's, the finer the grade of sugar you are purchasing. It actually indicates the number of holes per inch in the screening material used to form the size of the sugar crystals. If the package has four X's, then there were four holes per inch in the screen. A ten "X" sugar is usually a confectioners' sugar.

YEAST
A block of yeast is composed of millions of one-celled fungi that will multiply at a fast rate given their favorite carbohydrate food either sugar or starch in a moist environment. Yeast reproduces ideally at 110^0-115^0F except when used for bread dough and does best at 80^0-90^0F. Yeast causes the carbohydrate to convert into a simple sugar glucose, which then ferments into alcohol and carbon dioxide. It is the carbon dioxide that will leaven the baked goods similar to the reaction of baking powder expanding the air and creating steam. There is no risk from the production of alcohol, since the heat from the baking evaporates the alcohol as well as killing the live yeast cells. It is also an excellent dietary source of folic acid. Yeast and molds can be destroyed by processing the foods at boiling temperature.

Yeast should be tested before you use it in all instances. Just mix a small amount in ¼ cup of warm water that has ¼ teaspoon of sugar mixed in. The mixture should begin bubbling (happy yeasties) within about 5-7 minutes. If this does not occur, they are either dead or too inactive to provide the leavening function.

Always store your dry yeast in the refrigerator. The cold slows down the metabolic processes. This works for any product containing yeast.

However, make sure you allow it to warm to room temperature before using it. The yeast needs to get its act together again.

If you have ever wondered how sourdough bread is made, wonder no longer! It is made from a live fungal culture that is called a "starter."

The starter is made from tap water and white flour, which ferments and traps yeast spores from the air causing it to become sour. Starters may be kept for years. Only a small portion is removed when needed for bread making, allowing more to grow.

As a substitute for yeast, you can use one teaspoon of baking soda mixed with one teaspoon of powdered vitamin C. A similar chemical reaction will take place as with the baking soda. Ascorbic acid is just acidic enough to make the reaction work.

Yeast must always be added to water. Never place yeast in a bowl and pour water on it. The yeast is easily damaged and the weight of the water falling may harm too many of the little yeasties.

Compressed yeast has a higher level of moisture, about 70% compared to the standard dry yeast at 8%. Compressed yeast should be stored in the refrigerator and only lasts for about 2 weeks before losing its effectiveness. Dry yeast should always be stored in an airtight container since it absorbs water rather easily. The yeast is interchangeable with 1 packet of the active dry yeast being equal to the leavening power of 1 cake of the compressed yeast.

If you would like to slow down the rising time, just add one extra cube of yeast to the batter. It should slow things down about 45 minutes to one hour without changing the taste of the product.

Kneading is required to evenly distribute the yeast and other ingredients throughout the dough. If this is not done efficiently, the dough will not rise evenly resulting in a product with a shorter shelf life. Dough kneading machines make this chore easy and if you knead dough frequently a machine is a worthwhile necessity.

Science of yeast

Yeast is used to condition the dough and turn a heavy mass into an easily digestible product. Yeast also adds a percentage of food value to the product making it nutritious. It is a microscopic one-celled fungi, which multiplies by the process known as "budding." If you are using active dry yeast always store it in the refrigerator. Always test yeast if you are not sure if it is active or not. Just mix a small amount in $\frac{1}{4}$ cup of warm water that contains $\frac{1}{4}$ teaspoon of sugar. The mixture should begin bubbling within 5-7 minutes, if not they are dead and will not go to work for you.

ZZZZZ

ZEST

The oil found in the outer yellow or orange rind of citrus fruits. Avoid the white pith since it is bitter. The flavor of fresh zest from oranges and lemons will provide an excellent flavor boost to any dish. If you decide to use both the zest and the juice from a fruit, it would be best to remove the zest first. Zest will freeze for about 6 months and be active.

ZESTING

If you are going to use grater for zesting you will probably have a problem with the holes clogging. Try placing a piece of waxed paper on top of the grater. The waxed paper will trap the zest on top of the waxed paper instead of clogging the grater. A toothbrush will also remove the zest from a clogged grater.